AMERICAN WOMEN

images and realities

AMERICAN WOMEN
Images and Realities

Advisory Editors
ANNETTE K. BAXTER
LEON STEIN

A Note About This Volume

Daughter of a Kentucky congressman, Sophonisba P. Breckinridge (1866-1948) pioneered the professionalization of social work. First of her sex to pass the Kentucky bar and to earn a political science doctorate at the University of Chicago, she discovered through the Women's Trade Union League and Hull House the overwhelming problems of children, crime, schools, housing, blacks, and women workers, and she helped formulate Progressive Party policies on unions, slums and legislation. This book, done for the President's Research Commission on Social Trends, depicts, through primary sources, the increasingly important role of clubs, unions and professional organizations in advancing the participation of women in American life.

Women in the Twentieth Century

A Study of Their
Political, Social and Economic Activities

SOPHONISBA P. BRECKINRIDGE

ARNO PRESS

A New York Times Company
New York • 1972

Reprint Edition 1972 by Arno Press Inc.

Reprinted from a copy in The Wesleyan
University Library

American Women: Images and Realities
ISBN for complete set: 0-405-04445-3
See last pages of this volume for titles.

Manufactured in the United States of America

- - - - - - - - - - - - -

Library of Congress Cataloging in Publication Data

Breckinridge, Sophonisba Preston, 1866-1948.
  Women in the twentieth century.

  (American women: images and realities)
  Original ed. issued in series: Recent social trends
monographs.
  1. Women in the United States--History. I. Title.
II. Series. III. Series: Recent social trends
monographs.
HQ1419.B7 1972   301.41'2'0973   72-2593
ISBN 0-405-04450-X

WOMEN IN THE
TWENTIETH CENTURY

Women in the Twentieth Century

A Study of Their
Political, Social and Economic Activities

BY

SOPHONISBA P. BRECKINRIDGE

*Professor of Public Welfare Administration, School of Social
Service Administration, University of Chicago*

FIRST EDITION

McGRAW-HILL BOOK COMPANY, Inc.

NEW YORK AND LONDON

1933

COPYRIGHT, 1933, BY THE
PRESIDENT'S RESEARCH COMMITTEE ON SOCIAL TRENDS

PRINTED IN THE UNITED STATES OF AMERICA

THE MAPLE PRESS COMPANY, YORK, PA.

FOREWORD BY THE COMMITTEE

WOMEN IN THE TWENTIETH CENTURY by S. P. Breckinridge is one of a series of monographs published under the direction of the President's Research Committee on Social Trends, embodying scientific information assembled for the use of the Committee in the preparation of its report entitled *Recent Social Trends in the United States.*

The Committee was named by President Herbert Hoover in December, 1929, to survey social changes in this country in order to throw light on the emerging problems which now confront or which may be expected later to confront the people of the United States. The undertaking is unique in our history. For the first time the head of the Nation has called upon a group of social scientists to sponsor and direct a broad scientific study of the factors of change in modern society.

Funds for the researches were granted by the Rockefeller Foundation, an expert staff was recruited from universities and other scientific institutions, and a series of investigations was begun early in 1930 and concluded in 1932. The complete report contains the findings of the President's Research Committee on Social Trends together with twenty-nine chapters prepared by experts in the various fields.

Modern social life is so closely integrated as a whole that no change can occur in any of its phases without affecting other phases in some measure. Social problems arise largely from such unplanned reactions of the rapidly changing phases of social life upon the more stable phases. To give a few examples: changes in industrial technique react upon employment, changes in the character of adult work affect educational needs, changes in international relations affect domestic politics, changes in immigration policy affect the growth of population and the demand for farm products, changes in consumption habits affect the demand for leisure and facilities for enjoying it, changes in demands for social service by governmental agencies affect taxes and public debts, changes in methods of communication tend to standardize the mode of life in country and city. The effects noted in this list of illustrations in their turn cause other changes, and so on without assignable limits.

[v]

The usual practice of concentrating attention upon one social problem at a time often betrays us into overlooking these intricate relations. Even when we find what appears to be a satisfactory solution of a single problem, we are likely to produce new problems by putting that solution into practice. Hence the need of making a comprehensive survey of the many social changes which are proceeding simultaneously, with an eye to their reactions upon one another. That task is attempted in the Committee's report. Of course the list of changes there considered is not exhaustive. Nor can all the subtle interactions among social changes be traced.

To safeguard the conclusions against bias, the researches were restricted to the analysis of objective data. Since the available data do not cover all phases of the many subjects studied, it was often impossible to answer questions of keen interest. But what is set forth has been made as trustworthy as the staff could make it by careful checking with factual records. Discussions which are not limited by the severe requirements of scientific method have their uses, which the Committee rates highly. Yet an investigation initiated by the President in the hope that the findings may be of service in dealing with the national problems of today and tomorrow, should be kept as free as possible from emotional coloring and unverifiable conjectures. Accuracy and reliability are more important in such an undertaking than liveliness or zeal to do good. If men and women of all shades of opinion from extreme conservatism to extreme radicalism can find a common basis of secure knowledge to build upon, the social changes of the future may be brought in larger measure under the control of social intelligence.

The Committee's researches were not confined to preparing a general report laid out with proper regard for balance. Intensive investigations of considerable length were carried out in several directions where the importance of the subjects warranted and adequate data were available. Some investigators were rewarded by especially valuable developments of their programs on a scale which made it impossible to condense the results into a single chapter without serious loss. In these cases separate monographs are necessary to provide adequate presentation of the evidence and the findings. However, at least a part of the subject matter of each monograph is dealt with in the Committee's general report, which should be read by all who wish to see a rounded picture of social trends.

[vi]

PREFACE

In the following study an attempt is made to present the developments that seem to have been taking place in the activities and relationships of women other than those incidental to family life. As is pointed out below, opportunity is not offered to discuss the modern substitute for the women's direction of consumption which in the Domestic or Household Organization of Industry was incident to her direction of many productive processes.

Nor is this an undertaking to review the so-called Woman's Movement, although it is impossible to ignore the legacy which that movement has bequeathed to the women of the twentieth century. It is inevitable, however, that the connection should be noted between the manifestations in the late eighteenth century of interest in human rights, the quest for liberty, equality, fraternity, the beginning of women's struggle to obtain larger freedom for themselves so that they might aid in the effort to abolish slavery, the persistent attempts to industrialize industry by the factory acts introducing selective processes and eliminating the non-industrial worker, the gradual sharpening of the distinction between the domestic and the pecuniary interest on the part of women, between the industrial and the charitable on the part of the employer of women workers. These are all threads of interest so interwoven as to be separated only with great difficulty. If the attempt to deal exclusively with the extra-domestic is not entirely successful, indulgence is asked.

Three aspects of the activities of women have seemed to be specially suggestive; these are their varied organizations, their search for gainful occupation, and their relationship to government. A discussion of these subjects seems to call for different methods of presentation. In the discussion of women's organizations, a rather simple chronological presentation, roughly recognizing the ten-year periods, has seemed the most hopeful device for giving a reasonably adequate idea of the variety and number of groups in which women have allied themselves with other women. The sources of this discussion have had to be found largely in reports of clubs, in the proceedings of conventions,

[vii]

supplemented by correspondence and interviews with officials to whom grateful appreciation for this assistance is warmly acknowledged. It is impossible adequately to express the obligation under which I have been placed by the graciousness of the officers of organizations and societies.

Something of the same method seemed generally applicable to the political activities of women, and here again appreciative thanks should be expressed to those from whom help and information were secured.

In the discussion of women's occupations, however, greater reliance has been placed on figures than was the case in the other two discussions, and especially, of course, on the Census, to which more extended reference will be made at a later point.

Something should be said as to the relation of the discussion in the following pages and that in the chapter on the Activities of Women Outside the Home in the Report on Recent Social Trends in the United States. It has not been possible to avoid all repetition, but in general the conclusions thought to be justified by the data presented in that chapter are taken as the basis for the discussion in the following pages, so that a more comprehensive body of fact is made possible by increased space. An attempt has been made to supplement and not to reproduce the material presented in that chapter. It is hoped that both discussions are sufficiently comprehensive, but it has seemed unnecessary to refer again to certain portions of the development traced in that chapter, such as those in the field of protective legislation and the figures with reference to opportunities for professional education and the attitude of certain professional schools toward women students. While the chapter and the more extended discussion in the following pages should each be reasonably adequate, together they should give a more complete understanding of the developments and their significance, than either alone would give.

An account of any restricted group in its effort toward emancipation will include among other subjects those limitations growing out of prejudice or other attitudes of hostility, limitations sometimes removed in part by legislation, sometimes by administrative action when the appointing power may "walk right through the obstacle as though it were not there." When this has once been done, the unreality of the obstacle seems to have been always obvious. When reading the closing pages below in the light of policies adopted since March 4, 1933, it should be recalled that until some one is persuaded or persuades himself to walk through prejudice, it is an impenetrable as well as an immovable obstacle.

A few words more may be uttered here in acknowledgment of obligation. To Miss Marguerite Owen, formerly of the National League of Women Voters, now Secretary to Senator E. P. Costigan of Colorado, I owe much more than I can express. As I say below, the discussion has often benefitted, not only from data assembled by her, but from her vivacious and animated style and from her clear vision. To Dr. Alice Channing, formerly of the U. S. Children's Bureau, now of the Boston Council of Social Agencies, grateful acknowledgment is likewise expressed.

To that wise and able public official, who so brilliantly exemplifies the possibility of enriching the community services—Grace Abbott, Chief of the U. S. Children's Bureau—I offer grateful thanks for suggestions and critical sympathy. Mention may also be made of help from my colleagues, Dean Edith Abbott, long a student in the field of women's occupational interest, the late Professor Ernst Freund, whose concern for a larger measure of social understanding was a constant stimulus, and Professor-Emeritus Marion Talbot, whose confidence in the capacity of women to live freely has widely affected the university education of women, to them grateful acknowledgments are made.

S. P. BRECKINRIDGE.

CHICAGO, ILL.,
May, 1933.

CONTENTS

[xi]

WOMEN IN THE TWENTIETH CENTURY

INTRODUCTION

IN 1832, Lydia Maria Child published a History of Women;[1] in the following year Lucretia Mott spoke at the first convention of the American Anti-Slavery Convention in Philadelphia. In 1838, Georgia Female College inaugurated an experiment in collegiate education for women.[2] In 1840[3] American Anti-Slavery Societies sent among their delegates to the meeting of the World's Anti-Slavery Convention, held that year in London, a number of women[4] who were refused admission and who sat through the proceedings behind a grill in the gallery, with William Lloyd Garrison keeping them company and in the society of such English women as Lady Byron and Elizabeth Fry.[5] In 1848, at the first Woman's Rights[6] Convention presided over not by Lucretia, but by James Mott, a Declaration of Sentiments was discussed and adopted.[7] This declaraction, modeled after the Declaration of Independence, stated the various grievances from which women thought they suffered, "due to repeated injuries and usurpations on the part of man toward woman," including disfranchisement and the lack of political capacity, the legal incapacity resulting from marriage, unequal laws of divorce, the double standard in morals, occupational limitations, the denial of educational opportunities, subordination in church government—the whole amounting to "social and religious degradation," and calling for

[1] Thomas Woody, *A History of Women's Education in the United States* (New York, N. Y. and Lancaster, Pa.: Science Press, 1929), II, 414 *ff*.
[2] *Ibid.*, II, 161.
[3] *Ibid.*, p. 415; Elizabeth Cady Stanton, Susan B. Anthony, and Matilda Joslyn Gage, eds., *History of Woman Suffrage* (New York: Fowler and Wells, 1881–1922), I, 52 *ff*.
[4] Among them Lucretia Mott and Elizabeth Cady Stanton.
[5] Wendell Phillips pled their cause, but when defeated, participated in the deliberations of the convention.
[6] Stanton, Anthony, and Gage, *op. cit.*, I, 67.
[7] For copy, see Appendix.

the zealous and untiring efforts of both men and women for the over-throw of the monopoly of the pulpit and for the securing to women an equal participation with men in the various trades, professions, and commerce.

In the same year, 1848, the New York legislature enacted an extended Married Women's Property Rights Law.[1]

During the years 1843–1853, Dorothea Dix[2] was traveling the land over, presenting to the legislatures of all the states memorials with reference to the abuse of mentally ill persons, securing increased resources for their care and advising those responsible for the administration of great institutions in which the unfor-tunate insane were confined. About the same time (1849) Eliza-beth Blackwell, having succeeded in obtaining a medical education in Geneva, New York, and Philadelphia, was admitted to prac-tice in St. Bartholomew's Hospital, London, in all the wards except those in which women were treated.[3] In 1869, the Iowa legislature admitted women to the practice of the law.[4]

In 1862 Jenny Douglas began to clip the money in the Treasury, and the federal Civil Service was open to women; also about that time women began to take positions in the newly established public elementary school systems of the central and middle states.[5] In 1894, the doctrine of women's costal breathing as distinguished from men's abdominal breathing was disproved in a Harvard and in a Leland Stanford laboratory. In 1907 the United States Bureau of Labor, enabled by a special congressional appropriation, undertook an investigation of the conditions under which women and child wage earners worked; in 1909, the first White House Conference issued a declaration to the effect that children should, when possible, be cared for by their own mothers, and that a federal agency to keep the country informed concern-ing problems of child care should be set up.[6] In 1912, the United States Children's Bureau was established with a highly qualified

---

[1] *New York Laws*, 1848, Chap. 200.

[2] Francis Tiffany, *Life of Dorothea Lynde Dix* (Boston and New York: Hough-ton, Mifflin and Co., 1890).

[3] *Dictionary of American Biography*, under the auspices of the American Council of Learned Societies; edited by Allen Johnson (New York: C. Scribner's Sons, 1929), II, 320.

[4] Ruth A. Gallaher, *Legal and Political Status of Women in Iowa*, State Histori-cal Society (Iowa City, 1918), p. 59.

[5] Woody, *op. cit.*, I, 496 *ff*.

[6] *Conference on Care of Dependent Children, Washington, 1909. Proceedings held at Washington January 25, 26, 1909;* U. S. Sixtieth Congress, Second Session, Senate Doc. 721.

woman chief. In 1916, the United States Civil Service Commission in their report[1] took notice of the question of women employees and the Civil Service; in 1917, the federal government, in framing a policy with reference to the defense forces, abandoned in unmistakable terms the doctrine of "male necessity." In 1918, the Woman in Industry service, now the United States Woman's Bureau, was established; a woman was appointed on the United States Civil Service Commission; in 1920, the nineteenth amendment to the United States Constitution was ratified and at the November election of that year, women in all the states participated for the first time.

During these years industrial and domestic changes were taking place. Manufacturing processes that had been carried on in the home were more and more being organized outside, and American women were leaving their homes to work in cotton, woolen and silk mills. The principles of the factory system were being more and more widely applied to industry and commerce, while the development of the factory system was being resisted by tobacco, food and clothing manufacturers who tried to use as workshops, tenement homes that were not homes but places of sweated labor. In 1868,[2] Mrs. Croly, Jenny June, a well known writer, was refused admittance to the dinner given in honor of Charles Dickens at which her husband was a guest, and the woman's club movement was inaugurated. Something, we believe, of the significance of these events for the development of the American community during the first decades of the twentieth century can be extracted from a more extended view of certain aspects of the relation of women to the period.

It has been pointed out in another place[3] that women are seeking gainful employment in steadily increasing numbers as compared with the female population and when compared with gainfully employed men, that the women workers are older, more of them are married, and they come more largely from the group of native white than was true at an earlier time—all changes in a direction indicating that women may be expected to manifest a more universally professional, or industrial, or occupational habit of thought rather than the adventitious or casual attitude

[1] *Thirty-third Annual Report of the United States Civil Service Commission*, 1916, pp. 130, 131.
[2] Woody, *op. cit.*, p. 453.
[3] *Recent Social Trends in the United States*, Chap. XIV.

thought in the beginning years of the century to be characteristic of them.[1] This idea is expressed in various ways. Writers[2] discuss Woman's Coming of Age, ignoring the agelessly long road over which women's memory may travel as it seeks to restore the past in which they played their rôle as witches,[3] or when they acted as beasts of burden, gradually pulling themselves and then their companions on to the levels of industrialization and toward civilization; others rebuke them for desiring to throw off their bonds until they know and tell what they will do with their new freedom, while others express the simple, but for the time unfulfilled, desire to share the life of the community directly and yet completely, not partially on the one hand as celibates nor vicariously on the other as shut off by marriage from full participation in the productive work of the community. Can these developments be set out? At least an attempt can be made.

It is obvious that such an attempt faces difficulties not presented by developments in men's activities. These difficulties grow out of the difference in the degree to which the lives of men and of women are individualized. In the one case, the person is regarded as of immediate interest, as self-determining; professionally, or at any rate, occupationally-minded; in the habit of doing things which can be objectively judged. In the other case, there is still much that is vicarious. The married woman is supposed, or has until the very recent past been supposed, to have a husband who supports her. The unmarried woman may be a daughter or sister, called on to maintain by her presence and services, if not by her earnings, the family group. The ability to support the daughter or sister or wife in idleness, or at least in the absence of her gainful employment, has been a source of "honorific" satisfaction to the man and the woman's problem of her own choices was confused and accentuated by the effect that her gainful employment might have on the prestige of the male members of the household. It is not possible completely to set out the situation. It is sufficiently dealt with in the chapter

[1] William I. Thomas, *Sex and Society* (Chicago: University of Chicago Press, 1907); Thorstein Veblen, "Barbarian Status of Women," *American Journal of Sociology*, IV (January, 1899), 503–504.

[2] Samuel D. Schmalhauser and V. F. Calverton, *Woman's Coming of Age* (New York: Horace Liveright, Inc., 1931).

[3] Karl Pearson, *The Chances of Death and Other Studies in Evolution* (London, New York: E. Arnold, 1897), Vol. II, *Woman as Witch*.

on the Family[1] to justify limiting this presentation to the attempts of women to establish relationships with individuals and organizations other than those of the immediate family. There are three sets of such contacts not fully discussed in other portions of the project referred to, which may suffice to suggest the direction in which women's activities are developing, namely, the groups into which in innumerable and varied organizations women associate themselves to find refreshment, recreation, or culture, to cultivate some intellectual or social interest, to accomplish some public-spirited object, to secure the advantages of privacy and convenience of a home without the responsibilities of family life—a study of women's organizations will introduce the reader to the middle ground between the family life on the one hand and the world of gainful employment on the other.

Women have formed organizations for many purposes, and especially since the activities of the reform groups of the 1830's, 1840's and 1850's, women have been adding to the number and the variety of their organizations. Examination of those organizations during these latter years should reveal something of their changed point of view with reference to their place in society, their relation to their state, to the family, and to the occupational world.

The second set of data concerns especially the opportunity for employment and the response of women to that opportunity. Of the significance of this aspect of women's changing relationship it is not necessary to speak here. Further comment will be made at a later point.

The third body of data to which the study may profitably turn is that revealing to some extent the relationships of newly enfranchised women to the state. To understand the implications of those data, it will be necessary to review the decades preceding the ratification of the Nineteenth Amendment; but many of the important suggestions emerge from the study of the organizations.

The reader is asked to examine these three bodies of material in the hope that they may contribute to an understanding of the readjustment being made in the relationships of women to the community.

In the following study, then, opportunity is not offered to discuss the modern substitute for the woman's direction of con-

[1] *Recent Social Trends in the United States,* Chap. XIII.

sumption which in the Domestic or Household Organization of Industry was incident to her direction of many productive processes. When, after the economist's illustration of the Rule of Uses, she assigned so many hanks of yarn to socks and so many to vests,[1] she not only decided what and how many socks and vests should be made, but how the yarn should finally meet human needs. There are those who suggest that this responsibility will again be lodged with women,[2] but that is not the theme of this discussion.

As to methods and sources, mention will be made here only of certain difficulties connected with the use of the one ostensible comprehensive source—the United States Census. The Census itself calls attention to the unsatisfactory character of the figures at the different census dates because of the differences in the instructions given enumerators[3] and because of the differences in the time of the year when the enumeration was made, the Census of 1900 being taken on June 1; that of 1910 on April 15; that of 1920 on January 1; that of 1930 on April 1. When an attempt was made to review the development, a new classification for women's occupations was adopted, which was not available for men's occupations, which differs from the summary occupational classification used in the main census volumes for 1910 and 1920 in at least the following respects:

In the earlier census classification factory workers, dressmakers, seamstresses, and milliners, not in factories, are classified under the heading "manufacturing and mechanical"; laundry operatives in power laundries are classified under the heading "domestic and personal"; in the new classification, all factory workers and laundry operatives are included under the head "factory and mill workers" and the other groups are excluded. "Clerical"

---

[1] Alfred Marshall, *Principles of Economics* (6th ed.; London: Macmillan and Co., Ltd., 1910), p. 117.

[2] Sherwood Anderson, *Perhaps Women* (New York: Horace Liveright, 1931).

[3] In 1900, for example, no instructions were given with reference to women, with the result that the reporter for the census thought the figures an understatement; in 1910, instructions were given which are thought to have exaggerated the number of women farm laborers; while in 1920, the instructions probably led to an underestimate, so that in discussing the subject, the Census prefers to omit agricultural occupations from the consideration, although the figures for the three years are not inconsiderable, 770,483 in 1900; 1,397,224 in 1910; 896,057 in 1920; and 913,976 in 1930. For discussion of these defects see Joseph A. Hill, *Women in Gainful Occupations, 1870–1920*, Census Monograph IX, p. 16 *ff*.

occupations, according to the 1910 and 1920 census classifications included not only occupations usually thought of as clerical, but also canvassers, agents, collectors, messengers and errand girls; the new classification includes only typists, stenographers, book-keepers, cashiers, accountants and miscellaneous clerks; and excludes the canvassers, agents, and messengers. However, saleswomen and clerks in stores are here combined with clerical workers on account of the difficulty of differentiating clerks in stores from saleswomen in the earlier censuses. The heading "professional pursuits" in the usual census classification includes such occupations as attendants in doctors' and dentists' offices, and theatre ushers; this new classification includes only occupations usually thought of as professional, that of doctor, lawyer, teacher, artist, author, editor, librarian, photographer, trained nurse and the like. "Domestic and personal service" in the usual classification includes a great variety of occupations in addition to those of domestic servant, such as hairdressers, barbers, elevator operators, hotel keepers, laundry operatives, home laundresses, janitors and practical nurses; in the new classification servants and waitresses are separated from the other domestic and personal occupations.

In commenting on the Twelfth Census (1900), complaint was uttered because the reader was told the industry in connection with which the worker was employed but learned neither the nature of the work done nor the degree of skill required. In the Fifteenth Census (1930), the categories "operatives" and "laborers" conceal many facts, since they suggest only the degree of skill and neither the industry in connection with which the worker is employed nor the nature of the job. Only when those terms have been more completely analyzed will it be possible adequately to know to what extent, if at all, the range of women's occupational opportunity has widened.

PART I
WOMEN'S USE OF SPARE TIME

CHAPTER I

WOMEN AND THEIR ORGANIZATIONS[1]

IN THE following pages attention is drawn to a bewildering
number of organizations, from which it is hoped that something of the development of women's interests during the recent
past can be learned. It must be admitted that relative quantita-
tive data in this field are difficult to obtain. Women are joined
together by a common purpose to secure some object that seems
to them of great social importance; they are bound by common
occupational interests; they belong to lodges and benefit societies.
They express, as men do, an explicable pride in ancestry; they
seek now to obtain by organization many of the satisfactions
that were, in the earlier times, well nigh exclusively characteristic
of family life. Costly club houses provide shelter and living conditions that are comfortable and private—where a woman may
have "a room of her own," where she may exercise hospitality
without the burden of preparation. A woman may, however,
belong to several clubs, several of which may be united to federated organizations, and exact figures are therefore difficult, if not
impossible, to secure. It is true that the number of memberships
might be estimated, but the number of members, hardly. While
nothing like an exact measurement of effort or of achievement is
claimed, a statement with reference to the successive activities
will, it is hoped, give an idea of the extent and variety of·effort
devoted to these organizations, and show after what kinds of
satisfactions women strive, when, like the apostles, "being set
free, they go unto their own."

Although it is hoped that no significant organization has been
overlooked, the following study does not pretend to offer a
census of all women's organizations in the United States. Neces-

[1] Grateful acknowledgment is made to Miss Marguerite Owen, formerly of
the National League of Women Voters, now Secretary to Senator Edward P.
Costigan of Colorado. She is responsible for assembling most of the data, and to
her is due any vivacity of style. She is not responsible for interpretation though
great weight is due any judgment of hers with reference to any field of women's
interest.

[11]

sarily, the inquiry has been limited to those which deserve, on the basis of the distribution of their membership or the purposes of their existence, to be called national. And some consideration has had to be given to the accessibility of essential data.

Particular attention has been given to an examination of the club movement in the United States as it is reflected in the history of the General Federation of Women's Clubs. Women from all parts of the country and with all sorts of interests have been joined together in the Federation as they probably have been united in no other association. It antedates most of the specialized groups, yet it has survived their appearance and still holds a prominent place in the organization life of women in the United States. Changes in its composition, in its program and policies should therefore give an indication of certain changes in the thought and interests of women of whom the Federation is representative.

The sources of information utilized in the preparation of this study have been many and varied. Publications, reports, and proceedings of the various organizations have been examined. The information they yielded has been generously supplemented and clarified by correspondence and interviews. At best, however, the source material is not such as to make possible, even if it were desirable, an elaborate statistical analysis. It is no uncommon thing to discover in the same volume of a convention proceedings different statements as to size and distribution of the membership. It is not always easy, either, to separate the enthusiastic interpretation of a committee report from the data upon which it was based. Aspirations and achievements are sometimes inextricably mingled. An effort has, of course, been made to choose wisely and to report accurately those developments in women's organizations which will indicate the general trend. Detailed discussion of legislation supported or opposed by the organization is discussed in the section on women and government.

It has seemed best to present the first part of this report in roughly chronological order. It records the appearance of various new organizations and reports the apparent developments within the club movement in some detail for each decade, and yet the limits of the decades cannot be too closely adhered to. In the later section—covering the post-war period, the period of special interest but also of special difficulty—a summary of the developments within other organizations is attempted, and a few special topics are discussed that seem to throw light on the path of development. The period covered by this discussion must be apparently a long one. The decade of special interest, 1920 to 1930, can be understood only in the light of a much longer devel-. opment. The segment of the circle is from one with a longer radius than characterizes some series of events. The nineties, and a forecast of the new century, is perhaps as good a starting point as any, with the organization of the General Federation of Women's Clubs as the apparent occasion.

CHAPTER II

THE NINETIES—AN INTRODUCTION TO THE NEW CENTURY

THIS is how the General Federation of Women's Clubs began.

In 1889, Sorosis, a Women's Club in New York City, celebrated the twenty-first anniversary of its organization by inviting all the known women's clubs in the United States to send representatives to a club convention. Ninety-seven clubs were invited, and the call announced the following topics for discussion:

1. The enunciation of the Woman's Club idea and its point of departure from the society.
2. The data upon which to gauge the extent to which in twenty-one years club life has grown among women.
3. In what it consists, and how it differs from the club life of man.
4. The methods and their operation.
5. Results obtained and outlook for the future.
6. The influence exerted upon the communities in which they exist.

Sixty-one clubs responded by sending delegates, and as a result of that meeting the General Federation of Women's Clubs was launched in 1890.

I. A GLANCE BACKWARD

There were other national organizations of women existing when the General Federation was inaugurated. In 1869 two suffrage associations had been formed, The National Woman Suffrage Association and the American Women's Suffrage Association, to be combined in 1890 under a somewhat redundant title—The National American Woman Suffrage Association. In 1874, the Women's Christian Temperance Union had been organized, with its members earnestly pledging "to abstain from all distilled, fermented and malt liquors, including wine, beer and cider, and to employ all proper means to discourage the use of and traffic in the same," and including as a paragraph in its "Principles": "We believe in a living wage; in an eight-hour day; in courts of conciliation and arbitration; in justice as opposed to

greed and gain; and in peace on earth and good will to men."
But those two were "reform" organizations and their courageous
memberships were small in 1890 when the census reported 16,234,-
690 adult females in the United States.

Many of those "females over 21" who were members of the
Evangelical Churches were participating in the prayer circles and
the Dorcas Societies which were abundant, or perhaps in the
missionary societies. A smaller number of these same church
women were active in the Women's Christian Associations, for
though there was as yet no permanent national organization,
Women's Christian Associations were springing up all over the
country and by 1890 they were joined together for annual conferences. They had developed from the prayer circles of the great
religious revival of 1857–1858, and in admiring imitation of the
Young Men's Christian Association which had been organized in
the United States a few years earlier. The first one, a Ladies'
Christian Association in New York, was formed in 1858. The
duties of the members were outlined as follows:

They shall seek out especially young women of the operative class,
aid them in procuring employment and in obtaining suitable boarding
places, furnish them with proper reading matter, establish Bible classes
and meeting for religious exercises at such times and places as shall be
most convenient for them during the week, secure their attendance at
places of public worship on the Sabbath, surround them with Christian
influences and use all practicable means for the increase of true piety
in themselves and others.

A year later a proposal for a similar organization was made in
Boston, but it was discouraged by the ministers of the city, who
had assisted in the organization of a Young Men's Christian
Association a few years earlier. The project seemed to them to be
too ambitious for women to undertake. Organization in Boston
was delayed, therefore, until 1866. In the meantime the Civil
War had been fought and the capacity of women had been tried.
When the Boston organization was effected, the name, Young
Woman's Christian Association, was used for the first time in the
United States. It enunciated as the object of its solicitude "the
temporal, moral and religious welfare of young women who are
dependent on their own exertions for support." Other cities
followed, and in 1871 the Woman's Christian Association of
Hartford, Connecticut, invited the officers of all similar associ-

ations to a conference in celebration of the fourth anniversary of its organization. Eight associations were represented at the conference and reports of work undertaken in 13 other cities were heard. The call to the conference had emphasized the opportunity which it offered to discuss the common problems of those who were "striving to protect and to benefit in every way their young sisters, who are toiling for their own and others' support, with many trials and temptations."

The meeting was so profitable that a resolution was adopted providing for similar conferences at intervals of not more than two years. The next time, 36 city associations were reported in the United States, and in 1877 the conference was organized as the "International Conference of Women's Christian Associations," with mutual consultation about the work of the associations as its object.

While women of the Evangelical Churches were organizing Women's Christian Associations, women of the Protestant Episcopal Church were engaging in a somewhat similar activity in the Girls Friendly Society. Like the Christian Associations, it was an English plan which in 1877 was transplanted to Lowell, Massachusetts. Its purpose was to offer friendly assistance to the problems of growing girls.

Meanwhile, outside the churches and independent of the movement for social and political reform, still another national organization of women had been inaugurated in 1881 when a small group of collegiate alumnae met in Boston to form the organization now known as the American Association of University Women, and in the colleges themselves, especially in the coeducational universities, Greek letter sororities had been appearing with increasing rapidity since the first one was organized in 1867. There were more than eighty college chapters divided among eleven national sororities in 1891 when the National Pan-Hellenic Association composed of representatives from each one was formed. So many organizations of the Young Women's Christian Association flourished on middle western campuses that a national association had been formed by them in 1881.

One secret club of girls which had been organized in a college in Iowa in 1869 outgrew the campus limitations and as the P. E. O. Sisterhood offered to its middle western women members a taste of the delicious mysteries of a lodge. It was founded in Iowa Wesleyan College at Mount Pleasant, Iowa. Membership was invitational and the purposes were to further mutual friendliness and general improvement.

A few secret and benefit lodges for women were organized as auxiliaries to men's societies. They had been formed "to reconcile women," says one recorder, "to the life-long pledge of secrecy made by their husbands." Among the largest were the Daughters of Rebekah organized in 1851; the Degree of Honor organized in 1873, as an auxiliary to the Ancient Order of United Workmen; the Ladies of the Macabees organized in 1886, later to be divided into two opposing camps; and the Ancient Order of the Eastern Star, an auxiliary of the Masons which dates from 1876. In 1883, women relatives of members of the Grand Army of the Republic had organized the Woman's Relief Corps to supplement its activities.

Obviously, participation in sororities in college and membership in the secret lodges was limited to a relatively small number of women; the Christian Associations were in urban centers, directed by Evangelical Church women of sympathy and leisure; there were not many college graduates to join the Association of Collegiate Alumnae; the suffrage associations and the Women's Christian Temperance Union were still pioneers in their chosen fields. It was the appearance of woman's clubs all over the country which represented the general unspecialized leisure time activity of women, for which no prerequisite in the way of education, belief or male relationship was required. Clubs began to appear in the sixties and their growth marked the emergence of the middle-aged and middle-class woman from her kitchen and her home. The federation of those local, unrelated groups into a general affiliation, for no particular purpose other than the joy of mutual conference about problems not yet enunciated or apparent, was a significant introduction to the nineties.

II. THE FIRST TEN YEARS OF THE FEDERATION

The first Biennial convention of the newly organized federation was held in Chicago in May of 1892. There were 297 women in the delegate body, representing 185 clubs from 29 states. It was a conclave of "culture" clubs. Indeed Article IV of the adopted constitution provided that

clubs applying for membership in the General Federation must show that no sectarian or political test is required and that while distinctly humanitarian movements may be recognized, their chief purpose is not philanthropic or technical, but social, literary, artistic or scientific culture.

Sorosis, the mother of the Federation, had originated as a genuine feminine protest against a social discrimination. A club of newspaper men in New York City were giving a dinner in honor of Charles Dickens when he visited this country in the late sixties. Jennie June Croly—the wife of a member of that club and herself a writer—wanted to go. Her sex debarred her and in the energy of her exasperation she determined to secure for women some of the benefits that men were unwilling to share with them. So Sorosis was formed

For the promotion of useful relations among women, the discussion of principles which promised to exert a salutary effect upon women and on society, and the establishment of an order which should render women helpful to each other and to the world.

It is probable that even these general phrases placed Sorosis in a more advanced position than most of the other study clubs which answered her call in 1889. "It was," reports the Federation historian of the first Biennial, "the almost unanimous decision that clubs should adhere to the purpose of intellectual development and recreation, and that the club should serve as a 'resting place' from the regular absorbing duties of life."[1]

However, even in this early day there were leaders who were eager to promote public interests through the clubs. Jennie June Croly, who was perhaps responsible for Sorosis's pledge to "render women helpful . . . to the world," had said at the Federation Council banquet in 1891:

The eagerness with which women's clubs all over the country have taken up history, literature, and art studies, striving to make up for absence of opportunity and the absorption in household cares of their young womanhood, has in it something almost pathetic. But this ground will soon be covered. Is there not room in the clubs for outlook committees, whose business it should be to investigate township affairs, educational, sanitary, reformatory, and all lines of improvement, and report what is being done, might be done, or needs to be done, for decency and order in the jails, in the schools, in the streets, in the planting of trees, in the disposition of refuse, and the provision for light which is the best protection for life and property?[2]

[1] Mary I. Wood, *The History of the General Federation of Women's Clubs* (New York: History Department, General Federation of Women's Clubs, 1912), p. 50.
[2] It was presented by Dr. Sarah Hackett Stevenson and seconded by Mrs. Julia Ward Howe. *Ibid.*, p. 46.

So far as the records disclose, the discussion at the first Biennial concerned problems of club organization and management. There was no effort to record the opinion of the clubs by the vote of their delegates on general resolutions. That was an innovation at the second Biennial, held in Philadelphia in 1894, when a resolution was adopted which read:

Resolved, that the General Federation of Women's Clubs declares its belief that one standard is equally binding upon men and women, and that immoral conduct which debars one from public and social life should also debar the other.

In 1895 the *Cycle*, a magazine devoted to Federation interests, offered the following question for a symposium:

Would you have clubs limited to study and discussion of these subjects, or would you advise that they endeavor, by education and active cooperation, to promote a higher public spirit and a better social order?

The answer seems to have been in favor of promoting "a better social order" for, although the culture club and literary society continued to make up the bulk of the Federation membership, in 1896 the limiting Article IV of the constitution, which limited membership, disappeared and "philanthropic" clubs were no longer denied admission. Village improvement associations were joined with Shakespeare clubs, and cemetery associations supplemented Monday afternoon societies. The test for admission was no longer emphasis on "social, literary, artistic or scientific culture."

In 1896, when more than 400 women gathered at the third Biennial in Louisville, 100,000 women were estimated to be affiliated with the General Federation, and the clubs in 21 states were united in state federations. At this Biennial the first resolution affecting a public question was adopted when the delegates voted to study "forest conditions and resources and to further the highest interests of our several states in these respects."

Already, the trend toward public welfare interest was apparent. The Federation was now divided into Departments on Literature, Education, Philanthropy, Social Economics, the Home, and Finance. An examination of the reports from the various states, however, betrays a conspicuous inequality in the progress. A California club reported that "by its vigorous and aggressive campaign recently it succeeded in defeating an obnoxious measure attempted by the city council, which tried to bond the city to obtain funds to lay asphalt pavements." And, regardless of the merits of asphalt paving, participation in public, even political, affairs can be noted. At the same time the report from a neighboring state recorded the activities of a club organized in 1891. It was "devoted to study and conversation" and reported that its dazzling course of study had "embraced Greece, Rome, Italy, England, and France, with their traditions, history, literature, art, and government."

And while one club in Connecticut reported its study of the History of Civilization—"Wife Capture, and Slavery"—and another in the same state boasted a program embracing "electricity, literature and parliamentary law," the state of Delaware reported that one of its committees had been occupied "agitating a compulsory education law."

A club in Florida stated that money raised by the efforts of its members "is expended so far as necessary, in work on streets, in keeping them clean, and in making and repairing driveways and sidewalks." Another club in the same state had "fenced and improved a park, driven a public well, lighted streets with electricity, and planted more than one hundred shade trees." With catholic impartiality the Federation received this more romantic record of the work of the Edelweiss Circle in Arkansas:

For but a brief year has this "round table" group of women climbed the rugged sides of the mount of knowledge, and even now are plucking the dainty flower of culture from literature's lofty peak. Its success is assured by the earnest, faithful, and persistent work of its members. The Intellectual Development of Europe . . . has been the basis of study for the past year. . . .

Even though reports of literary activities predominate, there is evidence of a considerable number of programs on current events, and just four years after the determination of the Federation to keep club life as a "resting place," a Federation officer in Michigan reported, "There is a general feeling, so far as my correspondence with clubs, my visits to many of them and my observation in the state has revealed it, that we should give less time to merely literary work, and more of it to ethical and sociological culture." And from Ohio, "They are asking if their club does not stand for something better and higher than mere selfish culture."

All through the reports of work in the states the same contrast runs—while one club studies "Matthew Arnold as a critic, poet, and theologian," another provides "seats for public parks, two drinking fountains for men and dogs and granite troughs for horses." The Federation had adopted the motto, "Unity in Diversity." The unity was a thing of the spirit difficult to set down, the record of the diversity remains.

More than 800 delegates attended the 1898 Biennial at Denver, representing an estimated membership of 160,000 women in the country. For the first time a petition was dispatched to Congress. It was resolved that the General Federation "should send word to the Speaker of the House of Representatives, at Washington, urging the passage of Senator Hoar's bill providing for protection of birds."

A new alignment of Departments in the Federation shows the increasing interest in social problems, for the Federation now was divided into seven departments—education, art, home economics, industrial conditions as affecting women and children, civic clubs and town and village improvement associations, economic phases of club work, and literary clubs. Jane Addams and Mrs. Sidney Webb addressed the delegates on "The Industrial Problem as it affects Women and Children," and the convention adopted resolutions embodying standards for women and children in industry which are by no means realized today. The habit of resolution was already established in 1898. From the civic section came one resolving that all clubs

. . . make a study of measure of public sanitation, of matters of public comfort, and of methods of improving and beautifying our towns and cities. Also, that they carefully watch all municipal legislation in such directions as shall improve the physical and moral conditions of the community.

From the industrial section:

First, that the U. S. government be asked to establish a system of postal savings banks for the benefit of small wage earners.

Second, that no child under 14 years of age be employed in mill, factory, workshop, store, office, or laundry, and no boy under 16 years in mines.

Third, that adequate school facilities, including manual training, should be provided in the United States for every child up to the age of 14 years, and also that good school laws shall be secured and strictly enforced in every community.

Fourth, that in mill, factory, workshop, laundry, and mercantile establishment, the maximum working day for women and children shall not exceed eight hours, or forty-eight hours per week.

Fifth, that so far as possible uniform labor legislation shall be secured throughout the different states.

Sixth, that each club in this Federation shall appoint a standing committee whose special duty it shall be to inquire into the labor conditions of women and children in that particular locality. That each state Federation shall appoint a similar committee to investigate its state labor laws and those relating to sanitation and protection for women and children. That it shall also be the duty of these committees to influence and secure enforcement of labor ordinances and state laws of this character. That these committees at specified times shall inform their organizations of all conferences and conventions in the interest of social and industrial progress, also that the General Federation shall appoint a committee of five members, to be called the Committee on Legislation for Women and Children, whose duty it shall be to collect the reports of the above mentioned work and present the results at the next Biennial.

If the printed Proceedings are accurate, the resolutions were adopted without debate, so too much enthusiasm or understanding on the part of the delegates should not be taken for granted.

A resolution on Forestry was adopted. One urged the creation of a National Health Bureau, and one implored state Federations to advocate state legislation which would give a mother possession of her children.

The state reports in 1898 show an increase in interest in programs on current events, and a considerable variety of activities for town improvement. The support of libraries emerges as a major interest, and measures to raise the age of consent[1] are favored in state after state.

When the turn of the century came and the Federation met in Milwaukee in June, 1900, its trend was well marked. The diversity of its interests was still sharp. Resolutions on questions great and small were adopted—industrial problems, national conservation policies, and the merit system in the Civil Service. It is true that the reports from the states for the Biennium reveal a good many activities quite unrelated to the gallant resolutions adopted at Denver and it is likely that in 1900 comparatively few delegates understood completely or cared deeply about the resolutions they adopted. It is possible that the women whom they represented were concerned not at all. Nevertheless great strides had been made for a small number of women, and to

[1] That is the age of a girl below which a man or youth accused of having illegal sex relations with that girl child may not plead guiltlessness because of the girl's acquiescence in the act. The common law age of consent was ten years of age.

thousands the function of the club as a "resting place" already seemed an anachronistic blunder.

In the first decade of its life the Federation had grown by the addition of newly organized clubs and the federation of existing organizations. The first membership estimate of 100,000 was made in 1896. In 1900 with 155,000 estimated to be enrolled, a gain of more than 50 per cent had been recorded. The women's clubs had just begun their march.

III. NEW ORGANIZATIONS WHICH HAD APPEARED IN THIS DECADE

The General Federation was not alone in its growth during the ten-year period. New organizations of women had appeared during the nineties to take their places beside it. In 1890, for example, the National Society of the Daughters of the American Revolution had been organized in a feminine protest against the actions of the Sons of the American Revolution, which excluded women from its membership. Three women, in Washington, D. C., were founders, and only 18 completed the organization of the society which was to unite women descendants of soldiers and others who had given patriotic service in the Revolutionary army. The purpose of the organization was loosely described as "patriotic," and its first interests can be measured by three of the resolutions offered in the course of the organizing meetings:

1. That a monument be erected in Paris to the memory of George Washington.
2. That aid be given the Mary Washington Association.
3. That the Society should secure rooms and later a fire-proof building in which to deposit Revolutionary relics and historical papers.

In 1891 some friction developed and a New York chapter withdrew to start an independent similar national society—the Daughters of the Revolution—which also organized separate state societies.[1]

Two other organizations of women dependent upon ancestral records for membership appeared at about this time—the Colonial Dames of America in 1891—the National Society, U. S. Daughters of 1812 in 1892.[2] In 1894, the United Daughters of the Confederacy was born.

The Jewish Women's Congress which had assembled in Chicago in connection with the Parliament of Religions held at the World's

[1] In 1932, the original society was organized in 2,463 chapters and had enrolled 169,626 members.
[2] In 1931 they numbered 5,678 members.

Fair in 1893, resolved to form a permanent organization to unite in closer organization Jewish women "interested in the work of religion, philanthropy and education." At the time of the first convention of the National Council of Jewish Women, held in New York City in 1896, there were already 50 sections established in the United States and Canada, with a combined membership of 3,370 women.

In the nineties, two organizations of nurses were established, one the American Society of Superintendents of Training Schools, which later became the National League of Nursing Education, and the Nurses Associated Alumnae of the United States and Canada, now the American Nurses Association. The first group, like the Council of Jewish Women, sprang from the Chicago World's Fair where a nurses' section was included as a section of the Hospital and Medical Congress. It was one of the early organizations uniting women on a common occupational basis. Its platform stood for the development of adequate nursing education. Three years later this organization sponsored the second and in September, 1896, nurse delegates from twelve alumnae associations met in New York to form their national organization, "a quarter of a century after the organized system of nursing in the United States may be said to have begun."[1] The founders of the association intended that its policies should be broad enough to meet whatever demands a growing profession might present. The protection of the public and of the nurse by legislation requiring their registration through examination was immediately advocated by state associations, and although there were only a few hundred nurses in the association in 1900, a period of steady growth had begun.

In 1896 the National Association of Colored Women was formed by the merging of two groups which had been organized a few years earlier. In 1892 a Colored Women's League had been established in Washington and was carrying on active welfare work for the underprivileged women of that race. A similar group in the South had been inaugurated in 1893.[2] The organization of the National Association was hastened by the fact that colored women's clubs were not welcomed in the General Federation. Disappointed Negro women leaders determined that organized effort alone would prove Negro women worthy of responsibility.

[1] *Historical Sketch of the American Nurses Association*, p. 1.
[2] Under the leadership of Mrs. Booker T. Washington.

So the association in Article II of its constitution announced as its purpose:

Section 1. To promote the education of colored women and to hold an Educational Institute biennially at the convention.

Section 2. To raise the Standard of the Home.

Section 3. To work for the social, moral, economic and religious welfare of women and children.

Section 4. To protect the rights of women and children who work.

Section 5. To secure and enforce civil and political rights for our group.

Section 6. To obtain for colored women the opportunity of reaching the highest standards in all fields of human endeavor.

Section 7. To promote interracial understanding so that justice and good will may prevail among all people.

Twenty major departments with a variety of subdivisions were organized to carry out the general purposes.

In 1897, the National Congress of Mothers was organized. It was later to be known as the National Congress of Mothers and the Parent-Teachers Association. The organization took place when a meeting was called by Mrs. Frances Birney and Mrs. Phoebe Hearst in Washington, D. C., to which were invited representatives of Mother's Clubs all over the country. Its object was to confer on the problems of childhood and particularly to discover the material and experience available on the subject. The minutes of the early meetings fail to record the number of women then united in these Mother's Clubs all over the country. In 1900, the fourth annual convention was held in Des Moines, and, although the proceedings write of "crowded auditoriums," pioneers in the organization believe that the crowds were largely Iowa visitors. The delegate body was not large, for the movement was just beginning. The reports and speeches show a concentrated interest upon the problems of the child and the home, and a faint distrust of the effect on the child and the home of "higher education."

In 1899 four existing Consumers' Leagues joined to form a National Consumers' League. Mrs. Josephine Shaw Lowell had started the first League in New York. It was her influence which now prompted New York, Philadelphia, Boston and Chicago to join together, and although a man was elected president of the National League and it was never wholly a woman's organization, women prevailed in its membership, and undertook most of the responsibility it assumed in its campaign to arouse the conscience of the consumer to the abuses of industry.

The nineties had seen local organizations federate and con-
solidate into national groups, or had watched entirely new groups
begin their activities on a national basis. The beginning of the
era of centralization left its mark on women's organizations no
less plainly than on the business of the country. Besides that,
there were women whose horizons had been widened and whose
sense of public obligation found opportunity for expression.
There were innumerable homes where the children's reading
matter now included the books called for by the art or industry
departments of their mothers' clubs.

CHAPTER III

THE FIRST DECADE OF THE NEW CENTURY

IN 1900, the Women's Convention, auxiliary to the National Baptist Convention, was organized by the colored women affiliated with the largest denominational group of Negroes in the United States.

The organization in 1903 of the National Woman's Trade Union League of America was evidence of a new grouping within the labor movement. It was no novel thing for women in various trades to organize. There had been sporadic organizations since 1825, and women had been admitted on an equal footing with men to membership in the Knights of Labor, an organization which began as a secret society among the garment workers of Philadelphia in 1869, and grew until its membership reached 600,000 in the middle eighties, only to disappear in 1890. The American Federation of Labor which had been organized in 1881 had prospered, but the organization of the women in industry did not play a large part in its activities.

It was, however, with the cordial approval of the leaders of the Federation that the National Woman's Trade Union League was organized at the convention of the American Federation of Labor in 1903. From the first it included in its membership and among its officers not only women representatives of Trade Unions but women of leisure interested in its purposes, who were known as "Allies." The first objective of the League was stated to be:

> To assist in the organization of women wage earners into trade unions and thereby to help them secure conditions necessary for healthful and efficient work and to obtain a just return for such work.

In 1904, at the meeting of the American Institute of Homeopathy, the Women's Homeopathic Fraternity was organized for purely social purposes. It was the first national organization of women in the profession of medicine.

The American Home Economics Association appeared in 1908, with 700 charter members:

To bring together those concerned in developing the art of right living by the application of systematized knowledge to the problems of the home and the community.

The Trade Unionists, the women making of Home Economics a profession, and women physicians of homeopathic medicine— these are the groups having a common occupational interest which were organized in the first decade of the twentieth century.

Meanwhile the movement toward federation and centralization was increasing. In 1906 a union of the Women's and Young Women's Christian Associations was effected under the name of the Young Women's Christian Association of the United States of America, and a national board was elected.

Two years later, in November, 1908, the Council of Women for Home Missions was organized by uniting two Interdenominational Committees for Home Mission Conferences and a Home Mission text book society. Women's Home Mission Boards had been organized since 1877 to direct the missionary activities of women in the churches. Before that time the work which they carried on had been under the direction of Boards of men. The Constitution adopted by the new council stated:

The object of the Council shall be to unify the efforts of the National Women's Home Mission Boards, Societies and Committees by Consultation and by cooperation in action.

Nine constituent boards were members at the time of organization, and although the work of the Board in providing textbooks and pamphlets and promoting fellowship between and among denominations falls more naturally into an examination of trends in organized religion, it is not insignificant that the organization of the work of church women throughout the country responded to the apparently inevitable compulsion to federate and centralize. A similar organization was effected by the federation of the Woman's Boards of Foreign Missions. The work of the local missionary societies was not greatly altered by the change, nor was their object affected at all.

Although new organizations had appeared and administrative methods in old ones were changed, it is in the club movement that the changing interests of the ordinary women may be traced.

I. THE DECADE IN THE CLUB MOVEMENT

At the Sixth Biennial held in Los Angeles in May of 1902, the membership of the General Federation had passed the 200,000 mark—211,763 members were reported. Representatives of culture clubs were there in abundance, but they listened to Jane Addams speak on the "Social Waste of Child Labor" and voted, or at least a majority of them did, that for two years the General Federation should work to secure the initiation, maintenance and improvement of child labor laws. And they listened while Connecticut reported that

after three years of careful study and wise preparation, the committee on Equal Guardianship Rights carried its cause before the legislature and succeeded in having our Connecticut Guardianship law so amended that since June 3, 1901, no child can be willed away from its mother and every mother is the guardian of her children equally with their father.

In Colorado, club women reported that they were working for

better laws regarding school taxation, school registration, local option, the rights of women, and child labor.

Over 1,200 women attended the Seventh Biennial held in Los Angeles in 1904. Here Household Economics was for the first time recognized as a part of Federation work, with the committee objective the introduction of domestic science into every school and higher institution of learning.

The merit system in the Civil Service had been advanced as a proper subject for Federation support in 1900. It was presented then in five minutes! Two years later a committee on the subject was formed and an hour and a half given to its discussion. Now, in 1904, it was voted as one of the major issues for the next biennium, although it was pointed out that the reform was urged primarily for state eleemosynary and corrective institutions, to insure humane care for a state's wards rather than to secure honest and efficient government for all its citizens.

Traveling libraries appear by 1904 to be supported by the clubs in a majority of states. Forestry is still a subject of considerable interest. Numerous scholarships have been awarded.

By this time the standing Committees of the Federation were Art, Civics, Civil Service Reform, Education, Forestry, Household Economics, Pure Food, Industrial and Child Labor Legislation, and Library Extension.

Civil Service Reform, Forestry, Household Economics were comparatively new committees, but none so new as Legislation, a committee composed of representatives of the Committees on

Industrial Problems, Household Economics, Libraries, Civics and Forestry.

The creation of a federal agency concerned with the needs of children and "dumb animals" was advocated at this Convention, and thanks were extended to the Senate for its investigation of the practices of the Mormon Church. A resolution was passed urging

that each state federation urge upon its Senators to take such legislative action as will prevent the recognition of a power which undermines moral standards and will prevent the continuance of practices which are contrary to the principles of the American people.

So far as can be judged by the reports given and the resolutions adopted at the Biennial Conventions or from the pages of the General Federation magazine, the movement, at least so far as the leadership in the Federation was able to direct its course, was steadily and consciously away "from exclusive study clubs to inclusive social service organization."

In 1910, at the end of the second decade of its life, the General Federation of Women's Clubs claimed an approximate enrollment of almost 800,000 women, an increase of almost 500 per cent in only ten years. There can be no question but that a wide gap still remained between a majority of the club women in most communities and their leaders of the national movement. Notes from the states show an infinite variety of study programs, and although the extension of the merit system in the Civil Service had been selected by the Convention as a major item to support during the biennium, clubs still found time to debate the question, "Is housework incompatible with the higher life?"

The cause of Pure Food offered a rallying point for increasingly enthusiastic support in the states, and the fight against tuberculosis, which was just beginning to enlist the support of women in 1906, was at its height in 1910. Child labor laws were popular to advocate in its stead but the cause of Civil Service Reform languished in the clubs. State reports show that it was difficult to arouse interest in its consideration. Perhaps the reason for the general languor might be found in the candor of a report from North Carolina:

and this is also why Civil Service Reform has not been touched. It borders on politics, and our men have spoken in no uncertain terms concerning it.

Civil Service reform still held its place in the list of Resolutions, however, and the campaign for pure food was again embraced. Interest in conservation and the elimination of the White Plague were once more affirmed.

One Resolution urged the display of the American Flag at all club meetings; another requested each state to consider whether the mountain laurel should be urged as the national flower; and one in opposition to the publication of objectionable news in the press was adopted. School improvements of various kinds were endorsed in one long Resolution, and hostility to the White Slave Traffic was embodied in another. There were special recommendations for federal legislation—a pending bill for Vocational Education was endorsed, and a measure providing for a Department of Health. The use of the Hetch-Hetchy Valley as a source of water supply for San Francisco was opposed, the creation of a Department of Education in the Federal Government was urged. It was resolved that the Congress and the several state legislatures

should be requested to develop safety devices and better inspection of mines, mills, factories, and railroads, whereby industrial accidents might be reduced to a minimum.

The Biennial resolved that club women should study the world-wide movement for the substitution of a system of law for war, and that they should endeavor to create

an intelligent public sentiment before the third Hague Conference for settlement of all international differences by law instead of by violence.

Resolutions further to prepare a digest of laws relating to women and to create a new Department of Music, concluded the Federation's list of allegiances and hostilities for 1910

At this 1910 Biennial, for the first time, the question of suffrage for women was presented—with the position of advocates and opponents represented by speakers on the same platform. The Federation was slow to accept this reform which was regarded by many as the most effective weapon with which to secure all the other reforms advocated. Timid delegates might vote for decent labor laws for women and children and in favor of safety devices in mines without much consciousness of the existence of a contrary public opinion. Woman suffrage was different. The issue was clear and most women knew where they stood. They knew what their husbands thought about it. There was much opposing sentiment in the clubs even in 1910. The club movement was, from the feminist point of view, conservative, in spite of the fact that back in 1896 the Federation Council meeting had earnestly debated, before it was laid on the table, the provocative motion that all "delegates to all future Biennials go under their own names instead of their husbands'."

The sharp rise in the interest of the clubs in legislation will be discussed in another section of this report. It was great. Nevertheless, the familiar study-outlines on art, literature and history, which certain women's magazines had been offering to their subscribers from 1897, made up most of the service for club programs.

It is not unlikely that the growing interest in public affairs was responsible for much of the criticism of the club movement which assumed formidable proportions in this decade. Earlier laughter-provoking cartoons had been common, and a half-scornful reference to the clubs as the "middle-aged woman's university" was often quoted by Federation speakers. By 1905, however, the number of "club pages" devoted to the activities and interests of club women showed that the daily press took the movement seriously. The attacks which appeared in one woman's magazine were equally earnest.

In January of 1902, for example, an ecclesiastic of high rank wrote in the *Ladies' Home Journal:*

> The spirit of unrest has found easy victims in thousands of American homes, until the social condition which presents itself today, even among the best and most cultured classes, differs essentially from our standard heretofore held as inviolable. . . .
>
> As I have said before, I regard Woman's rights, women and the leaders in the new school of female progress as the worst enemies of the female sex.

And in the same magazine in March, 1902, the editor remarked:

> It has been one of my dispositions to study Woman's Clubs, both at close range and at a comfortable distance, and I must confess that which I have seen of them and read of them is not to their credit.

There was a clamor in answer to the editorial opinion and a convincing recital of various community projects undertaken by clubs of women.

Yet in 1905, a distinguished Ex-President of the United States wrote in the same magazine in the first of a series of two articles:

> I am persuaded that there are Woman's Clubs whose objects and intents are not only harmful, but harmful in a way that directly menaces the integrity of our homes.

It was this statesman's theory that the clubs were made up of neglected wives who joined the organization in retaliation for the inattention of their husbands. Some club activities were undoubtedly very silly, some husbands were unquestionably inattentive, but when these articles were written there were almost 500,000 women enrolled. A considerable number must have been cherished wives, and the record of some of the work they were undertaking stands as a fine tribute to their conception of the public welfare.

If there is any special characteristic of the period from 1900 to 1910, it may be the tendency toward cooperation between and among national organizations. For, while their own union was still new, representatives of the Federation were working on common projects with representatives of other groups. Seven national organizations were "affiliated" with the General Federation in a somewhat nebulous relationship. A new department of the National Education Association was composed of representatives of the Association of Collegiate Alumnae, the National Council of Jewish Women and the General Federation. It was called the Educational Department of National Organizations of Women.

At the request of the National Civic Federation representatives of the American Federation of Labor, the National Association of Manufacturers, the General Federation, and the American Economic Association met to investigate the whole subject of child labor. The Conservation Association, the Tuberculosis Association, the Peace Congress, the American Federation of Arts, the National Child Labor Committee, had invited Federation representatives to sit in conference. The President of the General Federation had been honored with a seat at the White House Conference of Governors in 1908. And at the convention in 1910 another cooperative relationship was forecast by the adoption of a resolution expressing the desire of the Federation to cooperate with the Audubon Society.

Often the impulse for cooperation must have come from the small specialized or professional groups, which looked upon the Federation membership as a fertile field for education and support.

The new decade which the great Federation was facing with such an amazing group of standards and such a diversified membership, was to see new groupings of women appear, old organizations increase, and at least one association disappear when the cause for which it was organized had triumphed.

CHAPTER IV

FROM 1910 TO THE WAR

THE decade naturally divides itself into two periods, that before the United States entered the World War, and the years after April 6, 1917.

In 1912 a new national movement for young women emerged to culminate later in the Association of Junior Leagues of America. The first Junior League had been formed in New York in 1901— its purpose being to organize the city's debutantes in active civic work. By 1912, six more Junior Leagues existed. They were in Baltimore, Boston, Brooklyn, Chicago, Philadelphia, and Portland, Oregon, and a conference of their representatives was held in New York. The membership of the Junior Leagues was confined to girls of leisure, those whose families represented, for the most part, the wealth and social leadership of their communities.

In 1912, the two existing nursing organizations formed a third— The National Organization for Public Health Nursing. Both lay and professional members were welcomed to membership.

A new occupational development, as well as a recognition of a social need, was discernible in the organization, at the annual conference of Charities and Corrections in 1915, of the International Association of Policewomen.'At that time, at least thirty cities employed women in their police departments. Although no women had had the title of "policewomen" until 1910, women had been associated with the police departments of various cities for a long time. The Woman's Christian Temperance Union had advocated their employment as far back as the seventies and eighties when its efforts had secured the appointment of police matrons in fifteen American cities. Later other women's organizations sponsored their employment and in 1915 there appeared to be a sufficient number to organize an association for the cooperative development of their program.

In the same year at a meeting in November of the American Medical Association, the Medical Women's National Association was organized in Chicago.

In 1916, the Federation of Teachers was organized from a local teachers' union in Chicago and affiliated with The American Federation of Labor. It was not exclusively a woman's movement, although a woman organized the federation, but the fact that public school teaching is so largely feminine makes its appearance worthy of mention as an achievement of women. It was the first national organization in the United States in which teachers were united, for it was not until 1918 that class-room teachers were recognized as part of the National Education Association, which had been organized in Philadelphia in 1857. Before 1918, the membership of the Association was largely composed of administrative leaders, college presidents, professors, and principals. Women did not bulk large in those positions, and only found a place in the organization when class-room teachers were admitted to its activities.

In 1916, out of a series of separate but related conferences the National Association of Deans of Women was organized, now a section of the Department of Superintendence of the National Education Association. Its history goes back to November, 1903, when, on the invitation of the Deans of Women at the University of Chicago and of Northwestern University, eighteen Deans of Women met in the first conference of Deans of Women of which there is record. The problems which they met to discuss were the natural concerns of their profession—the living conditions, the social life, and the organization of student activities, especially as those activities affected women students. Six resolutions were adopted, one of gratitude to the women who called the meeting and one welcoming the assistance of the Young Women's Christian Association in its work with students. Intercollegiate athletic contests for women students were disapproved, the principle of student government was advocated. One resolution considered the housing of women students away from their own homes and approved:

(1) Dormitories, preferably small; (2) cottages, belonging to and controlled by the institution; (3) approved lodging and boarding houses belonging to private individuals.

Of the social life of women students this first conference

Resolved, that social life should be regulated and that the tests of good health and high scholarship should be applied in extreme cases of social dissipation. In the opinion of this conference, the public have exaggerated impressions in regard to the amount of social dissipation

[35]

existing in coeducational institutions. The facts brought out in the reports of deans from such institutions point to the conclusion that the proportion of women students who give too much time to social affairs is very small.

This meeting was the first of a series of similar conferences at which old and new topics were considered. A conference of Deans and Advisers in State Universities was held at least biennially from 1905, and informal conferences of Deans of Women were held in connection with the meeting in 1909 of the Religious Education Association in Chicago and with meetings of the Association of Collegiate Alumnae. A conference of Deans of Women of Private Institutions occurred in Chicago in 1909; and finally the National Association of Deans of Women was formed. Its annual meetings now are held in connection with the meetings of the National Education Association and its membership in 1930 was 1,064. Its programs deal with the varied problems of women students, their adjustment to life on the campus and their preparation for life outside. The creation of the new post of Adviser or Dean of Girls in High Schools is due in large measure to the work of the Association.

In 1914, a militant left wing seceded from the National American Woman Suffrage Association and founded the Congressional Union, which two years later adopted a new name, The National Woman's Party, for the purpose of applying to the effort to secure the ballot the methods developed by the "suffragette" group in England.

Soon after the outbreak of the war in 1914, the Women's Peace Party was organized in Washington, and in January, 1915, 3,000 people attended a convention at which a program for peace was adopted. In the spring of the same year an international conference of women was held at The Hague and in January, 1916, The Women's Peace Party became the United States Section of the Women's International Committee for Permanent Peace which was organized then. Its stated object is:

To promote that peace between nations, races and classes, which is based on justice and good will, to outlaw war, to substitute law for war, and to cooperate with women of all countries in carrying out the policies formulated at International Congresses of the Women's International League for Peace and Freedom.

The new name was chosen at a meeting in Switzerland in 1919. The membership of the Women's International League for Peace and Freedom in the United States is not large, although its slow growth has been steady. In 1930 it had approximately 10,000 members. It has supported every effort toward peace, and has opposed all attempts to increase national defense, to glorify war, to embark on imperialistic national policies, or to discriminate against pacifist citizens. Two smaller peace societies for women were organized later—one the Women's Peace Society and the other, the Women's Peace Union.

So far, membership in organizations has been largely from domestic women; married women whose club activities provided an escape from household and family cares or from professions; women who were, as it were, furthering the interest of their profession—the nurses, physicians.

In the period after April 6, 1917, notice should be taken at once of the organization of the first of a group of five "service clubs for business women." That is, for the first time gainfully employed women were providing their spare time with opportunities for relaxation and for association with other similarly occupied women. Following the example of the Rotary, Kiwanis and similar clubs for men which had developed business and professional classifications as a basis for membership, the first Altrusa Club was organized[1] for women in Nashville, Tennessee, and added four others within the year. To quote the Altrusa Handbook:

To be eligible for active membership in an Altrusa Club, a woman must be actively engaged in an occupation in which she holds a responsible position of executive character; or she must be the owner of her own business, or be practicing a profession.

Good fellowship and friendship among women from various occupational groups is the primary object of membership in Altrusa; nevertheless the national association voted in 1924 to encourage each club to adopt vocational guidance as its general service activity. In carrying out this recommendation Altrusa clubs have cooperated with school groups, sponsored lectures, conducted surveys, maintained scholarships for vocational training, and assisted in placement. Books on the subject have been donated to schools and public libraries. In the recent past the Altrusa clubs have cooperated with the Institute of Women's Professional Relations, to which reference is made below, in connection with the development of professional interests among the

[1] By a man.

women,[1] in surveying the field of dentistry as a professional opportunity for women.

There were in January, 1931, 109 Altrusa clubs in 34 states, with a total membership of 3,000 women.

Quota, International, was the second such club to appear. The Christmas party at which the Kiwanis Club of Buffalo, New York, entertained its "ladies" in 1918, seems to have been the immediate cause of its organization. Five business and professional women were guests, women "keen of insight and broad of vision" according to the brochure issued by the headquarters. They planned the organization of Quota, and in 1919 Quota, International, obtained a charter.

The plans and standards and rate of growth of Quota are similar to those of Altrusa. In 1930 there were 30 Quota clubs with a total membership of 3,000. Service to girls is the essential activity of the Quota clubs with the suggestions to local groups that they work by

(1) Aiding existing organizations; (2) organizing or aiding girls' clubs and homes; (3) providing scholarships for girls; (4) doing personal or "big sister" work, with individual girls.

The third, Zonta Club, was organized in 1919, with a similar plan of organization and work, and in June, 1930, it reported 108 clubs with 3,200 members.

The Soroptimists were organized shortly afterward, in the autumn of 1921. Like the Altrusa clubs, this group was organized by a man—a professional organizer. Unlike the other three clubs, it was inaugurated on the western coast—in San Francisco. There were 8 members of the first club at the time of its organization. In 1930, 62 clubs were reported with a total membership of approximately 3,200.

The ideals of the organization are embodied in the five objects which are listed:

CIVIC.—To encourage meritorious civic movements and to urge cooperation for the betterment of local conditions.

MORAL.—To encourage the practice of the Golden Rule, and to foster high ethical standards in business and professional life.

SOCIAL.—To promote the spirit of service and true friendship among our members.

[1] *Recent Social Trends in the United States,* Chap. XIV.

PERSONAL.—To develop efficiency and the success to be derived therefrom; to foster the interchange of ideas and business methods as a means of increasing the efficiency and usefulness of SOROPTIMISM; to recognize the worthiness of all legitimate occupation of each Soroptimist as affording her an opportunity to serve society.

The fifth of these clubs is Pilot, International. It flourishes in the South.

And then the business and professional women took on a similarity to the groups organized within a definite calling.

In 1919, at St. Louis, the National Federation of Business and Professional Women's Clubs was organized by a group of less than 200 women representing 105 existing clubs.

In the meantime, while these new groupings within the constantly increasing ranks of wage-earning women were indicating the changing position of women in the United States, the older organizations continued to expand, so that the history of the General Federation in its third decade should now be briefly reviewed.

In 1912, the Federation of Women's Clubs, according to some statements in its record, passed the million mark in its membership, although the lower estimate of 800,000 which appears in the same Convention Proceedings is probably more nearly correct.

The leaders in the club movement were aware of the distance which lay between the resolutions adopted by the delegates at the Conventions and the actual activities of the clubs at home. In her address to the Convention in 1912, the president deplored the fact that little had been done to carry out the resolutions adopted in 1910. No one could claim that the Hague Conference, industrial accidents, or clean journalism had been greatly affected during the biennium by the attitude of clubs.

Nevertheless, resolutions were adopted at this Biennial with even greater facility than usual. Twenty different questions, ranging from forest fire prevention to sex education and Bible reading were involved in as many resolutions. And although the delegates voted "either to purify or to eliminate" the Comic Supplement, a resolution favoring woman suffrage was ruled out of order. A majority of the resolutions affected questions political, although the word was still dreaded. Discussion of their significance will, therefore, fall more appropriately in a later section of this report dealing with the subject of women's participation in politics.

Reports from the states deal with an extraordinary diversity of subject matter. Some clubs put wire waste baskets to collect refuse on street corners. Others trained the speaking voice.

A new subject was introduced in the next Biennial which met in Chicago in 1914 when for the first time the Federation clubs endorsed equal suffrage for women. A confusing array of subjects—sex education, fire prevention, health campaigns—were offered again for the attention of the delegates, and the Convention heard addresses by authorities, sang songs, and listened to reports. There was much protest against current styles of dress, indignation because of "slit skirts, transparent gowns and ridiculously narrow skirts" and distress because of immodest dancing.

No examination of Biennial records, of magazine files, or of state conventions can give a complete picture of the work being carried on all over the country; but it is safe to say that the interest in the award of scholarships was general—more than twenty states were then granting them to promising students. Traveling libraries and traveling art exhibits were numerous, and the Federation joined in the wave of public effort to reduce the deaths from tuberculosis and to eradicate the social diseases. There were numerous resolutions about the White Slave Traffic, one state Federation reporting that its clubs had been advised to put placards in railroad stations to warn arriving girls of the perils of the city.

A few states still boasted of exclusive clubs, and described the brilliance of their members' papers—but most of them added "civic" and legislative activities, and in several reports the sad habit of passing resolutions and then forgetting them was deplored.

The beautification of the Lincoln Highway assumed prominence in 1916 along with censorship of moving picture shows, and "Americanization" seems to have been the keynote of the convention which was held in New York City with 2,144 delegates registered and 15,000 women in attendance.

By the time the 1918 Convention came the activities of women had been diverted to war needs. Two million women was the estimate of the membership appearing in the reports at the time. The familiar committee reports were heard at the Biennial and it was natural that interest in conservation of foods should make the Home Economics committee the most outstanding. "Children's Year," when it was proposed, was heralded, and the talk of standardized dress for women found congenial atmosphere in a world of uniforms.

Nearly forty resolutions were adopted at this convention and the General Federation of Women's Clubs faced the fourth decade of its life with the habit of endorsement heavy upon it.

Unquestionably the resolutions were taken seriously by the leaders and indicate their conception of club women's interests. Material for study was prepared, speeches were made, articles were written in relation to the subject matter advanced. However, it is impossible to estimate the extent to which local clubs attempted to carry out the resolutions, but that club activities meant much in the lives of many women cannot be doubted.

CHAPTER V

THE POST-WAR DEVELOPMENT 1918–1932

DURING the period from the close of the war until the present time, the end of the second, the whole of the third, the beginning of the fourth decades, women's organizations have continued to multiply, the variety in purpose is greater than ever, the tendency toward cooperation or toward the development of interrelationships has perhaps been strengthened, the international interest has been expressed; but with all such movement of expression has gone, too, the provision for individual satisfaction or for purely social intercourse. The patriotic motive, the religious or sectarian bond, the scientific interest, the professional alliance, the altruistic impulse—all are conspicuous in the purposes of the organizations; at the same time, great sums of money are assembled for the provision of comfortable living quarters and of accommodations for bridge or other pastimes, having only the individual's satisfaction in mind. As has been said above, it is difficult to convey in brief statement the variety of these activities and the multiplicity of these organizations. If the purpose were to study the relative effectiveness of different forms of organization, a very different method of presentation might be employed. The purpose is not, however, to discuss methods of organization. It is certainly not possible to measure results of one or of the other form of association; nor is that the interesting problem. The interesting question is not what kind of organizations are formed, but what is the meaning to women of the organizations and how women express themselves through these activities.

The war had a disturbing effect upon women's organizations in at least two ways. It gave occasion for the development of new organizations based on the patriotic motive, and, through the mobilization of the youth of the land, widened the range of interest of the women. In the following pages the story of the national organizations, to which reference has already been made, will be continued and some account will be taken of the new ones that have come into existence. It is hoped that from these threads of activity may be discerned a line of development in women's relationship to the post-war generation.

There seem to be twenty-three organizations to which reference must be made, besides what might be termed four movements: (1) the development of adult education among rural women under the Department of Agriculture, (2) the further organization of Negro women, (3) the Pan Hellenic movement among sororities, and (4) the club house movement. Besides these movements, some reference should also be made to certain sets of problems such as that of international relationships and the question of budgets and sources of support. It is hoped that out of this kaleidescopic variety may come a discernible picture of women's effort to bridge the gap between their segregated and isolated status of the past and their possible future participation in the fullness of community experience.

The war meant great dislocation in family life, in industry, in government. What it meant for women in their organizations can be only suggested, not fully told. And, as one writes or reads, there should be kept in mind the multiplicity of interests involved in any one organization. Who can measure for example the significance of belonging to the Gold Star Mothers?

Perhaps the associations connected immediately with the war or its consequences may be mentioned first.

During the years since the war, new organizations have appeared and old ones have developed.

The Service Star Legion and the American Legion Auxiliary.— The war, of course, brought new alignments and caused unfamiliar groups of women to come into the field of organized activity. In the fall of 1917 the War Mothers of America was organized in Indiana and held its convention in Evansville, the home of Lance Corporal James B. Gresham, who was the first American boy to die in the service. After the Armistice, interest lagged, but the Baltimore branch, acting on a previous agreement to entertain the 1919 Convention, called similar organizations known to have been organized to work for the soldiers to meet with the War Mothers of America and proposed that all should be merged in one large association. Eleven organizations answered—Pershing's Own came from Kansas, delegates from The Sunset Trail were sent from Oregon, the Daughters of Democracy were represented, Sammies' Mothers Clubs, the Daughters of the Nation, and a half dozen

[43]

others. The Service Star Legion was adopted as the name of the new group and 50,000 women were enrolled as members with the objectives of their organization stated in the following seven declarations:

1. To serve God, Country and Humanity.
2. To promote Peace and Brotherhood among men and nations.
3. To guard the welfare of soldiers, sailors and marines who were engaged in the World War, and to lend aid and comfort to their families.
4. To preserve and cherish the memory of the men and women who sacrificed their lives for the liberty of the world.
5. To foster a spirit of sisterhood and democracy among women.
6. To cooperate in all civic and patriotic work.
7. To protect and preserve American ideals and traditions.

Some of the original War Mother's group refused to admit other women relatives. These withdrew and organized and took the slightly changed name American War Mothers.

In the same year the establishment of a women's auxiliary of the American Legion was promoted, and when the second national convention of the Legion was held in Cleveland in 1920, 1,342 local units of this auxiliary organization were reported. In 1921 the organization of the American Legion Auxiliary was completed and the first national convention called.

Inevitably membership in the independent Service Star Legion diminished. From 50,000 in 1919, it fell to 10,000 in 1925 and, although membership figures for succeeding years are not available, it is unlikely that it has shown any considerable growth. Under its general principles, it has undertaken to maintain an educational loan fund for the members of families of World War veterans, to give relief to needy veterans and to inaugurate or support various movements to commemorate the victims of the war. In addition, the Service Star Legion has supported proposals designed to provide peaceful methods for the settlement of international disputes.

The Legion Auxiliary in the meantime has grown from the 131,000 reported in 3,653 units in 1921 to 300,549 members divided among 6,635 units in 1928—a gain in seven years of approximately 129 per cent. By December, 1931, a total of 412,-063 members were enrolled. The Auxiliary assists the Legion itself in all its activities and undertakes special responsibilities toward rehabilitation and child welfare in relation to disabled veterans and their children, and the children of men who died in the service. Like the Legion, the Auxiliary is prepared to oppose any movement for a reduction of armaments. A sentence from the address of the National President at the 1930 Convention in Boston is typical of the attitude which finds expression in formal addresses and in committee reports. She said:

> The Auxiliary's efforts in this field have been devoted primarily to combatting sentimental pacifism among the women and counter-acting the activities of the radical pacifists among the women and the students of the country.

The National Society, Daughters of the American Revolution.—The American Legion Auxiliary has worked in increasing harmony with the Daughters of the American Revolution which, since the First Congress in February, 1892, has grown until on June 1, 1932, it was composed of 2,463 chapters with a total membership of 169,626. In 1920 its membership had totaled 107,723. Ten years earlier it was 79,713.

The objective of the founders was expressed in three paragraphs:

> To perpetuate the memory and spirit of the men and women who achieved American independence, by the acquisition and protection of historical spots, and the erection of monuments; by the encouragement of historical research in relation to the Revolution and the publication of its results; by the preservation of documents and relics, and of the records of the individual services of Revolutionary soldiers and patriots, and by the promotion of celebrations of all patriotic anniversaries.

> To carry out the injunction of Washington in his farewell address to the American people, "to promote, as an object of primary importance, institutions for the general diffusion of knowledge," thus developing an enlightened public opinion, and affording to young and old such advantages as shall develop in them the largest capacity for performing the duties of American citizens.

> To cherish, maintain, and extend the institutions of American freedom, to foster true patriotism and love of country, and to aid in securing for mankind all the blessings of liberty.

Certainly the objectives of the first statement of the founders have been honored and the country is greatly indebted to this volunteer body of women who have rescued historic sites, engaged in geneological research, beautified cemeteries, and erected commemorative monuments.

Scholarships have been generously awarded by the Daughters. Over $138,000 was expended through the Student Loan Funds in 1929 and more than 350 young men and women were assisted through college. An Industrial School for Girls is maintained in

South Carolina, and contributions are made to fifteen other institutions, the majority of them among the mountaineers of the South, as a further effort to carry out the objective in the second statement.

It is in heeding the third admonition of the founders that the organization has expressed itself on public questions and that these daughters of rebels have allied themselves with the militaristic theory of national defense, and with what was there recognized as the Tory, rather than the revolutionary, attitude toward political theories.

At its annual Congress in Washington in 1930 forty resolutions were adopted. Of these, besides eight expressions of courtesy, eleven were related to fiscal or organization management questions. One urged the adoption of the "Star Spangled Banner" as the National Anthem of the United States, another recommended the designation of April third as America's Creed Day. The establishment of a National Park on King's Mountain was approved, the creation of a Colonial National Monument on the sites of Jamestown and Yorktown in Virginia was endorsed, and the assistance of the organization to the George Washington Bicentennial Commission was pledged. Participation in the Yorktown celebration was projected in a Resolution. The erection of a Community House for midshipmen at Annapolis was approved and the invitation extended by the American Legion that the Daughters "have a salon" in its new building in Paris was accepted.

One resolution expressed a general policy and all the others related to public questions in which every citizen may properly have some concern. The policy resolution was this:

WHEREAS, it has always been a settled policy of the National Society, Daughters of the American Revolution, to avoid controversial subjects of a religious or political nature, as being outside of its province; and

WHEREAS, a restatement of this policy would prevent misunderstanding in the future as to the Society's attitude.

RESOLVED, That this 39th Continental Congress re-affirm the resolutions of the National Board of Management passed June 4, 1913, and April 18, 1914, which declare that all controversial or dividing topics such as religion, politics, and prohibition should be excluded from its deliberations.

The subject matter of the following Resolutions was then evidently regarded by the Congress of the Daughters as non-controversial. In regard to immigration the Congress resolved:

That we urge upon Congress the extension of the policy of restriction upon immigration to all geographic and political areas beyond the boundaries of Continental United States not specifically regulated by the Immigration Act of 1924; the enactment of legislation providing for the registration of aliens for the protection of all lawful entrants and the elimination of subversive and undesirable elements from our country; and the enactment of more strict legislation, supported by adequate appropriations, to effect the deportation of aliens who have surreptitiously entered the country, or who have succeeded in evading our laws designed to exclude the dangerously criminal and insane.

It endorsed the resolution of the Women's Patriotic Conference on National Defense, which determined to expose and combat so-called subversive influences in schools and colleges, and

WHEREAS, The schools and colleges are considered a fertile field for the dissemination of socialist and communist theories, often so subtly presented that the students fail to recognize their sigificance; and

WHEREAS, The press in many states have carried news stories describing forums that have been organized within educational institutions, to break down patriotism, to weaken the spirit of national loyalty, and to interfere with military training and other phases of national defense,

it approved requiring teachers to take the oath of allegiance as a further barrier "against the entrance of anti-American organizations into the schools." It declared its opposition to the recognition of Russia and to entangling alliances "which could operate to limit our full liberty in international affairs." It endorsed the objects and purposes of the Reserve Officers Training Corps organization and approved "just and necessary compensation for the commissioners and enlisted personnel of the Army, Navy and Marine Corps, Coast Guard, Geodetic Survey and Public Health Service." Adequate National Defense was urged in the following statement:

WHEREAS, The right of National self-defense is incorporated in the Constitution of the United States and confirmed by the laws of reason; and

WHEREAS, Organizations of doubtful intention are conducting propaganda to weaken the defenses of our country in the face of an armed world.

RESOLVED, That the National Society of the Daughters of the American Revolution reaffirm their traditional adherence to the principle that the institutions, liberty and property of the United States must be properly defended against all possible aggression from within or without; and

RESOLVED, That we urge the enforcement of the terms of the National Defense Act and the support of the Government and people of all organizations and programs for the proper training of our young men for national service in the event of need; we specifically urge the support of our naval and military establishments, of the National Guard, the Reserve Officers' Training Corps and the Citizens' Military Training Camps; and

RESOLVED, That we urge the Congress of the United States to make proper legislative and financial provision for the maintenance of a competent National Defense in all its branches.

And subversive organizations were opposed in the following Resolutions:

WHEREAS, Full information as to affairs affecting their government is a moral right of the people of the United States; and

WHEREAS, Certain influences inimical to the safety of the United States have been conducting a heavily financed propaganda in support of their aims; and

WHEREAS, These inimical influences use every possible effort to keep their operations secret from the public; now, therefore, be it

RESOLVED, That we strongly urge the unmasking of all subversive organizations of foreign or local nature by rigorous investigations conducted under competent governmental authority and that steps be taken to disrupt such organizations, deport the aliens participating therein and properly punish those of American citizenship who have lent their support to this form of disloyalty.

While there has been some protest in the membership against these activities of the leaders and some disagreement with the view of the society, the organization has evidently been fairly unanimous as to the principles enunciated.

A good many women who take slight interest in its public policies, undoubtedly become members of the organization in order to establish a family record. Those who do become active, attend congresses, and hold offices, seem to be harmonious in their attitude toward public questions. In 1929, an election year in the organization, there were 4,118 voting delegates and their alternates registered at the Congress. In 1930 the delegates and alternates numbered 3,628. The Headquarters in Washington, with a beautiful auditorium, a spacious library, and a museum, is valued at three million dollars.

Women's Overseas Service League.—As organizations of World War veterans multiplied, it was natural that the women who had served overseas should unite. In 1921, various groups of overseas women united in one national organization under the name, Women's Overseas Service League. Of the 22,000 women who served overseas with the government or with welfare agencies, about 2,500 are now enrolled in the Overseas League, which is organized in 56 units.

The League has inaugurated a fund for the care of needy disabled overseas women, particularly those who are not eligible for government aid. At the same time it advocates an extension of government responsibility to include care for all disabled women who served overseas with the government. It engages in welfare work not only for disabled overseas women, but for all veterans, for men and women now in the Service, and in some instances for the children of veterans.

These are mentioned as activities of the organization which enunciates its purpose in the following terms:

> To keep alive the spirit that prompted overseas service, to maintain the ties of comradeship both of that service, and to assist and further any patriotic work; to inculcate a sense of individual obligation to the community, state and nation; to work for the welfare of the army and navy; to assist, in any way in our power, men and women who served and were wounded or incapacitated in the World War; to foster and promote friendship and understanding between America and the Allies in the World War.

The National Council of Catholic Women.—The National Council of Catholic Women appeared in 1920. It is an affiliation of

> (1) National organizations of Catholic women enjoying ecclesiastical approval; (2) Diocene Councils, organized according to the plan and wish of the Ordinary; (3) State and local organizations of Catholic women; and (4) Individual Catholic women interested in work for the general welfare of the church.

In October, 1930, 1,700 local societies were affiliated and 50 Diocesan organizations in addition to the following National members: The Alumnae Association, National Catholic School of Social Service; The Alumnae Association, Trinity College; The Alumnae Auxiliary Association, Catholic Summer School of America; The Catholic Daughters of America; The Catholic Ladies of Columbia; The Christ Child Society; The Daughters of Isabella; The First Catholic Slovak Ladies Union: The International Federation of Catholic Alumnae; The Ladies Auxiliary, Ancient Order of Hibernians; The Ladies Catholic Benevolent Association; The National Alliance of Bohemian Catholics; The National Catholic Women's Union; The Supreme Ladies Auxiliary, Knights of St. John; The Theta Phi Alpha Fraternity;

and The Women's Catholic Order of Foresters; and these state organizations: The Catholic Daughters of America, Illinois State Court; The Catholic Daughters of America, Pennsylvania State Court; The Catholic Ladies Aid Society, California; The Sociedade Portugeuza Rainha Santa Isabel, California (Portugese Society of Queen St. Elizabeth); The a'Kempis Club of New Jersey; Young Ladies Grand Institute, California.

The Council is an official part of the program of the Catholic Church in the United States. It was organized at the call of the Chairman of the Department of Lay Organizations of the National Catholic Welfare Conference, an organization composed of the Archbishops and Bishops of the United States. Two hundred Catholic women, sent from their Dioceses by their Bishops, or representing various groups and organizations, met in Washington in March of 1920 and the Council was begun.

To quote its own outline, the purposes are:

To provide a channel of communication and otherwise aid in bringing into the currents of national life the messages from the Departments and Bureaus of the Council:
  (a) Acquainting Catholic women throughout the country with national legislation of vital interest to them and securing united action, when necessary, e.g., defense of Catholic education and parental rights;
  (b) Upholding existing federal laws threatened by such forces as Birth Control, Sterilization, Equal Rights Amendment, etc.;
  (c) Active work for the Catholic schools and colleges; encouragement of religious vacation schools and instruction classes for students not in Catholic schools and colleges;
  (d) Aid to the Catholic Press;
  (e) Immigration follow-up and religious care of the foreign born;
  (f) Rural Catechetical Instruction;
  (g) Welfare of Women in Industry.
To maintain a vigilant oversight of forces that endanger national well-being or threaten the fundamental Christian foundations of our country; to be a channel of communication to the Departments and Bureaus of the Council with reference to destructive trends and tendencies in Catholic lay life;
  (a) To study and promote Christian Social principles;
  (b) To study fundamental Catholic principles underlying international relations;
  (c) To maintain Christian standards in recreation, dress and literature.
To maintain representation at all meetings of a national or international character when vital principles are at stake or where matters of national well-being which should be our concern are under discussion.

To provide national conventions for conference on common problems and through adequate publicity given to these deliberations to place the Catholic attitude on questions of the hour before the general public.

To maintain National Headquarters—a reliable bureau of authentic information, cooperating with all other departments of the Council.

To maintain a trained staff to aid by correspondence the initiation or development of local projects undertaken by diocesan councils or other affiliated organizations.

To maintain the National Catholic School of Social Service to educate a corps of experts in social service technique who will be exponents of Christian principles and Catholic spiritual culture for the solution of social problems.

To assist, through affiliation with the International Union of Catholic Women's Leagues, in world-wide protection for the home and the defense of Catholic principles of social action.

The General Federation of Woman's Clubs of the Present.— The third decade of the century showed no new development or startling changes in the club movement. Some of the older clubs advanced to new heights of membership. At the 1922 Biennial 13 clubs were reported having a membership of more than 1,000, with one, the Friday morning club of Los Angeles, having more than 2,000. No estimate of the entire membership of the General Federation is given.

The program of the Federation is as diversified as ever, and the state reports disclose the same variety and inequality in progress. There is a slight decrease in the number of resolutions passed as compared with the two most recent Biennials. Perhaps the action of the 1926 Biennial, which resolved that "in the future the General Federation should guard its Resolutions more carefully," is responsible for the apparent change.

At the 1924 Biennial one chairman commented that "the clubs were returning to the literary program." In a good many communities they had, of course, never gone very far away. In 1922, the Headquarters Report included, as an evidence of the activities of the organization, an analysis by subject of the many requests for information which had been received at the Headquarters from the separate clubs. It is interesting to examine.

While nearly 50 inquiries were in the field of art, only 15 were related to civic interests—and "Civic Pride" is one topic included in that modest total. Citizenship questions number only 14— and this included an inquiry about the "Proper Form for the Flag Salute"! The Social and Industrial Problems of Women gave rise to 49 inquiries—but the women of Russia and the Dangers of the Woman Vote each counted in this total. Interest in Community and Social Service brought forth 22 questions; Conservation, 16; Home Economics, 10; while there were only 4 inquiries relating to International questions. Literature, however, had a list of approximately 100 inquiries.

In spite of the gallant effort during more than twenty years to keep the subject alive, interest in Civil Service reform has in this decade lagged at a new low level. Active anti-tuberculosis work and the campaign against venereal disease were much diminished. The motion picture committee, however, was active, and interest in Indian affairs assumed some prominence. The billboard nuisance had become an object of hostility.

It would be easy to be scornful of an assembly ready, as the Federation was in 1926, to favor, in Resolution 18, a pending federal measure directed against the contract system of prison labor and swiftly then to pass to number 19 which opposed the habit of weight reducing without a physician's advice. In 1924, 35 Resolutions of some importance were adopted. They range from statements expressing support of the practical proposal that prohibition agents should be placed under Civil Service, that the United States personnel classification board should be abolished, and that the first eligible postmaster should be selected for appointment, to a general resolution which registered the members' aversion to obscene literature.

The fact that the Federation is a federation should, however, never be forgotten. A small literary, art, music or purely social club may join the other clubs of the state in a state federation, and through the state federation is counted a member of the General Federation. The interest of its members in Conservation and Indian Affairs may be slight, their sympathy for a Federal Department of Education or prison labor reform may be incomplete, although these are subjects advanced by enthusiastic chairmen, and presented at the conventions to the Committee on Resolutions as subjects upon which delegates to the conventions will vote.

At the Biennial conventions the opportunity is given to hear addresses and discussions, reports of plans proposed and work accomplished. The number of delegates is limited and expediency must sometimes direct their choice. Often they are not the most capable in deliberation, nor the most penetrating in their comments and reports. And even in an era of small hats and short hair the average convention hall leaves something to be desired when several thousand women gather to hear and to try to be heard. The Biennial meetings are then an inadequate instrumentality for the education of individual club women in the significance of the program of the General Federation, and this service should not be expected of them.

In the last decade a new type of cooperation has appeared within the Federation, namely the cooperation of the clubs with commercial interests. It can be noted in connection with the work of the music committee, with publishing houses, with household equipment companies in the furnishing of club houses and in the Better Homes movement. It was most conspicuously apparent in an ambitious Home Equipment survey which was conducted by the Federation and financed by the National Electric Light Association. Unhappily the source of the fund was revealed at a time when the private utility companies were disclosed as the organizers of a far reaching campaign to influence public opinion in their own behalf. Although the accuracy and usefulness of the data which had been assembled were not affected by the revelation, the reaction in many quarters was so unfavorable that the Home Equipment Survey has failed to be as important a contribution to knowledge of the subject of home-making as had been anticipated.

The Congress of Parents and Teachers.—From its modest beginning in 1897, the National Congress of Mothers has grown until in 1930 it was one of the largest organizations of women in the United States. In 1908 the rapid development of Parent-Teacher Associations prompted a change in the name, and it became the National Congress of Mothers and Parent-Teachers Associations. In 1924 it became the National Congress of Parents and Teachers, in order that the men who were participating in the work of the Congress might not be obscured.

In 1931, 1,511,203 members of Parent-Teachers Associations were enrolled in 22,000 units in 49 state branches in the National Congress and united in the program of parent education and child welfare which has grown up around the public school system of this country. The first data available on national membership are for the year 1912. Then 31,672 members were enrolled. In 1917 the figure was 98,844. The rapid increase continued. In 1920 there were 278,721 members, and in 1928 the million mark was

[53]

passed. Colorado led in 1930 in the proportion of members to its population—using United States Census Bureau estimates for computation, 5.11 per cent of the estimated population of the state were then enrolled. The largest actual membership in 1931 was in California, with Illinois, Ohio, New York, Texas, and Michigan making up the top sextette, if both memberships and units were taken into account.

The activity of local Parent-Teacher Associations centers around the school and the usefulness and growth of the organization are affected by the good will or hostility of the school administration. Its program must be adjusted and its value tempered by the requirements of expediency. State reports in the Convention Proceedings show evidence of much activity in relation to the school plant. Playgrounds are established and improved. Pictures, pianos and radios are donated. Libraries are maintained all over the country through the activities of Parent-Teacher Associations. Thrift banking schemes have been adopted as a result of their initiative. They support school bands. County and school nurses have been secured and some are paid by Parent-Teacher funds. Pre-school clinics feature some reports. Student loan funds are reported from at least 20 states. One state reported over 2,000 grade school pupils assisted in 1928. Local work appears to vary in type and excellence just as the activities of the clubs have been unequal. It has, however, the unifying center. It is organized around the school.

The national leaders have offered programs of parent education at the conventions, with educators, psychologists and sociologists leading the discussions, and courses in Parent-Teacher work are conducted in cooperation with educational institutions. An annual national project is called the Summer Round-up. The United States Commissioner has approved it, and the American Medical Association, the National Education Association, the American Child Health Association and the American Red Cross cooperate in the effort to correct defects of childhood by a widespread campaign of physical examination followed by treatment. In 1928, 48 states participated in the campaign. In 1930, 55,526 children were examined.

The American Association of University Women.—The 66 women alumnæ of Vassar, Smith, Oberlin, Wellesley, Boston University, Cornell, the Universities of Wisconsin and Michigan who met in 1882 at the second meeting of the newly organized

Association of Collegiate Alumnae in Boston, agreed that the object of this association should be to unite alumnae of those institutions for practical educational work.

In 1884, the first branch was established in Washington, D. C. In 1889, the Western Association of Collegiate Alumnae was united with the Association of Collegiate Alumnae, and in 1893 there were 16 branches existing. In 1921, the Southern Association of College Women was merged with the Association of Collegiate Alumnae and the American Association of University Women was adopted as the name of the organization. In 1923–1924, there were approximately 18,400 members organized in 500 branches. In 1931, there were approximately 551 branches and 36,818 members.

The program of alumnae education which the Association has always sponsored has expanded until now it includes the study of pre-school, elementary and adolescent, as well as collegiate and university, education, the expression of interest in international relations, and the publication of a journal of high quality. In 1931, when the semi-centennial of its organization was celebrated, it was estimated that there were groups in 523 branches studying the educational questions and 232 devoting attention to international affairs.

The Association attempts, by means of an accredited list, to raise standards in colleges and universities attended by women, and from the beginning has encouraged the educational progress of young women by awarding scholarships, fellowships, and loan funds for high school, normal school, college, and university courses. In 1925, 86 branches were participating in this form of Association activity by contributing approximately $50,000 a year for the purpose.

The Association is not unique among organizations in maintaining scholarships. Many organizations do that. A more distinctive project has been the granting of fellowships to women whose capacity and interests lead them to seek advanced degrees and scholarly attainments. The first fellowship was awarded by the Association of Collegiate Alumnae in 1890. In 1900, 3 fellowships were granted; in 1925, 11; and in 1930, 14. Now a fund of over $158,000 is devoted to this purpose and a campaign for a $1,000,000 endowment for fellowships, both national and international, is in progress. A history of the Association, written by one of its founders and another of its past presidents, relates

[55]

the story of its connection with the development of educational opportunity for women in the United States.[1]

The Young Women's Christian Association.—In the years since the work of the Young Women's Christian Association was begun it has expanded and developed and, although its constitution has been reworded, it has largely held to the objective which was first, the aid of self-supporting young women. From the beginning boarding homes have been maintained, to be used as residences, lunch rooms, and centers of recreation for wage-earning girls. In 1930 511,640 guests were housed in 300 Association residences. Educational work of various kinds was undertaken by the first Associations in New York and Boston, with vocational guidance and placement following as a natural corollary. In 1930, over 400,000 women and girls enrolled as participants in health education courses offered by the Association all over the country; more than 100,000 were interested in its general education classes. Only a few more than 30,000 participated in religious education. The same development has taken place in the employment service. Two hundred and two associations and 46 colored branches reported on employment in 1930. More than 140,000 women and girls had been placed in business, household and industrial jobs; more than 23,000 were placed in business, and a few under 10,000 in industry, and over 81,000 found household employment. The nature of the employment of the rest is not described.

This diversification of interests early developed a distinguishing feature of the Young Women's Christian Association—the fact that much of its work has been carried on by a paid staff, and that for more than forty years the advancement of its program has offered a professional opportunity for women. There were so many association secretaries in 1889 that they met to discuss their professional problems at the organization conference. Special training courses have been developed for their preparation and in 1930 the work of the local Associations was directed by a professional staff of 3,473 members.

The history is interesting. The first worker with younger girls was employed in 1887; twelve years later the number of "Junior Department" secretaries had grown to ten. In 1909, the

[1] Marion Talbot and Lois Kimball Mathews Rosenberry, *The History of the American Association of University Women* (Boston: Houghton, Mifflin Co., 1931).

problems of the adolescent girl were the subject of a conference program and today more than 230,000 younger girls form the largest group having membership in the Association.

There are today approximately 1,145 Young Women's Christian Associations in the country, although 180 are unaffiliated with the national organization. Including those independent groups, 265 are located in cities, 142 in towns, 47 in rural districts, and the largest number, 691, are established in colleges and universities.

As membership in the Young Women's Christian Association has grown, the basis for affiliation has been modified. In 1906, when the Associations of the country merged, the basis of membership in the Association was affiliation in any Protestant Evangelical Church. For twenty years this was unchanged, until, in 1926, at its convention in Milwaukee an alternate plan was adopted. Now any Association may admit to membership "any woman or girl properly introduced or giving satisfactory references as to character . . . " "Any woman or girl over eighteen" may become an elector in the Association, provided she declares that she desires to enter the Christian fellowship of the Association and will loyally endeavor to uphold the purpose in her own life and through her membership in the Association.

An effort has been made in recent years to supplement the work of the City Association by the development of a Town and a Rural Communities Department. Concern for the welfare of Indian women and girls has resulted in the organization of an Indian division. There is a Department of Immigration and Foreign Communities. There are 63 colored branches of City Associations with about 28,000 women and girls listed as members.

In 1905, 60,427 women were enrolled in the Young Women's Christian Association. In 1907 185,501 were reported. The membership in 1920 was 500,000 and in 1930 it stood at 603,876. It should be remembered that this figure includes Girl Reserves, students, groups of business women whom the Association serves, and its paid staff. Only approximately 55,000 women serve as volunteers on boards and committees and as advisers throughout the country—inheriting the responsibility undertaken by the first Women's Christian Associations more than sixty years ago.

From the first building owned and displayed at the first conference at Hartford in 1871, the valuation of Association real estate has grown until in 1929 it amounted to $71,749,902, and includes Boarding Homes, Administration Offices, Community Centers, and Summer Camps.

The Girls Friendly Society.—The Girls Friendly Society has grown since its organization until in 1931 it had a membership of 46,000 in 1,181 communities. Although girls of any creed may be members, the adult leaders—called "Associates"—still must be communicants of the Protestant Episcopal Church. It provides lodges or residence clubs in 11 cities for girls with small salaries. It maintains 27 Holiday Houses, where members may spend their vacations. Through membership in its branches, girls are given the opportunity for recreation and study, and every year a new missionary object is selected for support, and study of its needs by the branches is advanced to bind the membership together in a common benevolence. In 1928, for example, the Girls Friendly Society gave $6,000 to the Woman's Wing of St. Mark's Hospital at Cape Palmas, in Liberia, as its missionary project.

The growth of the Girls Friendly Society has been uneven, and its membership in 1930 was smaller than it had been five years earlier. However, it still enlists the support of women of the Episcopal Church, and contributes to the lives of thousands of working girls.

The National Woman's Christian Temperance Union.—Although the National Woman's Christian Temperance Union has joined with other organizations in supporting local, state and federal movements which might well fall within the scope of an organization having "for God and Home and Every Land" as its motto, and has carried forward independent projects of reform, it is nevertheless the record of the Union in behalf of temperance, in support of prohibition and its enforcement, which differentiates it from all other organizations of women. It has grown steadily and in 1930 it reported approximately 600,000 members. It has waged campaigns against patent medicines containing alcohol, against the sale of cigarettes, and in opposition to obscene literature. In state and local branches, the Woman's Christian Temperance Union is zealous in the field of moral reform.

The National Council of Jewish Women.—The National Council of Jewish Women included in 1930 over 50,000 members in its sections. It has set up buildings and institutions representing a value of more than $1,250,000. Neighborhood centers are maintained, Girls Homes, Y. W. H. A.s, Vacation Camps and Council Houses.

The Sections have provided for Jewish women the opportunity for social intercourse and for study and recreation together, which is characteristic of the general club movement. However, service to the underprivileged and unadjusted members of the race bulks large in its reports of work accomplished. In some communities various aspects of its work for social welfare and relief have been recognized by subsidies from Community Funds or from the treasuries of Jewish social agencies.

Aid to Jewish immigrants is generously supported, organized on a world-wide plan of cooperation, of which the Immigrant Aid Service maintained at Ellis Island and other ports of entry is one link, and the program of education for citizenship and employment in local communities another.

In 1921, the Council sent a Reconstruction Unit of Social Workers to Europe to reconstruct Jewish agencies and Jewish communities disorganized during and after the war, and in 1923 it summoned a World Conference of Jewish Women's Organizations in Vienna to consider the problem of Jewish refugees.

Religious schools have been organized in communities lacking facilities for Jewish education, and calendars of Holy days have been distributed to educational institutions in an effort to eliminate important school activities on Jewish Holy days. Scholarships are maintained by sections generally.

American Home Economics Association.—In September, 1930, The American Home Economics Association reported a membership of slightly more than 10,000. The work of the Association is as varied as the professional field to which it is related.

It has conducted research and investigations; it publishes a journal; it awards scholarships and fellowships; and, by cooperating with other research and commercial agencies, has endeavored to raise the standard of the profession it represents and to contribute to the knowledge of the whole field of Home Economics which ranges from textiles and nutrition to child development and parental education.

Three National Organizations of Nurses.—In 1930, there were three national nursing organizations cooperating to advance the interests and increase the service of the profession.

The National League of Nursing Education is the oldest, for it will be recalled that as the American Society of Superintendents of Training Schools for Nurses it was organized by eighteen superintendents in 1893. Its program dealt with the problems of nursing education, the courses and the practices offered and denied in that field of training. Until 1912, the membership was restricted to superintendents of training schools, but in that year it was enlarged to include instructors, supervising and head nurses, and public health nurses who were engaged in teaching work. State Leagues were forming by 1912 and a new plan of organization brought them in and changed the name to the one now used.

The function of the League is unchanged. It has strictly limited its field to problems connected with the education of nurses. Methods of teaching have been considered and necessary improvements have been advocated. Conditions under which student nurses receive their education have been examined, uniform curricula have been advocated in order that a reasonable minimum of instruction might be assured every graduate nurse. The extension of education in nursing to colleges and universities, with professional training and work for a Bachelor's Degree advancing together, has been urged by the League. Indeed, one of its first projects was securing, in 1899, the establishment of a school for the preparation of those who would teach or administer nursing training. The course was given in connection with Teachers College of Columbia. In 1931 there were 1,802 schools of nursing in the United States with which the League cooperated, giving continuously generous counsel and aid. There were in that year 82,989 students registered.[1]

The second organization, called the Nurses Associated Alumnae, was founded by the first in 1896. Now, as the American Nurses Association, it is the official organization of registered nurses in the United States, with 76,000 registered nurses enrolled. In 1929, there were 52 state Associations, one in each of the 48 states, one in Hawaii, one in Porto Rico, one in the District of Columbia, and an alumnae association of the Freedman's Hospital (colored).

In 1910 the Association inaugurated an educational fund, now administered jointly with the National League for Nursing Education and the National Organization for Public Health Nursing. It has provided scholarships and fellowships for gradu-

[1] Walter J. Greenleaf, *Nursing*, U. S. Department of the Interior, Office of Education, guidance Leafleat No. 15, p. 11.

ate nurses desiring the opportunity for further study and has loaned money to graduate nurses taking advanced courses in nursing education or in public health work. In May, 1929, the Loan Fund amounted to $5,500 and the Scholarship and Fellowship Fund totaled $34,000.

In 1911, a relief fund for needy nurses was inaugurated. The report of May, 1929, showed 189 beneficiaries carried on that date. The principle of the Fund on that date was $146,404.31. Since that time it has been decided that the administration of relief on a national basis is unsound and that some other plan for the administration of the project should be devised.

In 1921, as a memorial to the American nurses who died in the World War, the organization presented a new school building to L'École Florence Nightingale connected with la maison de la Santé de Bordeaux. A total of $81,000 had been donated in 1929.

With seven other national health organizations, the Association engaged in 1926 in financing a five-year program of the Committee on Grading of Nursing Schools.

The present period of general unemployment has concentrated attention upon a problem of the nursing profession which has been the concern of the Association for a long time; that is, the chronic condition of unemployment in the private duty field due not only to the free lance character of the work, but to the faulty distribution of service. A study was undertaken which will include a survey of nurse registries and graduate nurse services. Legislative protection, consideration of various plans of financial safeguards for nurses and the responsibility of interpreting the nurse to the public—these are questions for which the Association assumes leadership.

In 1912, the two existing organizations formed a third, the National Organization for Public Health Nursing, for the "stimulation and standardization of public health nursing and the furtherance of cooperation between those interested in public health nursing measures." In this organization the emphasis is on the cause of Public Health Nursing, rather than on the nurses as a professional group. Lay persons were admitted to its membership which in 1931 reached 4,500 individuals, and 285 local groups. On all problems of Public Health Nursing the National Organization for Public Health Nursing is prepared to give information, advice and consultation to local groups. A technical staff of ten, seven of whom are nurses, serve the board and committees.

All three nursing groups work together in close cooperation and harmony, holding biennial meetings together, having joint committees and headquarters. Their growth represents the constantly more exacting standards of the profession. Their work dramatizes the progress which has been made since 1828 when the first students of nursing were introduced at the Philadelphia Dispensary.

The National Woman's Trade Union League of America.— The National Woman's Trade Union League has reported 27 local branches established from its founding in 1903 to 1929. It has given aid to women on strike, assisted in the organization of new Trade Unions and has constantly attempted to shelter and protect women in industry within and outside its membership by organization, legislation and education. For more than ten years the League maintained a Training School for Active Workers in the Labor Movement and awarded scholarships to 44 Trade Union girls. This pioneer educational program for working girls ended in 1926, but the idea has developed until now 5 colleges have opened their doors to summer schools for working girls.

The American Federation of Teachers.—The Federation of Teachers has grown until its membership approaches 40,000 now, and in the National Education Association 175,000 classroom teachers represent the profession of which women make up the major part.

Organizations for Women in Medicine.—The Woman's Homeopathic Fraternity, formed in 1904, and the Medical Woman's National Association, organized in 1915, have been joined by the Osteopathic Medical Women's Association.

It was a purely social relationship which, until the war, bound together the first group, the women in Homeopathic Medicine. Then they joined in a national effort to establish a hospital unit, a project which was almost concluded when the Armistice was signed. There are less than 500 members of the Fraternity, but a scholarship fund is maintained for the education of young women in the profession. The fund has been available for more than a decade, 9 of the scholarship students are already practicing, and several are in college at the present time. In October, 1930, the membership of the Medical Woman's National Association, which requires membership in the American Medical Association for eligibility, was just over 600.

The Osteopathic Women's National Association.—In 1914 women in the practice of osteopathic medicine recognized the need of some organization through which their common interests could be advanced, and presented the necessity to the Board of Trustees of the American Osteopathic Association. The Trustees responded by creating a Bureau of Public Health, with a Women's Department, which later became a Women's Bureau of Public Health.

For six years this Bureau functioned as an auxiliary, and under a national chairman and a committee appointed by the Trustees of the A.O.A. it organized units in each state.

It was the desire to cooperate and affiliate with other national women's groups which prompted the translation of the Bureau into the Osteopathic Women's Association, effected in 1920.

Its objects are:

To promote the welfare of women and children; to cooperate with other women's organizations; to stimulate state and local organizations and to secure combined action by our women.

Scholarships have been established by the Association, clinics are maintained, lectures on health subjects are given. The consideration of common professional problems and mutual friendliness bind its membership, which is now over 300.

The National Federation of Business and Professional Women's Clubs.—The National Federation of Business and Professional Women's Clubs, to which reference will be made in the discussion of Women's Earnings, is only a little more than ten years old; but in 1931 state Federations existed in 46 states, and there were approximately 1,100 local clubs, which were eligible for membership because 75 per cent of all their members were actively engaged in business or in a profession. About 56,000 individual members were enrolled. It is fitting that during the first ten years of its existence the Federation should be able to report the development of 500 local educational funds through which it endeavors to realize its slogan, "at least a high school education for every business girl." Approximately, too, it has directed surveys of vocational guidance facilities in local communities and in cooperation with the University of Michigan has fostered and published the results of an occupational survey of its membership which is a genuine contribution to data concerning the business woman's problems. It publishes a monthly journal, *The Independent Woman*, which has advocated increased recognition of the interests of business women, such as, for example, larger income tax exemption for single persons under the federal law.

The proceedings of its conventions show a considerable amount of time given to discussion of emblems, of dues, and of administrative relationships. Those time-consuming topics are characteristic of the first years perhaps, and at the same time the National Committees on Health, on Education, on International Relations and Research have reported ambitious plans undertaken and accomplished. They have fostered campaigns to interest business women in positive health, to meet and join with employed women of other countries, and to face the special problems of women's employment.[1] And in general the 1,100 local clubs have provided a means of recreation and relaxation for thousands of business girls to whom other women's organizations have been alien.

Curiously enough, the clubs federated in this group do not maintain many club houses. In April, 1929, there were only 17 club houses maintained by local clubs and just 126 clubs with rooms. The membership is composed of women who might seem to have particular use for the services of downtown club houses. The explanation given by an official is that business women have no time to give to the volunteer management involved in the operation of a downtown club house by a club supported by the dues of wage-earning women. Apparently the club house movement for some time must be sponsored by women of wealth and leisure. The business or professional women of large incomes join with them. For the smaller income group the facilities of the semi-philanthropic organizations are available for recreation. For meetings of business clubs hotels are commonly used, and it is a matter of pride to many to have their insignia in the hotel lobby along side of the organizations of business men who gather weekly to lunch and make motions and sing. In September, 1930, under the leadership of the American Association, an International Association was organized in Geneva.

[1] *Recent Social Trends in the United States*, Chap. XIV. Attention is called to the published results of their admirable research.

The Association of Junior Leagues.—In 1930, there were 109 Junior Leagues in the United States, one in Hawaii, three in Canada and one in Mexico. In all, 22,000 young women are affiliated with the Association "of the Junior Leagues of America, Inc.," which was formed in 1921 by the 30 Leagues then in existence. A headquarters office is maintained in New York City with an Executive Secretary in charge, and a secretary in the field. The members of local Junior Leagues volunteer their services to various welfare agencies, or maintain their own projects. Hospital libraries and occupational therapy departments are financed and maintained, milk stations, day nurseries and clinics are supported. Baby shelters and hospitals are operated. Settlement and community houses are assisted. Little "civic" activity appears in the summaries of work undertaken by the Leagues, but the donation of considerable money and much time by young women of leisure to the benevolent agencies of their communities is recorded.

The Junior League has invaded smaller cities each year and has probably diverted some girls who might otherwise have found regular occupation by lending social distinction to the rôle of the benevolent volunteer.

The National Consumers' League.—Mention has been made of the substantial part played by women in the National Consumers' League, which was formed by the Federation in 1899 of Leagues in New York, Pennsylvania, Massachusetts and Illinois; and which attempted to arouse the conscience of the buying public to guarantee adequate protection to industrial workers. A woman founded the movement and, although the national presidents have always been men, one woman, Florence Kelley, was general secretary from the beginning until the winter of 1932, and the work all over the country has been carried forward largely through women's efforts. Two years after it was organized the National Consumers' League numbered 30 branches in 11 states. Three years later there were 64 branches in 20 states. But the League was not destined to grow great in size. In October, 1930, only 17 branches of varying size were reported, and in addition approximately 41,000 individual members were directly affiliated with the National League.

It was largely through the efforts of the Consumers' League that the General Federation of Women's Clubs advocated a high standard of legislation for women and children in industry in the first years of its existence. The League has financed investigations and published reports which have directed the attention of other groups to the abuses of home labor and of contract labor, and has urged them to demand decent standards. It is possible that the adoption of those standards by other women's organizations may have frustrated the Consumers' League's own growth. It was also through the efforts of this organization that the attention of the U. S. Supreme Court was directed to a new type of evidence and a new approach to the question of legislative control over industry.[1]

The National League of Women Voters.—When the National League of Women Voters took the place of the National American Woman Suffrage Association in 1920, it was not expected, even by its initiators, to be a long-lived organization. It was recognized, however, that women as first voters needed to be informed about the exercise of their new duties and privileges. After ten years the hope of dissolution proves to have been as optimistic as Mrs. Croly's notion that the cultural activities of women's clubs would soon be out-dated. The League has undertaken a long-time job of non-partisan political education. All its work is intended to see women in their character as citizens.

Leaders in the League of Women Voters like to refer to it as an agency of adult education, "to promote the participation of women in government." It has sponsored citizenship schools, ballot marking classes, and institutes of political education in cooperation with educational agencies and independently. It has produced popular but authoritative pamphlets on subjects related to the field of government which have been widely commended. With great earnestness it has supported a program of federal and state legislation. Its conventions are comparatively small, limited in representation to match the size of the United States Congress. Social features are reduced to a minimum and the programs are crowded with the presentation of the subject matter of the League's program of work and its discussion. All of these conditions tend to make the League a very business-like, orderly, hard-working group.

From the beginning, the League has emphasized the importance of its paid, as well as the value of volunteer, service. This is in sharp contrast to the General Federation of Women's Clubs, which has taken pride in the fact that it has advanced through

[1] *Recent Social Trends in the United States*, vol. I, p. 732.

service which is almost entirely volunteer. The League maintains a general national office in Washington, D. C., with three other national activities—the Radio Committee, the Department of International Cooperation to Prevent War, and the Treasurer's Office, housed in New York.

There were in 1930, 17 members of the national staff occupying positions of executive responsibility, 5 of them in the field, and a clerical force which averaged about 20 members. Twenty-seven state Leagues had headquarters. Of that number 22 states employed executives. In all, there were 55 positions divided among them. In addition, 41 local leagues had headquarters, with staff members totaling 30. These figures do not include stenographers or clerical assistance employed in state or local Leagues. They reveal that more than 100 young women, almost without exception college graduates and in most cases with some special interest in politics and government, are finding a professional opportunity in advancing the League's program from some one of the 72 headquarters.

Unquestionably the League has contributed greatly to the political education of its members. It has encouraged the use of study groups, round tables, forums and discussion classes to promote the examination of public questions. The League does not do welfare or relief work, but it supports movements for welfare through government. It has remained non-partisan in policy, and, although in some communities it has incurred the displeasure of local party leaders, in general it is recognized to have an all-partisan membership. Campaigns for city charters have been initiated by city Leagues. Reorganized state governments have been demanded by state Leagues and much admirable state legislation has been enacted as a result of its insistence. As in every other organization, there is some variation in the quality of work undertaken by local groups and naturally there is a great difference in the attitude toward the study of political questions and active participation in controversial issues. There is a gap between the program of work adopted at the national and state conventions and the activities of some local groups. However, the fact that the regional directors—volunteer members of the National Board in charge of a group of states—travel extensively in their territories, assisted by paid secretarial help almost constantly in the field, and that national officers and members of the national headquarters staff are sent on frequent trips, does tend to standardize the methods and to minimize inequalities. The League seems to be fairly homogeneous throughout the country.

Perhaps it is because of its record of causes espoused, of serious work undertaken, that the League has not grown more rapidly. It is impossible to cite accurate figures of membership, as the National League is composed of state Leagues and has no complete record of individual membership. The League is now organized in 45 states, the District of Columbia and Hawaii. In only two states does the estimated membership exceed 10,000, and it is probable that the total number of individual members falls below the 100,000 mark for the whole country.

In the opinion of many who have been associated with the League from the beginning, it is smaller in membership now than it was the year of its organization, even when generous allowance is made for the improved methods of membership record keeping which the National League has encouraged the states to adopt. In the early years the enthusiasm of victory and the excitement of a novel organization brought numbers of women into its membership with no very definite idea of responsibility. The fact that the League is a hard-working organization has discouraged the casual "joiner"; that it has eliminated social features rather generally has disappointed some women; the fact that it occasionally espouses unpopular causes has served to alienate still others. Those who remain are pretty well tried, and in influence and accomplishments within its chosen field the record of the League is not undistinguished.

While the large majority of leaders and officers in the club movement have been married women, in the League it has been the reverse. Its officers and committee chairmen are apt to be professional women experts in the field they undertake to supervise, or unmarried women of leisure and independence. The League has had only two presidents, one a widow with no children, the other unmarried. Both have given full-time service with the regularity that is usually considered professional.

The National Woman's Party.—The National Woman's Party is a non-partisan organization of women in the United States that has as its objective, "to secure for women complete equality with men under the law and in all human relationships."

Some of the innumerable laws that have in the past differentiated between men and women are still found in every state.

Among the most important ones are eligibility to public office including jury service, admission to public employment, *e.g.*, teaching and civil service, marriage, divorce, property rights of married women, support of family, domicil, guardianship, inheritance from children, earnings of children, sex offenses, illegitimate parentage, maternal and infant hygiene, mother's aid, prohibited occupations, public health regulations, and regulation of terms and conditions of employment.

The National League of Women Voters, as successor to the National American Woman Suffrage Association, has advocated a step-by-step procedure in the removal of injustices to women. The National Woman's Party has proposed a new amendment to the federal constitution which as a blanket provision would *give men and women equal rights throughout the United States and every place subject to its jurisdiction and would give Congress the power to enforce the amendment by appropriate legislation.*

The arguments given for working for a national equal rights amendment are that it is more inclusive than state legislation, that it is more permanent than state legislation, and that it is a more dignified way to establish equal rights than is state legislation. The tactical advantages in campaigning for a national amendment over campaigning for state legislation are that it obviates the costly and difficult state referendums which frequently occur in state legislation; it unites the resources of women and makes these resources more effective than when divided among 48 state campaigns; it takes the issue of equal rights into the national political arena, and it "forces the politicians to take a position on the principle of equal rights and prevents their dodging the issue as in the case of state legislation." The amendment, advocated since 1921, has been introduced at each session of the Congress and has been the subject of hearings before the Judiciary Committees of both houses, recent ones being in February, 1929, and in January, 1931, and January, 1932.

Representatives from the National Woman's Party and from the Inter-American Commission of Women representing 21 republics of the Western Hemisphere, took part in a series of conferences at Geneva in September, 1930, which resulted in the organization of Equal Rights International to work for the complete equality of women throughout the world.

The work of the national headquarters of the Woman's Party can be illustrated by their organization and broadcasting through the press of a nation-wide protest against the discharge of married women and of women from night work, the demand that more women be called for jury service in the District of Columbia, the intensification of a nation-wide press campaign against industrial discrimination, conducting hearings on the Cable Nationality bills, arranging for deputations to the President and asking him to withstand industrial inequality and to uphold the Equal Rights Amendment, hearings on the Equal Rights Amendment before the Senate Judiciary Committee, remonstrances by deputation and by organized telegraphic protest to governors against legislation alleged to be discriminatory, an organized protest against the Department of Labor's sending to Geneva a representative who, it was believed, would uphold the no-night-work convention—a protest followed by a public announcement on the part of the Secretary of the recall of the representative.

A recent achievement is convincing the chairman and secretary of the U. S. Civil Service Commission that the ancient Rule 7, under which appointing officers could specify the sex of a prospective member of the staff, should be abrogated. On October 8, 1932, these officials requested the President to revise the rules so as to place women on an equal footing with men. Over the dissent of the third member of the Commission, the President complied with the request on December 23, 1932. This does not deprive the appointing authority of the power to exercise a choice, but a reason must be given when the candidate who is lower on the eligibility list is chosen.[1]

The Woman on the Farm.—In spite of the great increase in membership of women's organizations and the wide diversity of their interests, one large group of women has been largely missed. The farm women of the country have been very lightly represented in the organized activities with which the women of towns and villages have been so preoccupied.

The club movement had made scant headway in the open country, although a club of farm women claims to be the first woman's club organized in the United States. It was organized in May, 1857, at Sandy Springs, Maryland, and it still exists under its original name of The Mutual Improvement Association. Its constitution sets out so well the methods and indicates the

[1] *Equal Rights*, XVIII: 390, Jan. 7, 1933.

sense of necessary discipline so clearly that a few sections are quoted. It provided:

that our number be limited to fifteen persons who shall meet at the home of each, in rotation, on the last fifth day of each month . . . taking the names in alphabetical order. The hour of meeting being 3 p.m. from the 4th to the 9th month inclusive, and 2 p.m. during the rest of the year, in order to allow sufficient time for business before supper, which it is recommended should be simple and early.

The plan of the group was described in another paragraph of the Constitution:

That we shall offer for the benefit of the Association such information as we may have obtained, by experience or otherwise, in any way calculated to elevate the minds, increase the happiness, lighten the labor or add to the comfort of one another, our families or neighbors; . . .

And further:

That each member be called on by name for some communication; when she may either ask for information on any subject she thinks it desirable to discuss or give information of the right nature which she has acquired, or call attention to some passage or book she has read not familiar to the rest, and all shall be expected to give attention to the subject under consideration.

But clubs like this were few. Generally, the farm women's participation in organized activities came in relation to general farm movements, the rise of the Granges, through Farmer's Institutes, or Farmer's Clubs which included the entire family.

The Grange deserves special mention for the position which its women members have always occupied. From 1867, when the Grange was organized, women were admitted to membership on a basis equal with men. And indeed, in order to secure a charter for a subordinate Grange, the application of at least 13 persons was required, not less than 4 of whom must be women. It is probable that at all times the majority of Masters, and of other major officers in the Grange, have been men. Nevertheless women have been elected, too, in considerable numbers. So much so that in the beginning Grange leaders were accustomed to a certain amount of urban ridicule because of their capitulation to "petticoat government." The 1930 roster of major state officers—master-lecturer, treasurer and secretary—shows 26 unmistakably feminine names in a list of 128. Only a fifth, to be sure, but probably as good an average and as favorable to women as any other organization of men and women could show.

The Farmer's Institutes as an agency of adult education developed in the first half of the nineteenth century. The programs, at which a variety of farm problems were presented, generally included one woman speaker. Her contribution was usually inspirational and typical of her subjects were "The Beauty of Unselfishness" and "Little Deeds of Kindness."[1]

Women regularly attended the Institutes, however, and in 1898 the farm women of Illinois formed an auxiliary to the county Farmer's Institutes known as the Domestic Science Association, modeled on a plan of organization which had flourished for some time in Ontario. Twenty counties were organized the first year and by 1906, 55 of the 102 counties in Illinois were doing active work. The clubs met once or twice a month and studied subjects such as the value and cost of food, hygiene and sanitation, the care and diet of the growing child. By 1904, at a meeting of the American Association of Farmer's Institute Workers, organized work for women was of sufficient importance to be given a special place in the reports. Other states followed the example of Illinois and in Indiana, Oklahoma, Minnesota, Kansas and Nebraska separate organizations for women were formed. In 1912, 720 Women's Institutes were held in 8 states with a total attendance of 78,776 women reported.

In 1913, a report of the Secretary of Agriculture stated, "According to the testimony of many who are thoroughly familiar with conditions, the needs of the farm women have been largely overlooked by existing agricultural agencies." A year later the passage of the Federal Act,[2] which appropriated federal money for Extension work in Home Economics and Agriculture in the states, accelerated the work among farm women which had already been begun. Although the federal law was not enacted with the object of providing an organization for farm women, its administration has given farm women an opportunity to work and to study together, which is not unlike the city woman's club. Organized groups of women in cities sprang from wars, from the World's Fair, or from an obvious occupational or social need. The majority of farm women clubs are unique in that they were stimulated to organize by an Act of Congress, and they are

---

[1] Lucile W. Reynolds, "Adult Education with Special Reference to the Rural Woman" (A Master's thesis, available in the University of Chicago Library).

[2] Generally known as the Smith-Lever Act, *U. S. Statutes at Large* 38: 372, Sixty-third Congress, Second Session, Chap. 79.

perhaps fortunate in that from the beginning they have had professional leadership.

This is not the place for a discussion of the federal act, its administration or the general accomplishments under it. It is only necessary to say that funds authorized by it have provided for an educational program with farmers and their wives which has been carried on by county agents, specialists in the problems of agriculture, and home demonstration agents, skilled in the work of Home Economics.

The work varies by communities and by states and there have been from the beginning differences in the plans for the South and the North. In the South the project undertaken by the group is planned to vary with the seasonal needs. In the North one project will probably be developed throughout the year—clothing, recreation, gardening, home beautification or whatever the subject may be. Although a school or a community center may provide the meeting place, very often it is a farm home. Around the work and the transaction of necessary business, a club life of work and recreation has developed which duplicates that of some of the most desirable of the clubs of towns and cities. The meetings have a definite objective, and to some extent trained leadership. They are free, therefore, from some of the alleged weaknesses of the general club movement.

In 1915, 368 county agencies reported that they had enrolled 6,871 women and organized 250 rural community clubs in 15 southern states. The war emphasized work in food production projects, and in July, 1917, agricultural agents were in 1,436 of the 3,001 counties in the United States and Home Demonstration agents had increased to 1,715. They have worked through existing organizations like the Granges and farmers' clubs, and particularly through the Farm Bureau Federation since its organization in 1920, while some groups have been specially organized to learn in extension classes modern methods of canning, of home beautification, or child care. According to the report of the Department of Agriculture, there were, in 1922, 210,560 farm women enrolled in extension work. In 1930 the number had grown to 646,340.

In 1928, increased funds became available under what was known as the Capper-Ketcham Act,[1] and during the years 1928 and 1929, state and local funds were increased by $1,500,000.

[1] *U. S. Statutes at Large* 47: 1151.

On June 30, 1930, there were 1,352 County Home Demonstration Agents and the farm women were said to be participating in increased numbers as local leaders.[1]

A particular activity in Ohio should be noted as an example of a distinctive development within a state. There, in 1911, as a part of the extension program of a magazine for farmers, the *Ohio Farmer*, the organization of farm women's clubs was begun— "To study and work on farm home making problems, also to consider closer social contact with neighboring farm women." In 1913 there were 42 of these clubs in 26 counties and their Federation was concluded. Later this Federation of Farm Women's Clubs itself federated with the Ohio Federation of Women's Clubs. In 1925, there were 145 clubs in 38 counties in Ohio, with a total membership of 3,124 members. At the beginning of 1933, the *Ohio Farmer* reports 160 Clubs, with about 3,600 members in 40 different counties, with some counties still to be heard from.

The organization of the Farm Bureau Federation in 1920 gave another channel for farm women's activities through its Home and Community Service, in which the women of the Farm Bureau were enrolled. In two states—Illinois and New York—the Home Bureau for women is separately organized and financed independently of the Farm Bureau. More generally, however, it is affiliated.

There are entertainment and social features connected with the Grange, with the monthly meetings of the Farm Bureaus, and the recreational aspects of the Home Demonstration groups have developed. Pageants, plays and musical programs seem to be common.

For several years, *The Farmer's Wife*, a magazine with a circulation approaching a million, and one of the few magazines appealing directly to farm women, has conducted an elaborate inquiry into the interests and practices of farm women and has awarded an honor—that of being designated a Master Farm Home Maker—on the basis of its findings.

One of the questions on which the decision may rest concerns the organizations to which the candidate belongs. A cursory examination of a small number of these questionnaires showed them to be so interesting that the questionnaires, or Work Sheets,

[1] *U. S. Department of Agriculture Extension Service Report of Extension Work in Agriculture and Home Economics in the United States*, 1931, p. 22 ff.

of 1,499 women in 23 states[1] were examined, and the replies to a few questions tabulated. The women replying represent a selected group, and are not perhaps typical of the million farm women in the country. They were in touch with the Home Demonstration Agents, and were proposed for honorary notice by their neighbors. They are, it may be supposed, the more progressive women of the communities represented.

Only 145, or .09 per cent, of these women had failed to finish the eighth grade. Twelve hundred and forty had completed the common school learning. Two hundred and sixty-four, or almost 18 per cent, had attended high school, although they had not completed the full course. A large number, 449, just short of 30 per cent, were graduated from high school, and some of these persisted further. One hundred and sixty-four,[2] or just under 11 per cent, attended normal school, although they did not graduate, while 214, more than 14 per cent, spent some time at college or in a university. Sixty-eight had been graduated from a college or university and 20 had completed the normal course. That is, over 5 per cent had completed a college or professional curriculum, besides 45 who had attended business college, 36 who had been matriculated in a seminary, and 302 who had enrolled in extension or home study courses.

Certainly all of them could have been considered eligible to participate in the organized activities which tempt the leisure time of women today. Yet only 395 stated that they employed their leisure time in club and community work. The word "leisure" must have had a connotation of idle sociability for in a later section of the inquiry, in a section devoted to "Community Work," 698, only a little less than half of the total number of women, testified that they engaged in Community Club work.

The next largest number, 493, replied that their organization activities were confined to the Ladies Aid. An equal number went to Sunday School. Four hundred and forty-eight belonged to Home Demonstration Clubs. In the order of their numerical importance their interests are exhibited in the following tabular statement:

[1] Arkansas, Illinois, Indiana, Iowa, Kansas, Kentucky, Maryland, Michigan, Minnesota, Mississippi, Missouri, Nebraska, North Carolina, North Dakota, Ohio, Oklahoma, South Carolina, South Dakota, Tennessee, Texas, Vermont, Virginia, West Virginia.
[2] Presumably these were not all high school graduates.

Community club............................... 698
Ladies aid..................................... 493
Sunday school................................. 493
Home demonstration clubs...................... 448
Library and study clubs........................ 426
Parent-teacher associations or school clubs......... 425
Social clubs................................... 419
Missionary societies........................... 394
Farm bureau township groups................... 276
Women's federated clubs........................ 235
Town and community associations................ 210
4-H Clubs.................................... 161
Farm bureau units............................. 152
Leagues of women voters....................... 41
Women's progressive farmers associations......... 11

It is not practicable to ascertain with any degree of accuracy the activities of each organization by the names. Membership in certain national organizations is included in the total classified as "Library and Study Clubs." Exactly 100 of the 426 mentioned their membership in the Woman's Christian Temperance Union. Twenty-eight belonged to the Daughters of the American Revolution, and it is of interest to record that 57 women were members of Red Cross Chapters. Membership in fraternal orders is included among the total number active in "Social Clubs." One hundred and three of the 419 were members of the Eastern Star. Nine had been initiated into the Royal Neighbors and 2 were Rebekahs.

As the result of a series of interviews with individuals working with farm groups, it seems probable that many of the Community Clubs are the kind in which the whole family participates—a type of organization for recreation and self-improvement much more common in the country than in the city. Under this heading, membership in a Grange was mentioned sixty-four times. Farmers' Institutes, Farm Women's Councils, Farmers' Clubs, Rural Clubs, County Councils—the names of the organizations are similar, and it is probable that the activities are much the same.

For the rest, it is the church, with its Ladies Aid and Missionary Societies, the school with its related Parent-Teachers Association, and the home, leading to Home Demonstration Clubs and Home Bureau units, which appear to claim the major interest of these farm women.

A letter from a woman[1] identified with work among farm women of Ohio is of interest in this connection.

I would say (she wrote) that their primary interests outside their homes are connected with the church. They are ardent members of the Missionary Society and W. C. T. U. In many cases they belong to farm women's clubs of a civic or literary nature. . . .

Some of the most interesting clubs I have run across have been farmers' clubs attended by both men and women and often by the entire family. Meetings are held once a month, lasting all day, and include a royal good meal. Subjects under discussion are connected with both rural economics and civic life.

The evidence of slight interest in the League of Women Voters supports the admission of that organization itself, which recognizes the difficulty of enlisting farm women in its membership— a difficulty related of course to the problems of extension and finance. Only 5 women listed regular partisan political activity— 2 were members of political clubs of some nature. But before concluding that there is scant concern for government and politics on the part of women in the country, it should be noted that 1,284 of the group stated that they voted regularly. Eighty-two responded that they sometimes cast their ballot. Fifteen left the question unanswered. Only 94 confessed that they were habitual non-voters. And further it is possible that, in the Town and Community Associations, the Community Clubs, many of the local civic activities characteristic of Leagues of Women Voters may be carried on.

In the total engaging in the work of Town and Community Associations, 24 members of school boards are found, and 20 others participating in "School Improvement" Associations. Twenty-one women were members of cemetary associations. Eleven were found on Fair Associations or Boards. One served on a library and another on a township board. All these involve some relationship to political agencies.

Organizations of Colored Women Today.—The National Association of Colored Women has grown since its organization of 1896 until today there are 50,000 members, and state federations in 42 states. For 34 years, under a confusingly elaborate committee organization, the Association had endeavored "To

[1] A letter dated March 23, 1931, by Mrs. Lucia Johnson Bing who has been counselor at summer camps for farm women, and has had five years' experience with Institutes and other forms of recreational and educational activity among farm women.

show proof of improvement in the race along moral, mental and material lines."

In the variety of its interests, the Colored Women's organization has mirrored the diversity of the federated clubs. In 1930, however, the Association abandoned 38 of those Departments, and accepted as its responsibility only the activities relating to the 2 remaining. They are (1) Mother, Home, and Child; and (2) the Negro Women in Industry. The reason advanced for the constriction is that other national organizations, equipped to do the selected job with greater efficiency than the General Association, have appeared in the past few years, specializing in some particular aspect of Negro welfare.

Under the two Departments remaining the activities proposed are outlined by the president of the Association[1] as follows:

Through (1) *Mother and Child*, we would create better environment for Colored children; would carry on a program of adult education for mothers and fathers; and encourage Negroes to love home, and to create homes (we do not mean mansions, but places in which children may be born and have the proper cultural background).

Through department (2) *Women in Industry*, we propose to organize Colored Women of this country to the end that they may know their strength, gain power, and be active to the opportunities afforded in the fields of labor, commercial art, and other industrial pursuits.

It is possible that the simplification is largely a desirable administrative improvement and that little of the work actually undertaken will be abandoned. Only the multiplicity of aspirations will be affected. Nevertheless, the decision to analyze its resources and to survey other groups occupying the same field might well be faced by other national associations whose committee organization has only a slender relationship to the work of the local units, and none at all to the adaptability of the organization to the tasks involved.

The Association has a National Headquarters in Washington, D. C., and in addition owns the Frederick Douglass home which it is its intention to preserve and keep as a national shrine. There is evidence in the publications of the Association that this memorial undertaking has been such a drain on the financial resources of the group that other work has been neglected.

The organization in 1900 of the Women's Convention, auxiliary to the National Baptist Convention, was the second national

---

[1] *National Notes*, November, 1930, p. 3.

organization of colored women to appear. In 1930, over 2,000 women attended the annual Convention of the Auxiliary in Chicago. The increase from an income of $15 in 1900 to $50,000 raised in 1920, measures the growth of the organization which has depended largely upon the energetic idealism of its secretary.[1] In 1907, the Women's Auxiliary sponsored the organization of the National Training School for Women and Girls in Washington, D. C. It was opened in 1909—the only vocational school for Negro girls in the North and the only one in the country directed and supported by Negroes. In addition a series of pamphlets issued by the Auxiliary for the use of local missionary societies gives very spirited instructions and suggestions for the conduct of meetings and work.

In April of 1923 the College Alumnae Club of Washington invited other Negro college women to come together to consider the advisability of forming a national organization of Negro college women. A temporary national Association of College Women was formed at this time, with its aims outlined as follows:

I. *a.* To unite in one organization all of our college women for mutual benefit, and for united effort in benefiting our several communities.
    b. To promote friendliness among our college women.
II. To raise educational standards in colleges and to improve educational conditions among our people.
III. To promote scholarship—undergraduate and graduate.
IV. To bring together college women of the two races in the United States for conference in the interest of better understanding and better conditions of contact between them.

In 1924, a permanent organization was formed, and now almost 300 colored college women are members of the 8 branches which exist in Washington, Baltimore, Cleveland, Delaware State, Petersburgh, Virginia, Raleigh, N. C., St. Louis, and Talladega, Alabama.

At that time 300 local associations in 4 states[2] made up its membership of approximately 2,000. In 1929, 16 states[3] with an

---

[1] Miss Nannie H. Burroughs.
[2] Delaware, Georgia, Florida, and Alabama.
[3] Alabama, Arkansas, Delaware, Florida, Georgia, Kansas, Kentucky, Missouri, Mississippi, North Carolina, Oklahoma, Tennessee, Texas, Virginia, West Virginia and Louisiana. The states having the largest membership are Delaware, West Virginia and Arkansas.

approximate membership of 1,000 associations and 18,000 members were enrolled.[1]

The National Congress of Parents and Teachers acts in an advisory capacity to the colored group. Indeed, the call for organization was signed by the president of the National Congress, the chairman of the Committee on Extension of Parent-Teacher Associations among Colored People, and by the president of the Georgia Colored Parent-Teacher Association, who is now president of the National Association (colored).

The program of work and the objectives of the colored Parent-Teacher Association are, in so far as is practical, identical with those of the older organization.

With the cordial cooperation of the Congress of Parents and Teachers, but independent in organization, a National Colored Parent-Teacher Association was formed in 1926.

Negro college women had organized sororities as early as 1908 when Alpha Kappa Alpha was launched. Zeta Phi Beta is another national group and there are numerous local Greek letter societies. Unlike the sororities for white students, the Negro groups are not necessarily confined to the quadrangle. A chapter in Boston, for example, may have as its members women attending colleges anywhere in New England. In Chicago, the members may be in any one of several nearby institutions.

No summary of Negro women's organizations would be complete without mention of their generous participation in secret lodges. A number of lodges listed in the "Negro Year Book" have names which show that "Brothers and Sisters" are joined together in large numbers, although no accurate statistical information is readily available. And then there are the large auxiliaries to the secret societies which are exclusively male. There is an auxiliary to the Elks, a Household of Ruth to supplement the Odd Fellows, and an Order of the Eastern Star to grace the Masons. It should be remembered that the Negro orders are not connected with the white lodges of similar names, nor are the auxiliaries related.

The Sorority System in Colleges and Universities.—Reference has already been made to the appearance of sororities in their pioneering days, when higher education for women was itself a

---

[1] Letter from Mrs. H. R. Butler, president, February 23, 1931.

novelty, and their union into independent social groups even more so. The statistical material available is incomplete.[1]

A good many of the early chapters established did not survive the difficult first years, sometimes because of anti-sorority legislation, sometimes because of the fluctuating student population or other generally adverse conditions under which women students worked. Nevertheless the growth of the sorority system has been persistent. Barely 20 chapters established between 1870 and 1880 are reported[2] to have had an unbroken existence. Between 1880 and 1890, 63 chapters were established, the next decade saw 60 charters awarded, 200 were founded between 1900 and 1910, and in the following decade 400 more were inaugurated.

In 1907, there were 25 national sororities for women students, of which 17 were academic, 8 professional. There was a college membership of 8,200 and a total membership of 47,200.

In 1927, there were 44 sororities—26 of them academic and 18 professional. A college membership of 32,500 distributed in 150 institutions was reported that year and a total membership of approximately 210,000 distributed among 1,300 active and alumnae chapters. A further examination would be necessary to reveal whether the increase in members only keeps pace with the enlarged enrollment in the colleges or whether a greater democracy is evident in the selection of a larger proportion of women students.

Larger chapters are inevitable if the expensive chapter houses are to be maintained. In 1905, only 7 chapters were reported[3] as owning their own chapter houses—the first one erected by Alpha Phi at Syracuse in 1889 was valued at $10,000—while 35 chapters rented places of residence. In 1927,[4] a total of 385 houses are listed as being owned, with a total valuation of $10,602,550.

Obviously there must be considerable business connected with the acquisition and management of such substantial property interests. A closer relationship between the active and alumnae organizations is one consequence and today many of the more than 200,000 sorority women find their leisure time activities

[1] Baird's *Greek Manual* is the usual authority, and Ida Shaw Martin of Boston has issued *A Sorority Handbook* at intervals. These sources are not always in agreement and confess their data to be unsatisfactory.

[2] Martin, *op. cit.*

[3] Baird's *Manual*, 1905.

[4] *Ibid.*, 1927.

after graduation directed toward the management of sorority affairs. A few sororities have undertaken some form of welfare work as a responsibility, such as the support of a specific charity or school; almost all of them provide scholarships for their deserving members or for outsiders. But primarily the sororities exist for the mutual pleasure of their members. The social life for the women students in many colleges is organized around them. And the alumnae organizations are most concerned with the success, the growth, and the welfare of the neighboring college chapters. The alumnae assist in meeting financial problems, in conducting household affairs, in upholding standards of decorous conduct and scholarship. They act as advisors and friends. They give and they raise money.

The Club House Movement.—If there is any phase of the club movement which stands out with especial vividness in the modern development it is the increasing number of club houses. Not that club houses for women are a novelty. At the second Biennial of the General Federation, held in 1894 in Philadelphia, club houses were reported in Philadelphia, Wilmington, Indianapolis, Lansing and Milwaukee. Since that time there has been a steady increase until now approximately 1,200 club houses are reported by the General Federation. In value these club houses range from $300 to $3,000,000. The facts may be unrelated but it is of interest to report that the $300 club house serves its community as library and rest center, while the $1,000,000 plants are maintained to serve their members.

The small club houses—and there are many ranging in cost from $50,000 to $100,000—seem often to be planned as community assets, with the men of the community contributing counsel as well as making gifts of money. A number of such buildings house the public libraries of their towns, some provide the only auditorium available. With low dues—one club whose membership dues are $2 built a $15,000 club house—they must depend on the money-raising activities of their members for supplementary income and upon their volunteer efforts instead of professional service in the club maintenance and management.

The larger clubs—like the city clubs—a group of which Chicago's was a pioneer—offer the advantage of hotel comfort to resident members and transient guests.

The most costly club houses—both in plant equipment and in dues to the members—are the athletic clubs, which flourish with such conspicuous success in Los Angeles, San Francisco and Chicago. They offer an infinite variety in their service to their members. Comfortable bedrooms, luxurious libraries, good living rooms, all kinds of athletic equipment, reducing machines, Turkish baths and beauty parlors.

The Los Angeles Women's Athletic Club is valued at $1,500,-000, the Chicago Women's Athletic Club at $1,000,000, and the Illinois Woman's Athletic Club in Chicago at $3,750,000. The entrance fee to the San Francisco Club is $500, and the dues are $50 annually. The Club's payroll is $10,000 a month. And while the dues are high for a woman's club, these are modest compared with the fees required to affiliate with an athletic club for men offering similar advantages.

Country clubs for women are luxurious new developments of the club movement. The National Women's Country Club near Washington, D. C., has in its membership a number of wealthy and prominent women from all over the country. The Mount Vernon Country Club of Detroit has a membership of women of leisure. The Woman's National Golf and Tennis Club flourishes at Glen Head, Long Island.

The club house of the National Woman's Democratic Club in Washington and that of the Woman's National Republican Club in New York may be said to represent the social interests of party women. The headquarters of the American Association of University Women and the General Federation of Women's Clubs are each housed in national club houses in Washington which have some facilities for transient guests.

Two of the most pretentious club houses—luxurious hotels for women in New York—are Pan Hellenic House and the Clubhouse of the American Woman's Association. The first was built by the fraternity college women and is valued at $1,600,000. The latter is an $8,000,000 venture. The Junior League of New York is equipped for the work and recreation of its 2,000 members in its club house which cost $1,250,000.

Women's club houses provide a place for conference and meeting for the groups which in size have long outgrown the hospitality of their members. To many members they offer a residence and a place of recreation. They are a visible sign of the trend to entertain away from home. For small lunch parties, for teas or bridge, dinner or dancing, clubs all over the country have supplemented the hospitality of the homes of their members.

A brilliant English novelist, Virginia Woolf, has accounted for the relative paucity of women's, as compared with men's, productiveness whether in science, literature, or the other arts, by the lack of a "room of her own." It may not be far fetched to relate that earlier lack to the rapid increase in the number of these costly buildings, making provision for accommodations intended for women's activities not related to family life and rendering possible individual experience unrelated to domestic responsibilities or obligations.

The National Council of Women and Some Other Cooperative Relationships of Women.—As soon as there were national organizations, there were cooperative relationships between and among the members who met in committees, sat in conferences and joined each other in councils. The formation of the Pan Hellenic Association has been mentioned. More pretentious and earlier came the organization in 1888 of the National Council of Women of the United States. In 1891, it was incorporated and affiliated with the International Council of Women. Then its membership included the following associations:

The National Woman Suffrage Association
The National Woman's Christian Temperance Union
The Woman's Centenary Association of the Universalist Church
Woman's National Press Association
Wimodaughsis (a National Club)
The National Women's Relief Society
The Young Ladies National Mutual Improvement Association
The Illinois Industrial Reform School for Girls
The National Free Baptist Woman's Missionary Society
Sorosis (the club representing, by invitation of the Council, the club
    movement, "until the General Federation of Women's Clubs could
    be formed and affiliated").

As organizations multiplied the Council grew. In 1928 there were 38 organizations on its roster, but a year later the number had dropped to 21. In the early years of this century there are proud references to the Council in the records of other organizations. Then it was said to represent 6,000,000 women. In 1930, however, its influence had been almost extinguished. Most of the large groups having strong national organizations had withdrawn. Apparently the cycle of the Council had been run. However, the Council is the organization into whose keeping the representation of women's interests at Chicago's second World's Fair is entrusted. How enduring will be any strength newly acquired in connection with that undertaking only time can tell.

Later, as interest in legislation arose, women's organizations united to form legislative councils in the states. These, and the formation of the Woman's Joint Congressional Committee in Washington in 1920, will be discussed in a later section. During the War, the Council of National Defense had a Woman's Division under which a variety of women's organizations enlisted for the war period. Two later conferences are important as they record the adherence in common sympathy of two opposing groups of organizations.

In 1923, a proposal was advanced to unite in conference all the national women's organizations which professed to support some program for the peaceful settlement of international disputes, the substitution of law for war. The first meeting was held in 1925, and this Conference on the Cause and Cure of War, in which eleven organizations participate, has convened in Washington every succeeding year.

The member organizations are:

The National League of Women Voters
The National Board of the Y.W.C.A.
The National Federation of Business and Professional Woman's Clubs
The Council of Women for Home Missions
The Federation of Women's Boards of Foreign Missions of both Americas
The American Association of University Women
The National Council of Jewish Women
The National Women's Christian Temperance Union
The General Federation of Women's Clubs
The National Women's Trade Union League
The National Women's Conference of the American Ethical Union

The conferences' three-day programs have included addresses by experts in international law, in economics, and in military organization. Discussions have been encouraged, and the conferences have served as educational institutes upon which the delegates and constituent organizations have drawn heavily in the continued study and support of their programs in international relations. The "Peace Societies" are not included in membership, and the Conference has not been permitted to become an agency to promote any particular system for the promotion of peace although it has endorsed such proposals as the Kellogg Pact, and has advocated international tribunals and conferences.

Distrust of the purpose of the Conference on the Cause and Cure of War prompted the organization of a hostile conference. It is called the Women's Patriotic Conference on National Defense, and customarily meets in Washington immediately following the other. It is sponsored jointly by the American Legion Auxiliary and the D.A.R. and 40 organizations unite to oppose efforts to reduce armaments, to support increased provision for national defense, and generally to resist what they call subversive influences.

With the exception of the two major organizations upon whose leadership the Conference depends, the member groups are small. Some of them are local clubs, and almost all of them are composed of women who identify themselves in their relationship to the veteran of some war. The entire membership is as follows:

American Gold Star Mothers
American Legion Auxiliary
American War Mothers
American Women's Legion
Auxiliary to Sons of Union Veterans of Civil War
Bergen County Women's Republican Club of New Jersey
Colonial Daughters of the 17th Century
Daughters of the Colonial Wars, Inc.
Daughters of the Defenders of the Republic, U.S.A.
Daughters of the Union Veterans of the Civil War 1861–65
The Government Club, Inc.
Ladies of the Grand Army of the Republic
Ladies Auxiliary Veterans of Foreign Wars
National American Veteran and Allied Patriotic Organizations
National Auxiliary United Spanish War Veterans
National Patriotic Association
National Society, Colonial Daughters of America
National Society of Colonial Descendants of America
National Society, Daughters of the American Colonists
National Society, Daughters of the American Revolution
National Society, Daughters of Founders and Patriots of America
National Society, Dames of the Loyal Legion
National Society, Daughters of the Revolution
National Society, Daughters of the Union
National Society of New England Women
National Society, Patriotic Women of America
National Society, United States Daughters of 1812
National Society, Patriotic Builders of America
National Society, Women Descendants of the Ancient and Honorable
    Artillery Company
New York City Colony, National Association of New England Women

Service Star Legion, Inc.
Society of Sponsors of the United States Navy
The Guadalupe Club of 1848
The National Patriotic Council
The National Women's Relief Corps
The Security League of Westchester
Women's Naval Service
Women of the Army and Navy Legion of Valor
Women's Overseas Service League
Women's Constitutional League

International Relationships.—Coöperation at home has been followed by cooperation abroad, and most of the large organizations maintain some relationship with women's groups of similar aims in other countries.

In their names, the Woman's International League for Peace and Freedom and the International Policewomen's Association, proclaim that the boundaries of nationality do not limit their interests. The name "General" Federation of Women's Clubs was chosen instead of "National," in order that clubs around the globe might join. For a long time the position of "Foreign Correspondent" was an established one and the Biennial conventions learned of clubs in foreign lands, entertained their delegates and extended greetings.

In 1883, the National Women's Christian Temperance Union founded the World's Christian Temperance Union through the efforts of Frances E. Willard, who was elected its first president, and 8 round-the-world missionaries were sent out by the W.C.T.U. Now women of 50 nations participate in the general crusade which includes in its program the abolition of traffic in drugs as well as alcoholic liquors.

The National League of Women Voters is the branch in this country of the International Alliance of Women for Equal Suffrage and Citizenship. As a result of the Pan American Conference of Women, which the League of Women Voters sponsored in Baltimore in 1922, the Pan American Association for the Advancement of Women was organized, with the League the member for the United States. In 1925, the Association met in Washington and changed its name to the Inter-American Union of Women. Its aims were stated to be:

1. The promotion of the education of women and the encouragement of higher standards.
2. Working for the social welfare of women and children.

[87]

3. Obtaining and enforcing civil and political rights for women.
4. Safeguarding the interests of women who work.
5. Attaining for women the highest opportunity to cultivate and use the talents God has given them.
6. Stimulating the friendship and understanding among the American nations with the aim of maintaining justice and permanent peace in the Western Hemisphere.

Plans for further conferences have not materialized and the Inter-American Union of Women is now inactive.

The National Council of Catholic Women is a member of the International Union of Catholic Women's Leagues. In 1923, the Jewish Women of the World were called in conference in Vienna by the National Council of the United States. There are Councils of Jewish Women in nine European countries today due to its influence.

Earlier, in 1919, the National Women's Trade Union League of America had voted in its convention that it should call an International Congress of Working Women. As a result of that decision there convened in Washington, in October, 1918, the First International Congress of Working Women with 12 countries represented. A second meeting was convened in Geneva in 1921—this time called the International Federation of Working Women. A change in the organization which took place at this conference illustrates the difference in the attitude toward organizations of women workers in Europe and in the United States. Delegates from European countries proposed that instead of continuing as an autonomous independent organization of women the Federation should become a department of the existing International Federation of Trade Unions.

The emphasis among European women in industry was on workers as a class, while the League in the United States recognized the need for a woman movement within the Labor movement. The National Woman's Trade Union League of America, therefore, withdrew from membership, although a friendly relationship still exists.

The American Nurses Association is part of the International Council of Nurses, and the American Association of University Women is affiliated with the International Federation of University Women. Membership in the Fidac Auxiliary—affiliated with the international association of men who served in the allied armies—is maintained by the American Legion Auxiliary.

Quota Club is Quota International. Zonta boasts branches in Europe and Australia. The Soroptomists are international in scope of membership. The Federation of Business and Professional Women's Clubs had organized Continental trips for women which it has called Good-Will-Trips, and in 1930, in Geneva, consummated the organization of a formal International Association. The Association of Junior Leagues of America, Inc., already has a league in Mexico affiliated, and has made provision in its plans and constitution for the admission of Leagues in Europe.

The International Federation of Home and School was formed at the invitation of the Congress of Parents and Teachers of the United States and the sister group in Canada. In 1929, there were Parent-Teacher Associations in 32 countries and national associations projected in 8 other countries as a result of the International program.

In 1919, the Medical Women's International Association was organized in New York City. Congresses have been held in Geneva, London and Paris, and now there are 22 member organizations.

Usually membership in an International group means representation at International Conferences. It means the exchange of Bulletins and magazines, connection through correspondence and the entertainment of foreign guests. For the organization leaders at least it means that women of different nations take counsel together. In the end it seems that this widening of organization limitations must be a sound contribution to the cause of international good will.

Budgets and Support.—Only a few national organizations of women are self-supporting. Most of them depend for revenue not only on the dues and the heroic money-raising efforts of their members, but upon the donations of their friends. In some groups this is accomplished by having a sliding scale of membership, and members whose major participation is financial are made "contributing" or "life" members as the case may be.

The Y.W.C.A. is well established as a community service organization and has been able to raise much of its money by public appeals. In some communities the chests subsidize it; in others, special campaigns are waged.

The Council of Jewish Women spends nationally and through its sections about $500,000 annually, and owns property over

$1,250,000 in value. It is subsidized by community funds in some cases and generally makes appeals for contributions for its work to men and wealthy women not in its active membership.

In the years since its organization, the American Association of University Women has expanded its annual budget from $35 a year to approximately $94,000. Dues and contributions from branches are supplemented by Foundation subsidies to finance its program which includes the support of research and fellowships and makes a special appeal to certain research endowment funds.

Some of the money administered by the Home Economics Association was granted by one of the great Foundations. A total of $105,000 has been donated for the establishment of the Washington Child Research Center, and other grants for special research projects total about $35,000. Aside from these monies the budget for the organization for 1929–1930 was $53,900, raised largely within the Association.

The Nursing Organizations have enjoyed subsidies for research, too, and of the $110,000 which the National Organization of Public Health Nurses spends annually, membership dues and payment for services are a part, while contributions from interested persons are solicited and received.

The National Woman's Trade Union League of America has an annual budget of approximately $23,000. In 1928–1929 more than $17,000 of that total was received from individual donations.

The Woman's International League for Peace and Freedom raises approximately $25,000 to spend annually in the United States and sends $6,000 to the Geneva office as its share of the International expense. The membership fee is only $2.00, and the balance must be secured from individual gifts.

The annual income estimated by the 1930 Convention of the Federation of Business and Professional Women's Clubs was $69,212.20. The Federation, according to a statement of the secretary, has never received any large gifts, and is supported almost wholly by the dues and contributions of its own members.

The Congress of Parents and Teachers likewise reports that the $95,000 in its estimated budget for 1929–1930 was raised from the dues of its members.

The 1930 Convention of the American Legion Auxiliary reported disbursement of $80,616.13 for the fiscal year.

The National League of Women Voters has an annual budget of about $130,000. It is raised by contributions in the nature of "quotas" from state Leagues which are generously supplemented by contributions from men and women who are in sympathy with its program of political education for women. In 1929–1930 the League conducted, through its state Leagues, a campaign for an endowment fund of $100,000.

The success of the League's plan, which incidentally memorialized women's services to the cause of citizenship, parallels a similar campaign inaugurated by the General Federation of Women's Clubs in 1910 and successfully completed a few years later in honor of outstanding club leaders. In 1930 the Federation treasurer reported an income for the biennium of $14,122.55 from the memorial endowment. The balance from the war service fund has provided an additional biennial income of over $11,000 for Federation activities since the war.

In addition to these special funds and other smaller ones, the General Receipts which were reported by the Federation in 1930 for the two-year period ending March 31 of that year amounted to $236,025.17.

It should be remembered that the National Budget of most organizations does not include a record of expenditures for state or local work. It is only a small part of the money which is spent by women's organizations to carry out their programs in the United States today.

Chapter V

SUMMARY

IF AN attempt is made to review the salient features of this account, it will be noted there came first federation, then cooperation, then specialization. These seem to be the changing emphases in women's organizations. The new groups which appear and the older ones which grow are more restricted in the field they cover than the clubs united in the General Federation. Women who work are inclined to ally themselves with others of their profession or with other groups of women in the business world. Women of leisure with education and technical training are likely to join with others to promote some special program. It seems unlikely that the General Federation is growing now at as rapid a pace as in former years. Its very size and its proud diversity militate against such growth.

It has seemed impracticable, as has been pointed out, to give any adequate numerical comparison with former years because the membership figures have always been estimates and are far from exact.[1] The difficulty in estimating the actual number of women in the Federation, for example, is due to the fact that the organization is composed of clubs, not women. A single woman may belong to several federated clubs; an estimate of repeaters seemed hardly worth while. The leaders of the Federation believe the organization is growing. Careful observers sometimes disagree on the basis of experience in certain communities. As a cause they cite the fact that with an increase of general educational opportunity the literary programs are no longer attractive to so many women, and with a similar increase in recreational facilities in movies, in athletics, in bridge clubs, the social features no longer seem necessary. And the clubs are no longer exclusively the

[1] The Eastern Star reported 1,687,674 members at its last convention.

The Congress of Parents and Teachers reports that the million mark was passed in 1928.

The General Federation estimate is "over two million."

The Woman's Christian Temperance Union reported approximately 600,000.

These seem to be the largest national organizations of women.

center from which women enter or influence community activities. Much of the civic work in which they pioneered is now assumed as a public responsibility. Streets are lighted, for example, and playgrounds maintained by public agencies. Women, like men, can express their support or opposition at the polls.

It would probably be impossible to give to the clubs too much credit for their pioneering contributions to these now generally accepted public responsibilities. The American Library Association is reported to credit women's clubs with the responsibility for initiating 75 per cent of the public libraries now in existence in the United States.

But if, today, other organizations seem more skillful tools for professionally-minded women to use, the clubs still offer the "resting place" they sought to be forty years ago. The club house has a place in woman's life today and so far it is the general federated club which offers it most reasonably and most generously. Young women will join clubs with club houses whose services they enjoy. No other aspect of the club movement seems so well designed to attract the young woman of 1933.

One interest and one activity appears to be shared by almost every organization whose records have been examined. They all maintain scholarships. The P.E.O. Sisterhood and the Eastern Star share this activity with the D.A.R., the Congress of Parents and Teachers and almost every group which has been mentioned. Education is the thread of similarity which runs through all the groups—reminiscent of the Federation motto, "United in Diversity."

The facts with reference to women's organizations and their political activities are obviously external. There is revealed an uncalculable amount of energy going farther in uncharted directions. Whither and to what result, who can say? The comment of a brilliant observer from another environment may throw light on the subject, especially of the probable significance of the club movement and of the possible utilization of the middle years by women who have been equipped to enter the labor market but have allowed the experience of their family life to terminate their wage earnings. She wrote:

The channel through which so much of the American woman's social activity flows—the Woman's Club—seemed to me to be of immense importance politically because its routine is planned to be compatible with the domestic arrangements of married women. It has recently become obvious that the reason women have not produced nearly so many of the great as men have is, not that what we regard as the characteristically masculine activities demand different powers from those demanded by the characteristically feminine activities of wifehood or motherhood, but that they demand the same. For now that the raising of the marriage age and the lowering of the birth rate allow women to follow at any rate the initial stages of an artistic and scientific occupation, we find that the women who show most promise are usually those who are most sexually attractive. To take a conspicuous instance, there are probably no more beautiful women in England than our finest woman pianist and 'cellist of the younger generation. In fact, the women who would make the best artists, scientists, or politicians are the very ones who are more inevitably called to another career which is usually incompatible with any other. In the past this coincidence of sexual and creative powers meant utter frustration of feminine talent, since these were the very women who were most certainly doomed to marry young and be bound to such an unremitting toil of childbearing, childrearing, and housework that when their children were grown up they were in most cases too tired to do anything but rest.

Nowadays the physical conditions of life are so much improved that it is no more natural for a woman to be exhausted at the age of forty-five, after having been a wife and mother, than it is for a man to be exhausted at that age after having practiced as a lawyer or doctor. We must resign ourselves to the fact that, in spite of this improvement, it will be very difficult for such a women to return to the practice of an art or a science. She will have forgotten its technic, and since domestic life calls (above all things) for a chameleon adaptability of mind that can shift from object to object as emergency dictates, she will have impaired her power of concentration. But there are other careers, and in particular there is the political career. This is the ideal field for the middle-aged woman who has acquired a sense of values by many years spent in the cultivation of human relationships, if only she has meanwhile kept in touch with affairs. That is an immensely difficult condition; and the woman's club seems to be the best device yet framed for fulfilling it.

The development of this device in the United States may be due to the fact that in one important respect it has better material to work on than it would have in England. American women do not dislike men as much as Englishwomen do. Englishwomen probably love men more for, owing to the more sedative airs of Great Britain, they are apt to sit still and feel, while the exhilarated Americans run about and receive new impressions. But they do not like men. . . .

But the number of serenely energetic American Women between forty-five and sixty-five far surpasses the number in England who manage to preserve the integrity of their nervous system. . . .

My incredulity concerning the masculine aptitude for these matters was enormously increased when I visited the United States and saw how American men, compelled by the need of their country for economic exploitation to take less interest in politics than the European, overshoot the mark and take none at all; and my suspicion that women have more aptitude for the work—based on observation of the way the emancipated Englishwoman takes to politics, at the first opportunity, as a duck takes to water—was as enormously increased when I saw how an otherwise politically barren land blossoms forth from coast to coast in Leagues of Woman Voters. Indeed, it is almost beside the point to discuss whether the women of the United States have a special aptitude for the work, since they are the only people who seem to be ready to do it. And there are the vast carcasses of Russia and China—sprawling helplessly over the map, magnificiently endowed with population and natural wealth but insufficiently innervated by governmental systems—to prove what happens to a country that is not a political entity.[1]

[1] Rebecca West, "These American Women," *Harper's Monthly Magazine,* CLI (1925), 722–30.

PART II
WOMEN AND GAINFUL EMPLOYMENT

CHAPTER VII

WOMEN AS WORKERS

THE Census of 1900 attracted the attention of students to the steady increase in the number of women who were gainfully employed, and raised the question whether or not great changes were taking place in the amount and character of the work of women, so that they were both invading men's fields of employment and affecting the home disastrously. There was wide discussion in the press, and the period was also characterized by scientific discussions[1] in which it was shown that in the major industrial occupations women were not displacing men, and were as a whole probably doing no more work than they had always done. They were, however, in many cases offering their labor outside the home and collecting their own earnings, where, before, either they had rendered unpaid services in the home or their husbands or fathers had owned and collected their earnings.

It was even then clear that the occupations of women in connection with family life had been of fundamental importance in the production of the commodities or services available and likewise in the determination of the ways in which those commodities and services should be enjoyed. There were, to be sure, always women for whom the home did not make satisfactory provision;[2] and, it is interesting to note that, except in the matter of inheritance under the law of primogeniture, the common law made no distinction between the unmarried adult woman and the man. For the married woman, on the other hand, the difference in legal capacity was very great. So far as her activities were concerned, however, her occupations were largely connected with the domestic organization, as wife, mother, daughter, or sister, or as hired assistant in the performances of tasks of a domestic character. When, however, the factory system developed and products hitherto produced in the home were manufactured elsewhere,

---

[1] Edith Abbott, *Women in Industry* (New York: D. Appleton and Co., 1909).

[2] Lina Eckenstein, *Women under Monasticism* (Cambridge University Press, 1896).

women and children were employed under the new conditions. This process of women following, not the flag, but the job, is still continuing, with resulting changes of attitude on the part of both men and women, and confusion on the part of both as to what effects of the change on important social institutions are to be anticipated.

Interest in these questions led, during that early decade of this century, to the investigation by the United States Bureau of Labor,[1] to which reference has been made, which brought out the facts with reference to the dependence of great numbers of families on the wage-paid labor of women and girls as well as of men and boys, which destroyed the myth of the pin-money girl, emphasized the bargaining disadvantage as compared with the employer under which women and girls sought employment, and made obvious the relative inequality between men and women as wage bargainers. From that time, the inequality of women as compared to men with respect to occupational opportunity has been recognized as one of the chief disadvantages under which they have suffered, and has resulted in an effort to widen the range of their employment and to mitigate the results of their relative weakness. Especially it has been recognized that these features of their employment retard and impede effective organization among them.[2]

The results of this bargaining weakness manifested themselves in excessively long hours, in frequent employment at night which rendered enormously difficult the maintenance of home standards or of sound family life, in lack of Saturday half holidays or Sunday rest, in conditions of work less than decent or morally safe, and in wage scales inferior to those of men workers even where skill or professional equipment might characterize their work.

From the recognition of these features of women's employment developed efforts, some educational, like trade education and vocational guidance, to remove the pressure of competition at the lowest level; some social, like the mothers' pensions, to remove

[1] U. S. Bureau of Labor, *Report on Condition of Woman and Child Wage Earners in the United States*, Vol. III, *Glass;* Vol. V, *Department Stores;* Vol. VI, *Why Children Leave School*, etc. Sixty-First Congress, Second Session, Senate Document 645 (Washington: Government Printing Office, 1910). See *Recent Social Trends in the United States*, vol. I, p. 731.

[2] See for interesting recent discussion of this view, Sylvia Anthony, *The Place of Women in Industry and in the Home* (George Routledge and Co., Ltd., London, 1932), Chap. IV.

the non-industrial person from the working group; some legislative, apparently protective in character but really an item in the program of emancipation, taking the form of efforts (1) to secure legislative regulation of conditions of work; (2) to secure a statutory minimum wage for women since trade unionism seemed unable to accomplish this in the case of women; (3) and to formulate standards by which employment might be judged. This last effort was restricted largely to public employment.

This new occupational and domestic position, together with the granting of suffrage, has been giving women a wider share in the life of the community. It is not the purpose of this study to discuss that share in its entirety. The participation of women in family relationship and family life is not presented here; but, in the following pages, an attempt is made to discover and to discuss some of the activities of women outside the home and the direction taken by those activities. The selection of material is not simple, nor is the order in which the data should be presented perfectly obvious. It has seemed best to review the recent figures with reference to women's employment. The subject of their voluntary association in clubs and organizations of various kinds has preceded and their relation to government since the ratification of the Nineteenth Amendment seems to follow the discussion of their employment. These three groups of data it is hoped may indicate the direction in which the activities and their influence are tending.

With reference to their employment, a few preliminary remarks will make clearer the later discussion.

Although it is not intended here to devote any considerable space to the changes that have been brought about in the law of the family group, which by 1900 had been substantially revolutionized with reference to reciprocal rights and duties both of husband and wife[1] and of parent and child,[2] there are several aspects of the subject, in its relation to the employment of women, on which it is worth while to comment. Under the older family organization, the services of both the wife and the daughter or their wages if they were gainfully employed, belonged

---

[1] *A Survey of the Legal Status of Women in the Forty-eight States* (National League of Women Voters, 532 Seventeenth Street, N. W., Washington, D. C.).

[2] Sophonisba P. Breckinridge and Edith Abbott, *Delinquent Child and the Home* (New York: Charities Publication Committee, 1912), Appendix III, p. 247.

to the husband and father. Whether work was done within or outside the home, the goods, services or earnings accrued to the composite family income,[1] to which much attention has been given during these recent years by students of family life, of the labor problem, and of the problem of poverty.[2] Services rendered in the home by the wife or minor children were unpaid, without other compensation than provision of support, which, being a poorly enforced obligation, gave excuse for characterizing marriage as a sweated trade.[3]

By the beginning of the twentieth century nearly all the states had enacted laws giving to married women the right to collect and control their earnings as well as to manage their property and to be held responsible for their contracts or their actions of a tortious character.[4] On the other hand, the right of the legitimate mother to share with the father in the custody of her child's person and in the direction of her child's life was somewhat later in being recognized, and the change in the attitude of the law and of the courts in recognizing that the determining question is neither the right of the father nor the right of the mother, but the well-being of the child, belongs to the second and third decade of the century. With the enactment of the so-called Juvenile Court legislation, beginning in Illinois in 1899 and followed by 1930[5] in forty-six of the other forty-seven states, the doctrine enunciated in 1827 by the great Lord Chancellor Eldon, that when the Court of Chancery could obtain jurisdiction, and when that court could both learn what was the need of the child whose interests were neglected by the father, and meet that need,

---

[1] For statement of the law see James Schouler, *A Treatise on the Law of the Domestic Relations* (Boston: Little, Brown and Co., 1870), Chap. V, "The Effect of Coverture upon the Wife's Personal Property"; Chap. VI, "Upon the Wife's Chattels and Real Estate." See also A. V. Dicey, *Lectures on the Relation between Law and Public Opinion in England during the Nineteenth Century* (London, New York: Macmillan and Co., Ltd., 1905), Lecture XI, "Judicial Legislation," pp. 369–96.

[2] *Recent Social Trends in the United States*, Chap. XVI. For Family Income, see for example, *Report of the United States Immigration Commission*, Vol. VI, *Immigrants in Industries: Bituminous Coal Mining*, pp. 55 and 209; Vol. XXVI, *Immigrants in Cities*, pp. 139, 226, 318, and 403; *Woman and Child Wage Earners* (1912), especially Vol. XVI, *Family Budgets of Typical Cotton Mill Workers;* United States Bureau of Labor Bulletin No. 175; Children's Bureau Publication No. 20, *Welfare of Children of Maintenance-of-Way Employees*, pp. 24, 33 *ff.*

[3] Cecily Hamilton, *Marriage as a Trade* (London: Chapman Hall, Ltd., 1912).

[4] *Recent Social Trends in the United States*, Chap. XIII.

[5] U. S. Children's Bureau, Legal Chart No. 17. *Analysis and Tabular Summary of State Laws relating to Jurisdiction in Children's Cases*, etc.

there was no question of power,[1] was made a principle of decision on which the courts could rest determinations in cases of individual children. During these decades the right of the mother to be made guardian was granted in many states,[2] but in the case of the mother, as of the father, the question will be decided in the light of the child's interest.

In 1930, there remained certain questions of the married woman's rights to enter into partnership without her husband's consent,[3] or without some public record,[4] but these limitations, like those upon a husband or wife testifying when the other was interested, rest upon other considerations than those of the wife's legal incapacity.

With reference to the legislation remaining to be enacted, there are differences of opinion among the organized groups of women, due to the fact that the value of the wife's participation in the family life has never been formulated. In the states in which the so-called Community Property[5] System prevails, the idea of equality between husband and wife is applied except in management; in the other states, the differences of opinion as to the ways in which the interest of the wife and widow can best be protected prevent such uniformity of legislative policy from characterizing the efforts in the various states as was true of the effort to secure to her the control of her own property.

In this connection, reference may be made to the anomalous position of the unmarried mother, whose claim to her child being that of possession, while not quite that of the legitimate father, was better than the claim of anyone else. With the increased emphasis on the protection of the child's interest, the legislative program increasingly lays enforceable duties on the fathers of children whether born within or without wedlock.[6]

The legislative program for the emancipation of the married woman is then well nigh complete. However, the fact that, in

---

[1] The Wellesley Case, *Wellesley* v. *Beaufort*, 2 Russell 1; conveniently available *Social Service Review*, 4: 67.

[2] See *A Survey of the Legal Status of Women in the Forty-eight States, 1930* (National League of Women Voters, 532 Seventeenth Street, N. W., Washington, D. C., Revised Edition, March, 1930), p. 23.

[3] As in Illinois, *ibid.*, p. 66.

[4] As in Florida, *ibid.*, p. 53.

[5] *Ibid.*, p. 11.

[6] U. S. Children's Bureau, Legal Chart No. 16, *Summary of Laws Dealing with Illegitimacy.* It will be helpful for the reader to note at the same time U. S. Bureau Publication No. 148, *Adoption Laws in the United States.*

general, the husband's domicil determines the wife's, affects the mobility and hence the opportunities of the married woman who would earn; but the problem is one of very great complexity about which it is extremely difficult to obtain definite information, so that often the result of attempting to work out these conflicts of interest can be discovered only by examining the records of the divorce courts.

While no evidence is given, to the effect that women are capable of doing the various tasks which they/have chosen, notice may be taken of the theory of different physiological structure, mentioned above, which at an earlier date seemed to justify the exclusion of women from higher academic opportunities. It was generally thought that nature, in making special provision for child bearing, caused women to breath costically while men breathed abdominally, and that this "deep-seated structural difference affecting every organ, every cell in the body—making a difference throughout the entire structure, the brain included,"[1] rendered it forever impossible for men and women to be treated alike in the things of the mind. From the point of view of those who would exclude, the sequence proceeded from the incapacity of childhood, to the incapacity of adolescence, to the incapacity of child bearing and child caring, and through the incapacity of the menopause to the incapacity of senility. It was complete. But that theory was abandoned before the beginning of the century and it may be assumed that such evidence would now be superfluous.

However, it may perhaps be profitable to recall the fact that for much of the work for which a long period of training was formerly necessary—craftsmanship—the machine or the altered organization has reduced the period of preparation. During the war, for example, women would learn, in a few weeks, processes, which would enable them to replace the men called to the front, for which the period of training previously required by the trade union was longer than the whole period of the war. In other words, the requirements for apprenticeship and other previous preparation had often for their purpose not only the maintenance of high standards of work but also the limitation of the supply of workers, the reduction of the competitive pressure, and often the exclusion of a less dignified or less respected group of

[1] Clelia Duel Mosher, *Personal Hygiene for Women* (Stanford University Press, 1927), p. 1.

workers—women, Negroes, aliens, and other possibly ignoble groups.

In some cases, the exclusion was secured by developing ideas of superiority. The "legal mind," for example, was a masculine mind of peculiar quality and the exclusion of women was based on mere economy and on consideration for the feelings of women to prevent their inevitable humiliation and embarrassment. It is also true that the duties of various public offices, *e.g.*, jailor, sheriff, member of the House of Representatives, governor, United States senator, were characterized by features of public honor, and were supposed to require certain characteristics of personal vigor, courage, ability to command respect. It has, however, been found appropriate to fill positions in each of these categories by persons whose qualifications have consisted in having been married to a person holding such an office and being widowed. More than once in most of the offices named, the widow has replaced the deceased husband, and has successfully continued to hold the prisoners in safe-keeping, to direct the protective or law-enforcing agencies of the county, to take her place among the representatives in Congress or to direct the governmental activities of a sovereign commonwealth. In fact, the artificial glamour by which many occupations have been surrounded has not infrequently been competitive, and those seeking the "opportunity," as in the clever verse of Charlotte Perkins Stetson, are learning to walk "right through the obstacle as though it were not there." It should be easy to understand these developments. To the feminists perhaps it seems a survival of the attitude so satisfying to the author of *Paradise Lost*.[1] On

[1] . . . "Though both
Not equal, as their sex not equal seemed:
For contemplation he and valour formed,
For softness she and sweet attractive grace;
He for God only, she for God in him."
(*Paradise Lost*, Book IV, lines 295–99)

"To whom thus Eve, with perfect beauty adorned:
'My author and disposer, what thou bidd'st
Unargued I obey; so God ordains:
God is thy law, thou mine: to know no more
Is woman's happiest knowledge, and her praise.'"
(*Ibid.*, Book IV, lines 634–38)

The student of women's vocational struggle is also reminded of the attitude of the English craftsmen toward the capacity of widows to carry on. *Economic Journal*, 5: 209, at 225 (1895), E. Dixon, *Craftswomen in the Livre des Metiers*.

further examination, it is a manifestation of the rough common sense of the English guildsmen, as over against the logic of the French craftsmen, that let widows of deceased guildsmen "carry on," although wives and daughters were excluded from the opportunity to qualify.

Attention should also be called to the effect of widening the competition and thus raising the marginal level. The worker on the lower margin who is displaced may suffer, but the community gains unless the rate of displacement is too swift. This does not accept mere and disastrous cheapness as an element in efficiency. To the extent to which any group of workers offer only cheapness, or chiefly cheapness, they threaten the entire structure. The question must, however, be raised: Are there obstacles deterring the workers' progress against which cheapness alone will prevail?

For sources, reliance is placed so far as practicable on the publications of the Census Bureau, especially the Census of Occupations[1] and of Manufactures, on publications of other official authorities, such as the United States Bureau of Labor Statistics, the United States Woman's Bureau, or of State Departments of Labor.

As has been said, the problem was competently stated during the decade 1900–1910, when the figures for 1870, 1880, 1890, and 1900 were discussed. At that time it was pointed out that the employment of women, while one problem so far as the effect of limited occupational opportunity is concerned, assumes many aspects, each of which must be distinguished from the others if the true development is to be understood. There is, first, the question of the place of the woman known until 1930 as the "gainfully employed" woman, in relation to the non-gainfully employed woman, who, however, as a wife or daughter, has been held to the performance of domestic duties, since the husband or father was entitled to companionship and services. What proportion of women are gainfully employed, what proportion of the gainfully employed are women, what is the range of their employment, are the first questions to which the following discussion will be devoted.

It should be noted that the entrance of women into the world of gainful occupation causes an increase in the supply of labor,

[1] And especially the Releases of the *Fifteenth Census*, June 28, 1932, *Occupation Statistics;* October 12, 1932, *The Marital Condition of Gainfully Occupied Women;* October 31, 1932, *Home-Makers by Employment Status.*

and clearly in connection with any addition to the labor supply many questions arise. The interests of those already in the working group cannot be ignored. With the growing number of women offering their labor power, there are in fact two main questions. First: Is the pressure of poverty, the disorganized state of industry, the low scale of men's industrial or agricultural earnings, forcing women, mothers of small children, to remain breadwinners when the technical resources of industry and commerce could provide conditions under which they could more successfully perform their marital and maternal duties? A second question is whether or not in a world in which the productive forces are so developed as to make possible a shorter day, a shorter week, and a fuller life, the access of women to the satisfactions of life must either require celibacy or continue to be vicarious, or indirect through a husband, or whether the contact of a woman, married or single, may be immediate and her participation in productive life and in domestic life be individual and direct

Chapter VIII

WOMEN'S SOURCES OF INCOME

IT IS not to be forgotten that there are men whose inherited wealth enables them to live without the necessity of offering their services in the labor market, but from Table 1 it can be seen that in the United States the proportion of men who are not gainfully occupied is, for the adult groups, small, slightly increasing with the decrease in employment demands and the increase in wealth, with the reduced demand for boy labor and the increased regulation of boy labor, but very small and not affected by the domestic status of the man. With the women the situation is different. The question is not merely, Is she gainfully occupied? but, Is she gainfully occupied or married? so that the proportion not gainfully occupied, while decreasing, is still, for each age period, the great body of the female population.

TABLE 1.—Percentage of Population Gainfully Occupied in the United States by Sex, 1870–1930[a]

Population group	1870	1880	1890	1900	1910[b]	1920[b]	1930
Population 16 years and over							
Total................................	52.2	54.0	55.8	56.7	59.0	58.1	57.1
Males................................	88.6	90.6	90.5	90.5	91.1	90.5	88.0
Females...............................	14.8	16.0	19.0	20.6	24.3	24.0	25.3

[a] Figures supplied by Ralph G. Hurlin; see *Recent Social Trends, in the United States*, Chap. VI, for his explanation of his use of the Census data.

[b] Adjustments were made by Ralph G. Hurlin in the occupation figures used for 1910 and 1920, because of probable over-enumeration of women and children in agriculture in 1910, and probable under-enumeration of farm laborers due to the date of census in 1920. For the total population the percentage gainfully occupied according to the published census figures was, in 1890, 41.5 instead of 40.6; in 1920, 39.4 instead of 39.6. See also Fifteenth Census of the United States, 1930, Release, June 28, 1932: Occupations Statistics, Abstract Summary for the United States.

As has been already pointed out, this does not mean that women have not always worked; it means that their position in the wage market is treated as anomalous, and their employment for wages is often discussed as though husbands and fathers had been commonly out of their own efforts not only willing but able to provide for their wives and daughters. There is something amusing in the discussion. For just as, when the bridegroom uttered the solemn words, "with all my worldly goods I thee endow," he was about to become the legal owner of the wife's personal goods and entitled to the income from her real estate, so when husbands and fathers discuss the support of the women of the family they fail to recall the fact that the services of the wife, marital and domestic, and of the daughters have belonged to them. There was, to be sure, in the case of the wife, the reciprocal duty of providing necessaries; in the case of the daughter, there was probably no duty to her, but only an obligation to the community that she should not become a charge on the poor rates. With the development, then, of the factory system and the individualization of the demand for women's labor, came the question of women's bargaining capacity, of women's scales of pay, of widening opportunity and of rendering immediate the participation of women in the community's activities.

The situation in the family group of women who are not gainfully occupied but depend wholly upon the husband's support or upon invested wealth is not to be discussed here; but something of the occupational opportunity open to those women who wish or need to enter it, is of great interest in the attempt to understand the place of women in current American life.

First, it must be kept in mind that by "women" in this discussion are meant not merely those of mature years, or those who have reached their legal majority, be that eighteen years, as in some states, or twenty-one years of age, as in others; but anyone sixteen, or possibly ten, years old or older. And, from the point of view of industrial protection or lack of protection, the sixteen-year-old workers are truly women, for the child labor laws of the separate states furnish no protection beyond that age, although until she reaches her majority, unless she has been emancipated by her father's act or by her own marriage, a girl's earnings belong to her father.

How many women workers? This is a question with a triple implication. How many, compared with the number of other decades? How many, compared with the female population? How many, compared with the employed men?

There were, when the Census of 1930 was taken, 10,752,116 of them.[1] They have steadily increased in number since 1870,

[1] This is the number of those ten years and over. Release cited, p. 3. See Table 1.

when the first census was taken separating women from men and when there were 1,836,288. They have not only increased absolutely, but they have increased when compared with the female population, and they have increased when compared with the gainfully employed men.

It should be kept in mind that the period under consideration is one characterized by the development of business, the expansion of the distributive processes, the increasing application of the principles of subdivision of tasks and of interrelation of functions, and by an enormous increase in the productivity of industrial processes. It may not be surprising then that, as the Census shows, the proportion of men gainfully employed as compared with the total male population was less in 1930 than in 1920. The proportion of women gainfully employed, on the other hand, increased so that while in 1920, 21.1 per cent of those ten years old or over, and 24 per cent of those sixteen years and over, were gainfully occupied, in 1930 the percentages were 22 and 25.3 per cent. Or, looking over the whole period, 148 in 1,000 women and girls sixteen years and over were gainfully employed in 1870; in 1930 there were 253, or an increase of 105 in a thousand in sixty years. This increase in the proportion of women and girls who enter the labor market assumes greater significance when it is compared with the smaller increase in the female population sixteen years of age and over.[1]

In noting the difference between the development in the case of men and of women, it should be kept in mind that if a man is not gainfully occupied the other possible categories in which he may be found are "in school," "in institutions," or "not accounted for," whereas in the case of the women there is the additional category of "housewives." From Table 2 it appears that in the case of men there is a decline in the proportion gainfully occupied, in the number at school and in the number not accounted for. In the case of the women there is an increase in the proportion gainfully occupied, the number at school, and a slight increase in the number unaccounted for, but a decrease in the proportion of the female population who are housewives not gainfully occupied.

Attention will be called to the increased number of housewives who are gainfully occupied, and the increased number of

[1] See more elaborate statement, *Recent Social Trends in the United States*, Chap. XIV.

WOMEN'S SOURCES OF INCOME

TABLE 2.—ATTEMPTED PER CENT DISTRIBUTION OF MALE AND OF FEMALE
POPULATION BY ACTIVITY GROUPS, 1910, 1920, AND 1930[a]

Activity group	1910		1920		1930	
	Male	Female	Male	Female	Male	Female
Total..............................	100.0	100.0	100.0	100.0	100.0	100.0
Children under 5 years..................	11.4	11.8	10.9	11.0	9.3	9.3
Children 5 to 15 years not at school or gainfully occupied........................	2.9	4.7	3.4	4.0	2.7	3.0
All persons attending school...............	19.0	20.0	20.1	21.0	22.5	23.0
All persons gainfully occupied..............	63.6	17.1	61.8	16.5	61.3	17.7
Housewives not gainfully occupied..........	0.0	43.7	0.0	44.0	0.0	43.2
Adults in institutions.....................	.7	.4	.7	.4	.7	.4
Not accounted for.......................	2.4	2.3	3.1	3.1	3.5	3.4

[a] Figures supplied by Ralph G. Hurlin.

gainfully occupied women who are housewives, but those combinations of tasks are not presented here.[1]

I. THE AGE OF GAINFULLY OCCUPIED WOMEN

When, during the early years of the century, interest was aroused in the increase in gainful employment among women, the youth of great numbers of them attracted especial attention. From the point of view of the group from which the young ones came, it was evidence of lack of economic well-being in the family; it was a source of waste to the school system, and it made possible the development of the "parasitic trades," the industry living, as it were, on the future industrial and physical well-being of the worker. It is therefore a great satisfaction to see a distinctly smaller proportion of the youngest age group drawn into the labor market and to have evidence that the increase in numbers is found not wholly in the next higher group, but rather among the more mature. From Table 3 it appears that the more mature are contributing larger quotas.

This fortunate change also reflects itself in the altered distribution of workers among the age groups, as is shown in Table 4. From these figures it appears that the redistribution among age groups sends considerably more into the higher levels of age while

[1] In connection with this discussion, the reader is especially reminded of Chapter VI in *Recent Social Trends*, I, 268, and Hurlin's illuminating discussion of *Shifting Occupational Patterns*.

materially reducing the number of working children. Naturally it would be from the younger group that the school girl would come; it is likewise from the younger group that the great

TABLE 3.—PERCENTAGE OF POPULATION GAINFULLY OCCUPIED, BY AGE AND SEX, 1890–1930[a]

Age	1890	1900	1910	1920	1930
Total population:					
10 to 15 years............................	18.1	18.2	13.7	8.5	44.7
16 to 44 years............................	57.1	58.3	61.8	60.7	59.5
45 years and over........................	52.3	52.1	52.0	52.3	52.2
45 to 64 years........................	55.5	55.9	....	58.2	58.0
65 years and over......................	41.8	39.0	....	34.2	33.2
Males:					
10 to 15 years............................	26.0	26.0	18.6	11.3	6.4
16 to 44 years............................	90.6	91.4	93.3	92.4	89.2
45 years and over........................	90.3	88.1	85.5	86.6	85.8
45 to 64 years........................	95.2	93.5	....	93.8	94.1
65 years and over......................	73.8	68.4	....	60.4	58.3
Females:					
10 to 15 years............................	10.0	10.2	8.7	5.6	2.9
16 to 44 years............................	21.7	23.5	28.1	28.3	29.7
45 years and over........................	11.6	12.9	14.8	14.0	16.1
45 to 64 years........................	12.5	14.1	....	17.1	18.7
65 years and over......................	8.3	9.1	....	8.0	8.0

[a] Department of Commerce, Bureau of the Census, Release September 28, 1932. *Age of Gainful Workers.*

TABLE 4.—PROPORTION OF GAINFULLY EMPLOYED WOMEN BY AGE, FOR THE UNITED STATES, 1920–1930[a]

Age	1920	1930	Age	1920	1930
	100.0	100.0			
10 to 13 years...............	1.4	0.7	20 to 24 years...............	21.2	21.8
14 years....................	1.0	0.4	25 to 44 years...............	40.0	42.3
15 years....................	1.7	0.8	45 to 64 years...............	15.8	17.8
16 years....................	3.2	1.9	65 years and over..........	2.3	2.5
17 years....................	3.9	2.9	Unknown...................	0.2	0.1
18 and 19 years.............	9.4	8.8			

[a] Department of Commerce, Bureau of the Census, Release September 28, 1932, *Age of Gainful Workers.*

number of the gainfully occupied came, many of them staying only until they married. It has long been recognized that age affects the gainfully occupied women, so that the high level of gainful occupation is the period between twenty and twenty-five, with a marked drop for the twenty-five to thirty group and a marked drop for the thirty to thirty-five group, whereas an examination of the figures relating to men would show that the proportion of gainfully occupied among the men sees no decline from the five-year-age groups until fifty years is reached and a serious reduction in number only at sixty-five.[1] It is therefore of special interest that the tendency is now seen to be for the age periods of greatest employment to shift upward. If the working group is separated on the basis of age, it appears that in 1920, 20.5 per cent of the employed women were less than twenty years of age while in 1930 only 15.5 per cent were under that age.

The change in age grouping is so important that its possible significance may be pointed out at slightly greater length. In 1920, 56 in 1,000 little girls between 10 and 15 years were em-

TABLE 5.—GAINFUL OCCUPATION OF CHILDREN AND SCHOOL ATTENDANCE 1880–1930[a]

	1880	1890	1900	1910	1920	1930
Percentage of children 10 to 15 years old gainfully occupied						
Total	16.8	18.1	18.2	13.7	8.5	4.7
Male	24.4	25.9	26.1	18.6	11.3	6.4
Female	9.0	10.0	10.2	8.7	5.6	2.9
Percentage of children 5 to 15 years old attending school						
Total	65.5	66.1	67.6	74.0	79.1	84.4
Male	66.2	65.8	67.5	73.6	78.8	83.5
Female	64.8	66.3	67.7	74.3	79.4	85.4

[a] Figures supplied by Ralph G. Hurlin.

ployed, in 1930 there were only 29; the number of fourteen-year-olds, too, was more than halved, the drop being from 82 to 40 in 1,000, and in the fifteen-year-olds from 154 to 76. The sixteen-year-old girls sent 279 out of 1,000 into the labor market in 1920, in 1930 only 170. The seventeen-year-old proportion dropped from 357 to 275, the eighteen-year-old and the nineteen-year-old from 423 to 405. That is, the group from sixteen to twenty in 1920, sent considerably larger proportions than in 1930. Whereas, in 1930, the older group, namely from twenty-one to twenty-

[1] See *Recent Social Trends in the United States*, Chap. XIV, and especially Chap. VI, p. 278, 279 for discussion of age of women workers. See, for elaborate and interesting discussion, Johanna Lobsenz, *The Older Woman in Industry* (New York: Charles Scribner's Sons, 1929).

[113]

five, received a larger contribution than had been the case ten years earlier. From Table 5 it appears that the younger members of the community were still in school.

All of these changes point to a greater possibility of organization and a less transient attitude toward work, which is of importance from the point of view of the employer's attitude toward women as well as from that of the worker's attitude toward her job.

II. THE NATIONALITY AND RACE OF WOMEN WORKERS

Attention has been called to the fact that the racial and national emphasis in the gainfully employed group is changing and that the native born white group are supplying larger proportions than other groups to the gainfully employed. This may be further evidence of increasing professionalization, since it is largely from the native born that the leisure class is found if there is one. If a large proportion of the native white are taking employment, it may definitely signify a weakening of the leisure class influence and the growth of more independent and self-respecting attitudes on the part of women.

TABLE 6.—NUMBER AND PROPORTION OF WOMEN TEN YEARS OLD AND OVER GAINFULLY OCCUPIED, BY COLOR AND NATIVITY, 1920 AND 1930[a]

	Total number, 1920	Per cent gainfully occupied, 1920	Total number, 1930	Per cent gainfully occupied, 1930
All classes............................	40,449,346	21.1	48,773,249	22.0
Native white[b]........................	30,210,818	19.3	37,287,838	20.5
Foreign-born white[b]..................	6,078,195	18.4	6,138,705	18.8
Negro.................................	4,043,763	38.9	4,727,666	38.9
Mexican..............................	....	....	454,378	14.8
Indian...............................	85,379	11.5	115,512	15.4
Chinese..............................	5,189	14.1	9,742	16.0
Japanese.............................	25,432	20.8	36,693	18.4
All other............................	570	18.8	2,515	27.0

[a] *Fifteenth Census of the United States*, 1930, Release June 28, 1932, *Occupation Statistics, Abstract Summary for the United States*, p. 4.
[b] In 1920, Mexicans were included for the most part in the white population.

There is a slight increase as shown in Table 6, in the proportion of foreign born white and a distinct increase in the proportion of Mexican women who, as discovered by the enumerators in 1920, were often counted among the white. The proportion of Negro women who seek paid employment is of special interest, because in the case of the Negro one could not know what to expect at the end of the decade. Negro women have in the past continued wage earning after marriage, and few have been economically able to refrain from working. Therefore a larger proportion of Negro women than of other racial groups were found in the wage-earning group. Because, however, of the slight proportion they constitute of the population, they were relatively unimportant from the point of view of the racial distribution of the working group. To the extent to which they have been able to move into the economically more advantaged group, the idea of refraining from working would have special weight, but the Census shows their group sending exactly the same proportion into wage earning in 1930 as in 1920.

III. MARRIED WOMEN AND GAINFUL EMPLOYMENT

The number of married women who seek employment is increasing. The proportion of gainfully employed who are married is increasing. From Table 7 it can be seen that among 1,000 married women in 1890, 4.6 were employed; in 1900, the number had risen to 5.6; in 1910, to 10.7; in 1920, it fell back to 9.0; in 1930, there were 11.7. Among 1,000 gainfully employed in 1890, 139 were married; in 1900, 154; in 1910, 247; in 1920, 230; in 1930, 289. Marriage is evidently not the only basis for double responsibility for family care and gainful occupation. While the Census[1] gives 11.7 per cent of the married as occupied, a statement from the same source[2] shows 13.8 per cent of the home-makers gainfully employed. The Census supplies, in fact, two sets of figures: (1) the one[3] telling the numbers of married women who are gainfully employed and the number of gainfully employed who are married; and (2) the other,[4] the number of home-makers who are employed and the number of gainfully employed who are home-makers.

The two questions of marital status and domestic responsibility, while closely related, are quite separate. The two involve questions of the length of the day's work, of the effect on gainful employment of variety of task, with its inevitable distraction

[1] Bureau of the Census, Release October 12, 1932, *Marital Condition of Gainfully Occupied Persons.*
[2] Release October 31, 1932, *Home-Makers by Employment Status.*
[3] Release October 12, 1932, *Marital Condition of Gainfully Occupied Women.*
[4] Release October 31, 1932, *Home-Makers by Employment Status.*

and division of interest and possibility of increased lost time because of conflict of responsibilities. The problem of the married woman involves, however, as the other may not do, the effect of the emotional as well as the physiological strains of child bearing, of infant care, of adjustment to personal demands made on the

TABLE 7.—NUMBER AND PROPORTION OF WOMEN FIFTEEN YEARS OLD AND OVER GAINFULLY OCCUPIED, BY MARITAL CONDITION, FOR THE UNITED STATES; 1920–1930[a]

	Women 15 years old and over			
	Total number	Gainfully occupied		
		Number	Per cent of total	Per cent distribution
1910				
Total............................	30,047,325	7,639,828	25.4	100.0
Single and unknown.................	9,001,342	4,602,102	51.1	60.2
Married...........................	17,684,687	1,890,661	10.7	24.7
Widowed and divorced...............	3,361,296	1,147,065	34.1	15.0
1920				
Total............................	35,177,515	8,346,796	23.7	100.0
Single, widowed, divorced, and unknown[b]........................	13,858,582	6,426,515	46.4	77.0
Married...........................	21,318,933	1,920,281	9.0	23.0
1930				
Total............................	42,837,149	10,632,227	24.8	100.0
Single and unknown.................	11,359,038	5,734,825	50.5	53.9
Married...........................	26,170,756	3,071,302	11.7	28.9
Widowed and divorced...............	5,307,355	1,826,100	34.4	17.2

[a] Bureau of the Census, Release June 28, 1932, *Occupation Statistics*, p. 5.
[b] This group was not subdivided in 1920.

wife or expressed by the wife that are not present in the case of the mother, the sister, the daughter, who assumes these duties. These questions can be competently discussed, of course, only in relation to the continuous adjustment of family life to the new aspects of the composite income; and, in this connection, they can be only mentioned, not elaborated. However, the figures are interesting because of the divergences and such implications as may be drawn are suggestive.

According to the first statement, the proportion of married women who were gainfully occupied increased from 46 in 1,000 in 1890 to 117 in 1,000 in 1930. The proportion of gainfully occupied who were married increased during the same period from 139 in 1,000 to 289. In the case of home-makers, as distinguished from married women, the numbers are given only for 1930, but the figures here are for 3,923,516, whereas the figure for married gainfully employed is 3,071,302. The Census does not account for the discrepancy of 852,214, which may contain some home-makers under fifteen years of age, and otherwise some of the widowed or divorced of whom, in 1930, there were 1,826,100.

In the case of both groups the geographical distribution is interesting. The high proportions of married women gainfully employed are found in the District of Columbia (299 in 1,000 married women) where undoubtedly domestic service, Civil Service and teaching would offer opportunities; in South Carolina, 240 in 1,000; in Mississippi, 227 in 1,000, where agriculture as well as domestic service would bring Negro married women into the labor market. Among the gainfully employed home-makers in the District of Columbia, 169 of 1,000 are found in office work, 314 are servants or waitresses. In South Carolina, 284 of 1,000 gainfully occupied are in agriculture, 214 are servants and waitresses, 139 are in industrial occupations. In Alabama (331), in Mississippi (586), in Arkansas (353), the large proportion of the gainfully employed home-makers are in the cotton picking that is called agriculture. Professional groups of impressive size, that is, more than one in ten of the gainfully employed home-makers, are found in Maine (110), Vermont (121), Connecticut (103), New York (131), New Jersey (103), Illinois (102), Michigan (121), Minnesota and Iowa (118 each), North Dakota (138), South Dakota (163), Nebraska (129), Kansas (112), West Virginia (134), Oklahoma (133); and in the so-called mountain and Pacific states, in every case, the number is considerable, the lowest in these states being 131 in 1,000 in Washington, and the highest, 184, in Montana.

Perhaps a word should be said on the subject of the meaning of "home-maker" in the terminology of the Census. It is not very definite. It is that woman member of the family who is responsible for the care of the home and the family. The figures already published give no clew to the number of other wage earners, the size of the family, or the nature of the responsibility. The publication of these data will be welcomed as confirming or disproving the conclusions that seem to rest on the studies already made.[1]

As is to be expected, the proportions vary greatly in the different national and racial groups. That is, while 11.7 per cent of the native white home-makers are employed, and only 10.2 per cent of the foreign born, 37.5 per cent of the Negro home-makers are in the labor market. However, the question of women's having the right to combine marriage and wage earning is by no means settled. It is still raised, and not infrequently married women are barred from admission to certain employments and employed women lose their positions because of marriage. Both of these situations have been the occasion for research and for discussion. The idea that a married man can and does adequately support his wife is often assumed to be sufficient justification for applying special principles to the employment or retention of married women workers. A recent bulletin of the Association of Deans of Women reports incidentally and without comment the action of a Board of Trustees of one of the state universities prohibiting the employment of married women and the resulting displacement of the dean of women, who was married, by an unmarried successor.[2]

One important question of the gainfully occupied married woman is that of her domestic responsibilities. The Mother's Pension Movement registers the generally accepted view that mothers of dependent children are not to be forced by economic necessity to assume the responsibilities both of support and of care. These laws, however, do not contemplate support under

[1] The U S. Women's Bureau, *e.g.*, Bulletins Nos. 38, 41, 49, 67; Day Monroe, *Chicago Families, A Study of Unpublished Census Data* (Chicago: The University of Chicago Press, 1932); Irene Graham, "Family Support Among Chicago Negroes," *Social Service Review* 3: 345; Alma Herbst, *The Negro in the Slaughtering and Meat Packing Industry* (Boston and New York: Houghton, Mifflin Co., 1932), p. 90 *ff.*; also, Myra Hill Colson, "Negro Home Workers in Chicago," *Social Service Review* 2: 385.

[2] This action seems to have been taken without protest on the part of the woman member of the Board of Trustees, of the university women in the state, or of the faculty. It was an item in an economy program, and its appropriateness seems to have been taken for granted. Similar action by the Trustees of the University of Missouri is noted in the Metropolitan Press, February 1, 1933. It is in strange contrast with the action of Barnard College, quoted, p. 122.

conditions of normal family life and generally provide only for the widow or the wife of the incapacitated man.[1] There is also the question of the labor supply and those with whom the married women may compete. The recent reports, for example, of the Royal Commission on the Civil Service in Great Britain states that the young workers in the Service, those for whose tasks only slight preparation is required, favor retaining the bar that now exists against the employment of married women, while the higher professional groups of women in the Service were demanding the removal of the bar.[2]

It is important from the point of view of the work, through its effect on the turnover, as well as through any effects that marriage may have on the quality of the work. The effect on the turnover is suggested by figures with reference to the reasons for vacancies in certain schools recently reported on.

In 1930–1931 approximately one-sixth of the vacancies [reported on after a National Survey of the Education of Teachers] were due to teachers who married and left teaching. The creation of new positions, due either to increased school enrollments or to reorganization within the schools, was the only other factor accounting for more than 10 per cent of the vacancies filled by "new" teachers in 1930 and 1931.[3]

The degree to which teachers would marry and leave their position varied, however, with the grade of school under consideration. For example, in the elementary schools, this was the cause of 16.4 per cent of the vacancies, in the junior high schools it was the cause of 13.6 per cent of the vacancies, and there were in the junior high schools two other sources which provide larger proportions of vacancies than this, namely, "leaving to teach elsewhere" and "newly created positions." Among the senior high school teachers, the per cent due to this cause was again the third in order, causing 12.7 per cent of the vacancies.

[1] U. S. Children's Bureau, Chart No. 3. *Tabular statement of the laws governing mother's pension.*

[2] *Great Britain, Report of Royal Commission on Civil Service,* 1929–31 (Cmd 3909; London, 1931), p. 112.

[3] E. S. Evenden, Associate Director, National Survey of the Education of Teachers, "Teacher Supply and Demand in the United States 1930–31."

This question is discussed at some length and of course very competently by Marguerite B. Benson, *Annals of the American Academy of Political and Social Science,* Vol. CXLIII, No. 232, May, 1929, *Women in the Modern World* (American Academy of Political and Social Science, Philadelphia. Editor in charge of this volume: Viva B. Boothe), p. 109. There are also interesting suggestions in the figures of relative wages of women who remain in one position as compared with those of women who change positions.

What will be the effect of a marked increase in the number of married women workers can indeed not be foretold. To the extent to which the employment of married women is the result of the disorganization of industry through seasonal employment or underpayment of men or of inadequate social provision in the shape of mothers' pensions or children's allowances, it is a handicap to true industrial organization and an unfair burden on the really occupationally minded women. To the extent to which it means permanence of employment and a gradual lessening of the casual attitude, the turnover will be lessened. The absenteeism may, however, be increased through the recognition of the necessity for maternity leave, and part-time work may provide possibility of continued child care.

As to the effect of marriage on the quality of work, there is as yet no possible statement. Generalizations are indulged in because employers often act from mixed considerations and try to rationalize their activities. In December, 1931, for example, a representative in the Reichstag reported married women employees to be so inefficient that the Budget Committee decided that the married women could be asked to resign if the authorities thought that their families could be maintained without their earnings. In March of 1932, however, the Berlin Labor Court held that marriage was no ground for dismissal.[1]

From the point of view of many professional women the question of continuing employment after marriage is of grave importance, since the possibility of working after marriage alone provides the conditions under which the woman may continue to share in the life of the group directly as an individual and not vicariously. This has seemed so important that two independent enterprises have been undertaken, one at Smith College, to discover ways and means of enabling married women to participate on a part-time basis,[2] one a special undertaking in the field of research to discover the possibilities of developing these opportunities.[3] This has resulted in the establishment in January, 1929, of the Institute of Women's Professional Relations, financed by private individuals, sponsored by the American

[1] *Metropolitan Press*, December 10, 1931, March 28, 1932.
[2] Lorene Pruette, Ph.D., "The Married Woman and the Part Time Job," *Annals*, CXLIII, No. 232, (May, 1929), XXV (1929), 301, *Woman in the Modern World*.
[3] Chase Going Woodhouse, "The Status of Women," *American Journal of Sociology*, XXXV (1929–30), 1091.

Association of University Women, with headquarters at the North Carolina College for Women. Briefly stated, the objectives of the Institute are

to act as a clearing-house for information on the opportunities and requirements for college women in business and the professions; survey and chart present opportunities for college women; study new opportunities; cooperate with business and professional groups in securing facts on necessary aptitudes and training; cooperate with educational institutions in planning for functional education; and study the problems involved in the changing position of women in economic life and in the home.

As a matter of fact, when the question is asked as to why a married woman seeks gainful employment, the reply is generally that she does this, just as the single woman or the man takes gainful employment, namely, to support herself or help to support her family. This purpose, as has been said, is now generally accepted in the case of the single woman.[1] From the report on Women and Child Wage Earners it became evident that among the groups studied it was well nigh universal for the daughters to work either from economic necessity or because the standard of their class demanded wage earning on the part of the daughters as well as of the sons, or because of both these motives. There is still, however, a great deal of discussion as to why a married woman works. So far as the married woman in factory, store, or laundry is concerned, there can be little question whether or not the woman prefers housework to work in the factory; she must do both. Figures will be given showing that the combination of domestic and factory tasks accounts for a considerable amount of the lost time in certain industrial establishments.[2] It should be noted, too, that in 1920 four-fifths of the gainfully occupied married women, exclusive of those in agriculture, were in manufacturing, trade and domestic and personal service, that is, in work whose reward is the pay check, while less than one-tenth were in professional and semi-professional pursuits. When the 1930 figures are more completely available, interesting light will be thrown on the subject.

The occupation and income of the husband, of course, often determine the decision of the wife as to whether or not she will

[1] *Report on Condition of Woman and Child Wage Earners,* Vol. 18, *Employment of Women and Children in Selected Industries.* See U. S. Bureau of Labor Statistics Bulletin Whole No. 175, pp. 19, 20, 69, 70, 105, 160, 203.
[2] See p. 163.

take gainful employment, and in another place attention was called to the statements of a number of educated women on this subject.[1]

A corollary to the employment of married women is the recognition of the right of married women workers to have maternity leave without sacrificing their positions. This, too, has been recognized in certain jurisdictions in which the question has been raised, as in New York State, where the Commissioner of Education ruled[2] that absences for maternity were not different from any other absences and were therefore no basis for dismissal. "The teacher has not been dismissed nor has she resigned her position," he replied to a request that he declare such a teacher to have resigned. "Her tenure of position is protected by the education law. She cannot be removed from her position except on charges, and absence for purposes of maternity does not constitute cause for dismissal."

A recent action in this direction, reported by the Dean of Barnard College, is so interesting that her statement is quoted in full.[3]

One of the most perplexing problems [Dean Gildersleeve writes] thrust upon women by the economic and social changes of recent years has been the necessity of combining marriage, motherhood, and careers. Partly because of our location in a great city and our connection with a large university, where careers for husbands were conveniently at hand, Barnard has for many years had married women on its teaching staff. Recently, when the question of children arose, the President and the Trustees in several special cases arranged for the mother, when the birth of a child was expected, a half-year's leave of absence with full pay.

It has seemed desirable to the Trustees to decide whether such a policy is a reasonable one and if so to regularize the practice. Accordingly a special committee of the Board was appointed to study the question, and on its recommendation the following resolution was adopted at the Annual Meeting of the Trustees in December:

Resolved, That a woman member of the administrative or instructional staff of Barnard College, on Trustee appointment for full time, who is expecting a child, be granted a leave of absence for a half year on full salary or for a full year on half salary, the period of the leave to be determined by the Dean after consultation with the individual concerned.

The administration is much gratified by this enlightened and progressive action. We have felt for many years that a women's college was

[1] *Recent Social Trends in the United States*, Chap. XIV.

[2] *New York Times*, March 9, 1931.

[3] *Annual Report of Dean Gildersleeve of Barnard College*, 1932 (New York City), p. 7.

a peculiarly appropriate place in which to experiment with solutions of the new problems faced by women, and to attempt to arrive at some wise adjustment. Our observations have shown that the combination of rearing children and carrying on college teaching is a difficult one, but in some cases certainly very desirable. It is of the greatest importance that our teachers should be normal and interesting human beings, with as full and rich lives as may be. Neither the men nor the women on our staff should be forced into celibacy, and cut off from that great source of experience, of joy, sorrow and wisdom, which marriage and parenthood offer.

Another corollary is the probable increase, on the part of women continuing in employment, in the practice of retaining the maiden name after marriage. This subject seemed of great importance to some of those connected with the early feminist movement, whether the woman was or was not gainfully employed. Lucy Stone's[1] name suggests itself at once in connection with this demand. Less is said on the subject now and the question is not often raised, although as recently as 1921 a Lucy Stone League was formed with this as an item in its program, and it is necessary under the statutes of certain states for a married woman to register under her husband's name.[2] The law on the subject seems to be that the wife may retain her maiden name or acquire by custom a new one. When legal papers are to be signed, however, as, for example, in applying for a passport, evidence of the marital status is required in order that the obligation of public authorities may be defined. The passport regulations require that if a wife apply in her own name she shall state that she is married and give the name of her husband. However, the subject receives relatively little attention.

[1] Alice Stone Blackwell, *Lucy Stone* (Boston: Little, Brown and Co., 1930), Chap. XII, p. 171.

[2] The question was raised in the autumn of 1932 in connection with the candidacy for the House of Representatives in Connecticut of Elsie Hill (Mrs. Albert Levitt), who has never taken her husband's name. Interest was again aroused by the appointment as U. S. Secretary of Labor of the Hon. Frances Perkins, who has always retained in public life her maiden name.

Chapter IX

HOW WOMEN EARN

I. OLD NAMES WITH NEW FACES

HOW does a woman choose a job? The question of the social status of occupations has been the subject of elaborate statistical inquiries.[1] Undoubtedly, the social attitude toward women's occupations has a very real influence upon those who look toward employment and those who advise prospective workers. These questions involve considerations of opportunities for employment, of cost, and of the time necessary for preparation, the general social and economic position of the family, and other facts of that kind. A clear line must be drawn, of course, between gainful employment which the girl may seek and the opportunity of being a home-maker into which she is supposed to pass by the way of matrimony, finding the opportunity at the request of the young man. Those questions belong rather to the discussion of the place of the woman in the family, than of the place of women in the labor market. It is interesting that several studies with reference to the prestige of occupations, differing in various respects, agree in putting medicine at the head of the list as bestowing the greatest prestige upon those who practice, and also in the general order in which they rank the occupations of lawyer, high school teacher, elementary teacher, bookkeeper, salesperson, factory operative, and waitress, placing them in that order of relative social advantage; while they likewise agree in placing what they call "home-making" relatively low on the list. It should be noted, however, that nothing is said as to how one enters these occupations or what the main rewards are.

One of the interesting movements of the last twenty-five years is the so-called Vocational Guidance Movement, growing out of the appreciation of the "wasted years" of young persons leaving school to go to work. Educational and social workers in the United States followed similar groups in Germany and Great

[1] See, for example, *Teachers College Record*, XXXIII (May, 1932), 696; Clara Meyer, "The Social Status of Occupations for Women." References are made in this article to previous studies by G. S. Counts, *School Review*, XXXIII, 16, and by Lehman and Witty, *Journal of Educational Sociology*, V (1931), 101.

Britain in attempting to bridge the gap between school and work, to prepare the child and aid in the selection of a job, a process that earlier was closely tied with the social and occupational status of the family. But selection of a job depends not only on aptitudes and ambitions; it is likewise related to the demand for workers and this raises the question of the range of opportunity open to women to which reference has been made above. When the question is asked whether or not that range is widening, the apparent answer is "yes," and the real answer may likewise be in the affirmative. To say just what the development has been, however, it will be necessary to await further analyses of the Census data than are now available.

It is clear that women have assumed a larger place among the gainfully employed during the past three decades, but the tendency to concentrate in relatively few occupations is evidently still very great. Whether or not this tendency is as marked now as it was in 1900 cannot be definitely stated until the Census figures are more completely available.[1]

Reference has been made to the altered classification used by the Census. In some cases, new categories are constituted by breaking up old categories, in other cases they are constituted by combining old categories. For example, "operative" and "laborer" are terms characterizing the degree of skill rather than the nature either of the particular task or of the occupational organization with which the worker is associated. Until much more complete analysis of these terms is available, it cannot be known whether the number of paths leading from the home to the possible job is greater or smaller than before. No account of the occupational prospect nor of the occupational experience can be quite complete, either, until the question of the changed conditions under which the processes of what might be called household management are carried on, is amenable to statement and analysis. It is, as a matter of fact, the possible combination of domestic obligation and employment that presents so absorbing a question to many women. While much more information about women in relation to the occupational organization remains to be revealed,[2] a number of interesting developments can be discovered and their significance set out.

[1] *Recent Social Trends in the United States*, Chap. XIV.
[2] Possibly by a companion volume to *Statistics of Women at Work, 1907, Twelfth Census*, and to Hill, *op. cit.*

The Census of 1900, for example, made it clear that agriculture as a claimant for women's services was already declining. The scriptural fields knew their Naomi and their Ruth, the stretches of Eastern Europe are still harvested in part by the weary hands of women; the Negro women have picked cotton; the foreign born

TABLE 8.—PERCENTAGE DISTRIBUTION OF FEMALE GAINFULLY OCCUPIED PERSONS SIXTEEN YEARS OF AGE AND OVER, 1870–1930[a]

Occupation group	1870	1880	1890	1900	1910	1920	1930
Agriculture	20.5	20.0	16.7	16.5	14.9	10.9	7.4
Manufacturing	20.0	26.0	26.7	26.4	24.1	22.6	17.6
Trade and transportation	1.0	2.2	3.5	5.5	8.0	10.7	11.7
Clerical service	.4	.9	2.6	4.5	8.1	17.1	18.8
Domestic and personal service	52.6	43.4	41.8	38.1	35.5	27.9	32.6
Public service (not elsewhere classified)	.0	.1	.1	.2	.2	.2	.3
Professional service	5.5	7.4	8.6	8.8	9.2	10.6	11.6
Total	100.0	100.0	100.0	100.0	100.0	100.0	100.0

[a] These are the figures supplied by Mr. Ralph G. Hurlin after treatment to harmonize the 1930 returns with those of 1910 and 1920.

TABLE 9.—DISTRIBUTION OF WOMEN TEN YEARS OF AGE AND OVER AMONG GAINFUL OCCUPATIONAL GROUPS, 1910–1930[a]

Occupational group	1910	1920	1930[b]
Agriculture	22.4	12.7	8.5
Extraction of minerals			
Manufacturing and mechanical	22.3	22.6	17.5
Transportation	1.3	2.6	2.6
Trade	5.8	7.9	9.0
Public service	0.2	0.1	.2
Professional service	9.1	11.9	14.2
Domestic and personal	31.3	25.6	29.6
Clerical	7.3	16.6	18.5

[a] These are from the Census of Occupations of 1910, 1920 and Release of June 28, 1932, Occupation Statistics, and are given here because more easily available.
[b] Agriculture includes forestry and fishery.

have worked in the truck gardens of the "Eastern Shore" and of the Middle Coast, but the place of agriculture among the occupational groups has been declining for both men and women. Where in 1870, 205 of 1,000 women workers were in agriculture, in 1930[1] only 74 were farmers or farm laborers. This is shown by figures in Tables 8 and 9. Manufacturing, too, which first drew

[1] These do not include the children between ten and sixteen years of age.

women from their homes to work in large numbers in one place
under conditions quite beyond their control, where in 1870, 200
in 1,000 or more than one-fifth of the gainfully occupied were to
be found, now calls for only 176. The textile, clothing, food
industries—changing raw materials into articles ready for use—
either are less needed (note the difference in women's garments
due to fashion) or the need can be met with relatively fewer
hands. In domestic and personal service the difference between
1870 and 1930 is not so great as between 1910 and 1920 nor as
was anticipated for 1930. In 1870, over half the gainfully occupied
found their opportunity in this group of occupations and their
domestic service really meant domestic service—cooking, laundering, waiting on table—doing for another for wages what women
did as unpaid service or in fulfillment of marital or filial obligations in their own homes. Since 1910 considerably less than one-
third of the gainfully employed women are in the group; but the
decline has not been a steady one, for in 1920 only a few over a
fourth, 279 in 1,000, were in this group; that is, the number went
down and rose again. But when it rose it was not service in the
home of another but service on the whole somewhat professionalized, that made up the total, for barbers and beauty parlor
employees made up a respectable share of this increased number.

The space vacated by the agricultural, manufacturing or
personal service worker has been filled by the workers who assist
in the great volume of distributive services or in enabling persons
separated in space to communicate with each other, that is,
they make telephone connections, they may be air-pilots or radio
announcers, or sell the innumerable articles for many of which
the demand has been stimulated. They, also, perform the mass of
services generally characterized as clerical. These groups have
grown from 13 in 1,000 to 117, and from 4 to 188. Two other
groups are to be accounted for. The professional group claimed in
1870, 55 in 1,000, mostly teachers; they now contain 116 and
among them are still mostly teachers, but also trained nurses,
lawyers, doctors, actresses, skilled press-women, dentists, chem-
ists, and many others for whom opportunities for professional
equipment are more or less adequately available. To one other
group the Census calls attention, *Public Service, not elsewhere
classified.* Women under these classes have increased so that
where there was none in 1880 and only 1 in 1,000 in 1890, they are
now 3 in 1,000 or 17,583 in all. They are policewomen and

probation officers in whose hands may lie a large share of the leadership in reconstructing the behavior not only of women and child offenders with whom they come in contact, but of those responsible for the treatment of all offenders. Further reference to these occupations will be made at a later point.

Since agriculture is so definitely a declining occupation,[1] no further comment will be made on that subject except to say with what special interest the figures from the Census showing the redistribution geographically of Negro women will be awaited, although a considerable volume of the change due to the migration of the Negro from the southern states to the northern industrial centers had already taken place in 1920. It is true that a discussion of that phenomenon belongs rather with the subject of racial relationship or of population, or possibly of the labor supply, than with the subject of women's activities. Those figures would perhaps help in an adequate understanding of the effect of changed circumstances on group thinking with reference to married women's employment, rather than to a

---

[1] This does not mean that the subject lacks interest, and, in fact, a very competent study by Ruth Allen, *The Labor of Women in the Production of Cotton*, University of Texas Bureau of Research in the Social Sciences Study No. 3 (Austin, Texas, 1931), pp. 172–73, gives interesting information about certain aspects of the employment of women in the agriculture of that state. Certain conclusions of the study seem worth quoting:

"In regard to the women who do field work for their families, certain conclusions seem justified:

"1. Unmarried women living at home will with few exceptions do field work for their families.

"2. Married women work in the fields largely as the result of poverty, as indicated by a large percentage in the families of tenants.

"3. The larger percentage of unmarried girls is found among the families of owners, indicating that the force tending to keep a girl at home is a comparatively good standard of living.

"4. The refusal on the part of these girls to do unpaid field labor would probably force many farms to stop producing cotton, which is a consummation devoutly to be wished.

"5. The burden of the mother who has no one to help her with the housework and yet works in the field is very heavy, more so probably than the double burden of the industrial worker.

"6. Families having two or more adult women are in a very favorable situation with regard to labor costs in the production of cotton.

"7. Groups like those mentioned in Paragraph 5 are significant because of their effect upon the wages of labor on the cotton farm and, through them, upon the wages of all unskilled labor.

"8. The unmarried girl who stays at home is likely to do some work for hire, as indicated by the small percentage in this group as compared to the percentage among the hired workers."

general discussion of women's activities. Negro women are not of a group for whom unpaid work in their own home was the common experience, and how Negro women are responding to the changed circumstances of northern communities would make an interesting chapter in itself. In this connection, it need, however, claim no more attention. However, it will be noted below that a few women have qualified in the United States Forestry Service, and where there were two women listed in 1920, under the category of foresters, forest managers and timber cruisers, in 1930 there were 15.

But if women in agriculture need not detain the student, attention should be given to the other classes of occupations, and Domestic and Personal Service contains many interesting implications. Some occupations, for example the steam laundry, listed in the group have taken on aspects of the factory. Some are on their way toward the professional. The beauty culture business is taking this route. Brief statements about these two may indicate some of the questions connected with the choice by a woman of her job.

II. DOMESTIC AND PERSONAL SERVICE

Between 1900 and 1920 a steady decrease in the number of women in domestic and personal service occupations had been likewise taking place. The decrease in the number of servants, cooks, waitresses and laundresses was especially noticeable during this period, and the character of the job was changing in that the habit of "living in"[1] was declining. In 1920, for example, almost half the servants, 49.6 per cent, were found to live in their own homes, while in 1900,[2] only a third had lived at home. The others had taken part pay in kind besides being where a limitation of the day's work was difficult. The decrease in laundresses (not in laundries) continued up to 1930. The number was 385,956 in 1920 and 356,468 in 1930. On the other hand, the number of women employed in power laundries increased from 80,747 to 160,473 during the same period. In 1930, however, the number of women in all occupations classified as "domestic and personal" (see Table 10) had increased by 45 per cent, that is, from 2,186,682 to 3,180,251. Part of this increase was due to the

[1] That is, sleeping on the employers' premises and being paid partly in room and board.
[2] Hill, *op. cit.*, p. 138.

growing numbers of women in occupations not ordinarily thought of as domestic, carried on outside the home and wholly lacking the character of personal relationship. They belong in the category only because of the nature of the utility resulting from the effort put forth. That is, there was an increase in the numbers of

TABLE 10.—MEN AND WOMEN EMPLOYED IN DOMESTIC AND PERSONAL OCCUPA-
TIONS, 1910–1930ᵃ

Occupation	1910		1920		1930	
	Men	Women	Men	Women	Men	Women
Total...................	1,225,395	2,530,403	1,193,313	2,186,682	1,772,200	3,180,251
Barbers, hairdressers, manicurists.......................	172,977	22,298	182,965	33,246	261,096	113,194
Boarding and lodging house keepers..................	23,052	142,400	18,652	114,740	17,093	127,278
Boot blacks.................	14,000	20	15,142	33	18,747	37
Charwomen and cleaners......	7,195	26,839	11,848	24,955	20,943	40,989
Cleaning and dyeing shop workers......................	12,215	2,645	17,094	4,573	66,515	21,603
Elevator tenders.............	25,010	25	33,376	7,337	55,255	12,359
Hotel keepers and managers....	50,269	14,235	41,449	14,134	39,538	17,310
Housekeepers and stewards....	15,940	173,383	17,262	204,350	20,383	236,363
Janitors....................	91,629	21,452	149,590	29,038	273,805	35,820
Laborers, dom. & personal service......................	50,265	3,215	31,224	1,669	67,337	4,350
Laundresses (not in laundry)...	13,693	520,004	10,882	385,874	4,565	356,468
Laundry owners.............	17,057	986	12,239	1,453	22,482	2,063
Laundry operatives..........	35,909	76,355	39,968	80,747	80,229	160,475
Midwives...................	....	6,205	....	4,773	....	3,566
Nurses (not trained).........	15,926	110,912	19,338	132,658	13,867	139,576
Porters (except in stores)......	84,055	73	87,683	485	127,436	52
Restaurant keepers...........	50,316	10,516	72,343	15,644	125,398	40,008
Servants						
Cooks....................	117,004	333,436	129,857	268,618	194,297	371,095
Other servants.............	145,672	976,113	128,956	743,515	169,877	1,263,864
Waiters and waitresses........	102,495	85,798	112,064	116,921	161,315	231,973
Other......................	180,716	3,543	61,381	1,919	33,830	1,808

ᵃ Figures taken from volume on *Occupations 1910*, Thirteenth Census, and Release June 28, 1932, *Occupation Statistics*. The numbers seem interesting in themselves.

laundry and cleaning and dyehouse operatives, of beauty parlor operatives and manicurists and of elevator operators. In 1930 the number of women enumerated in these three occupations was 181,728 larger than in 1920. It should, however, be noted that the increase in the numbers of women in the old domestic occupations of cooks, servants and waitresses was greater, for there were in 1930, 737,878 more of these than in 1920.

It has been suggested that domestic work in the home has taken on new aspects. Home laundering meant the wash tub—it may now mean the electric washing machine and the electric iron manipulated by members of the family or by the woman who comes in by the day and washes, dries, and irons. Work in a power laundry, on the other hand, means division of tasks so that men manage the heavy mechanical operations for washing. What the balance will be between the more effective organization of the power laundries and the provision of the utensils for facilitating home washing together with the reduction in the number and general volume of garments now in use cannot be measured. But some examination of conditions of work in power laundries may help in interpreting the situation, and serve as a basis for further understanding of the elements in women's choices of jobs.

A report concerning women in power laundries, written in 1913, called attention to "the army of women leaving their homes to follow in the wake of tasks transferred to the machine equipped factory."[1] Another report in 1927 on women in power laundries in New York State described the growth of the laundry industry in the last few years as "phenomenal."[2] As has been the case with the making of clothing and other kinds of work formerly done by women in the home, the transfer to the establishment outside the home has meant that men have replaced women to some extent.

The subject of power laundries and the division of work between men and women suggests the interesting question referred to before—as to whether or not women are replacing men or men, women. There were many shifts during and again after the war which left no trace of the Census figures. It may simply be noticed here from Table 11 that women constituted in 1930 a somewhat smaller proportion of the total number employed in this group of occupations, 642 in 1,000 rather than 674; that among charwomen and cleaners, women are fewer by 117 in 1,000; so with janitors and cooks, as well as laundry operatives; whereas the beauty

[1] Marie L. Obenauer, *Employment of Women in Power Laundries of Milwaukee*, U. S. Department of Labor, Bureau of Labor Statistics Bulletin No. 122 (1913), p. 9.

[2] *Hours and Earnings of Women in Power Laundries of New York State*, prepared by Bureau of Women in Industry, New York State Department of Labor, Special Bulletin No. 153 (1927), p. 6.

culturists, the boarding and lodging house keepers, the cleaning and dyeing shop workers, the elevator tenders, the laundry owners, servants other than cooks and waitresses, have increased relatively to the men.

Steam laundries were originally chiefly used for the laundering of collars and cuffs and for flatwork, such as sheets and towels,

TABLE 11.—PROPORTION OF WOMEN OF ALL PERSONS EMPLOYED IN DOMESTIC AND PERSONAL OCCUPATIONS, 1910–1930[a]

Occupation	1910	1920	1930
Total..	67.4	64.7	64.2
Barbers, hairdressers, manicurists.......................	11.4	15.4	30.2
Boarding and lodging house keepers.......................	86.1	86.0	88.2
Book blacks..	(b)	(b)	(b)
Charwomen and cleaners...................................	78.9	67.8	66.2
Cleaning and dyeing shop workers.......................	17.8	21.1	24.5
Elevator tenders...	(b)	18.0	18.3
Hotel helpers and managers..............................	22.1	25.4	30.4
Housekeepers and stewards...............................	91.6	92.2	92.1
Janitors...	18.9	16.3	11.6
Laborers—domestic and personal service..................	6.0	5.1	6.1
Laundresses—not in laundry.............................	97.4	97.3	98.7
Laundry owners and officials............................	5.5	10.6	8.4
Laundry operatives......................................	68.0	66.9	66.7
Midwives..	100.0	100.0	100.0
Nurses (not trained)....................................	87.4	87.3	90.9
Porters (except in stores)..............................	(b)	(b)	(b)
Restaurant keepers......................................	17.3	17.8	24.2
Servants			
Cooks...	74.0	67.4	65.6
Other servants..	87.0	85.2	88.2
Waiters and waitresses..................................	45.6	51.1	58.9
Other occupations.......................................	1.9	3.0	5.3

[a] Bureau of the Census, Release June 28, 1932, *Occupation Statistics*.
[b] Less than 0.1 per cent.

from hotels, restaurants, railroads, steamships and the like. During the last decade, however, with the improvement of machine methods of laundering and with social changes which have taken place, apartment house life for example, and the high cost of domestic labor, the use of the steam laundry for the family wash has grown. Wet wash, rough dry and other family services have been greatly developed. Only since 1909 has the Census of Manufactures considered power laundries of sufficient importance to collect data from them, and it still classifies laundries separately from manufacturing industries. Owing to differences in the methods of obtaining the information there is considerable discrepancy between the number of women enumerated as laundry operatives by the Census of Occupations and the number reported by the Census of Manufactures as wage earners in power laundries. According to figures from the Census of Manufactures, probably the more reliable source, the number of all wage earners in power laundries increased 20 per cent from 1909 to 1919 and 54 per cent from 1919 to 1927. On the other hand,

TABLE 12.—NUMBER OF WAGE EARNERS, NUMBER AND PER CENT OF WOMEN EMPLOYED IN POWER LAUNDRIES, 1909–1927[a]

Year	Total number	Number of women	Per cent women
1909............................	109,484	78,004	71
1914............................	130,641	89,741	69
1919............................	131,879	93,226	71
1925............................	169,200	111,470	66
1927............................	203,216		

a Figures for 1909 to 1919 from *Fourteenth Census*, 1920, Vol. 10, *Manufactures*, p. 1030; *Biennial Census of Manufactures*, 1925, p. 1266; and *Biennial Census of Manufactures*, 1927, p. 1292. The figures for 1927 include only laundries reporting receipts of $5,000 and over a year and are not quite comparable to earlier figures which include smaller laundries also. The figures given by the *Census of Occupations* for workers ten years and over are 1910, 68.0; 1920, 66.9; 1930, 66.7.

evidence of a decrease in home laundresses is available from the Census of Occupations and seems to show that the number of laundresses who worked outside of steam or power laundries, either in the home of the employer or "taking in washing" in the home of the worker, decreased 25 per cent between 1910 and 1920,[1] that is, from 520,004 to 385,874, and between 1920 and 1930 by 8.8 per cent, or from 385,874 to 356,468; while, as can be seen from Table 10, between 1910 and 1930 the men operatives increased from 35,909 to 80,229, or by 123.3 per cent.

In the home the woman did all the work of laundering, washing, wringing out and ironing the garments; when this work was removed from the home to the factory men were substituted for women in some of the machine operations. Men operated the washing machines and extractors, as the machines are called which wring the water from the linen, and also sometimes operate the steam presses. Women sort and mark the soiled linen, shake

[1] Hill, *op. cit.*, p. 33. Census Release June 28, 1932, *Occupation Statistics, Abstract Summary for the United States*, p. 19.

it out after it is removed from the extractor, pass the flat work through the mangle, sometimes operate the steam presses and do the hand ironing.

The proportion of women in the total number of workers depends largely on the type of laundry; in wet wash laundries, where most of the work consists of washing and extracting the water, there is little work for women. A recent survey covering 19,758 women laundry workers in 23 cities in various states, but not including wet wash laundries, found that women comprised 81 per cent of the working force, a higher proportion than is shown in the United States Census figures.[1]

Whether or not women employed in the power laundry are any better off than they were when employed as washerwomen in the home, bent over the washtub or operating the new electric washing machines, is another question. The conclusion of a study of the New York State Department of Labor concerning the hygienic conditions of steam laundries was that work in the model laundry need not be injurious to the health of the workers.[2] But work in the hot, steamy atmosphere of the ordinary steam laundry with the irregular hours, long standing, and necessity of working treadle machines is not a pleasant occupation, although the machines which men tend do the heaviest and wettest part of the work.

Another occupation classified as Domestic and Personal is that of hairdressing, or, to use the term preferred by the trade, cosmetologists. This is now considered work for a "specialist," but is a form of personal service in which women were formerly employed in private homes, and which has opened up increasing opportunities to women for work. With the style of short hair and the increased expenditure of women on various aids to "beauty" the number of women employed as hairdressers or "cosmetologists" has rapidly grown. It has been estimated that the number of barbers, hairdressers and manicurists of both sexes increased from 216,211 in 1920 to 374,290 in 1930. On the basis of material recently gathered it is estimated that from 12,000 to 15,000 women are employed in this business in New York City alone, an increase of from 225 to 300 per cent since

---

[1] U. S. Department of Labor, Women's Bureau Bulletin No. 78 (1930), p. 10, *A Survey of Laundries and their Women Workers in 23 Cities.*

[2] *A Study of Hygienic Conditions in Steam Laundries and their Effect upon the Health of Workers.* Prepared by the Division of Industrial Hygiene, New York Department of Labor, Special Bulletin No. 130 (1924), p. 86.

1920.[1] At one time, beauty shop operators were almost exclusively women, but the fashion of bobbed hair gave men a chance to enter this occupation, and in New York City they have probably replaced women to some extent and now do permanent waving, other forms of waving, and even shampooing.[2]

Beauty shops employ women not only as general beauty operatives to shampoo, wave and cut the hair, and as manicurists, but also as other specialists, electrolysis operators and even as chiropodists. Many women are proprietors.[3] A national organization of hairdressers and cosmetologists was formed in 1921 and now has 126 branches. The requirements of education and special training for beauty shop operatives are rising. An occupational monograph written in 1923 described hairdressing as a trade for girls in which limited school experience was no handicap.[4] Since that time, however, at least 21 states have passed registration laws requiring licenses for beauty parlor operatives and establishing standards of special training and general education including usually at least graduation from grammar schools.[5] In some states which have no registration laws, bills for registration have been presented to the legislatures. In Massachusetts such a bill has been before the legislatures for three successive years. In that state girls who have graduated from the sixth grade and meet the other requirements of the child labor laws for work certificates may now enter the occupation.[6]

During these two decades, between 1910 and 1930, women workers in cleaning and dyeing shops increased from 2,645 in 1910 to 21,623, or by 739 per cent. Women boarding and lodging house keepers declined 11 per cent, while hotel keepers and managers increased 22 per cent, a trend which indicates, perhaps, a change in the type of housing. Women elevator operators have

[1] Frieda G. Miller, *Hours of Work in Beauty Shops in New York City*, New York State Industrial Bulletin, X, No. 4 (January, 1931), 132–33.

[2] Of the 2,157 employees in beauty shops covered by this study, 26 per cent were men.

[3] See the lists of occupations of Classified Women's Clubs, as the national organizations of the Quota and Altrusa Clubs show.

[4] In Philadelphia, Ruth Woodruff, *The Hairdresser* (Philadelphia: White Williams Foundation), Occupational Monograph Series, No. 3 (1923), p. 5.

[5] For a review of the registration laws in effect in 1927 see *The Hairdresser*, revised. Ruth Woodruff, Junior Employment Service, Board of Public Education (Philadelphia, 1929), Occupation Study No. 2.

[6] In general, the occupation of beauty operative seems to be progressing from a form of domestic and personal service to an occupation which only specialists with training may enter.

[135]

apparently continued to increase. The 1910 Census enumerated 25 women elevator operators; in 1930 there were 17,310, or 31.4 per cent of the total number.

Other great increases are found in the numbers of women restaurant keepers and waitresses in which the trends are indicative of modern urban dwelling. In the former, women are nearly

TABLE 13.—PER CENT DISTRIBUTION OF MEN AND WOMEN EMPLOYED IN DOMESTIC AND PERSONAL OCCUPATIONS, 1910–1930[a]

Occupation	1910		1920		1930	
	Men	Women	Men	Women	Men	Women
Total.....................................	100.0	100.0	100.0	100.0	100.0	100.0
Barbers, hairdressers, manicurists..........	14.1	0.9	15.3	1.5	14.7	3.6
Boarding and lodging house keepers........	1.9	5.6	1.6	5.2	0.9	4.0
Boot blacks.............................	1.1	(b)	1.3	(b)	1.1	(b)
Charwomen and cleaners..................	0.6	1.1	0.9	1.1	1.2	1.3
Cleaning and dyeing shop workers..........	0.9	0.1	1.4	0.2	3.8	0.7
Elevator tenders........................	2.0	(b)	2.8	0.3	3.1	0.4
Hotel keepers and managers...............	4.1	0.6	3.5	0.6	2.2	0.5
Housekeepers and stewards...............	1.3	6.9	1.4	9.3	1.2	7.4
Janitors................................	7.5	0.8	12.5	1.3	15.5	1.1
Laborers, domestic & personal service......	4.1	0.1	2.6	0.1	3.8	0.1
Laundresses (not in laundry)..............	1.1	20.6	0.9	17.6	0.3	11.2
Laundry owners.........................	1.4	(b)	1.0	0.1	1.3	0.1
Laundry operatives......................	2.9	3.0	3.3	3.4	4.5	5.0
Midwives...............................	.....	0.2	.....	0.2	.....	0.1
Nurses (not trained)....................	1.3	4.4	1.6	6.1	0.8	4.4
Porters (except in stores)................	6.9	(b)	7.3	(b)	7.2	(b)
Restaurant keepers......................	4.1	0.4	6.1	0.7	7.1	1.3
Servants................................	29.8	54.1	31.1	51.6	29.6	58.7
Cooks..............................	9.5	13.1	10.9	12.3	10.9	11.7
Other servants......................	11.9	38.6	10.8	34.0	9.6	39.7
Waiters and waitresses..................	8.4	3.4	9.4	5.3	9.1	7.3
Other...................................	14.7	0.1	5.1	0.1	1.8	0.1

[a] Bureau of the Census, Release June 28, 1932, Occupation Statistics.
[b] Less than 0.1 per cent.

four times as numerous as in 1910, while men increased but two and one-half times. Women as cleaners, janitors and housekeepers also increased, as they did in the occupations of cook and other servants. More than one-third of the women in domestic and personal service are listed as servants, a proportion which has changed little over the twenty-year period.

It may be said in summary that in the census classification of domestic and personal service women are increasing, but in the period from 1910 to 1930 they have increased only 36 per cent as compared with a rise of 56 per cent for men. Moreover, as can be seen from Table 13, several major changes are taking place among the individual occupations within the larger group.

Chapter X

WOMEN IN SELECTED MANUFACTURING OCCUPATIONS

IT IS of course to the manufacturing and mechanical group of occupations—the old occupations of women—that special interest attaches. Cotton and other textile manufacture, the manufacture of clothing, of shoes, of tobacco, glass, and printing have long employed great numbers of women.[1] Since the occupational classifications in the different Census compilations are not identical, however, it is not yet possible to discuss at length the changes that have occurred in these occupational groups.

But with reference to the position of women in factories, in general, it may be noted that the Census of Manufactures is probably a more satisfactory source of information than that of Occupations, and certain data taken from that source may supplement the data taken from the Occupations compilation, and both sets of facts indicate that the status of women in factories has changed little during recent years. Large numbers of women have worked in factories ever since the early days when the making of cotton cloth first became a factory industry. Decade by decade up to 1920, the number of women, like the number of men, employed in factories steadily increased; but in 1930 there was practically no increase in the number of women, and, according to figures from the Census of Manufactures there was a decrease in the number of men. The proportion of women in the total number of factory employees has remained approximately the same for the last fifty years. In spite of the many changes in the various industries and occupations within the industry, one change has apparently offset another change in so far as women's employment was concerned.

It is to be regretted that it is not possible to get from the Census of Occupations classification the number of persons employed either in all manufacturing industries or in specific

[1] Edith Abbott, *Women in Industry;* and *Woman and Child Wage Earners,* Vols. I, II, III, XIII, XVI.

manufacturing industries. The difficulty is that persons employed in manufacturing and mechanical industries are combined; the term "mechanical" covers a great variety of occupations, both skilled workers and laborers in the building and other trades. The term "operative" excludes both skilled workers and laborers who are employed in factories; the figures for "operatives" are therefore not comparable to the Census of Manufactures figures for all wage earners employed in manufacturing industries, and the proportion of women among "operatives" is larger than among all wage earners in factories.

From the Census of Manufactures, figures for the number of all employees in manufacturing industries are available from 1880 to 1929, when the last census, which gives the numbers separately for men and women employees, was taken. According to these figures, the proportion of women to the total number of employees was 19 per cent in 1880, 20 per cent in 1909 and 21 per cent in 1929. The figures for 1929 include women ten years of age and over, and for the preceding years women sixteen years of age and over; probably, however, this discrepancy does not affect the proportion of women to all employees.

From the Census of Occupations, figures are also available for the number of persons employed in manufacturing and mechanical industries and for operatives, who are generally employed in manufacturing industries. The proportion of women to all persons employed in manufacturing and mechanical industries slightly decreased between 1910 and 1930, from 17 per cent in 1910 to 13 per cent in 1930. In contrast to the figures from the Census of Manufactures, which show a slight increase in women wage earners in factories, the proportion of women employed as operatives also slightly decreased, from 39 per cent in 1920 to 38 per cent in 1930.

As has been said, relatively few women are found in the occupations which are generally regarded as skilled, and classified as manufacturing and mechanical, except in dressmaking, millinery and tailoring. Women have formerly monopolized the occupations of dressmaking and millinery, and were in 1910, 19 per cent of the tailors, and in 1930, 12 per cent. During the last twenty years, however, as can be seen in Table 13, the number of women in all three of these occupations has greatly decreased, probably because of the transfer of much of the work from the home and small shop to the factory. In the printing trades, too,

TABLE 14.—WOMEN IN SELECTED OCCUPATIONS[a] IN MANUFACTURING AND
MECHANICAL INDUSTRIES (OTHER THAN OPERATIVES AND LABORERS),
1910–1930[b]

Occupation	1910	1920	1930
Apprentices	(c)	9,433	3,897
Bakers	4,779	4,593	8,916
Compositors, typesetters	14,051	11,306	10,269
Dressmakers, seamstresses	447,760	235,519	157,928
Filers, grinders, buffers	2,846	2,470	2,336
Foremen and overseers (mfs)	19,741	30,171	28,467
Jewellers and watchmakers	2,537	1,678	1,254
Manufacturers (proprietors)	4,301	4,945	5,711
Managers and officials	1,863	8,331	10,422
Milliners	122,447	69,598	40,102
Painters, varnishers[d] and glaziers	2,541	3,335	524,150
Paperhangers	797	406	1,456
Tailors	40,813	31,828	21,807
Upholsterers	1,293	2,267	1,293

[a] Occupations in which 1,000 or more women were enumerated in 1930.
[b] Bureau of the Census, Release June 28, 1932, *Occupation Statistics*.
[c] Comparable figures for 1910 not available.
[d] Painters and varnishers includes painting operations in factories.

TABLE 15.—PROPORTION OF WOMEN IN TOTAL EMPLOYED IN SELECTED OCCU-
PATIONS IN MANUFACTURING AND MECHANICAL INDUSTRIES (OTHER THAN
OPERATIVES AND LABORERS), 1910–1930[a]

Occupation	1910	1920	1930
Apprentices	(b)	6.6	5.5
Bakers	5.3	4.7	6.3
Compositors, typesetters	11.0	8.1	5.6
Dressmakers, seamstresses	99.6	99.8	99.7
Filers, grinders	5.7	4.1	2.9
Foremen, overseers	11.2	9.8	8.4
Jewellers, watchmakers	7.8	4.2	3.2
Manufacturers	1.8	2.7	2.7
Managers and officials	1.5	3.3	3.3
Milliners	95.7	95.0	89.2
Painters, varnishers[c] and glaziers	1.8	1.0	3.8
Paper hangers	3.1	2.1	5.1
Tailors	19.9	16.6	12.9
Upholsterers	6.4	7.6	4.5

[a] Bureau of the Census, Release June 18, 1930, *Occupation Statistics*.
[b] Comparable figures for 1910 not available.
[c] Painters and varnishers includes painting operations in factories.

the number of women employed as typesetters and compositors
was also less in 1930 than in 1910.

As forewomen and officials in manufacturing industries women
are shown by the Census to have made a very slight progress

during the last twenty years. Although the actual number of women enumerated as forewomen and overseers in manufacturing was larger in 1930 than in 1910 (see Table 14) relatively their number was smaller in 1930. Of all the foremen and overseers in 1910, as shown in Table 15, 11 per cent were women, when in 1930 they were only 8 per cent. In 1910, on the other hand, women constituted 1.5 per cent of all managers and officials in manufacturing. In 1930 they were 3.3 per cent.

TABLE 16.—NUMBER OF WOMEN TEN YEARS OF AGE AND OVER CLASSIFIED AS OPERATIVES IN MANUFACTURING INDUSTRIES, 1910–1930[a]

Industry	1910	1920	1930
Total...	1,087,538	1,428,727	1,458,799
Building industry...............................	1,521	20	23
Chemical industry..............................	13,676	19,129	28,863
Cigar and tobacco factories.....................	71,845	83,960	67,948
Clay, glass and stone industries.................	9,461	13,165	15,712
Clothing industries.............................	237,270	265,643	346,751
Food and allied industries.......................	38,439	73,097	88,586
Iron and steel industries........................	23,557	57,819	60,763
Metal industries (except iron and steel)...........	20,859	30,447	30,803
Leather industries..............................	65,507	82,794	91,750
Lumber and furniture industries..................	13,947	18,640	19,596
Paper and printing industries....................	59,574	67,845	63,490
Textile industries..............................	385,947	438,363	432,250
Cotton.....................................	140,666	149,185	145,683
Knitting...................................	65,338	80,682	89,803
Silk.......................................	50,360	72,768	73,690
Dyeing and finishing........................	5,203	5,582	5,666
Woolen and worsted.........................	52,056	61,715	49,060
Other......................................	72,324	68,431	68,348
Miscellaneous industries.........................	104,132	192,264	182,364
Industries not specified..........................	41,803	85,551	29,900

[a] Bureau of the Census, Release June 28, 1932, *Occupation Statistics.*

It should also be noted that a great many shifts have taken place in women's occupations in factories. Some of the older industries which formerly employed many women have become less important; some occupations which employed women are disappearing; other new industries and new occupations are taking their place. Technical changes due to improved machinery have caused many changes; women have replaced men in some occupations which have become simplified by machinery; men have replaced women in other occupations, particularly those in which heavy and elaborate machinery has replaced simpler hand or machine processes. Women have continued to do that part of the work which requires little training or strength, but in which quick, agile fingers and speed are an asset. Historically, the cotton mill was the first important women-employing industry, and cotton manufacturing is still important from the point of view of the number of women employed, but is becoming less so.

TABLE 17.—PROPORTION OF WOMEN OF ALL PERSONS TEN YEARS OF AGE AND OVER EMPLOYED AS OPERATIVES IN MANUFACTURING INDUSTRIES, 1910–1930[a]

Industry	1910	1920	1930
Total..	38.3	37.1	37.3
Building industry.............................	12.9	(b)	(b)
Chemical industry.............................	34.4	27.2	24.6
Cigars and tobacco factories..................	47.3	57.8	65.5
Clay, glass and stone.........................	10.7	15.4	16.3
Clothing......................................	61.4	64.9	70.9
Food and allied industries....................	28.1	35.7	39.5
Iron and steel industries.....................	6.4	8.4	9.3
Metal industries..............................	29.9	33.4	33.5
Leather industries............................	25.8	29.6	34.3
Lumber and furniture..........................	8.3	11.0	11.0
Paper and printing............................	48.4	43.6	38.3
Textile industries............................	56.0	55.3	52.9
Cotton.......................................	50.2	49.3	48.2
Knitting.....................................	74.4	74.9	67.0
Silk...	63.4	62.9	58.6
Dyeing and finishing.........................	31.8	31.5	28.9
Woolen and worsted..........................	49.5	48.8	48.2
Other.......................................	59.9	55.9	51.1
Miscellaneous industries......................	40.1	35.8	34.0
Industries not specified.......................	(c)	(c)	(c)

[a] Bureau of Census, Release June 26, 1932, *Occupation Statistics.*
[b] Less than 0.1 per cent, 1910 figures probably not comparable.
[c] Figures not comparable for 1930 and 1910 and 1920.

The shoe industry and the clothing trades continue to be important women-employing industries, especially since women's dresses and underwear have become a factory product. The food industry—candy factories, bakeries and canning establishments—continue to employ women. Women are now also an important part of the working force in industries which traditionally have nothing to do with their work in the home; large numbers are employed in the paper box industry, in electrical and radio equipment factories, and in cigar factories. In the metal industries, where light metal parts are handled, women are employed to some extent, but in most occupations in metal manufacturing they are not yet accepted as desirable workers.

TABLE 18.—PRINCIPLE MANUFACTURING INDUSTRIES EMPLOYING WOMEN, AVERAGE NUMBER OF WAGE EARNERS TEN YEARS OF AGE AND OVER, NUMBER AND PER CENT OF WOMEN 1929 AND PER CENT OF WOMEN 1919[a]

Industry	1929 Total wage earners	1929 Number of women	1929 Per cent[b] of women	1919[c] Per cent of women
All manufacturing industries...............	8,838,743	1,860,240	21	20
Cotton goods............................	440,197	179,271	41	43
Silk and rayon goods.....................	130,467	74,648	57	61
Knit goods..............................	208,488	133,907	64	71
Woolens and worsted.....................	146,959	61,563	42	44
Clothing, men's.........................	209,990	133,130	63	59
Clothing, women's.......................	187,500	131,725	70	68
Tobacco manufacturing...................	116,119	76,439	66	59
Boots and shoes.........................	205,640	84,637	41	38
Electrical supplies......................	328,722	93,683	29	26
Canning................................	112,478	54,090	48	49
Confectionery and ice cream..............	85,900	41,059	48	53
Printing and publishing..................	280,309	40,987	15	21
Bread and bakery products...............	200,841	35,301	18	26
Rubber goods...........................	149,148	35,275	24	13
Paper boxes............................	55,654	27,491	49	59
Millinery and laces......................	39,060	26,900	69	76
Rayon and allied products................	39,106	15,535	40	

a Figures from Fourteenth Census, 1920, Vol. 8, *Manufactures*, Table 14, pp. 22–36. Cotton goods includes cotton small wares; men's clothing includes men's shirts and button holes; tobacco manufacture includes smoking tobacco, cigars and cigarettes; canning includes fruit, vegetables, preserves, fish, oysters; rubber goods includes rubber shoes and rubber tires; printing and publishing includes books, newspapers and periodicals. Figures for 1929 unpublished from Census of Manufactures.

b Per cent of total wage earners. The figures include wage earners of all ages.

c Exactly comparable figures for sex for 1909 are not available for employees in manufacturing industries who were ten years of age and over. In 1909, figures for children under sixteen were given separately from those for employees over this age, and the sex of the children was not given.

According to the Census of Manufactures, roughly, half of all women wage earners in 1929 were employed in what might be considered the older women-employing industries, in the textile, shoe, clothing, candy and ice cream establishments, in canneries and in establishments manufacturing bread and bakery products. Tobacco manufacture, printing and publishing, electrical and radio supply and paper box manufacture employed a considerable number; the remainder were distributed among the iron and steel, metal, automobile, rubber and glass and miscellaneous industries. The industries in which women formed an especially important part of the working force in 1929 are listed, as shown in Table 18, together with the proportion they formed of all employees.[1] In the textile industries women and girls were approximately half of the workers, the proportion ranging from 42 and 44 per cent in the cotton and wool industries to 71 per cent in the hosiery industry. In the clothing industry they were approximately three-fifths to two-thirds and in the shoe industry about two-fifths of all employees. About one-half the employees in the canning, candy and ice cream industries were women and only one-fourth in the bread and bakery industries. In tobacco and paper box industries women outnumbered men; in electrical supplies and in printing and publishing they were roughly from one-fifth to one-fourth the employees.

During the last thirty years the technical changes in some of the industries have affected the proportion of women employed; in the cigar and shoe industries, for example, the proportion of women employed has greatly increased; in the textile industries there has not been such change in the proportion of women in the industry as a whole, but there have been many changes in the occupations in which women are employed. The causes of these changes appear to be entirely outside the woman's control; technical changes within the industry, the doing away of some products and the substitution of new products as well as the available labor supply of men are some of the main factors which contribute to the result. Despite differences in the industry classification and in the occupations included in the Census of Manufactures for all wage earners and in the Census of Occupations for operatives in manufacturing and mechanical industries, the two sets of figures show the same general trends from 1910 to 1930. The relative number of women to all employees in the textile industries has decreased, but the relative number of women has increased in the clothing, tobacco and cigar and leather and shoe industries. The figures from the occupations census for women employed in the iron and steel and

---

[1] These figures include girls between ten and sixteen years—the proportions of women sixteen years and over in the total number of employees given, for example, for the cotton industry, p. 143, is of course slightly smaller.

metal industries show a relative increase in the number of women.

While it would be illuminating to trace the effect of these changes on the older occupations, such as cotton, woolen, and silk manufacture, to which so much interest attaches from the point of view of the group of women who have long been a part of the labor supply, space does not allow this, but it seems necessary to note certain new industries, such as the manufacturing of rayon, and the revolutionized condition in others such as tobacco and cigarette manufacture, in order that the actual situation may be fairly well understood. A brief statement about these two will therefore be given. Something will also be said about the employment of women in the so-called metal trades, because it has been in these that perhaps there has existed the strongest prejudice against their employment, which yet became so important during the war.

I. THE RAYON MANUFACTURING INDUSTRY

Rayon manufacturing offers a new field for women's employment, which is becoming increasingly important with the rapid growth of the industry. The 1925 Census of Manufactures first gave separate information for the manufacture of rayon or artificial silk fibre, an industry formerly included with the chemical industries. In that year there were 19,128 wage earners; in 1927, 26,341; in 1929, 38,938.[1] How many of these employees were women was not stated in the Census. In 1924, however, the United States Women's Bureau obtained information from two rayon plants employing about 7,000 persons, 42 per cent of whom were women,[2] and in a more recent study of the wages and hours of labor in rayon manufacturing, the Bureau of Labor Statistics included 18,743 men and 13,549 women,[3] or about the same proportion as was found in the plants reporting to the Women's Bureau.

In the chemical part of the production, converting wood or cotton cellulose into crude rayon thread, women play little part;

---

[1] U. S. Bureau of the Census, *Biennial Census of Manufactures*, 1927, p. 717. *Census of Manufactures*, 1929, Summary of Industries Release December 31, 1930.

[2] *Effects of Applied Research on Employment Opportunities of Women*, U. S. Department of Labor, Women's Bureau Bulletin No. 50 (1926), p. 23.

[3] "Wages and Hours of Labor in Rayon and Other Synthetic Textile Manufacturing," U. S. Department of Labor, *Monthly Labor Review*, XXXI (December, 1930), 151.

they are employed rather in the reeling of crude thread into skeins, inspecting and grading skeins and in subsequent processes which are similar to those which women perform in silk throwing mills. Indirectly, also, the increasing popularity of rayon has affected the employment of women in knitting and other textile industries where rayon has been substitued for silk or cotton.

II. THE CIGAR AND CIGARETTE INDUSTRIES

The cigar industry furnishes an especially good example of the effect of improved machines on the distribution of processes between men and women, and likewise on the location of industrial establishments. Formerly making cigars by hand was a skilled trade in which only men were employed; now cigars are largely machine made and women operate the machines, so that, like the clothing and textile industries, cigar manufacturing is regarded at the present time as a "woman's" industry. To find cheap woman labor,[1] cigar manufacturers have left New York City and have moved to places where they do not have to meet the competition of other women-employing industries; for, from the point of view of the woman worker, the cigar factory, with its odors and likelihood of staining fingers and clothes with tobacco, and the low wages offered, is an undesirable place to work. Thus cigar factories are located in the cities of New Jersey which manufacture chemicals and metals, and in the steel and metal working districts of Pennsylvania where men are employed and there is little other work for their wives and daughters— and also in such southern states as North Carolina and Florida where other industries are few. It is said that on account of the desire for cheap labor some manufacturers have made a special attempt to get married women and have so arranged the hours that women can be at home to get the family meals and start the children to school and still work in the factory.[2]

The trend of women into the cigar and cigarette industry is shown very clearly by the Census figures. In 1880 women were less than one-fifth of the employees in these two branches of the tobacco industry; by 1900 they formed over one-third and by 1919 three-fifths of the employees.

[1] Lucy W. Killough, *The Tobacco Products Industry in New York and Its Environs* (New York: Regional Plan of New York and Its Environs, 1924), pp. 42, 43.

[2] *Ibid.*, p. 26. See U. S. Women's Bureau Bulletin No. 100. *The Effects on Women of Changing Conditions in The Cigar and Cigarette Industries.*

These figures represent chiefly changes in the cigar industry, since until recently the number of persons employed in cigarette manufacture was relatively small. In 1919, 79,569 women, 60 per cent of the employees, were employed in cigar manufacture and 13,932 women in cigarette manufacture, 55 per cent of all the employees in that branch.[1] Since 1919 the production of cigarettes has enormously increased[2] and the production of

TABLE 19.—AVERAGE NUMBER OF WAGE EARNERS EMPLOYED IN THE CIGAR AND CIGARETTE MANUFACTURE, 1900–1929[a]

	Total number	Number of women	Per cent women
1900	103,365	37,740	37
1909			
1919	138,773	83,238	60
1929	105,077		

[a] Figures from *Census of Manufactures*, 1905, Part 3, p. 556 and *Fourteenth Census*, 1920, VIII. 34, and 1929 *Census of Manufactures*, release December 31, 1930. The figure for women in 1900 includes only women sixteen years and over; in 1919 and 1929 it includes all females ten years of age and over. For 1909 the figure for all tobacco manufactures are combined. The percentage of women in the total number of employees in all tobacco manufacture was 37 per cent in 1900, 47 per cent in 1909 and 59 per cent in 1919.

cigars has declined; however, the growth in the cigarette industry has not been sufficient to offset the decline in the cigar industry. In 1929 the number of wage earners in the two branches of the industry was smaller than in 1919 and but little greater than in 1900. The great increase in the per capita output of the worker in the tobacco industries as a whole between 1909 and 1925[3] was due to the growth of cigarette production and the substitution in consumption of machine-made cigarettes for hand-made cigars. The increase in the number of machine-made and decline in hand-made cigars no doubt was also a large factor in the result.

From the beginning, the cigarette industry has employed large numbers of women. Machines were early devised to cut, dry

[1] *Fourteenth Census*, 1920, VIII, *Manufactures*, p. 490.

[2] According to Internal Revenue figures 47 billions of cigarettes were manufactured in 1919 and nearly 120 billions in 1930. See *Wages and Hours of Labor in the Cigarette Manufacturing Industry*, U. S. Bureau of Labor Statistics Bulletin, No. 532 (1931), p. 7.

[3] Conference on Unemployment, Washington, D. C., 1921, Committee on Recent Economic Changes, *Recent Economic Changes in the United States: Report of the Committee* (New York: McGraw-Hill, 1929), II, 458.

and shred and later to roll the cigarettes.[1] Since 1919 the industry has undoubtedly employed a larger number of women but whether there are any changes in the proportion of women employed seems doubtful. A recent study of wages and hours of work of 14,266 employees in this industry in three southern states showed approximately the same proportion of women employed as was given in the 1920 Census for this industry.[2]

It is the cigar-making industry in which the technical changes have most strikingly influenced women's employment. As far back as 1907 the report into the condition of Woman and Child Wage Earners explained that the relative increase of women in the cigar-making industry was due to the growing use of machines which "required little training, strength or intelligence on the part of the operator."[3] Women as well as men were capable of making cigars by hand but the study showed that in factories where machines were largely used, the proportion of women and children was large; but where hand work was the rule, men predominated.

The so-called machines, really mechanical contrivances for which little mechanical power was used, were introduced as early as 1878[4] to strip tobacco and do part of the work of bunching and rolling, that is, the operations of making the cigar. As the machines were improved more women were employed; men continued to make the high-grade cigars entirely by hand, but women as well as some men were employed to bunch and roll the cheaper grades of cigars with the help of the machines, that is, by the "mold" or "suction table" methods, according to the terms used in the trade. Not until the last decade was the cigar-making industry revolutionized by the perfection of an automatic power machine for making cigars of good quality. Four girls who require but little training can tend this machine, which is run by electricity[5] and can produce 4,000 cigars a day, while a skilled

[1] *Report on the Condition of Woman and Child Wage Earners*, Vol. 18, *Employment of Women and Children in Selected Industries*, pp. 77–78. See also *Effects of Applied Research on Opportunities of Women*, United States Department of Labor, Women's Bureau Bulletin No. 50, p. 33.

[2] *Wages and Hours of Labor in the Cigarette Manufacturing Industry*, United States Department of Labor, Bureau of Labor Statistics, Bulletin No. 532 (1931), p. 2.

[3] Edith Abbott, *Women in Industry* (1906), Chap. IX. *Woman and Child Wage Earners*, XVIII, 91, 102.

[4] *Effects of Applied Research on Employment Opportunities for Women*, U. S. Department of Labor, Women's Bureau Bulletin No. 50, p. 32.

[5] Lucy Killough, *op. cit.*, pp. 22, 25.

hand-worker can produce but 300 a day, according to a statement in the *American Federationist*.[1] The decrease in the number of men wage earners and the increased proportion of women workers in the Ohio tobacco industry between 1914 and 1924 is noted in the report on Employment Trends of Men and Women in Ohio published by the Federal Women's Bureau.[2] According to this report the small Ohio plants which employed men on old style hand work were unable to compete with the large plants equipped with automatic machines and were forced out of business. In these large plants women and but few men were employed. In 1924, the automatic machine was still regarded as experimental according to a manufacturer's publication; but since then the installation of the machines has gone ahead rapidly. In 1928, it was estimated in the same publication that, excluding only cigars of the very highest quality, 50 per cent of the total production of cigars were manufactured by the automatic machine.[3]

Figures prepared by the Cigar Makers Union from replies to questionnaires sent out to local unions, show the displacement of men hand cigar makers by the automatic machine and the employment of women to tend the machine. According to this source, in 1927 there were 81,708 cigar makers and packers in

TABLE 20.—NUMBER OF EMPLOYEES BY SEX IN CIGAR-MAKING OCCUPATIONS, 1925, 1927[a]

	1925		1927	
	Men	Women	Men	Women
Making cigars by hand.....................	6,243	1,574	5,249	104
Making cigar by mold work system...........	8,609	899	13,575	1,417
Hand or mold team system..................	11,413	12,221	8,345	18,928
Breaking bunches by machine...............	1,040	8,280	1,352	6,699
Rolling machine-made bunches by suction table method.................................	831	24,303	2,582	18,257
Work on automatic machine.................	157	3,371	40	5,160

[a] The figures for 1923 and 1925 are given in the *American Federationist* in an article entitled "Women in the Cigar Industry" by George W. Perkins, September, 1925, p. 809. The figures for 1925 and 1927 were furnished by the present president of the International Cigar Maker's Union.

[1] "Facts in Figures," *American Federationist*, April, 1931, p. 458.

[2] *Variations in Employment Trends of Men and Women in Ohio*, United States Women's Bureau, Bulletin No. 73 (1930), p. 50.

[3] *Annual Review of the Tobacco Industry* (New York: Charles D. Barney Co., 1926), p. 13 and (1928), p. 16.

the country, both union and non-union, of whom 50,565 were women. The decline in the number of hand cigar makers and the increasing use of the automatic machine is obvious even taking into consideration possible inaccuracies in the figures. The number of employees who made cigars entirely by hand in 1923 was 13,305; in 1925 the number was 7,817 and 5,313 in 1927. The number of employees working on the automatic cigar-making machine in the same years, respectively, was 1,928, 3,528 and 5,200. The great majority of the hand cigar makers, though not all, were men and most of the automatic machine tenders were women. The figures in Table 20 from union sources give the number of men and women in the various types of cigar-making occupations for 1925 and 1927 and show the large number of women employed to make cigars with the help of the mold and suction table methods, the old machine processes, and the use of women in preference to men on the new automatic machine.

III. THE METAL TRADES

Women have never been accepted in the metal trades as they have been in the fabric, food and cigar industries. "In no industry studied was there found such violent prejudice against women's employment because of the mere fact that they were women."[1] Both employers and the men members of the organized labor unions have been hostile to the employment of women in the various branches of the metal trades. Laws have been passed prohibiting women from work as metal polishers and welders and attempts have been made to prohibit women from making cores in foundries. The Metal Polisher's Union has stood out against the employment of women metal polishers on the ground of the hazardous nature of the work and the danger from the dust. However, there are a few women members of the Metal Polisher's Union. The Molder's Union has not accepted women members and in the past had a provision in their constitution expelling male members who gave any time to the instruction of "female help in the foundry" or in any branch of the trade.[2] In 1929, a resolution to permit women to become members was put before the officials of this union but the question had not in April, 1931,

[1] *The Effects of Labor Legislation on the Employment Opportunities of Women*, United States Women's Bureau, Bulletin No. 65, (1928), p. 220.
[2] *The New Position of Women in American Industry*, United States Women's Bureau, Bulletin No. 12 (1920), p. 158.

been voted upon.[1] Undoubtedly the opposition to the admission of women is largely based on a fear that women would be hired for lower wages than men. A local of the Machinist's Union in New York issued a statement after the war to the effect that, "It is not our intention to drive women out of the industry provided that they desire to remain, but we do intend to insist that wherever they may be employed they ought to receive at least as much as men."[2]

Women, however, have worked to a limited extent in the various branches of the iron and steel and other metal industries. They have made light cores in foundries for many years, have been employed on metal-working machines, feeding automatic presses, in varnishing and lacquering small parts and in wrapping, packing and labelling.[3] The number of women, however, has been but a small fraction of the employees. In the steel mills and rolling mills the number of women has been negligible; in the foundries and machine shops, according to 1919 Census figures, women were about 3 per cent of the total; in automobile factories they were about 4 per cent of the working force. In the metal industries manufacturing small products there has been a much larger field of employment for women, but numerically these industries are not of great importance. In 1919 approximately half of the employees in the needle and pin industry were women, and from one-third to one-sixth in the manufacture of jewelry, typewriters, screws and hardware.[4] Although proportionately women are not important in the metal industries, the actual number employed in some of the branches is not inconsiderable. Over 16,000 were employed in foundries and machine shops alone in 1919 and about 15,000 in factories manufacturing automobiles and automobile parts.[5] In 1930, 60,763 were in iron and steel, and 30,803 in other metal industries.

[1] Statement of secretary of International Molder's Union, April, 1931.

[2] *Industrial Replacement of Men by Women.* Prepared by the Bureau of Women in Industry, New York Department of Labor, Special Bulletin No. 93 (1919) p. 45.

[3] *The New Position of Women in American Industry,* United States Women's Bureau Bulletin No. 12 (1920), p. 25. See also *Report of the Condition of Women and Child Wage Earners,* Vol. XI, *The Employment of Women in the Metal Trades,* pp. 12, 33–53.

[4] Percentages computed from Fourteenth Census, 1920, Vol. 8, *Manufactures,* Table 14, pp. 21–35.

[5] *Ibid.,* Table 14, pp. 21, 26.

At the time of the World War a great impetus was given to the employment of women away from the clothing and textile industries toward the iron and steel and other metal trades, toward the chemical, electrical, instrument and optical goods and other industries manufacturing products for war purposes. The replacement of men by women was most marked in the metal industries. Women were first substituted for men in the less skilled and repetitive occupations, such as the light machine work which they had previously done in some places, but as the war went on their work became heavier and required more training. The woman in overalls in front of heavy machines or wearing goggles as protection against dust and sparks became common. Sometimes mechanical devices were installed to do the heavy lifting, or men were employed to do the heavy work, as in core rooms where they wheeled the sand while women worked on the cores.

The employment of women during the war probably extended into every branch of machine shop manufacture.[1] Although the majority of women worked in ammunition plants, the work they did there was practically the same as that done in any machine shop, on the same type of machine and with the same type of tool. With reference to the extent to which women were substituted for men, according to reports of 562 firms after the Second Army Draft, 58,717 women had been substituted for men in the various industries, 37,683 of them in the metal trades.[2] By far the largest number of women replacing men in the metal trades, about 33,000 of them, worked in machine shops operating punch presses, drill presses, lathes, milling machines, gear-cutting machines and other metal-working machines, or they did assembling and inspecting or were employed in tool and drafting rooms. Some women had the opportunity of learning to read blueprints, to use micrometers, gauges, rules and compasses, to set up work on machines and adjust the mechanism of machines. A considerable number replaced men as grinders and polishers, welders, rivetters and even as crane operators. Others worked in core rooms handling cores. The heaviest cores successfully made by

---

[1] According to a study made by the United States Women's Bureau in 1919 based on the returns to the War Industries Board from 15,000 firms employing over 2,500,000 workers. *The New Position of Women in American Industry*, United States Women's Bureau, Bulletin No. 12, pp. 36, 37.

[2] *Ibid.*, pp. 94–96.

women were reported to weigh 45 pounds.[1] Ordinarily women make cores which are light in weight; some of the smallest ones are delicate and require very careful handling, work which women, according to employers, are well qualified to do.[2]

The significance of women's work during the war in the metal trades lay in the demonstration of their ability in the new lines of work rather than in the actual number employed, for the number of women considered in relation to the number of men was not very large. In the iron and steel industries reporting to the War Industries Board, there were after the second draft 491,160 men and 60,694 women, that is, something over 12 per cent of the employees were women.[3] Figures from the Ohio Division of Labor Statistics show that the number of women in the iron and steel industries in the state almost doubled in the twelve months from 5,770 in November, 1917, to 10,276 in November, 1918. The proportion of women in the total number of wage earners in these industries, however, rose only from 2.1 in 1917 to 3.8 in 1918.

The success achieved by many women in the new occupations which they attempted is well known. Over four-fifths of the 278 metal-working firms reporting on this subject in 1919 considered the output of the majority of women in the occupations for which they had been substituted for men as satisfactory or even better than the output of men.[4] A large proportion of the firms planned to retain women in these occupations. The attitude of employers responding to a questionnaire sent out by the New York State Department of Labor was similar. Failures according to the latter study were chiefly due to the lack of physical strength required for heavy lifting or to administrative causes, such as the expense of installing the special sanitary conveniences for women required by law, or to friction with the foremen. The difficulty was noted of getting an open-minded attitude toward women on the part of foremen "who had the usual masculine contempt for feminine mechanical ability."[5] The type of work which women had done

---

[1] *Ibid.*, p. 108.

[2] Core-making is a branch of the molder's trade. Cores, which are made from sand and baked until hard are used to form the holes in castings.

[3] *The New Position of Women in American Industry*, United States Women's Bureau Bulletin No. 12, p. 57, Table 10.

[4] *Ibid.*, pp. 95–96.

[5] *Industrial Replacement of Men by Women*, New York Department of Labor, Bulletin No. 93 (1919), pp. 33, 37.

in the war industries was the same as that carried on in machine shops during normal conditions; nevertheless, many women were of course discharged when the manufacture of munitions and other war supplies came to an end. The business depression of 1920 and 1921 and the plentiful labor supply of men also militated against the continued employment of women.

At the present time the indications are that women have not been able to maintain the opportunities opened up to them in the metal trades during the war and that, except where small

TABLE 21.—NUMBER OF MEN AND WOMEN WAGE EARNERS IN THE IRON AND STEEL INDUSTRIES OF OHIO IN NOVEMBER, 1915–1927[a]

	Men	Women	Per cent women
1915	188,027	3,414	1.8
1917	265,813	5,770	2.1
1918	260,514	10,276	3.8
1919	228,180	8,031	3.4
1921	146,372	4,473	2.9
1923	227,783	6,642	2.8
1925	224,942	7,322	3.1
1927	199,957	7,100	3.4

[a] Figures 1925–1927 from *Rates of Wages and Fluctuation of Employment in Ohio*, Department of Industrial Relations, Division of Labor Statistics, Report No. 19 (1928), p. 50. Comparable figures for 1915–1923 are published in *Variations in the Employment of Women and Men in Ohio*, United States Department of Labor, Women's Bureau Bulletin No. 73 (1929), p. 57.

metal products are manufactured, they are not employed to any great extent. Unfortunately in the absence of satisfactory figures the trend of their employment cannot be shown with any certainty.[1] Figures for women in the iron and steel industry of Ohio from the Ohio State Division of Labor Statistics have been published but they include so many different types of industries, from steel works, foundries and machine shops to the manufacture of office machines, bolts and rivets, screws, springs and the like, that it is not possible to tell in which branch of the industry and in what types of occupations women were employed during the war and have been retained. However, it is worth noting that while the number of women employed in the iron and steel industry in the state as a whole dropped from 10,276 at the time of the Armistice in November, 1918, to 4,473 in November, 1921, at the time of the business depression, by November, 1927, it

[1] The Occupation Census figures of interest in this connection are of filers, grinders, buffers. There were in 1910, 2,846; in 1920, 2,470; in 1930, 2,336.

[154]

had risen to approximately 7,000. The proportion of women to the total number of employees in 1927 was approximately 3 per cent, the same as in 1918.

More suggestive of the tendency of women to be eliminated from the occupations to which they had been admitted during the war is the fact that at the end of 1912 there were 12,500 women members of the Machinist's Union; in 1931, there was none.[1] Either the policy of the Union in organizing women had changed or men have displaced women. Studies have been recently made of a large number of employees in several branches of the metal trades with reference to the wages and hours of work. The number of women employees covered by these studies is relatively small. Among nearly 150,000 wage earners included in a motor vehicle industry study in 1928, only 4,134 or less than 3 per cent were women.[2] Similarly only 1,915 or about 1 per cent of over 130,000 employees in machine shops and foundries were women.[3] The women who were employed in automobile factories and machine shops did assembly work, inspecting, and a very small number were employed on metal-working machines of various kinds. According to estimates made by the Molder's Union in 1928 approximately 5,000 women were employed in foundries and core rooms. Most of the women foundry workers[4] were core makers. Aircraft manufacture was another of the war industries in which women were employed. A recent study of 11,079 wage earners employed in the manufacture of airplanes revealed only 234 women, many of whom were employed on types of work similar to those always open to women, such as machine sewing and fabric covering.[5]

Occupational studies of the metal trades made from the point of view of vocational guidance also indicate that there is little place for women. Studies made in 1924 of occupational opportunities in the metal trades of Cincinnati and Cleveland on the basis of visits to a comprehensive number of firms listed core-making

---

[1] *The New Position of Women in American Industry*, United States Women's Bureau Bulletin No. 12, p. 33. Information for 1931 from statement made by Miss Thorne, American Federation of Labor.

[2] *Wages and Hours of Labor in the Motor Vehicle Industry*, United States Department of Labor, Bureau of Labor Statistics Bulletin No. 502 (1929), p. 5.

[3] *Wages and Hours of Labor in Foundries and Machine Shops*, Bureau of Labor Statistics Bulletin No. 522 (1930), pp. 9, 10.

[4] At least those covered in recent Bureau of Labor Statistics studies.

[5] *Wages and Hours in the Manufacture of Airplanes and Aircraft Engines*, United States Bureau of Labor Statistics Bulletin No. 523 (1930), pp. 5, 7, 8.

as the principal occupation open to women and girls.[1] It was noted that women and girls sometimes did light assembly and light machine work, and in Cincinnati a few women were found in the drafting room. There is no reason, according to this report, why a girl who is interested in drafting and has training in mechanical drawing and has other qualifications should not become as skilled a draftsman as a man; the report also states that opportunities for women in this work are opening up in several cities.

As a result of an investigation of the present status of women in the metal trades, undertaken as part of the more comprehensive study of the effect of labor legislation on the employment of women, the United States Women's Bureau came to the conclusion that women had lost ground in the metal trades since the war and that the future of women in these industries depended on the manufacture of small metal products and the development of light processes as well as on the general attitude of the employer toward women on machine work.[2] A decrease since the war was found both in the number and proportion of women employed in twenty-two Michigan firms manufacturing automobiles and other metals products, which were visited both in 1919 and in 1927. In 1919 women formed 5 per cent of 81,024 employees in the automobile manufacturing plants, but only 2 per cent of 97,389 employees in 1927. The opposite tendency was shown in plants which manufactured automobile accessories; here the proportion of women had risen from 30 per cent to 44 per cent, but these plants employed a relatively small number of persons.[3] There is apparently no lack of desire on the part of women to work in these plants, for in the course of another study of women workers in Flint, Michigan, it was found that 3,338 women had applied for work at one large automobile establishment during a single year, but only 8 per cent of them had been taken on. In this city also, the proportion of women in the automobile accessory plants was considerably larger than in the plants manufac-

[1] *The Metal Industries in Cincinnati*, Vocational Pamphlet No. 4, Vocation Bureau of Cincinnati Public Schools (1924), pp. 101, 27, 63. *The Metal Industries in Cleveland*, Prepared for Cleveland Public Schools, Consumer's League of Ohio (1924), pp. 108, 32, 67.

[2] *Effects of Labor Legislation on the Employment Opportunities of Women*, United States Women's Bureau Bulletin No. 65, pp. 219–20.

[3] *Ibid.*, p. 221.

turing automobiles; 30 per cent and 7 per cent respectively of all employees were women.[1]

At the present time women occasionally work as metal polishers and grinders but their employment in this occupation appears to be unusual. According to information from the headquarters of the Metal Polisher's Union, women in one city who work in a typewriting shop on bolts, screws and nuts are union members. A small number of women metal polishers was also reported during the investigation of the United States Women's Bureau. Five of the twenty-two Michigan metal manufacturing plants visited had employed women metal polishers during the war, four in 1919 and one in 1927 employed women. Welding is also an unusual occupation for women at the present time. Four plants visited during this study had employed women in acetylene or electric or other types of welding during the war but in 1927 only one of these plants had retained women for this work.[2] One employer, in explaining the discontinuance of the employment of women welders, frankly said that "The job pays more than the company is willing to pay women."[3] During the course of a further inquiry in 1927 concerning occupations prohibited by law in some states, 526 women were found employed as metal polishers and grinders and 127 women as electric or acetylene welders.[4] These women were interviewed and most of them made favorable comments regarding their work. It was "interesting," it paid well and, according to a number, in spite of metal dust or danger from sparks, it was "easier" work than that previously done in domestic service or work in a cotton mill, a silk mill or a garment factory.

IV. ELECTRICAL AND RADIO SUPPLY INDUSTRY

In the manufacture of electrical supplies, in which women handle the small metal parts and do much work similar to that done in metal establishments which manufacture small articles, their employment is increasing. Part of this increase is due to the great growth of the industry. According to the Census of Manufactures the number of wage earners increased from 40,308 in

[1] *Women Workers in Flint, Michigan*, United States Women's Bureau Bulletin No. 67 (1929), pp. 12, 13.
[2] *Effects of Labor Legislation on Employment Opportunities of Women*, Bulletin No. 65, p. 226.
[3] *Ibid.*, p. 333.
[4] *Ibid.*, pp. 313, 320.

WOMEN IN THE TWENTIETH CENTURY

1900 to 329,361 in 1929. In that year the General Electric Company alone employed approximately 75,000 employees in its various plants, one-fourth of whom were women.[1] In the industry as a whole women increased not only in actual numbers but in

TABLE 22.—AVERAGE NUMBER OF WAGE EARNERS, NUMBER AND PER CENT OF
WOMEN IN THE MANUFACTURE OF ELECTRICAL APPARATUS MACHINERY
AND SUPPLIES 1900–1929[a]

	Total number	Number of women 16 years+	Per cent women
1900	40,308	6,158	15
1909	87,256	19,831	23
1919	212,374	55,820	26
1929	329,361		

[a] For figures see Twelfth Census, 1900, Vol. 7, *Manufactures*, p. 7; Thirteenth Census, 1910, Vol. 10, *Manufactures*, p. 285 and Fourteenth Census, 1920, Vol. 10, p. 945; Census of Manufactures, 1929, Release December 31, 1930.

relation to men at least up to 1919; in that year they were 26 per cent of the working force as compared with 15 per cent in 1900. An indication that the status of women in this industry has changed little since the war is given by employment figures for women in this industry in Massachusetts. That the actual number

TABLE 23.—AVERAGE NUMBER OF WAGE EARNERS, NUMBER AND PER CENT OF
WOMEN EMPLOYED IN THE MANUFACTURE OF ELECTRICAL MACHINERY,
APPARATUS AND SUPPLIES, MASSACHUSETTS, 1920–1928[a]

	Total number	Number of women	Per cent of women
1920	28,561	7,098	25
1922	19,064	4,212	22
1924	24,523	5,007	20
1926	27,899	6,426	23
1928	24,788	6,246	25

[a] Total figures are published in *Annual Reports of the Massachusetts Department of Labor and Industries;* figures for women were obtained from the records of the Department.

of wage earners in the electrical supply industry in this state was no greater in 1928 than in 1920 is a local condition and not typical of the situation in the industry as a whole. Although there was some fluctuation in the relative number of men and women

[1] *Facts About the General Electric*, Publicity Department, C. M. Ripley (1929), p. 16.

[158]

during this period, one-fourth of the employees were women both in 1920 and 1928.

During the war period the employment of women in the electrical supply industry became more common than had previously been the case. According to a study made by the United States Women's Bureau in 1919 on the basis of reports made to the War Industries Board, the number of firms manufacturing electrical supplies which employed women greatly increased. Although the war did not open up new types of occupations to women, they were employed in increasing numbers to do the same type of work which some women had previously done.[1] After the first army draft women formed 21 per cent of the employees of 172 firms reporting to the War Industries Board and after the second army draft they were 27 per cent of the working force.[2] Twenty-two firms which reported to the Women's Bureau the kind of work in which women had replaced men, reported 897 substitutions of women in jobs hitherto done by men. In the great majority of cases the output of the women substitutes in these firms was said to be satisfactory.[3]

The term "electrical supplies" covers a wide variety of products, from the manufacture of heavy turbines and motors for electric locomotives to small batteries and small motors and all kinds of miscellaneous electrical appliances. The opportunities of women to work vary according to the size of the product manufactured. A later investigation in 1927 included 106 establishments manufacturing electrical supplies employing 55,907 men and 17,055 women. The proportion of women in the various plants ranged from 2 to 90 per cent.[4] In the manufacture of heavy products, such as turbines, large motors, storage batteries, elevators and elevator parts, women were conspicuously absent, but their number was nearly as great as that of men in the manufacture of electric light bulbs, small motors, electric heating appliances, ignition systems and wiring devices and the like. The development of radio manufacturing, a development which has taken place largely since 1920, has opened up another and growing industry to women. The number of women nearly equals

[1] *The New Position of Women in American Industry*, United States Women's Bureau Bulletin No. 12, p. 113.

[2] *Ibid.*, p. 78.

[3] *Ibid.*, p. 94.

[4] *Effects of Labor Legislation on Employment Opportunities of Women*, United States Women's Bureau Bulletin No. 65, p. 396.

that of men in the manufacture of radio sets and greatly exceeds that of men in the manufacture of radio tubes, the number of women employed depending on the amount of assembly work and machine work, women being used for the former and men, to large extent, for the latter type of work.[1] The kind of work women do in all kinds of electric supply plants and radio supply plants is very similar regardless of the kind of product manufactured. They assemble parts, wind and insulate coils, by hand or machine, operate light punch and drill presses and other machines, inspect and test motors and coils. In the manufacture of electric light bulbs women wind and mount small filaments, assemble parts, exhaust and test the bulbs and cement them to the base. Women are especially fitted for this work because, according to one employer's statement, "Lamp making is too delicate work to be done economically by men."[2] The distribution of women in the occupations in the manufacture of small electric appliances is indicated by figures from one plant which manufactured generators, starters, horns, ignition systems, switches and tail lights; 685 women were assemblers, 302 winders, 176 punch or drill press or other machine operators and 115 inspectors.[3]

The manufacture of radios is highly subdivided. The making of condensors in one Chicago factory, according to a recent vocational monograph, involves 19 different operations, most of which girls did. Soldering done with a hand iron is a frequently repeated process.[4] A remark of one girl interviewed during the study of the United States Women's Bureau indicates the monotonous nature of the work: "Soldering hundreds and over a thousand little wires a day made me crazy."[5] For assembly

---

[1] *Fluctuations of Employment in the Radio Industry*, United States Women's Bureau Bulletin No. 83 (1930). This study covered firms that produced from 80 to 90 per cent of the sets and tubes manufactured in the United States in 1929. The average number of men and women employed during 1929 in these plants was as follows: (pp. 4 and 14)

    Receiving sets.................... 10,879 men   9,800 women
    Tubes........................... 1,755 men   7,906 women

[2] *Effects of Labor Legislation on Employment Opportunities of Women*, United States Women's Bureau, Bulletin No. 65, p. 420.

[3] *Ibid.*, p. 418.

[4] *A Study of the Radio*, Vocational Guidance Bureau, Board of Education, Chicago, Occupational Study No. 21 (1930), p. 14.

[5] *Fluctuations of Employment in the Radio Industry*, United States Women's Bureau Bulletin No. 83, p. 28.

work women are preferred to men and boys because of their greater finger dexterity, but the work requires little training, from three to ten days being considered sufficient to acquire speed.

Although new occupations as such in the electric supply industry were not opened up to women during the war, they seem to have been employed on heavier products than before the war; they worked on turbine coils and field coils which weighed from 32 to 59 pounds, which, however, were lifted into place by men; they replaced men in testing motors up to 500 volts and coils up to 5,000 volts, the latter regarded as a hazardous occupation; they also operated machines similar to the machines in metal-working establishments.[1]

Since the war more efficient automatic machinery has been installed. Improved winding machines, automatic punch and drill presses, automatic tapping machines and improved machines for making electric light bulbs have all probably affected women's employment. The installation of automatic machinery for mass production tends to increase the number of women employed. "When only a few parts are the product it is a man's job; when it becomes mechanical it is a woman's job,"[2] was the attitude of the employer. To what extent women have been retained in the more difficult operations in the electrical supply industry which they had performed during the war is not known. A number of the employers have stated that they keep women in the tool rooms, to do hand filing and for calibrating and balancing work in which men had formerly been employed. On the other hand, one firm reports that they have taken women off machines because the work on punch presses was heavy and dangerous. "Men watch the machines to see if things are going wrong; women repeat the operation but do not notice the condition of the machine," this employer commented.[3] It is probable that the possibility of employing women in machine shops first occurred to many employers during the war and has changed the general attitude toward "what can be women's work."[4] However this may be, it seems clear that the future opportunities of women in this industry will be determined largely by the increase in the manu-

[1] *The New Position of Women in American Industry*, United States Women's Bureau Bulletin No. 12, pp. 113–15.
[2] *Effects of Labor Legislation on Employment Opportunities of Women*, United States Women's Bureau Bulletin No. 65, p. 100.
[3] *Ibid.*, pp. 419–20.
[4] *Ibid.*, p. 93.

facture of small electrical products for the handling of which agile fingers and speed are essential but for which training and physical strength are not needed.

It has been in connection with manufacturing occupations that two questions related to women's occupational status have presented themselves, to which brief attention should be given. The first question is, namely, the relative amounts of time lost by women workers as compared with men workers, and with this the relative frequency with which women workers must be replaced or the question of turnover. Attention will be called to this question, from another point of view, somewhat later in the discussion.[1]

Lost time or relative greater absenteeism on the part of women than men is alleged to constitute a basis for the wage discrimination as between men and women, so characteristic of most occupational relationships. And the more temporary character of women's employment, the greater likelihood of a woman's giving up her employment and returning to domestic life seems to justify treating her work as of less worth while she is working. The subject of turnover, then, is one on which it would be important to obtain more information. As a matter of fact, personnel studies are throwing light on the subject.[2] However, the discussion has reached the stage of analysis in which one becomes increasingly aware of the factors and consequently increasingly cautious with reference to sweeping and generalized statements. There is no question that in many establishments the turnover of women is much greater than of men. Most of the studies have, however, been in manufacturing occupations, where men do the more and women the less skilled work. In these studies the turnover of women is universally higher than of men. However, there are no adequate studies of other groups in which the level of skill of the women is higher, the women coming possibly from an older level, and the rates of turnover apparently rather favoring the women than the men.

With reference to absenteeism the *prima facie* case is certainly in favor of the man. In the cotton industry, for example, the

[1] See p. 221.

[2] See, for example, the study made by the U. S. Bureau of Labor Statistics *Monthly Labor Review*, January, 1929, p. 39. There are many interesting citations suggested by Miss Marguerite B. Benson, "Labor Turnover of Working Women," *Women in the Modern World* (*Annals of the American Academy of Political and Social Science*, CXLIII No. 232 (May, 1929), 109*ff*.

time lost by women was found to be 21.9 per cent and by the men 16.2 per cent, the women's work period being slightly longer than the men's.[1] These are very high percentages, the rate for women being higher than in any other study that had been made up to that time,[2] and for men higher than any except in steel shipyards during the war. The problem is shown to be a highly complicated problem, with marked variations among mills in the same section of the country and more marked differences between mills in the South and mills in the North, the time lost by both men and women being greater in the South, where there are fewer holidays, where the work day is longer as a rule, and where there is less time for rest, housework, or recreation than in the North. The figures are extremely interesting, but space permits only brief mention to be made of the reasons for their absences given by the workers, which may be grouped into (1) personal reasons, (2) mill reasons, and (3) general reasons. Illness of the worker accounting for 23.2 per cent or almost a fourth of all the time lost—and illness does not include pregnancy, confinement or accident— illness of members of the family, accounting for an average of 4.2 days per worker who lost an average of 10.2 through her own illness—is the most prolific cause. Home duties caused 19.8 per cent of the time lost, recreation and vacation accounted for a portion, 4.1 days per worker in the North, 2.4 days in the South. Hunting a job in another mill, when there was a rumor of better wages, or a worker's husband had had a row with the boss in her mill, or pure restlessness,[3] accounted for 3.9 per cent of the women's lost time in the northern mills, and 10.2 per cent of that in southern mills. Pregnancy and confinement accounted for only 3.2 per cent of the total time lost. This was because the number of women was small, for the time lost by those women who were confined averaged 68.3 days for each woman. This cause accounted for more time lost in the South than in the North because there are more married women in the southern group. A second group of causes, grouped as "mill causes," meaning short hours, employing what were called "spare employees" more than was

---

[1] U. S. Women's Bureau Bulletin No. 52, *Lost Time and Turnover in Cotton Mills: A Study of Cause and Extent*, 1926, p. 38. The subject of lost time is one to which the U. S. Bureau of Labor Statistics, various departments of labor, and the National Industrial Conference Board have devoted attention, but often without distinguishing on the basis of sex.

[2] Various studies cover paper novelties, munition factories, etc.

[3] So skillfully portrayed by Sherwood Anderson in *Perhaps Women*.

really called for, accounted for 5 per cent of the lost time, and accidents accounted for 0.7 per cent. Besides these, there are some general causes given, such as disputes with the bosses and weather, accounting in all for less than 2 per cent of the absences.

Many factors entered into the relative absenteeism. The age group between sixteen and twenty lost least time. Married women lost most. Living at home increases lost time, and the size of the family affects it.[1] It is also in accord with what should be expected. The cotton mill family in the South is not industrialized, but the man is perhaps nearer industrialization and his obligations are far less complicated, his duties less varied, other claims on his time less insistent than is the case with the woman. Interesting testimony could be drawn from the figures with reference to turnover, but the point applicable to this discussion is the desirability of developing a situation in which the relation of the women to the gainful occupation should be more clearly distinguished from the unpaid services of the family, that are, where there is not domestic discord, in part at least, their own reward. This will mean increasing reliance upon objective tests of competence or of efficiency, with wages related to the job and not to the worker. It is this for which industrial or truly occupational women ask as distinguished from casual or occupationally more retarded domestic women. It is in fact, the general conviction that while there may be differences in the return of the man as compared with the return of the woman, the differences in pay are greater than their respective differences in productivity, and to that extent the work of women is characterized by what may be termed pure cheapness, a most disastrous influence in the occupational world.

The other question is that of their capacity for organization in behalf of their own interests. Much space has been devoted in the preceding discussion to the organizations of women intended to secure for themselves the satisfactions of culture, of social intercourse, of influence on public policy, and so forth. These organizations have, however, been largely the result of spare time activity on the part of older women. In the case of the gainfully employed women, in the past their relative youth, their lack of skill, and the transient attitude of many toward work because of prospective marriage, have constituted serious obstacles in the way of organization so that, for example, they have formed a relatively small

[1] *Ibid.*, p. 88*ff.*

element in the general trade union movement.[1] This does not mean that they have shown themselves or show themselves less than fully capable as trade unionists. Many of the industries in which they have been employed have, because of the character of the men's work as well as of the women's, been difficult of organization, or efforts at organization have been successfully resisted. The history of a number of the great strikes which brought into the crowded quarters of great cities or of textile communities the miseries of industrial warfare contains the names of the girls and women who in some cases led the first protest, as in the shirt waist strike in New York[2] or in the great clothing strike in Chicago in 1910, out of which came the Hart, Schaffner and Marx agreement and then the protocol and the resulting development of constitutional government in the clothing industry,[3] or in the Lawrence Strike in 1912 when a girl again precipitated the conflict and the women with the men sustained the struggle.[4] In 1926–1927 there was the Passaic, New Jersey, strike; in 1927, a textile strike in New Bedford, Massachusetts; in 1928, the Kenosha, Wisconsin, corset workers "tasted the bitterness of an economic fight."[5] That women can be organized, even when unskilled and low paid and young, there can really be no question.[6]

The question of the best kind of organization, whether the separate woman's local, or membership in the same local, whether there should be special concessions in initiation fees and dues

[1] These points are elaborated by Theresa Wolfson, *The Woman Worker and the Trade Unions* (New York: International Publishers, 1926).

[2] Louis Levine, *The Women Garment Workers* (New York: B. W. Huebsch, Inc., 1924), p. 145.

[3] *The Survey*, XXIV, 701, 823, 847; XXV, 273, 413, 424, 490, 613, 796, 942; XXIX, 491, 631, 661, 804; XXX, 13; XXXI, 723.

[4] *The Lawrence Strike* (1912), U. S. Sixty-second Congress, Second Session, Senate Document No. 870.

[5] Theresa Wolfson, "Trade Union Activities of Women," *Women in the Modern World* (*Annals of the American Academy of Political and Social Science*, CXLIII, No. 232, May, 1929), 127.

[6] Wolfson, *The Woman Worker and the Trade Unions*, p. 150. Dr. Wolfson enumerates four "ifs": "*If* the trade union broadens its structural boundaries to include the unskilled worker—and women are for the most part unskilled. *If* the union officials, responsible for organization policy, consider carefully and incorporate in their plans the psychology and racial transitions of the women to be organized. *If* the policy of special dues, initiation fees, and special duties are carefully considered as factors which reflect the existing differential in wages between men and women, and which tend to give this differential, trade union benediction, resolutions on 'equal pay for equal work' notwithstanding. *If* women workers generally will learn to consider themselves a permanent group in industry despite the impermanence of the individual" (pp. 157–58).

[165]

with lowered benefits or equal burdens for equal returns, are questions like those that confront women in government, in the church, in education. The separate organization seems to have its definite value for the novice, the timid, the inexperienced, but the history of women's locals is said to have been a "record of failures."[1] In the past, the part of women in the life of the union has not been unlike their part in political life. There are elements of difficulty and confusion. There are the different standards of order and cleanliness and attractiveness making meeting places that do not offend men sources of discomfort to women; there are conflicts with domestic obligations—the woman wage earner usually has home responsibilities as well; there are canons of safe and respectable conduct, the question of late hours away from home; there are questions of the immediateness or remoteness of the business transacted or the cause for which the sacrifice is asked. They have shown fine capacity as shop chairladies;[2] they are not infrequently secretaries; there have been a few business agents, practically never when appointed by the president and not so often as would be suggested by their skill as shop chairladies, but the selection of women for these positions is not unlike the election of women in positions of governmental responsibility.

As to numbers, the lack of records makes definite statements very difficult. The following figures suggest the effect of the war and reveal the decline in post-war activity. Dr. Wolman estimated 69,957 in 1910, the American Federation of Labor published figures claiming 365,500 members in 1920, Dr. Wolfson learned of 206,570 in 1924, exclusive of women organized in separate independent unions.[3] A later estimate includes 1927, when the number had increased from 210,648 to 260,095,[4] but it was estimated that while about one man among 9 men would be in a union, only one woman among 34 would be found allying herself with her fellow workmen. The decrease among both men and women is explained by the changing productive processes, and what will happen in the future can only be related to the question of possible increased planning with reference to the participation of labor in the control of working conditions.

[1] *Ibid.*, p. 164.
[2] *Ibid.*, p. 178.
[3] *Ibid.*, p. 214.
[4] Quoted from Dr. Leo Wolman by Dr. Theresa Wolfson, "Trade Union Activities of Women," *Women in the Modern World* (*Annals of the American Academy of Political and Social Science* CXLIII, No. 232, May, 1929), p. 123.

Chapter XI

WOMEN AND THE WORLD OF BUSINESS

THE domination of the selling motive over the desire to produce utilities obviously lacking in the life of the community was brilliantly set out during the early years of the century.[1] That vendability rather than serviceability determined the organization has been accepted as a defect of the present order. The wastes and ineffectualities of the supply of goods and the lack of adjustment between needs and goods is made clear in a recent survey.[2] When reference is made therefore to women in business, it is opportunities for employment that are in mind and not the part they play in determining consumption. Attention has been called, too,[3] to the very great concentration of women in a relatively small number of occupations in this field of activity that has so increased in its demand for the labor of women and girls. Of the almost 300,000 women classified under Transportation and Communication, 94 per cent are telephone operators, and this is an increase of almost a third, 32 per cent, since 1920. Among almost 1,000,000 women and girls in trade—973,000 according to the corrected figures, 962,680 in the published figures of the Census—more than four-fifths were in 1930 salespersons and clerks in stores or retail dealers. In the almost 2,000,000 who make up the clerical group, as shown in Tables 24, 25, 26, 27 over a third, 706,553, were clerks, and almost a fourth, 482,711, were bookkeepers and cashiers.[4] In both cases, there was a marked increase as compared with 1920. In the case of the store clerks and retail dealers there was a slight increase as compared with the total group, while in the case of the different "clerical" occupations the increase was marked. In the case of salesmen and saleswomen however this is not true. Where in 1920, 30.6 per cent

[1] Thorstein Veblen, *The Theory of Business Enterprise* (New York: Charles Scribner's Sons, 1904).
[2] *Recent Social Trends in the United States*, Chap. XVII, Robert S. Lynd, "Consumption."
[3] *Ibid.*, Chap. XIV.
[4] These figures are from the Census Release of June 28, 1932, *Occupation Statistics*.

of the salespersons were women, in 1930, they were only 27.1 per cent of the group. Something that should also be noted is the fact that a relatively smaller number, 11.4 per cent, of those engaged in all trade occupations, as compared with 11.8, were retail dealers, and a relatively larger number, 58.2 per cent in 1930, as compared with 54.4 in 1920, were salespersons.

There are two questions: (1) the reallocation of jobs; (2) the relative numbers of women as compared with men. A marked percentage increase is found in the number of window dressers, from one in 1,000 of those engaged in trade, to 6 in 1,000 and, as compared with men, the proportion changed from 82 in 1,000 of those engaged in window dressing to 309 in 1,000; but the numbers are small and the occupation is again one concerned with multiplying sales. No one can examine these figures without being impressed with the extent to which the great selling expansion has drawn on the activities of women and girls to perform services that have something of an adolescent character. They are not machine tenders, as many of the women and girls are in the factories and laundries; they are parts of a great organization, passing on goods possibly toward the satisfaction of a natural want, frequently toward a transaction for which high power salesmanship must take all the credit.

However, large numbers of women and girls find their livelihood in these occupations and the nature of the organization and development has very great interest from the point of view of current social progress. Attention may therefore be briefly devoted to the facts concerning the conditions under which so many women have been seeking and finding their jobs. Telephone operating and the clerical group of occupations take on a special interest.

Before discussing them, however, notice may be taken of a few occupations in which the numbers of women are yet small, but the fact that any have found a foothold in them gives promise of wider opportunity. Under Transportation and Communication there were listed 46 radio operators, which renders of interest the following facts. Under the federal radio act of 1927[1] all licensed radio stations must be operated by licensed radio operators. The qualifications for a license depend upon the class of station to be operated and the class of licensed operator such station must

---

[1] *U. S. Statutes at Large*, Sixty-ninth Congress, Second Session, Ch. 169, Vol. 44, Part I, p. 1162.

employ. There are ten classes of licenses at the present time. During the early years of radio there were only three, but the additional classes have become necessary because of the development of new radio services such as broadcasting, police radio, aviation, and radiotelephone.[1] In 1930 there was a total number of 16,796 operators of all classes licensed and in 1931 there were 20,703. An amateur radio station may be operated only by the holder of an amateur operator license.[2] In 1930 there were 18,402 licenses issued for amateur radio stations,[3] and approximately 148 amateur stations were owned by women.

It is also interesting to notice that there are classified in the group of aviators, 66 women[4] and 7 laborers in air transportation and 5 proprietors or managers in air transportation not otherwise specified are women.

Mention was made above, too, of certain factory occupations in which women were engaged during the war. There were other non-factory occupations for women which came into prominence during the war. Women were substituted for men on the rapid transit lines, and in driving taxis. Women were employed before the war and are still employed as ticket agents, but women street car conductors and women taxi drivers are now rarely seen. Whether or not the dismissal of women street car conductors after the war, especially in New York State, was because of the ten-hour-day and night-work legislation, has been a matter of wide discussion.

With these preliminary considerations in mind, an attempt will be made to set out the facts about the two groups of whom mention has been made.

I. WOMEN AS TELEPHONE OPERATORS

The increasing opportunity for work in the telephone service is a better example than in sales occupations of the expansion of non-industrial employment and of the growing opportunity for

[1] *Annual Report of Radio Division*, U. S. Department of Commerce (1931), p. 2.

[2] *Radio Service Bulletin*, Radio Division, U. S. Department of Commerce, No. 182 (May 31, 1932), p. 13.

[3] *Annual Report of Radio Division*, U. S. Department of Commerce (1931), p. 11.

[4] Of the 17,739 licensed pilots registered with the Department of Commerce, January 1, 1932, 532 were women. Fourteen women out of 267 held glider licenses, and 5 out of 9,016 were registered as aircraft mechanics. In 1933, these numbers had increased to 588, of whom 57 were transport, 43 commercial, 1 industrial, 1 autogyro, 486 private (U. S. Daily, January 18, 1933).

women's work in other than the older domestic and industrial fields. The telephone was invented before 1880 but it was a long time before its increased use demanded large numbers of women workers. The great advance in the mechanical perfection of the telephone during recent years, and especially the gradual installation of the automatic switchboard (the dial system) during the last decade, has apparently only kept pace with the phenomenal increase in the use of the telephone for both local and long distance communication. Although operators in the future may be needed only for complaints, adjustments, information and long distance calls, the number of women employed in all branches of the telephone service, in the clerical and commercial as well as

TABLE 24.—NUMBER OF MEN AND WOMEN AND PER CENT OF WOMEN EMPLOYED IN THE PUBLIC TELEPHONE SYSTEMS, 1907–1927[a]

Year	Total	Men	Women	Per cent women
1907.....................	131,670			
1912.....................	183,361			
1917.....................	262,629	91,510	171,119	65
1922.....................	312,015	104,433	207,582	66
1927.....................	375,272	131,802	243,470	65
1930.....................	....	....	321,027	

[a] U. S. Bureau of the Census, Census of Electrical Industries, *Telephones*, p. 48, and U. S. Bureau of the Census, *Telephones and Telegraphs* (1912), p. 48.

in the operating branch, continued to increase up to 1927, the date of the last quinquennial census of electrical industries. Nearly as many women were employed in all branches of the telephone service in 1927 as there were women employed in the cotton and silk mills combined in 1920. In the ten years which had passed since 1917, the first date when census figures for women are separated from those for all employees, the number of women had increased 42 per cent; during the same period the number of men had increased 44 per cent. Both in 1917 and in 1927 women constituted about two-thirds of all the employees in the public telephone companies.

The great majority of women in the telephone service are of course operators. In the early days of the telephone service operating was the work of men and boys, but women soon replaced them; as long ago as 1910, men were no longer employed in that occupation except sometimes at night in lonely and unprotected exchanges.[1] Unfortunately data for women telephone operators as distinct from those for men were not obtained at the last quinquennial census so that the effect of the installation of the automatic switchboard on the number of women operators cannot be shown. The full effect of this invention will probably not be felt for several years, until 1940, at which date it was stated, several years ago, that the New York Telephone Company expected to complete the installation.[2] Up to 1922 the number of women operators increased from 70,061 to 158,626. Between 1912 and 1917 the increase was much greater than during the next five years, 45 as compared with 15 per cent, probably because of this mechanical improvement.[3] The increase noted by the Census of Occupations is from 266,406 in 1920 to 321,027 in 1930, or 20.5 per cent.

TABLE 25.—NUMBER OF MEN AND WOMEN EMPLOYED AS TELEPHONE OPERATORS IN PUBLIC TELEPHONE SYSTEMS[a]

Year	Men	Women	Per cent increase of women employed
1907	2,457	70,061	
1912	1,972	94,360	33
1917	1,679	137,292	45
1922	932	158,626	15

[a] U. S. Bureau of the Census, *Telephones and Telegraphs* (1912), p. 48. U. S. Bureau of the Census, *Electrical Industries, Telephones* (1922), p. 52.

Women are also employed by telephone companies in routine clerical positions, and to some extent in supervisory work, as chief operators, personnel directors, assistants to traffic and district superintendents, and as service representatives. A half-dozen traffic supervisors and managers of telephone companies are listed among the members of the National Federation of Business and Professional Women's Clubs, showing that women sometimes attain the more important executive positions.[4]

[1] *Investigation of Telephone Companies*, Sixty-first Congress, 2nd Session, Senate Document No. 380 (1910), p. 99.

[2] *Effects of Applied Research on the Employment Opportunities for Women*, U. S. Department of Labor, Women's Bureau Bulletin No. 50 (1926), p. 39.

[3] A survey which the U. S. Women's Bureau is at present carrying on will no doubt throw light on the recent effects of the installation of the automatic switchboard on the employment of telephone operators.

[4] Margaret Elliott and Grace E. Manson, *Earnings of Women in Business and the Professions*, Michigan Business Studies, III, No. 1 (September, 1930), 178–79.

From Table 26 it can be seen that there were in 1930 almost 963,000 women in the occupations classified under the heading of *Trade*. In these occupations, which include those of sales clerks, bank officials, real estate and insurance agents, store proprietors and the like, the total number of persons employed

TABLE 26.—NUMBER OF MEN AND WOMEN EMPLOYED IN OCCUPATIONS CLASSIFIED AS TRADE, 1910–1930[a]

Occupation	1910		1920		1930	
	Men	Women	Men	Women	Men	Women
Total......................	3,160,562	472,703	3,585,701	671,983	5,118,787	962,680
Advertising agents..............	(b)	......	(b)	......	43,364	5,656
Apprentices....................	(c)	......	(c)	......	2,337	107
Bankers, travellers..............	103,170	2,684	156,309	5,304	212,312	9,192
Commercial travellers..........	161,027	2,593	176,514	2,806	219,790	3,942
Decorators and window dressers..	4,902	439	7,698	1,155	13,911	6,238
Delivery men..................	229,469	150	170,039	196	159,328	116
Floorwalkers, foremen..........	17,641	3,075	22,367	4,070	33,368	4,795
Inspectors, samplers............	11,685	1,761	12,683	1,031	10,923	5,820
Insurance agents and officials....	95,302	2,662	124,713	5,389	271,530	14,705
Laborers, warehouse............	80,452	673	124,713	896	113,027	642
Laborers (stores)..............	98,169	4,164	116,602	8,405	199,296	9,392
News boys....................	29,435	273	27,635	326	38,576	417
Proprietors and managers.......	21,352	1,010	33,715	1,061	42,201	3,104
Real estate agents..............	122,935	2,927	139,927	9,208	208,243	31,787
Retail dealers..................	1,127,926	67,103	1,249,295	78,980	1,593,356	110,166
Store clerks...................	275,589	111,594	243,521	170,397	238,844[d]	163,147
Salesmen and saleswomen.......	677,390	262,335	826,866	365,333	1,508,283	560,720
Undertakers..................	19,921	813	23,342	1,127	32,192	1,940
Wholesale dealers..............	50,123	925	72,780	794	81,837	1,688
Other occupations..............	34,068	7,572	52,106	15,505	96,069	29,106

[a] Bureau of the Census, Release June 28, 1932, *Occupation Statistics*.
[b] Classified as clerical, 1910 and 1920.
[c] Classified as manufacturing and mechanical 1910 and 1920.
[d] This decrease in the number of clerks in stores in 1930 as compared with 1920 probably does not indicate a real decrease. According to the explanation of the Census Bureau, "this group was more strictly confined in 1930 than in 1920 or in 1910 to persons specifically returned as 'clerks' in stores."

has rapidly increased during the last twenty years. Women form but a small proportion of the total number; they were 11 per cent of the total in 1910 and 15 per cent in 1930. But the rate at which their employment in this occupational group has grown exceeded that of the men in the decade between 1910 and 1920 and equalled that of the men in the decade between 1920 and 1930. In 1930 the number of women in this occupational group was 43 per cent greater than in 1920 and in 1920 it was 42 per cent greater than in 1910.

The women in this occupational group have been and still are chiefly saleswomen and store clerks. Compared with about one-third of the men in *Trade*, three-fourths of the women were classified as salespersons or store clerks in 1930. Another large

TABLE 27.—PER CENT DISTRIBUTION OF MEN AND WOMEN IN OCCUPATIONS CLASSIFIED AS TRADE, 1910–1930[a]

Occupation	1910		1920		1930	
	Men	Women	Men	Women	Men	Women
Total......................	100.0	100.0	100.0	100.0	100.0	100.0
Advertising agents...........	(b)	(b)	(b)	(b)	0.8	0.6
Apprentices.................	(b)	(b)	(b)	(b)	(c)	(c)
Bankers, brokers.............	3.3	0.5	4.4	0.8	4.0	0.9
Commercial travelers.........	5.1	0.5	4.9	0.4	4.3	0.4
Decorators and window dressers	0.2	0.1	0.2	0.2	0.3	0.6
Delivery men.................	7.3	(c)	4.7	(c)	3.1	(c)
Floorwalkers, foremen........	0.6	0.7	0.6	0.6	0.6	0.5
Inspectors, gaugers..........	0.4	0.4	0.4	0.2	0.2	0.6
Insurance agents.............	3.0	0.6	3.6	0.8	5.3	1.5
Laborers, warehouses.........	2.5	0.1	3.5	0.1	2.2	0.1
Laborers, stores, lumber yards.	3.1	0.9	3.3	1.3	3.9	0.9
Newsboys and girls...........	0.9	0.1	0.7	(c)	0.8	(c)
Proprietors, managers........	0.7	0.2	0.9	0.2	0.8	0.3
Real estate agents...........	3.9	0.6	3.6	1.4	4.1	3.3
Retail dealers...............	35.7	14.2	34.8	11.8	31.1	11.4
Store clerks.................	8.7	23.6	6.8	25.4	4.7	16.9
Salesmen and women..........	21.4	55.5	23.1	54.4	29.5	58.2
Undertakers.................	0.6	0.2	0.7	0.2	0.6	0.2
Wholesale dealers............	1.6	0.2	2.0	0.1	1.6	0.2
Other.......................	1.1	1.6	1.5	2.3	1.9	3.0

a Bureau of the Census, Release June 28, 1932, *Occupation Statistics*.
b Comparable figures not available for 1910 and 1920.
c Less than 0.1 per cent.

group of both sexes, three-tenths of the men and about one-tenth of the women, were retail store dealers.

The opportunities for women's employment, however, appears to have widened during the last decade. From Table 27 it appears that the proportion of women employed as saleswomen was approximately the same in 1930 as in 1910 and was a little over one-fourth of the total number of salespersons. Larger numbers of women in 1930 than previously, however, were returned as bank officials, inspectors, real estate and insurance agents and window decorators. In every 1,000 bank officials 29 were women in 1910 and 63 in 1930; in every 1,000 insurance agents but 27 were women in 1910 and 53 in 1930; in every 1,000 real estate agents in 1910 only 23 were women compared with 132 in 1930; of 1,000 window dressers and decorators in 1910 only 82 were women compared with 309 in 1930. However, in some occupations

TABLE 28.—PROPORTION WOMEN ARE OF ALL PERSONS IN OCCUPATIONS CLASSIFIED AS TRADE, 1910–1930ᵃ

Occupation	1910	1920	1930
Total....................................	11.8	15.8	15.8
Advertising agents......................	(b)	(b)	11.5
Apprentices............................	(c)	(c)	4.4
Bankers, brokers.......................	2.5	3.3	4.1
Commercial travelers...................	1.6	1.6	1.7
Decorators, window dressers............	8.2	13.0	30.9
Delivery men..........................	0.1	0.1	0.1
Floorwalkers and forewomen............	14.8	15.4	12.6
Inspectors............................	13.1	7.5	34.8
Insurance agents......................	2.7	3.9	5.3
Laborers (warehouses).................	0.8	0.7	0.6
Laborers (stores).....................	4.1	6.7	4.5
News girls............................	0.9	1.2	1.1
Proprietors, managers.................	4.5	3.1	6.9
Real estate agents....................	2.3	6.2	13.2
Retail dealers........................	5.6	5.9	6.5
Store clerks..........................	28.8	41.2	40.6
Salesmen and women...................	27.9	30.6	27.1
Undertakers..........................	3.9	4.6	5.7
Wholesale dealers.....................	1.8	1.1	2.0
Other occupations....................	18.2	22.9	23.3

ᵃ Bureau of the Census, Release June 28, 1932, *Occupation Statistics.*
ᵇ Classified as clerical in 1910 and 1920.
ᶜ Classified as manufacturing and mechanical in 1910 and 1920.

there appeared to be little or no change in the status of women, and in some cases they declined in number; among floor walkers in stores, for example, the relative number of women had decreased. In 1910, 169 in 1,000 were women and only 142 in 1930. That women are by no means limited at the present time to selling in stores, the lists of occupations of the members of various women's clubs indicate, but whether or not this is a recent development is uncertain. Among 40,000 members of the National Federation of Business and Professional Women's Clubs, there were 6,340 members employed in occupations classified under the heading of *Sales*. About one-third of these women were sales clerks in stores, the others were proprietors, managers of retail stores, partners in stores, heads of departments, buyers, sales agents for real estate and insurance companies, canvassers, demonstrators and the like.[1] The importance of women in these occupations and as managers of specialty shops dealing in clothing and millinery for women and children, florist and gift shops is brought out by the lists of occupations of members of the classified women's clubs,[2] those clubs to which only women who own or manage a business or are executives in other occupations are eligible.

II. OFFICE AND CLERICAL OCCUPATIONS

Clerical occupations, from the simple routine jobs which require little or no training to occupations almost professional in character, in 1930 employed 110,523 more women than were employed in manufacturing and mechanical occupations. With the invention of the typewriter and the labor saving office machines, the calculating machines, comptometers, multigraphing and other machines, the employment of women during the last thirty years has greatly increased.

The term "clerical work" is used to cover a great many different kinds of work from secretarial work, bookkeeping and some types of stenographic work for which trained workers are needed, to simple routine jobs such as filing, addressing envelopes, folding circulars or sorting mail, jobs which any intelligent girl with little or no training can do. A tendency toward requiring specialized work for each position, a trend toward substituting workers with technical training for those without such training and a lessening of the opportunities for promotion from the lower to the upper levels of commercial occupations, is probably discernible.[3] Especially in large business offices clerical jobs are becoming highly specialized and the tasks subdivided; stenographic, typing and filing work is centralized. Typists do typing only, the duplicating machine operator operates that machine only, and stenographers take dictation and do not act as private secretaries. The idea that a girl with a knowledge of stenography and bookkeeping entering a subordinate office position has a chance to rise to a position of responsibility is said to be becoming out of date.

[1] *Ibid.*, pp. 161–66.
[2] See the official Directories of the National Association of Altrusa Clubs 1930 and the *Quotarian*, February, 1931, official organ of the Quota Club International.
[3] *Biennial Survey of Education*, 1926–1928, U. S. Bureau of Education, p. 235.

WOMEN IN THE TWENTIETH CENTURY

TABLE 29a.—NUMBER OF MEN AND WOMEN EMPLOYED IN CLERICAL OCCUPATIONS, 1910–1930[a]

Clerical occupations	1910		1920		1930	
	Men	Women	Men	Women	Men	Women
Total.....................	1,129,849	588,609	1,689,911	1,421,925	2,038,494	1,986,830
Agents, collectors.............	82,345	4,187	149,427	11,640	182,680	13,477
Accountants and auditors......	35,653	3,586	105,073	13,378	174,557	17,014
Bookkeepers and cashiers......	263,892	183,569	270,491	345,746	273,380	465,697
Clerks.....................	597,833	122,665	1,015,742	472,163	1,290,447	706,553
Stenographers and typists......	53,378	263,315	50,410	564,744	36,050	775,140
Messenger work.............	96,748	11,287	98,768	14,254	81,430	8,949

TABLE 29b.—PER CENT DISTRIBUTION OF MEN AND WOMEN EMPLOYED IN CLERICAL OCCUPATIONS, 1910–1930

Clerical occupations	1910		1920		1930	
	Men	Women	Men	Women	Men	Women
Total.....................	100.0	100.0	100.0	100.0	100.0	100.0
Agents, collectors.............	7.3	.7	8.8	.8	8.9	.7
Accountants, auditors.........	3.2	.6	6.2	.9	8.6	.9
Bookkeepers and cashiers......	23.4	31.2	16.0	24.3	13.4	23.4
Clerks.....................	52.9	20.8	60.1	33.2	63.3	35.6
Stenographers and typists......	4.7	44.7	2.9	39.7	1.8	44.7
Messengers and errand work...	8.6	1.9	5.8	1.0	3.9	1.9

TABLE 29c.—PROPORTION OF WOMEN OF ALL PERSONS EMPLOYED IN CLERICAL OCCUPATIONS, 1910–1930

Clerical occupations	1910	1920	1930
Total.........................	34.3	45.7	49.4
Agents, collectors....................	4.8	7.2	6.9
Accountants, auditors................	9.1	11.3	8.8
Bookkeepers, cashiers................	41.0	56.1	63.0
Clerks..............................	17.0	31.7	35.4
Stenographers and typists............	83.1	91.8	95.5
Messengers and errand work..........	10.4	12.6	9.9

ᵃ Bureau of the Census, Release June 28, 1932, *Occupation Statistics.*

The increasing demand for clerical workers, offset in part, especially during the last decade, by the increased use of office machines, has affected the employment of women more than that of men. The increase of women in clerical occupations between 1910 and 1920 was 140 per cent; the increase in 1930 over 1920 was 40 per cent. During these two decades the number of men in clerical occupations also increased but not so fast as the number of women; between 1910 and 1920 the increase of men was 50 per cent and between 1920 and 1930 it was only 21 per cent.[1] Therefore, either women have replaced men to some extent in clerical occupations or new opportunities have developed of which they have taken advantage; from constituting 34 per cent of all persons employed in clerical occupations in 1910, women were 45 per cent in 1920 and 49 per cent in 1930.

It is true, however, that women are concentrated in the occupations of typing, stenography, bookkeeping and cashiering and office machine operating; the men are in miscellaneous clerical work including shipping and stock room work, timekeeping, weighing, all classified as "clerical" by the census. Formerly men were employed to some extent as typists and stenographers but by 1930 women practically monopolized this field; the proportion which women were of all typists and stenographers was 83 per cent in 1910 and 95 per cent in 1930. Women have also been increasingly employed as bookkeepers and cashiers, an occupation in which men were formerly more important. Not only have the actual numbers of women in this occupation been greatly increased, but also their number in relation to that of men. In 1910 women were 41 per cent of the bookkeepers and cashiers and in 1930 they were 63 per cent. The employment of women has also become more common in miscellaneous clerical work. In 1930 they predominated as office machine operators, while men predominated as shipping room clerks. Women were no doubt also important as file clerks, but the census includes this occupation with that of "other clerks." In all the occupations classified as "clerks," women were only 17 per cent of the total in 1910, but in 1930 this proportion had increased to 35 per cent. In the particularly skilled occupation

[1] The transfer of advertising agents, most of whom were men from the classification of "clerical" to the classification of "trade" in 1930 does not account for the relatively small increase in the number of men in clerical occupations between 1920 and 1930.

of accounting and auditing, however, women have made slow progress. About one-tenth of the auditors and accountants enumerated at the last three decennial censuses were women. An increase in the proportion of women in 1920 was not maintained in 1930. In the occupations of agents, collectors, demonstrators and the like, women have taken little part.

Whether or not women have been replacing men since 1920 in any of the clerical occupations in which men formerly predominated, the surveys which school and other organizations have made of clerical workers are not sufficiently comprehensive or representative of office workers as a whole to show. Proof is hardly needed of the replacement of men stenographers by women. However, a recent study made by the Vocational Bureau of the Chicago schools to find out if there was any opportunity for boys in stenography and bookkeeping should be mentioned. This study covered 57 large firms employing over 46,000 clerical workers, selected from the point of view of occupational opportunities for boys. Among the adult workers 2 per cent of the men, as compared with 22 per cent of the women, were stenographers, secretaries and typists; 2 per cent of the men and 1 per cent of the women were bookkeepers.[1] Also suggestive is a study of office practice published in 1927 as one of a series of the Harvard bulletins in education, a study which included 34,513 office workers in 31 different cities employed in offices sufficiently large to have office managers, representing different types of business establishments and factories. The office managers regarded typing, stenography, office machine operating, bookkeeping machine operating, filing, and secretarial work as "women's trades"; "men's trades" were those of correspondent, receiving clerk, shipping clerk, timekeeper and stock clerk; both sexes might be employed as bookkeepers, cashiers, mail clerks, payroll clerks, cost clerks, ledger clerks and statistical clerks. However, when the occupations of the relatively small number of persons reporting sex were analyzed, considerable numbers of women as well as

---

[1] The figures for occupations of adult workers in Chicago are published in the *Journal of Commercial Education* for January, 1928, in an article entitled "Commercial Occupations," Lloyd L. Jones, p. 21. The information regarding opportunities for junior workers is published by the Chicago Board of Education, Vocational Guidance Bureau, Occupational Study No. 15, 1928, entitled *Clerical Positions for Boys in Large Chicago Offices*.

men were found in all of the occupations considered primarily as work for men.[1]

How far women are now employed in the better paid and upper grade clerical positions and whether their number in the upper grade positions is increasing, are other questions which cannot be definitely answered. There is no doubt that considerable numbers of women have high grade clerical positions, but the proportion of women in these positions is probably relatively small. The great mass of women workers do miscellaneous kinds of work which must include many very routine jobs. As a result of the Harvard study of office practice just mentioned, it was concluded that the percentage of stenographers and bookkeepers among clerical workers as a whole was very small,[2] but this study does not give figures separately for men and women in these occupations. In the firms which the Chicago study covered, secretaries, stenographers and bookkeepers were relatively few; the majority of women were in work classified as miscellaneous.[3] A study of nearly 4,000 clerical workers of Minneapolis, conducted by the Sociology Department of the University of Minnesota in 1925, showed a somewhat larger proportion of women in stenographic and secretarial positions: 3 per cent of the women were secretaries, 14 per cent stenographers and 10 per cent bookkeepers.[4] Differences in the types of establishments selected for these studies as well as differences in the kinds of work classified as secretarial or stenographic may account for many of the differences in the results.

If lists of occupations of members of women's business clubs are consulted, considerable numbers of women are found in the higher grade clerical occupations, private secretaries, court reporters, public stenographers, bookkeepers and accountants. However, the type of woman who belongs to these clubs, to the Business and Professional Women's Clubs as well as to the Quota, Altrusa and other classified women's clubs, are no doubt the aristocrats among clerical workers.[5] The survey of the occu-

[1] Frederick G. Nichols, *A New Conception of Office Practice*, Harvard Bulletins in Education No. 12 (Cambridge University Press, 1927), pp. 49, 79.

[2] *Ibid.*, p. 42.

[3] Jones, *op. cit.*, p. 21.

[4] M. C. Elmer, *Women in Clerical and Secretarial Work in Minneapolis*, Women's Occupational Bureau (1925), p. 9.

[5] For lists of members in the classified women's clubs see the *Quotarian*, official organ of Quota Club International, February, 1931, and official directory of the National Altrusa Clubs, 1930.

pations and earnings of members of the National Federation of Women's Business and Professional Clubs included nearly 6,000 women whose occupations were classified as clerical. Among these over 1,000 women were either secretaries or private secretaries, 53 were court reporters and 57 accountants.[1] The latter term as used in this study included cost accountants; whether any women were also included who belonged to the highly skilled professional group of certified public accountants is not stated. According to a recent publication on occupations for women considerable prejudice exists against women in this occupation,[2] and in 1920 at least the American Institute of Accountants had only 7 women in a membership of nearly 1,500.[3]

The claim that men have more initiative, take responsibility better and are more regular in attendance at work than women no doubt still militates against the progress of women in the upper grade clerical positions, although they are accepted as indispensable for certain types of work in the more routine positions.

That men predominate at the present time in the better paid clerical occupations and in the higher salary groups within each occupation is demonstrated by a comprehensive study of clerical salaries made by the National Industrial Conference Board which covered 27,000 odd clerical workers employed in 427 manufacturing, insurance, banking and mercantile establishments, public utilities and other kinds of businesses in 18 of the large cities of the country. Positions classified as chief clerks, head bookkeepers, senior clerks and cashiers were those in which salaries were the highest.[4] The number of women who held positions classified as chief clerks, head bookkeepers and cashiers was 284 as compared with 1,333 men; 1,435 women and 1,880 men were employed as senior clerks. Women were the great majority of the stenographers, but in secretarial-stenographic positions where the greatest skill was required, men were 10 per cent as compared with 3 per cent of the persons classified as junior stenographers.[5] The median salary of the women was less than that of the men in

[1] Elliott and Manson, op. cit., appendix 2, pp. 126–27, and appendix 3, p. 133.

[2] O. Latham Hatcher, Occupations for Women, Southern Women's Educational Alliance (1927), p. 122.

[3] Training for the Professions and Allied Occupations, New York Bureau of Vocational Information (1924), p. 162.

[4] Clerical Salaries in the United States, National Industrial Conference Board (New York, 1926), pp. 11–14.

[5] Ibid., p. 17.

every occupation except that of mail clerks, an occupation frequently undertaken by boys just out of grammar school. The median salaries paid men and women[1] in certain occupations in which considerable numbers of both sexes were employed indicate that women did not receive equal pay for the same kind of work, although in giving these figures the report states that it is not possible to tell how far the work for which the salaries were reported for men and women was identical although called by the same name.

TABLE 30.—SALARY PAID TO MEDIAN MAN AND MEDIAN WOMAN

	Men	Women		Men	Women
Mail clerks	$14.68	$17.16	Payroll clerks	$30.68	$21.12
Order clerks	21.84	20.01	Cost clerks	31.95	20.00
Labor saving machine operators	22.31	21.82	Senior clerks	36.41	24.16
Junior clerks	24.25	18.61	Cashiers	41.59	31.19
General clerks	25.75	17.36	Head bookkeepers	44.08	33.21
Ledger clerks	29.81	22.88			

The ambition of the school girl to "work in an office" in preference to work in a factory has often been commented on by vocational counsellors and others in touch with girls who are seeking their first jobs. The social status of office work and the relatively pleasant surroundings as compared with the factory attract the girl rather than the prospect of an adequate financial return. The lower grades of office work are notoriously poorly paid. The New York State Bureau of Women in Industry (before the present industrial depression) collected material from employment offices and classified newspaper advertisements concerning the salaries offered in New York City, for different kinds of office work. According to these figures office operators were offered $14 a week; clerks a general average of from $15 to $18 a week; typists from $15 to $22 a week and stenographers from $15 for a beginner to $35 for an expert.[2] However, the average earnings of all women office workers employed by manufacturing establishments including those in supervisory positions were much higher than this and more nearly correspond to the earnings quoted in the National Industrial Conference Board study. According to figures from the New York State Department of

[1] Ibid., p. 30.
[2] "The Trend of Women's Wages in New York City," New York Industrial Bulletin, New York State Department of Labor, X, No. 6 (March, 1931), p. 191.

Labor the average earnings of women office workers in New York City factories in 1929 were $27.57 a week.[1] Earnings of women wage earners in factories in New York City were lower; in January, 1929, they varied from $23.57 a week in the clothing and millinery industry to $18.71 in the textile and $17.58 in the metal industries.[2]

With the rising standards of schooling set up by school attendance and child labor laws and with the increasing enrollments in high schools and commercial courses in high schools, there can be no doubt of the growing number of girls with high school training available for clerical jobs. But opinions conflict as to whether or not educational qualifications for clerical workers have risen during the last ten or twenty years. According to the director of the Boston Vocational Guidance Department of the Public Schools, employers in that city now demand high school graduates for clerical jobs whereas fifteen years ago one or two years of high school sufficed. A personnel director of the Commercial Department of the Telephone Company in the same city believed there were more high school graduates applying for jobs than formerly, so naturally more were employed. It is stated in an occupational monograph issued by the New Orleans public schools that firms who formerly employed seventh and eighth grade graduates as clerical workers, now employ only those who have had two years high school training and prefer graduates of a full time high school course.[3] On the other hand, the growing specialization and subdivision of work in large offices has no doubt greatly increased the number of simple routine jobs, for which little education is needed. In 1924, the Women's Educational and Industrial Union of Boston made a study of the public schools and women in office service and pointed out that machines had taken over much of the specialized part of bookkeeping, and that comptometers, adding and billing machines, provided an opportunity for young women of limited education to work.[4] In 1928 one writer, in discussing the mechanization of the modern

[1] "Office Workers' Earnings," *New York Industrial Bulletin*, New York State Department of Labor, X, No. 6 (March, 1931), 193.

[2] "The Trend of Women's Wages in New York City," *New York Industrial Bulletin*, New York State Department of Labor, X, No. 6 (March, 1931), 193.

[3] *The Office Worker in New Orleans*, New Orleans Vocational Information Series, No. 10 (1929), 8–9.

[4] May Allison, *The Public Schools and Women in Office Service*, Women's Educational and Industrial Union (Boston, 1914), p. 93.

office, points out that office machine companies conduct training courses for machine operators in which they accept grammar school graduates, and concludes that with the simplification of many office processes by machine "an increasing proportion [of women] in some of the more routine positions will be admitted at a lower educational level."[1]

No statements about educational requirements for office workers in general should be made because of the differing demands for the various kinds of clerical work. That varying amounts of education are needed was recognized in the recommendations of the federal reclassification commission for clerical workers in the federal civil service. In 1920, the Commission recommended for civil service employees in Washington that a common school education be required for positions classified as "under" file clerks and "junior" file clerks, other "under" clerks, addressing machine operators, multigraphing and mimeographing machine operators; for junior typists two years high school or graduation from business school, for senior file clerks, senior typists, junior and senior stenographers, private secretaries, billing machine and calculating machine operators and statistical clerks, high school graduation was recommended.[2] For most of these positions some experience but not business school was required. In 1930 the Personnel Classification Board made very similar recommendations for civil service workers in these types of work in the field service outside of Washington.[3] That these recommendations have been made is a significant sign of the changing point of view, for up to the present time no educational qualifications at all have been required for most of these positions.

Similarly office managers whose opinions were asked concerning general educational requirements during the Harvard survey of office practice distinguished between the different kinds of office work. The concensus of opinion was that common school training was sufficient for receiving and shipping clerks; junior high school training for file clerks, mail clerks, billing clerks, payroll clerks, timekeepers and duplicating machine operators;

---

[1] Grace L. Coyle, *Recent Trends in Clerical Occupations* (New York City: Woman's Press, 1928), pp. 33–34.

[2] *Report of the Congressional Joint Commission of Reclassification of Salaries,* Sixty-ninth Congress, Second Session, House Document No. 686, Part 2 (U. S. Printing Office, 1920), pp. 91, 105–106, 115–120, 190–197, 824.

[3] *Preliminary Class Specifications for Positions in the Field Service,* Personnel Classification Board (U. S. Printing Office, 1930), pp. 628–48, 733–35.

senior high school training for stenographers, bookkeepers, cashiers and typists. For secretarial-stenographers, correspondents and statistical clerks opinion was divided between the value of college training as compared with high school training.[1] As a matter of fact, the development of vocational schools and special courses to prepare young people is one of the striking developments in the history of the school system. The need was urgent and at first the public schools did not meet that need so that private schools arose in great numbers. The United States Office of Education publishes the figures. The number of girls enrolled in business courses or business schools during the period 1914–1924[2] increased so that there were 419,141 in 1924. The Bulletins for 1927–1928 and 1929–1930 do not classify the registration by sex; but in 1929, 651 private commercial and business schools reporting to the Office had a total enrollment of 179,756 students, of whom 121,215 were women, 67 per cent of whom were in day classes.[3] The development of curricula in this field is of great interest to women, and the Office of Education reports an increase in interest on the part of the Junior Colleges,[4] and the last two decades have seen the development in the colleges and universities of "Schools of Commerce and Administration," or "Schools of Business Administration," or "Schools of Business." The number of women students taking these courses has not been so great, but there has been a fairly steady numerical increase, and figures in the following table indicate for the end of the decade an increase as compared with the men, and a marked percentage increase. It may be that business, too, is opening more attractive prospects and permanent careers for women and that this is reflected in the larger attendance at the higher levels of preparation.

The figures show an increase in the number of university registrations in courses in commerce and business administration during each year except 1921–1922 when there was a slight decrease in the number of women registered. There has been little variation in the per cent of women of the total registered each year

[1] Edith Abbott and Sophonisba P. Breckinridge, *Truancy and Non-Attendance in the Chicago Schools* (Chicago: University of Chicago Press, 1917), p. 150.

[2] Biennial Survey, 1924–1926, Bulletin of the Bureau of Education, 1928, No. 4, *Commercial Education, 1924–1926.*

[3] U. S. Department of the Interior, Office of Education, Bulletin, 1930, No. 25, p. 1, Proffitt, *Statistics of Private Commercial and Business Schools.*

[4] *Ibid.*, Bulletin, 1931, No. 20, p. 32. Biennial Survey, 1928–1930, chap. v, Mallott, "Commercial Education," p. 32.

although the trend on the whole has been upward. The per cent
of increase in women's registration has varied from 3.5 to 33.5
per cent and there has been an increase for every year except
1921–1922 when there was a decrease of 2.3 per cent.

TABLE 31.—NUMBER OF WOMEN AND MEN REGISTERED IN COURSES IN
COMMERCE AND BUSINESS ADMINISTRATION IN THE UNIVERSITIES
1919–1930, THE PER CENT OF WOMEN OF THE TOTAL REGISTERED
EACH YEAR, AND THE PER CENT OF INCREASE IN WOMEN'S
REGISTRATION FOR EACH YEAR[a]

Year	Number of women	Per cent women of total	Per cent increase of women
1919–1920	3,149	8.7	
1920–1921	4,204	8.9	33.5
1921–1922	4,110	8.0	−2.3
1922–1923	4,254	7.6	3.5
1923–1924	4,564	7.6	7.3
1924–1925	5,328	8.6	16.7
1925–1926	5,664	8.6	6.3
1926–1927	5,980	8.5	5.6
1927–1928	6,216	8.6	3.9
1928–1929	7,235	9.5	16.4
1929–1930	9,654	11.0	33.4

[a] Based upon Delta Sigma Pi survey of universities offering organized courses in commerce and business administration.

Vocational monographs prepared by school vocational guidance bureaus stress the need for a four years' high school education
as well as technical training for stenographers and bookkeepers
and some high school training for the minor clerical jobs of
typing, office machine operating, and filing. In one vocational
monograph prepared by the Boston University College of Business Administration it is stated that a junior high school education
is sufficient for most types of filing and for multigraphing,
mimeograph and adding machine operators, but advocates more
training for calculating machine operators.[1] That no girl should
enter business today without a high school education is the
position taken by the Business and Professional Women's Clubs.
For the work of service representative in the New England
Telephone Company, work which involves meeting customers,
and adjusting difficulties as well as miscellaneous clerical work,
college women are recently being tried. Of about 350 women
service representatives in this organization in metropolitan

[1] *Vocational Monographs*, Nos. 1, 2, 3, Boston University, College of Business
Administration (1931), pp. 11, 22, 31, 33.

Boston about 40 are college graduates.[1] According to publications dealing with vocations for the trained woman, secretarial work has for many years been considered a field suited for college graduates.

[1] Statement made by Miss Pick, Personnel Director, Commercial Department, Boston Metropolitan Division of New England Telephone Company.

CHAPTER XII

PROFESSIONAL AND NEAR-PROFESSIONAL WOMEN

I. THE INCREASE IN NUMBERS

A RECENT student of the subject of women's education commented on the degree to which women had professionalized themselves, and the rapidity with which they had done it.[1] Writing in 1925, Professor Woody said:

> The population of the United States, since 1890, increased from 62,947,714 to 105,710,620 in 1920. The ratio of men to women in this period has been about the same. The population increased 68 per cent between 1890 and 1920; men in professional service for the same period increased 78 per cent; while women increased 226 per cent.

During the next decade the increase was not so spectacular but in 1930 over a million and a half women were employed in activities characterized by the Census as professional, and these women formed almost half of all the persons enumerated in the professional group. Large as this number and proportion is, it still appears that while the proportion of women among professional workers increased between 1920 and 1930 the relative number of men and women in professional activities was approximately the same at the beginning and at the end of the decade. In 1910, the proportion of women in the professions was 429 in every 1,000; in 1920, the proportion was 468; and in 1930, 469 of every 1,000 persons employed in professional occupations were women. The figures with reference to women in the professional occupations[2] are of special interest (see Table 32), for if the door-

---

[1] Woody, op. cit., II, 381.

[2] In this connection it should be noted that the census included under the heading "professional service" not only occupations usually regarded as professional, but also occupations followed in connection with the professions. In 1930, the sub-professional occupations were classified in two groups, an arrangement somewhat different from that followed at the previous decennial censuses. Under the heading "semi-professional and recreational" are included such occupations as religious workers, healers, chiropractors, keepers of charitable institutions, radio announcers, laboratory assistants; under the heading "attendants and helpers" are included theatre ushers, attendants in doctors' and dentists'

ways to·the professions are opened, the pressure on occupations
hitherto crowded may be lightened and the pathway from the

TABLE 32.—NUMBER OF MEN AND WOMEN TEN YEARS OF AGE AND OVER IN
PROFESSIONAL OCCUPATIONS, 1910–1930

Professional occupation	1910*a*		1920*b*		1930*b*	
	Men	Women	Men	Women	Men	Women
Total........................	976,523	734,752	1,154,221	1,017,030	1,727,650	1,526,234
Actors and showmen..............	35,293	13,100	33,818	14,354	54,511	20,785
Architects.....................	16,311	302	18,048	137	21,621	379
Artists and art teachers...........	18,675	15,429	20,785	14,617	35,621	21,644
Authors, editors, reporters.........	32,511	6,239	32,129	8,736	46,922	17,371
Chemists......................	15,694	579	31,227	1,714	45,163	1,905
Clergymen.....................	117,333	685	125,483	1,787	145,572	3,276
Dentists.......................	38,743	1,254	54,323	1,829	69,768	1,287
Designers, draftsmen..............	44,437	3,012	62,987	7,664	93,518	9,212
Lawyers, judges, justices...........	114,146	558	120,781	1,738	157,220	3,385
Musicians and teachers...........	54,832	84,478	57,587	72,678	85,517	79,611
Photographers..................	26,811	4,964	27,140	7,119	31,163	8,366
Physicians, surgeons and osteopaths	142,117	9,015	141,125	8,882	151,532	8,388
Teachers......................	133,920	480,985	145,857	649,316	244,111	880,409
School......................	118,442	476,864	116,848	635,207	190,049	853,967
Athletics and dancing..........	2,768	1,163	5,677	4,034	12,288	6,311
College (includes presidents).....	12,710	2,958	23,332	10,075	41,774	20,131
Technical engineers..............	88,744	11	136,080	41	226,136	113
Trained nurses..................	5,819	76,508	5,464	143,664	5,452	228,737
Veterinary surgeons..............	11,652	......	13,493	1	11,852	11
Other professional pursuits........	7,585	8,092	14,441	19,265	43,847	70,546
Semi-professional and recreational..	71,900	29,541	113,453	63,488	143,365	55,184
Attendants and helpers...........					170,384	55,625

a Thirteenth Census, *Population* Vol. IV, *Occupations*, p. 93.
b Bureau of the Census Release June 28, 1932, *Occupation Statistics.*

domestic inactivity, which has been characterized as a "consum-
ing dead weight,"[1] may more easily swing outward.

The transfer from the non-professional to the professional
emphasis is however not peculiar to women, for the per cent

offices, library assistants. Because of the relatively small numbers in the sub-
professional groups, changes in the 1930 classification by which certain occupations, such as apprentices, technicians and laboratory assistants, were transferred
to the professional service group from the manufacturing and mechanical and
domestic service groups are not particularly important. However, it is clear that
comparisons of professional groups with female population should be with older
groups.

[1] *Recent Social Trends in the United States*, Chap. XVII Lynd, "Consumption."

increase of men and women in professional occupations in 1930 as compared with 1920 was about the same (see Table 33);

TABLE 33.—PER CENT DISTRIBUTION OF MEN AND WOMEN IN PROFESSIONAL OCCUPATIONS, 1910–1930[a]

Occupation	1910		1920		1930	
	Men	Women	Men	Women	Men	Women
Total..............................	100.0	100.0	100.0	100.0	100.0	100.0
Actors and showmen.....................	3.5	1.8	2.9	1.4	3.1	1.3
Architects.............................	1.7	(b)	1.6	(b)	1.3	(b)
Artists and art teachers..................	1.9	2.1	1.8	1.4	2.1	1.4
Authors, editors, reporters................	3.3	0.8	2.8	0.9	2.7	1.1
Chemists..............................	1.6	0.1	2.7	0.2	2.6	0.1
Clergymen.............................	12.0	0.1	10.9	0.2	8.4	0.2
Dentists..............................	3.9	0.2	4.7	0.2	4.0	0.1
Designers, draftsmen.....................	4.5	0.4	5.5	0.7	5.4	0.6
Lawyers, judges, justices.................	11.7	0.1	10.5	0.2	9.1	0.2
Musicians and teachers...................	5.6	11.5	4.9	7.1	4.9	5.2
Photographers.........................	2.7	0.7	2.4	0.7	1.8	0.5
Physicians, surgeons and osteopaths........	14.5	1.2	12.1	0.8	8.8	0.5
Teachers..............................	13.7	65.5	12.6	63.9	14.1	57.7
School.............................	12.1	64.9	10.1	62.5	11.0	56.0
Athletics, dancing.....................	0.3	0.2	0.5	0.4	0.7	0.4
College..............................	1.3	0.4	2.0	1.0	2.4	1.3
Technical engineers......................	9.1	.....	11.8	.....	13.1	
Trained nurses.........................	0.6	10.4	0.5	14.1	0.3	18.9
Other professional pursuits...............	1.7	0.2	1.3	1.9	2.5	4.6
Semi-professional and recreational..........	7.3	4.1	9.8	6.2	8.3	3.6
Attendants and helpers...................					6.6	3.6

[a] Bureau of the Census, Release of June 28, 1932, *Occupation Statistics*.
[b] Less than 0.1 per cent.

women in the professions increased 50.6 per cent and the men 49.6 per cent. During the same period the population of women increased 25.1 per cent, and of the men 17.1 per cent, but the changes in men's interests are not the concern of this discussion except as they affect the occupational fate of women.

The distribution of women among the occupations listed as professions is of equal importance with their number. The number of teachers who are women has been commented upon and it is not surprising to find that the teaching profession claims almost three-fifths, 57.7 per cent, of the professional women; and yet this is a relatively smaller share than in 1910 and 1920. Professional opportunity is spreading somewhat. It is to be noted, however, as shown in Table 34, that the proportion of teachers

[189]

who are women is also somewhat smaller than at the earlier dates. It is important, too, to note that, while women were principally teachers in schools rather than in colleges or universities, the proportion in the latter group increased from 4 in a thousand to 13, a not inconsiderable increase. And attention will be called to the subject of athletics or physical education in which there

TABLE 34.—PER CENT WOMEN ARE OF TOTAL PERSONS EMPLOYED IN PROFESSIONAL OCCUPATIONS, 1910–1930[a]

Professional occupations	Per cent		
	1910	1920	1930
Total..	42.9	46.8	46.9
Actors and showmen...........................	27.1	29.8	27.6
Architects.....................................	1.8	0.7	1.7
Artists and art teachers.........................	45.2	41.3	37.8
Authors, editors, reporters......................	16.1	21.4	27.0
Chemists......................................	3.5	5.2	4.0
Clergymen.....................................	0.6	1.4	2.2
Dentists.......................................	3.1	3.3	1.8
Designers, draftsmen...........................	6.3	10.8	8.9
Lawyers, judges, justices........................	0.5	1.4	2.1
Musicians and teachers..........................	60.6	55.8	48.2
Photographers.................................	15.6	20.8	21.2
Physicians, surgeons and osteopaths..............	5.9	5.9	5.2
Teachers			
School..	80.1	84.5	81.2
Athletics and dancing.......................	29.6	41.5	33.9
College (includes president).....................	18.9	30.2	32.5
Trained nurses.................................	92.9	96.3	98.1
Other professional pursuits......................	....	....	61.6
Semi-professional and recreational................	....	....	27.8
Attendants and helpers..........................	....	....	32.0

[a] Bureau of the Census, Release June 28, 1932, *Occupation Statistics.*

was also a gain from 2 to 7 in a thousand, and in which very interesting developments are taking place. It is also interesting to note that the percentage of professional men in teaching and the proportion men were of the teaching group increased. Men may be driving women out, as well as keeping them out of the higher ranges of employment.

This excess of women in the schools gives rise to discussion, and sometimes to criticism. The feminization of the school system is sometimes named as the source of unsatisfactory educational and social results. For example, in the *Chicago Tribune* of July 17, 1932, the lack of interest of the young men of this generation in public affairs is attributed to the fact that they have been so largely educated by women teachers who are not in the habit of thinking politically. The phraseology used by the *Tribune* was as follows:

. . . There are, of course, young men who vote the Democratic ticket and young men who vote the Republican ticket, but they haven't been going places. Perhaps that is the fault of their early education, which has been intrusted almost exclusively to women unaccustomed to thinking politically. Perhaps the disrepute into which politics has fallen has had something to do with it. Probably the Utopian nonsense of much that is taught in the higher institutions has soured the oncoming generation.[1]

On the other hand, in 1918, in a letter with reference to the United States Army abroad, Rudyard Kipling made the following statement:

I heard the story of a regiment that had recovered some of its men mutilated by the Hun. No detail was slurred, and the tale ended: "The Germans did that to frighten us, sir."
"What happened next?" I asked.
The voice told me what had happened, and it was not at all a pleasant happening for the Hun. Yet the same man, a minute afterward, carefully used a watered down euphemis for an elemental fact which an Englishman, or for that matter an Englishwoman, would have got at in one word. The Americans were inclined this way a generation ago, because even then they were generally educated by women, and women's share in their education has increased since. They deliver themselves of whole sentences, through which one can almost see *the keen, tense, "up-lifting" woman-kind, who gave the entire virile sentiment its funnily feminine cloak.*
But of all creatures, *the woman-taught man is quite the most unprofitable to irritate or bully.* In addition to normal wrath his acquired delicacy is outraged and he finds himself at white hot feud with the system which makes such things possible. Then he goes to the limit and beyond, and *is as impertinent as a woman afterward.*
Like a woman, too, he cleans up behind him with acids and disinfectants.
This, as the boy said when he showed up a list of the kings of Israel for his English essay, is not all my own idea, but arose long ago out of a talk with that wise philosopher, Mark Twain.[2]

A few words may be said concerning another extremely interesting development suggested by the Census figures; namely, that of physical education and the increased provision of opportunities for athletic achievement. This development relates itself

[1] *Chicago Sunday Tribune*, Editorial Column, July 17, 1932.
[2] *Chicago Daily News*, August 17, 1918.

to a quite different source in this country from that from which such activity has been derived in Great Britain.[1] There the question of race deterioration was raised after the South African War, and while, after studying the subject, because of lack of knowledge of previous conditions, it could not be said that the English population was deteriorating, it could be said that the physical condition was not what it should be, and school feeding, physical education, nursery schools, and mothers' classes were developed as items in a program of conservation. In the United States, it was rather to meet the strange policy of exclusion urged by those who thought, as has been said, that there were deeply rooted, in fact ineradicable, differences in the physiological structure of men and women rendering women forever unfit for the inner sanctuaries of the intellectual world.

These limitations that were the basis of exclusion from academic equality were likewise a basis for protection in the wage bargain. Reference has been made to the emphasis laid on the physical limitations of women as prospective mothers[2] in factories and workshops. *Fatigue and Efficiency*,[3] Josephine Goldmark's commercial form of Mr. Justice Brandies' brief in the Oregon Ten-Hour case,[4] contained a great volume of testimony, rather than evidence, on the subject. Now, no one would argue that a ten-hour day is not long enough for the most vigorous worker whether woman or man, and the question of the actual economy of endurance was one that was in process of being reduced to terms of scientific statement but was not so reduced during the war.

This material assembled by Miss Goldmark was, as has been said, testimony rather than evidence; but it was directed toward bases of classification of function, not bases for judgment as to essential capacity in comparable fields. Its purpose was to prevent the use by the employer of his bargaining strength to a degree dangerous to a woman worker and through her to the community.

There were, in fact, widely held two views both tending to restrict the intellectual effort of women. One rested on the conviction that there was a permanent uneradicable difference to

[1] Sir Lewis Amherst Selby-Bigge, *The Board of Education* (London and New York: G. P. Putnam's Sons, Ltd., 1927), p. 106. Sir Arthur Newsholme, *The Ministry of Health* (London and New York: G. P. Putnam's Sons, Ltd., 1925) p. 88.

[2] *Recent Social Trends in the United States*, Chap. XIV.

[3] Published in 1913 by the Russell Sage Foundation.

[4] *Muller* v. *Oregon*, 208 U. S. 412 (1908).

the intellectual disadvantage of the woman; the other pointed out the peril of study to the individual girl student without reference to the effect of study on the youth of the other sex. The latter view, namely, that study was dangerous for the girl, was to a degree defensive and protective, and determined to a considerable degree the type of physical education provided by schools and colleges for girls, in order that the "distortions" of the spine and other maladies thought to be the unavoidable result of study might be cured,[1] and yielded before the end of the nineteenth century to the view that ill-health need not result from study, so that physical education took on a preventive aspect. The purpose of prevention in physical education gave way, likewise, before 1900, to the view that the physical education of girls should have in mind the functional training of the body, which, it was believed, would not only result in the general well-being of the body but carry over into everyday living in poise and self-control. Since 1910, however, an even broader theory has prevailed, to the effect that physical education is a branch of general education, that should concern itself not only with physical gain but with opportunities for the mental, moral, and social development of the student. It is under the influence of this principle that the physical education curricula of the women's colleges today are so largely shaped.

Attention may perhaps be called to the fact that, in the case of girls as well as boys, there has been a marked tendency to give increased attention to sports. In 1923, 200 leaders in physical activities for girls met in Washington and formed the Woman's Division of the National Amateur Athletic Federation.[2] Resolutions were then drawn up expressing what the leaders believed most necessary in athletics for girls.

As a result of the interest manifesting itself in part by the conference, it may be said that training teachers for physical education has been accepted as a part of the responsibility of the colleges and universities as well as of the normal schools and teachers colleges. In addition to these courses for prospective teachers much research is going on both in the United States and in Europe, which has to do with the effect of uninterrupted exercise upon the menstrual period and upon the reproductive

[1] Dorothy Sears Ainsworth, *History of Physical Education in Colleges for Women* (New York: A. S. Barnes and Co., 1930), p. 102.

[2] Woody, *op. cit.*, II, 130–32.

capacity of women. Some of the results seem available and the achievements of women in the field of sport and athletics bear out the conclusions of the laboratory and the gymnasium.[1]

It is, then, not simply a matter of the exceptional athletic achievement; there is the great organization for recreation in which women play their part, in which girls with boys are given the opportunity to develop themselves after the classical pattern of "sound minds in sound bodies," and there is the attempt to put this service on a truly scientific basis.

A few of the findings now tentatively, at least, held by students of the problem of their proper physiological treatment may be briefly stated. They are to the effect, for example, that there are wide differences among women in the adjustments they make from the point of view of circulation as the result of standing, and the *very best trained women make perfect adjustments*.[2] On the subject of weight carrying and the degree of energy that may be developed, undoubtedly interesting material will come from the observations that are being carried on in the Russian factories, but equally interesting observations are being made in the gymnasiums of the American colleges and universities and in the European play fields and festivals where the effect of exercise on the condition of the unmarried girl and the effect of exercise on the child bearing and child caring capacity of expectant and nursing mothers is being noted with an ever increasing basis for sound council in individual cases and an ever widening body of evidence that, given reasonably normal health, increased power of control on the muscles means better health, greater joy in mere physical existence, a greater range of satisfactions and at least equal ability to bear and to rear healthy children. None of these experiences of normal physical existence need be regarded as a handicap in the field of industry, of athletic enjoyment or of intellectual effort.

During the war millions of women carried on every kind of labor; in the Russian and Turkish[3] armies women's battalions

[1] *Physical Education in American Colleges and Universities*, U. S. Bureau of Education, Bulletin No. 14 (1927). On the subject of Causes of Lost Time in Factory Work, see above, p. 162.

[2] *American Journal of Physiology*, 81; 197–214 (1927), 87; 3, 667 (1929), 94; 507 (1930). *Damez elat Journal A.M.A.* 86: 1420–22; 5/8/26. Gound, *Research Quarterly of the A.P.E.A.* I, No. 4, p. 36. *Okeenewa Arbeits Physiologie* 2: 6: 363, 434 (1930).

[3] Note the career of Halide' Edib.

took their places in the trenches, or women took their part with the men at the front as the Chinese women are doing today. In the field of athletics or of sport, where the conditions of competition are fair, they gradually make their way, not only in competition with their own sex but in open competition with men. One has only to name them: Gertrude Ederle, the first to swim the English Channel; Mary Bell, a fourteen-year-old girl who swam the Niagara, August 10, 1931; Ruth Nichols; Amy Johnson, Alys McKay Bright, the aviator and deep sea diver; Flora E. Hollister, who made a 400 foot ocean descent (Bermuda); Mary Bradley who explores African jungles with her husband, taking her daughter along; Elizabeth Steen, Ph.D., who explored in Brazil; Eleanor Holgate Lattmore, who made a forty-day trip from Siberia to Chinese Turkestan; Annie S. Peck, who took an 1,800 feet high airplane trip to view the Andes she had explored; Anita Grew,[1] who swam first the breadth and then the length of the Bosphorus—these are a few of those whose exploits are part of the commonplace of the daily press. They are hardly news any more, but the words of the President spoken June 21st, 1932, as he pinned the Medal of the National Geographic Society on Amelia Earhart after her solo flight across the Atlantic, may well be quoted here:

Her success has not been won by the selfish pursuit of a purely personal ambition, but as part of a career generously animated by a wish to help others to share in the rich opportunities of life, and by a wish also to enlarge those opportunities by expanding the powers of women, as well as men, to their everwidening limits.

Mrs. Putnam has made all mankind her debtor by her demonstration of new possibilities of the human spirit and the human will in overcoming the barriers of space and the restrictions of nature on the radius of human activity.[2]

The organization for physical education is, therefore, one of the interesting educational developments of the century, opening up another field for professional opportunity and preparing the way for achievement on the part of women in the field of sport and athletics.

In connection with these achievements the emancipation of women from social restraints should also be noted. It is difficult to recall the list of those indulgences which were entirely proper

---

[1] She was the daughter of the United States Ambassador to Turkey, later transferred to Japan.

[2] *New York Times*, June 22, 1932, p. 3, col. 1.

and respectable for men but forbidden by social condemnation to women.

In the earlier, more primitive conditions of life, old women of certain types might take snuff or smoke the corn-cob pipe, but the cigar and cigarette were taboo. Even in prison, the taboo prevailed. The feminist journal, *Equal Rights*,[1] announced in January, 1931, that the women had at last secured equality in prison so that the convicts in the Auburn Prison for women had received permission to smoke in their cells. The consumption of malt and alcoholic beverages, the wearing of comfortable clothing, and above all, companionship with men in the absence of other women, all these were without the range not so much of elegant as of respectable conduct.

II. WOMEN IN COLLEGES AND UNIVERSITIES

It remains to speak briefly of women on college and university faculties and in research. Again it may be recalled that women have steadily increased in numbers in the student bodies of these institutions and among those taking the highest degrees. It is estimated by the Office of Education that 1,170 degrees were conferred between 1926 and 1930, on women. In 1930, for example, of 2,624 degrees of Doctor of Philosophy granted, 332 were to women candidates.

The question of the Doctorate is of great interest in the field of Education and as a factor in securing opportunities for research. It should be recalled that the degree is never given as an honorary degree, but implies at least three years of graduate work including the preparation of a dissertation which makes a contribution to the field of knowledge. Fortunately there is available an able study of 1,025 women[2] who have taken degrees from thirty-nine institutions since 1877 through 1924, in forty-eight different fields of study. They were distributed in general among the great divisions of learning as follows: 313 were in Language, Literature, and the other Arts; 371 in Natural Science and Mathematics; 341 in Social Science; 597 were in teaching; 110 in administrative and executive work; 81 in research; 77 were in miscellaneous positions, and 160 were not gainfully employed.

[1] *Equal Rights*, January, 1931.
[2] Emilie J. Hutchinson, *Women and the Ph.D.*, Bulletin No. 2 of the Institute of Women's Professional Relations. Published by the North Carolina College for Women.

Research opportunities were more frequent in the field of the Natural Sciences; three-fourths of those in research were in the sciences, and 15 per cent of those who took degrees in that field were in research. The proportion of others was negligible. Of 597 women engaged in educational work, over five-sixths were in colleges and universities—those of professional ranks chiefly in colleges rather than in the university. The reverse was true of those of lower rank.

The earnings ranged from $750 to $15,000 with the median at $2,732. Nearly 80 per cent of these scholars earned between $1,750 and $3,750. That the Ph.D. has a definite economic value is evidenced by a comparison of earnings before and after receiving the degree, an increase being generally shown. This has been shown to be true of other groups of university women.[1]

Holders of the Ph.D. in the majority of cases (over 70 per cent) held more than one graduate degree.[2] The Ph.D. degree was regarded as more necessary in the teaching profession than in any other, and more necessary for teaching in colleges and universities than in secondary schools. Only rarely was the financial cost of the degree easily met; scholarships or fellowships were held by nearly 70 per cent during their graduate work, but these stipends were not sufficient to cover expenses. In general it had been necessary for the graduate student to earn part of the money for tuition and living expenses; occasionally the money was borrowed. After studying the experience of these women one soon recognizes that the Ph.D. is not won by scholarship alone; in most cases a very steadfast courage seems to be the first requisite. Not only were these women as a rule self-supporting, but they were frequently responsible in some measure for the support of others. Of the 485 who answered the question on dependents, 337, or more than two-thirds, had had dependents either during or after their graduate work; while an undeniably heroic 25 per cent of these had been entirely responsible for the support of others at some time during their careers.

The capacity of women to carry work of high intellectual grade without injury to their health had already been demonstrated.

[1] Chase Going Woodhouse, "The Occupations of Members of the American Association of University Women," *Journal of the American Association of University Women*, June, 1928, pp. 121, 122.

[2] Hutchinson, *op. cit.*, p. 14.

The great land-grant colleges of the middle west, which were becoming true universities, had opened their doors to women; and the establishment of the University of Chicago in 1893, where, in accordance with the suggestion of the founder, equal rights for men and women students rested upon provisions in the charter, had made inevitable the opening up of graduate and research facilities to women on the part of the privately endowed universities of the East. The problem of education for women assumed then new aspects and the interest of organizations concerned with it turned to questions of content of curriculum and of provision of resources enabling competent women scholars to continue their work beyond the baccalaureat degree. The interest of the Association of Collegiate Alumnae, now the American Association of University Women, for example, was directed to the establishment of fellowships making possible for women advanced work both in the United States and in European institutions.[1]

During this decade questions arose as to the place in the educational system of preparation for domestic administration so that courses and departments in home economics, domestic science or household administration were developed in the land-grant colleges with agricultural and mechanical arts; and the gradual transfer of the emphasis in the field of domestic science from the arts of cooking and sewing to the facts of consumption and to problems in the scientific basis of the domestic arts is a marked feature of the period. The women's colleges were slow to yield to this influence, but the establishment at Vassar in 1924–1925 of an Institute of Euthenics under a name suggested[2] in the early nineties is evidence of a constantly widening influence of the principle that women students should be prepared for their lives as women as well as for the lives they share with men.

Together with the question of university and college instruction was presented the problem of industrial and trade education for girls. During this period, in the home as in public organization and in business, the idea of cost accounting and of planned expenditure, i.e., reliance on the budget, was receiving attention in connection not only with the Cost of Living studies among wage-earning and dependent families, but among those students who hoped that an art of consumption might be developed.

---

[1] Talbot and Rosenberry, op. cit., Chap. XI, p. 156.
[2] By Mrs. Ellen H. Richards. Talbot and Rosenberry, op. cit., p. 177.

That certain household processes would be retained for considerable portions of time was anticipated, but data were being assembled with reference to the over-worked[1] as well as of the under-occupied housewife and questions of self-determining relationships between individual housewives and the productive agencies developing to supply food ready to eat were being studied.[2] In general it might be said that Cost of Living studies and studies in efficient domestic management were being made from at least two points of view: first, there was the purpose of discovering the distribution of low incomes among the various demands of life in order that something of a pattern for a minimum wage might be framed;[3] and second, the drafting of a standard budget[4] for the use of charitable agencies.

Stress was also being laid on the possibility of developing an art of selection and use, a true art of consumption, and for the earlier idea of thrift as synonymous with postponed consumption was being substituted the idea of wise and careful use and fuller satisfaction.[5]

But these subjects were occupying relatively few of the students in the graduate schools of the universities, and the question was, What was the opportunity for those whose work lay in the older fields of the physical, the biological, or social sciences, or the humanities?

Women were taking advanced degrees, the Master's degree in considerable numbers, the degree of Doctor of Philosophy in smaller but increasing numbers.[6] The men who took degrees went in considerable numbers on to the faculties of the colleges and universities. The women could, it is true, only in relatively small

[1] Abraham Myerson, M.D., *The Nervous Housewife* (Boston: Little, Brown and Co., 1920).

[2] The idea of the National Kitchen.

[3] An illustrative list would include the British Board of Trade Cost of Living Studies, the Studies of the Immigration Commission, the Studies of the U. S. Bureau of Labor including the Woman and Child Wage Earners, and the labor Studies on the basis of which wage adjustments were made during and after the war.

[4] Nesbitt, *The Chicago Standard Budget*. First published as an Appendix to Amelia Sears, *The Charity Visitor*, Chicago School of Civics and Philanthropy (1913); later as a separate pamphlet.

[5] The Thrift Budgets issued by the Treasury Department during the War are interesting.

[6] Woody, *op. cit.*, II, 337. In 1900–1901 the degree of Ph.D. was granted on examination by 42 institutions to 312 men and 31 women, the M.A. degree to 1,106 men and 295 women; in 1909–1910, the Ph.D. was conferred on 362 men and 44 women, the M.A. on 1,172 men and 465 women, and the M.S. on 278 men

numbers avail themselves of those opportunities. But, as the Census shows and as other evidence confirms, they are reaching higher ranks in greater numbers. This is true of women in many countries. The opportunities do not correspond to evidence of capacity, but there is evident gain.[1] The International Federation of University Women, at the meeting of their Council in Edinburgh in July, 1932, through their Committee for award of international fellowships, made available figures bearing on the same question. Their report on the Position of Women on the Teaching Staffs of Universities gives data with reference to the relative numbers and percentages of men and women students in the universities, of men and women professors and of men and women lecturers in twenty-four countries.[2]

The percentage which women constitute of the student body varies from 7.72 in Greece (Athens) to 28.67 in Rumania, 30.84 per cent in Ireland, 33.10 per cent in Estoria, to 34.82 in Finland. These high percentages are of course not found identified with the greatest numbers, for these countries are among the small nationalities. In Germany the number of women is 12,884 but the percentage only 16.66; in Great Britain the number is 13,686, the percentage 26.95 of the whole; in France the number is 15,184, the percentage of total students 21.34. The figures for women on the faculty are very different. In nine countries[3] there are no women professors. In Great Britain there were 13, in Italy 11, in South Africa 9, in Ireland 8, in Canada and France 7 each. But these countries constituted 1.54 per cent; in Italy, .73; in South Africa, 3.84; in Ireland, 3.97; in Canada, .85; in France, .63. In

and 39 women. In 1919–1920, the Ph.D. was conferred on 439 men and 93 women, the M.A. on 1,650 men and 1,180 women, the M.S. on 585 men and 103 women. In 1930, 74 colleges and universities reported 1,692 Ph.D. degrees to men and 332 to women.

[1] *Bulletin of the American Association of University Professors*, VII (October, 1921), No. 6. Committee W. on the Status of Women, Professor A. Caswell Ellis, Chairman. See *Recent Social Trends in the United States*, Chap. XIV. The question of rank should be discussed with the subject of salary scale, but it has seemed better to present the figures relating to academic salaries with the figures of other salary scales in presenting the problem of the unequal pay of men and women, even when standards of achievement are identical.

[2] Australia, Belgium, Bulgaria, Canada, Denmark, Estoria, Finland, France, England, Germany, Greece (Athens), Holland, Ireland, Italy, Jugoslavia, Latvia, Lithuania, Luxembourg, New Zealand, Norway, Rumania, South Africa, Sweden, Switzerland.

[3] Austria, Denmark, Estoria, Greece (Athens), Jugoslavia, Latvia, Lithuania, Luxembourg, Sweden.

regard to the lecturers, the figures are more favorable; there the numbers rose to 227 for Italy and 585 for Great Britain. These were 3.50 per cent of the total for Italy and 15.86 for Great Britain. On the other hand, the variety of subjects taught shows that in all countries women are following their intellectual curiosity and some are finding the opportunity to demonstrate their capacity. One thousand three hundred and twenty-two were accounted for teaching in thirty-three fields of learning.[1] The numbers ranged from one in Aeronautics in Great Britain and one each in Theology and Comparative Religion in Switzerland and in Veterinary Science in Austria, to 155 in Medicine in every country listed except Estoria and Lithuania, and 192 in Biology in 26 of the 33 countries. Seventy-five of these were in Great Britain and 45 in Italy. There were 63 teaching Mathematics, of whom 29 were in Great Britain, 21 in Italy, 3 in Austria, 2 each in Canada, Germany and South Africa and one each in Ireland, Norway, Rumania, and Switzerland.[2] The variety in subject matter and in the jurisdiction adds new evidence of women's capacity for higher fields of intellectual opportunity, and of an actual if meager success in making use of their scientific equipment.

But attention should be directed to other aspects of the professional status of women. The striking features of the educational world are the substantial monopoly by women of elementary and secondary classroom instruction and the substantial monopoly of the collegiate and university field of instruction and of the administrative field by men; in the other profession in which there are large numbers of women (228, 737, from Table 32)—trained nursing—there is an actual monopoly of women. Among 1,000 trained nurses in 1930, only 19 were men. And more women relatively are going into nursing, as out of 1,000

[1] Aeronautics, Agriculture, Anthropology, Architecture, Art and Archaeology, Astronomy, Commerce, Domestic Economy, Economics and Social and Political Science, Education, Engineering, Geography and Meteorology, Geology, History, Indology, Law, Librarianship, Literature, Mathematics, Medicine, (Pharmacy, Hygiene, Dentistry, Surgery, etc.), Music, Philology (including Classical and Modern Languages), Philosophy, Phonetics, Physical Culture, Physics, Physiology, Psychology, Theology and Comparative Religion, Veterinary Science.

[2] The comment of the Committee on these figures is, "It is obvious that the number of women professors is very low in comparison with the number of women university students. There is therefore urgent need to increase the opportunities which will give highly qualified women the means of fitting themselves for the higher university posts. This aim has always been before the Committee."

professional women in 1930, 189 were nurses where only 141 had entered that profession in 1920. These figures are interesting in view of the decline in the number of midwives and of nurses not trained, as shown in Table 10, and suggest that women seek where possible the job resting on principles of reasonable equipment; and it is not far fetched to suggest that the figures with reference to "healers," of whom in 1930 there were 7,866 as compared with 7,902 in 1920, and "chiropractors" of whom there are 9,203 in 1930, suggest a new category in the semi-professional group. Interesting questions suggest themselves in connection with these bare statistical data of women and professional employment. The community, through its organization for medical instruction, puts obstacles in the way of women entering the medical profession,[1] and they crowd into the profession related to the care of the sick and also seek irregular and unorthodox opportunities. In the ministry, the educational path is not very smooth, so far as many professional schools are concerned, but Madame Blavatsky's Theosophic successor, in the person of Miss Tingley, Mary Baker Eddy, and Aimee McPherson Hutton, span the decades with which this study is concerned by an archway of religious appeal to which literally tens of thousands of individuals respond. No one perhaps can say what the precipitate will be, or where that margin, to which reference has been made, determined by capacity to meet community needs, will be found.

There are still other occupations of which notice should be taken. There is, for example, an absolute increase but a relative decline in the number of actors and showmen. There is a real decline in the group of artists and teachers of art (see Table 33), and of musicians and teachers of music, but an increase in the number of authors, editors and reporters. The designers and draftsmen are relatively more numerous in 1930 than in 1920, and there was a marked increase in the number of photographers. As for the so-called learned professions, their doors are still only partly ajar. Women doctors are decreasing both in comparison with the number of men or with the whole number of professional women; for, while in 1910 and 1920, 59 out of 1,000 physicians were women, in 1930 only 52 are women, and where in 1910, 12 in 1,000 professional women were doctors, in 1930 only 5 in 1,000 women had undertaken the practice of that great profession. The lawyers increased as compared with the total group between

[1] *Recent Social Trends in the United States*, Chap. XIV.

1910 and 1920, and stayed at 2 only among 1,000 professional women; but as compared with the total number of lawyers women increased from 5 to 21 in 1,000. Attention will be called at a later point to the recognition women are receiving in the appointment or election to judgeships, though in general the professional path trod by them is a rough and often not an ascending path.

There are a few other straws showing perhaps the direction of the wind. In 1920, social and welfare workers were included in the "semi-professional" group of "religious, charity and welfare workers." Now they are separated out and 24,592 women with 6,649 men constitute a new item in the professional list, a new profession in which women find an opportunity and constitute 78.7 per cent of the total number of practitioners.

Librarianship has been and remains largely a woman's profession. In 1920, women were 88.4 per cent of the total; in 1930 they were 91.3 per cent. And there is a slight increase in the number as compared with the whole group of professional women, for in 1920, 13 in 1,000 were librarians; in 1930, there were 17. In both of these professions interesting questions of education and training are occupying the minds both of members of the profession and of university educationists. How the experimental educational programs that are being undertaken will develop can only be known in the future.

Attention may be likewise at this point directed to the Census category, *Public Service not Other Wise Classified*, in which are found two important occupations for women new within the present century, which will undoubtedly, like the nurses and the social workers, be brought up to professional status, namely, probation officers and policewomen. These are occupations in which women are becoming more important. The occupation of probation officer is, of course, a relatively new one and is generally classed with that of social worker. In 1910, as the following figures show, most of the persons enumerated as probation and truant officers were men; by 1930, not only had the actual number of all probation officers greatly increased, but a much larger proportion of them were women. Women police officers were not enumerated in 1910; in 1930, however, the Census reports that nearly 1,000 women were police officers.

The introduction of women into the police system could be discussed below in connection with the general subject of women's relation to the state. They represent, however, rather an effort to assume on a wider platform specific domestic duties of a protective character than is suggested by their association with a division of the municipal administration generally regarded as the embodiment of the community's ultimate force. That "all police officers, men as well as women, should regard themselves as protectors not of the law but of the children, boys and girls who go about unattended in public places" was the injunction phrased in these rhythmic terms by a chief of police some years ago;[1] but this admonition is more honored in the breach than in the observance, and the desirability of diluting the old respect

TABLE 35.—NUMBER OF PROBATION AND TRUANT OFFICERS AND PER CENT WOMEN, 1910–1930

	Total	Women	Per cent women
1910	1,043	188	18.0
1920	2,679	780	29.1
1930	4,270	1,555	36.4

TABLE 36.—NUMBER POLICE OFFICERS AND PER CENT WOMEN 1910–1930

	Total	Women	Per cent women
1910	61,980		
1920	82,120	236	.3
1930	131,687	849	.6

for force with a new protective interest is more or less widely recognized. The two occupations represent the two extremes of the criminal law enforcement procedure, as the policeman appears at the beginning and the probation officer at the end of the series of acts growing out of an actual, or an alleged, or a threatened violation of the law.

The use of women in connection with the custody of women accused or found guilty of crime, as early as 1845, took the form first of police matrons in jails and police stations, when the American Female Reform Association of New York City secured the appointment of six prison matrons. By 1900 the propriety of this measure was widely recognized so that all the principal cities had installed matrons, and two states, Massachusetts and New

[1] Chief George W. Shippy. Commissioner of Police in Chicago, April 13, 1907 to August 15, 1909.

York, had enacted legislation requiring cities of 20,000 or more to appoint them.

With the experiences of the great fairs the need for something on a public scale like the old chaperonage became obvious. In Portland in 1905, at the time of the Lewis and Clark Exposition, the representative of the Travelers' Aid Society[1] was given power of this kind in order to carry on protective work for women and girls. After the exposition had ended she was placed in charge of a new department of Public Safety for the Protection of Young Girls and Women, which was made a part of the police administration. The members of the staff were, however, reluctant to become known as "police officers" and remained outside the police circle.

The first woman, then, to be known as a policewoman was Mrs. Alice Stebbins Wells, who became a member of the Los Angeles Police Department in September, 1910. The importance of this new approach to the problem of protection of women and girls was immediately recognized, and, by 1915, sixteen cities had appointed women officers to their police departments. By the time of the meeting of the National Conference of Social Work in 1915 (Baltimore) their number seemed to justify the organization of an Association.[2] They were given different titles and responsibilities,[3] but all were a part of the municipal police organization.

Later the number of cities employing women police increased. In 1924, the International Association of Policewomen estimated on the basis of questionnaires sent to the cities of the country that of 268 cities from which information was obtained, 58 employed none, 71 employed both matrons and women police, 52 employed women police, 65 employed matrons, and 22 employed persons who perform both kinds of duties.[4] For a later date, January, 1931, a census of policewomen in the United States taken by the International Association of Policewomen listed 523 policewomen employed by 148 cities in 38 different

---

[1] Mrs. Lola Baldwin; see Chloe Owings, *Women Police*, Publication of the Bureau of Social Hygiene (New York: Frederick H. Hitchcock, 1925), pp. 29–30. Also see p. 92.

[2] The International Association of Policewomen.

[3] Dr. Owings lists, p. 105, a woman supervisor of women police in Dayton, a superintendent of a division of women police in Seattle, an inspector in Denver, and in Milford, Ohio, a chief of police who held office for two years.

[4] Owings, *op. cit.*, pp. 121, 283. Dr. Owings gives a number of facts with reference to qualifications, methods of selection, salary and general type of organization.

states. The increase of only three in the number of cities between 1924 and 1931 seems small compared with the increase between 1917 and 1924, when the number of cities lacked only one of being double what it had been before. The interest stimulated by the war organization has evidently been somewhat dimmed, and as in other lines of employment, as women have come to be recognized as a permanent factor or competitive element in the situation, the resistance on the part of the men becomes more fixed and determined. There are, however, elements of real difficulty in the differences of opinion between those in control of the police organization and those who wish to have introduced into the police practice the methods and purposes of social work.

One of the noteworthy episodes in the struggle for recognition of certain minimum standards was the adoption by the International Association of Chiefs of Police at their annual convention in 1922 of a resolution in which certain standards were proposed. This resolution set up the following requirements for policewomen appointees:[1]

Graduates from a four-year course in a standard high school or the completion of at least fourteen college entrance units of study and not less than two years' experience, recent and responsible, in social service or educational work.

Graduation from a recognized school for training nurses requiring a residence of at least two years; or

Completion of at least seven college entrance units of study or two years in a standard high school and not less than two years of responsible commercial work involving public contacts and responsibilities, tending to qualify the applicant to perform the duties, or possessing the equivalent of a college education through experience, such as secretarial work.

To what extent the members of this Association succeeded in maintaining these minimum standards in their own departments cannot be demonstrated.

[1] *Public Personnel Studies* (Bureau of Public Personnel Administration, 923 E. 60th St., Chicago, 1931), V, No. 12 (December, 1927), 249. It might be noted that the entire number of this publication was devoted to a discussion of the "Functions and Work of the Woman's Bureau of a Police Department, and Tests for the Selection of Policewomen." The Bureau of Public Personnel Administration had carried on a project looking toward the standardizing of tests that might be used as the basis for civil service examinations for candidates for the position of police-woman. Their outline of the partially standardized tests is as follows: (1) Memory for oral directions; (2) laws, ordinances, rules and procedure; (3) police situations; (4) ability to understand and follow written directions; (5) social intelligence; (6) education and employment record; (7) personal traits; (8) physical condition.

PROFESSIONAL AND NEAR-PROFESSIONAL

The standards proposed by the police chiefs are recognized as being too low for the performance of skilled protective work. To do that kind of work the policewoman "needs," in the words of another student of the problem,[1]

to be a mature woman with the education of a university and the professional education of a good school of social work. She needs courses in family case-work, child welfare, public welfare administration and the discipline of statistics and economics as well as courses in criminal law, criminology, and theory and practice in the narrower field of social hygiene and protective work.

With reference to the use of women probation officers, notice must be especially taken of the effect of federal action at the time of entering the Great War. As in the case of the demand for the so-called equal wage for equal work, the demand for general recognition of the fundamental dignity, both of men and women, met an unexpected response in the statements of the War and Navy Departments, especially the War Department in 1917. The stage had been prepared by the experiences on the Mexican border in 1916,[2] which were graphically described in the American press, and in the prior publication by the Bureau of Social Hygiene of Abram Flexner's epoch-making discussion of *Prostitution in Europe.*

Notice must be taken first of the doctrine of "male necessity" under which prostitution was practiced. That this view was widely held is shown by the positiveness and vigor with which it was denied in 1917, when the United States Government undertook to adopt as a part of its military program, a new principle, partly to keep the "men" fit for service, partly to keep their mothers and fathers acquiescent under a program of conscription. "It used to be thought that the sex organs had to be used if they were to be kept healthy. This is a lie," are the words of the Commission on Training Camp Activities, endorsed by the Surgeon General.[3]

But it had been the generally accepted view, which carried its inexorable corollary that opportunity must be provided for their exercise even when marriage did not make this use natural or

[1] Edith Abbott, "Training for the Policewoman's Job," *The Woman Citizen,* April, 1926.

[2] Max Joseph Exner, "Prostitution in Its Relation to the Army on the Mexican Border," *Journal of Social Hygiene,* III (April, 1917), 205–20.

[3] Quoted conveniently in Edith Houghton Hooker, *Laws of Sex* (Boston: R. G. Badger, 1921), p. 221.

[207]

lawful. With the view of necessity for men went the attitude that the slightest extra-marital experience was fatal to the value of the woman, so that women were inevitably divided into two groups, one made up of those who had value, the respectable and "good," and those who had their uses but were disreputable, or "bad." The "good" could not even know of the "bad," upon whom the safety of their homes depended.[1] A woman who, however involuntarily, had had certain experiences outside the marriage bond was thereby damaged beyond restoration. She was less than fully woman in her claim to protection under the law.

Then came the episode on the Mexican border when the American military force was sent down and when flagrant opportunity for sex indulgence by the men was provided. The publication of the conditions existing there in the summer of 1916 brought home to many a realization of dangers more terrifying to American fathers and mothers than the loss of their sons' lives in patriotic sacrifice. And then the World War! The government then speedily announced that "alcohol and prostitution which had heretofore been regarded or largely tacitly recognized as necessary evils in connection with army life were no longer to be tolerated,"[2] and there were set up two Commissions on Training Camp Activities which secured the cooperation of law-enforcement groups and the protective groups so that the well-being of the men was made a matter of responsible concern of a Law Enforcement Division and of a Committee on Protective Work for Girls. The program of the Protective Committee

---

[1] See A. Maude Royden, *Women and the Sovereign State*, Chap. III, "The State and Prostitution" (London: Headley Bros., 1917).

[2] The account of this episode can be found in an article by Walter Clarke, First Lieutenant, Sanitary Corps, U.S.N.A., "The Promotion of Social Hygiene in War Time," *Annals of the American Academy*, Vol. 79, 168, p. 178. See also the Selective Service Law, 1917, *U. S. Statutes at Large*, 40, chap. 15, secs. 12–13; the Interdepartmental Social Hygiene Board Act, 7–8–18, *U. S. Statutes at Large*, 40, chap. 153, p. 886; *Annals of the American Academy of Political and Social Science*, LXXIX, p. 30, Fosdick, "War and Navy Departments Commissions on Training Camp Activities"; *ibid.*, p. 143, Anderson, "Making the Camps Safe for the Army"; *ibid.*, p. 152, Additon, "Work among Delinquent Women and Girls"; *ibid.*, p. 160, Mrs. Falconer, "The Segregation of Delinquent Women and Girls as a War Problem"; *National Conference of Social Work*, 1918, p. 656, Maude E. Miner, "Protective Work for Girls in War Time"; *ibid.*, p. 666, Tippen, "Specific Problems in Camp Communities"; *ibid.*, Miner, "The Police Woman and the Girl Problem"; *ibid.*, p. 212, Pierce, "The Federal Campaign v. Venereal Disease"; Owings, *op. cit.*, chap. vii.

included patrol work, protective bureaus, proper detention facilities, women probation officers, needed new legislation, new provision for correctional treatment for women and girls, and additional activity along educational lines. This program called for services like those of the public chaperon and considerable numbers of women were added to the group. It must be kept in mind that many of these women might be described as social workers. They were of higher occupational type than the usual policeman or than earlier police matrons. It must also be kept in mind, however, that protective work had not been put on as sound a professional basis as family welfare work; that, fundamentally, the interest in the girl was still secondary; and that the true object of the organization was to keep the men fit and to make their parents satisfied under a conscription policy for which they had been wholly unprepared.

Since then the developments have been, from 1900 and the years at the close of the old century to the present, in the following directions, among others:

1. Toward the dissolution of traditional secrecy and mystery on the subject of prostitution, and the inauguration of investigation, study, and frank discussion of the physical, social and economic problems in that field.

2. Toward the elimination of white slavery practices and of international and interstate commerce in women and girls, with no apparent lessening in pressure on that score up to the present time.

3. Toward the provision of ample protection for minors, through the passage of statutes designed to serve that purpose and the creation and development of effective machinery for the application of those statutes, and through the establishment of agencies whose purpose was to safeguard youth. Primary among these agencies was the policewoman's unit for the supervision and patrol of places frequented by young people, and the constructive handling of individual cases.

These programs contemplate the use of women police and of the probation officer. They also contemplate the establishment of specialized tribunals, or morals courts, and they include specialized treatment for women and girls for whom protracted detention seems indicated. Law enforcement involves not only problems in detention in anticipation of trial and in evidence of guilt or innocence, but in commitment after trial as well.

The vice commissions which were set up in many cities during the first years of the century included in their reports accounts of the conditions under which women were detained in city and county jails and pointed out the degrading and demoralizing conditions obtaining in many of the police and municipal courts where women and girls accused of offenses under the vice laws and ordinances were brought to trial. They recommended among other things the establishment of separate specialized courts in which should be heard all cases involving the so-called moral charges. These specialized "morals courts" were to be created with a view to improving the actual physical and psychological conditions in which such cases were heard, and for the purpose of bringing about more careful study and treatment of the offenders, to the end that as many as possible might be reclaimed for legitimate occupations and socially acceptable modes of life.

Such specialized courts were established, and are still functioning, in several of the metropolitan areas in the United States, where the volume of cases is sufficient to make the maintenance of a legal agency of this general character feasible. They are branches of inferior criminal courts. Due to the multiplicity of laws and ordinances dealing with sex delinquencies, the jurisdiction of these courts becomes too complicated for discussion within the bounds of a few paragraphs. Some sex delinquencies are felonies, some are misdemeanors, and some are classed as "offenses" or "quasi-criminal actions" under city ordinances. In some cities all persons charged may demand jury trial. Experienced offenders, with court-wise legal counsel, take advantage of that right to escape the jurisdiction of the specialized court whose judge usually remains long enough in contact with these problems to become conscious of the need for effective action to curtail rather than to license the business of commercialized prostitution and of the possibility of taking action toward that end. These are some of the factors that so scatter the hearing of sex delinquency cases as to make these courts often more specialized in theory and name than in actual practice. Some of the specialized courts are limited to the trial of women defendants. This is true of Chicago's and New York's courts, which are designated as "Women's Courts."

Stated in brief, the primary purposes of the specialized, or perhaps more aptly termed socialized, court are: to remove hearings on sex offenses from the general police or municipal court room with its mixed crowds of curious onlookers; to provide a place and personnel of such character as to assure all persons charged with these offenses of a fair and full hearing, and the community of an intelligent safeguarding of its interests in the process of determining which persons have been rightfully accused of acts destructive of social well-being; and to put an end to the system under which "treatment" of the offender consisted either of a fine, which constituted a license to carry on, or of penal commitment, which represented the now vanishing vindictive attitude of society—substituting for those penalties the facilities for studying each individual case and for applying in each instance the type of constructive correctional treatment that would insure to the individual an opportunity to return to good standing in a community anxious to reclaim as many hitherto lost productive units as possible.

To carry out such a program with even a moderate degree of success calls for personnel of a high order. To assist the judge in making the kind of disposition of cases consistent with the aims of the specialized court, there should be a staff including, in addition to the usual bailiffs and court attendants and clerks, physicians and psychiatrists to conduct physical and mental examinations of the individuals to be treated; social workers to discover and report on the complete social history; and probation officers to supervise carefully the offender's return to social standing and to carry out any suggestions for social or medical treatment that may have been recommended by the examining experts. For cases in which probation is not advised the court has need of commitment facilities of a reformatory character sufficient to meet the needs in a reasonably effective manner.

The movement to provide such institutions has had a slow growth in the United States. Prior to 1869 there had been provided for the commitment of women, no facilities other than state prisons for women convicted of felonies, and city or county jails and houses of correction for women found guilty of misdemeanors. In 1869 Indiana took steps to establish a separate prison for women, thus taking the lead in recognizing the need for a distinction between the problems which confront a state in the matter of handling its delinquent men and its women offenders. Although this institution was more prison than reformatory in its early years, its establishment was an important step forward. Two other states, Massachusetts and New York, made similar provision for the separate treatment of women before the opening of the new century, and Iowa followed suit in the year 1900. During the first decade of the twentieth century the movement was at a standstill so far as action was concerned, though the slow process of experimentation and the arousing of interest in the possibilities inherent in such a program no doubt moved forward quietly and continuously. The following table, published in 1922, lists the institutions that had been established for the reformative treatment of the woman offender up to that year.[1]

TABLE 37.—INSTITUTIONS ESTABLISHED FOR THE REFORMATIVE TREATMENT OF THE WOMAN OFFENDER, 1869–1922[a]

Date of legal establishment	Institution	Date opened
1869...........	Indiana Woman's Prison	1873
1874...........	Massachusetts Reformatory........................	1877
1881...........	New York House of Refuge for Women (Hudson. Since 1904 the New York State Training School for Girls)	1877
1890...........	New York House of Refuge for Women (Albion)	1893
1892...........	New York State Reformatory	1901
1900...........	Iowa Women's Reformatory	1918
1910...........	New Jersey State Reformatory for Women	1913
1911...........	Ohio Reformatory for Women	1916
1913...........	Pennsylvania State Industrial Home for Women	1920
1913...........	Wisconsin Industrial Home for Women	1921
1915...........	Minnesota State Reformatory for Women	1916
1915...........	Maine State Reformatory for Women	1916
1917...........	Kansas State Industrial Farm for Women	1917
1917...........	Michigan State Training School for Women	(Not yet opened in 1922)
1917...........	Connecticut State Reformatory for Women	1918
1919...........	Washington Women's Industrial Home and Clinic	(Opened but discontinued)
1919...........	Arkansas State Farm for Women	1920
1919...........	Nebraska State Reformatory for Women	1920
1919...........	California Industrial Farm for Women	1922
1921...........	Vermont State Prison and House of Correction for Women	1921
1922...........	Rhode Island State Reformatory for Women	

[a] A federal reformatory for women offenders against federal laws was authorized in 1924, and constitutes the only important addition to institutional provision during the past decade. See p. 308 for citation and reference to the superintendent and the women members of the Board of Directors.

The essentials of an adequate institution for the care of women offenders include non-partisan management, well-qualified officials, the indeterminate sentence, adequate social records,

[1] Helen Worthington Rogers, "A Digest of Laws Establishing Reformatories for Women in the United States," *Journal of Criminal Law and Criminology,* XIII, No. 3 (November, 1922), 385.

thorough physical, mental, and psychiatric examination—freedom of transfer between the reformatory and other institutions, educational facilities, industrial training, with employment planned for the teaching of useful trades, adequate recreational facilities, a credit system, skillful parole supervision. It is assumed that the groups housed together will not be too large, that the spirit will all be hopeful and reconstructive, and that the purpose will be the speedy return of the woman to community life as a healthy, law-abiding self-supporting member.[1]

Naturally the statutes in the nineteen states in which reformatories have been established conform to an extent to requirements formulated by "exacting penologists"; but they likewise naturally fall far short of conforming to all. All of them provide educational work for the inmates, and employment as a particularly efficacious reformative agent. They provide ample acreage where open-air life is made possible. Free transfer among state institutions serving different needs has been made possible. Parole has been made a part of the system for reformation, and the indeterminate sentence for the woman offender has been recognized as desirable, although not specifically provided for in practice in many of the acts. Classification of inmates has been required in twelve instances. On the other hand, many of the institutions lack provision for the cottage system, fail to supply the facilities for physical and mental examination and treatment, rely upon deficient records, and, most important of all, fail to require the commitment of all delinquent women of all classes to these reformatories, instead of to the jails, penitentiaries and prisons.

Following a period of considerable action during 1917 and 1919 there seems to have been a distinct slowing-up in progressive accomplishment in this field, at least so far as the establishment of new institutions is concerned. However, that there is constructive work being done in these institutions is recognized by the Commission on Law Observance[2] who concur in the statements of the National Society of Penal Information[3] in which is found the following paragraph:

[1] *Ibid.*, p. 405.
[2] U. S. National Commission on Law Observance and Enforcement, No. 9, *Report on Penal Institutions, Probation and Parole* (Washington, D. C.: Government Printing Office, 1931), p. 249.
[3] Paul W. Garrett and Austin H. MacCormick, *Handbook of American Prisons and Reformatories* (New York: National Society of Penal Information, Inc. (1929)), Introduction, p. xxxii.

We concur in the statements that women's institutions are on the whole better staffed and better administered than institutions for men, that their purposes are less punitive and that they have a higher degree of success with those who experience incarceration in them. Men's institutions, we think, have much to learn from women's institutions.

This discussion justifies calling attention to the so-called semi-professional occupation described as "keeper of charitable and penal institutions." Here the number of women increased from 4,931 in 1920 to 5,552, or by 12.6 per cent in 1930, while the number of men increased from 7,953 in 1920 to 9,468, or by 17.8 per cent, in 1930. This is not a vocation in which women are increasing at the expense of men. They are, however, finding an opportunity to do socially important work, to which attention may well be directed, and are in transit from the sub-professional to the professional group.

Chapter XIII

WOMEN'S EARNINGS

ATTENTION need hardly be called to the double aspect, generally discussed, of the problem of women's wages and earnings, namely (1) that they have been and are low when measured by the demands of health, decency and comfort, and (2) that different scales of pay usually exist for so-called women's and men's jobs, and different scales often exist for individual men and women when the occupational equipment is alike and the quality and volume of work substantially identical. That wages were and are low need hardly be urged. The rates were low, the earnings low. The question is, Are they rising or falling, and are the gaps between men's wages and women's wages growing narrower or wider? A Census study of factory wages furnishes much information on the subject within the range of its data, and those data can be supplemented by the Studies of the National Industrial Conference Board.[1]

The wage rates fixed for women's work have been, and are often now, low. This refers rather to 1929 than to 1932 when many are not earning at all. Moreover, through lost time, underemployment or underemployability, while women lose possibly relatively less than men lose, there is a great and a grave difference between the nominal and the actual earnings of women.[2]

[1] While the National Industrial Conference Board (*Wages*, 1914–31, p. 17) divides men into two classes: (1) skilled and semi-skilled, and (2) common and unskilled, all women are grouped into one class, which is said, however, to be in general the skilled or semi-skilled.

[2] Paul F. Brissenden, "An Analysis of Pay-Roll Statistics," *Earnings of Factory Workers, 1899 to 1927*, Census Monograph No. X, Department of Commerce, Bureau of the Census, p. 156. See also p. 162. This was not found to be the case in 1930–1931, when women's reductions were greater than men's. National Industrial Conference Board, *Wages in the United States*, 1931, p. 24. See p. 220. Report prepared for Twelfth Census by Professor Davis R. Dewey. Figures found in *Publications of American Statistical Society*, IX, 142; U. S. Bureau of Labor Statistics Bulletin No. 175, *Summary of Report on Conditions of Woman and Child Wage Earners*, p. 22. The Chicago Vice Commission, *The Social Evil* (1911), p. 198; the Illinois Vice Commission (1913), pp. 28, 311. See *Recent Social Trends in the United States*, Chap. XIV.

Already before the beginning of the century the discrepancy between the earnings of women and girls and the recognized cost of living had been made the basis for slanderous implications that certain types of employment, *e.g.*, department store work, generally necessitated the supplementing of women's respectable earnings by disreputable conduct. These implications were vigorously rebutted,[1] and it was pointed out that the wages were rather "meager wages of righteousness" than adequate wages of sin; but the figures have only to be quoted to substantiate the statement, and the second decade brought the widespread testimony as to the relative normal earnings of those who were drawn into the toils of organized vice.

The low rates at which women worked were accounted for by their youth, their lack of technical preparation, the narrow range of their opportunity, the difficulties of organizing them to which reference has been made elsewhere, and the transient attitude resulting from the prospect of matrimony, which was supposed, since household management had not been professionalized, to introduce them to an experience of lessened effort.

The Census figures apply only to wages and earnings in manufacturing occupations which, as has been shown, are offering no greater and, as a matter of fact, probably fewer opportunities to women than at an earlier date. In the occupations for which the Census assembled data,[2] the women's nominal full time earnings, as estimated by the Census, increased steadily by decades, from $314 in 1899, to $353 in 1904, to $391 in 1909, to $430 in 1914, to $858 in 1921, and $925 in 1923. The real full time earnings likewise increased except between 1909 and 1914, when they fell from $449 to $430. The increase in the actual earnings, too, failed in the period between 1919, when the figure was $726, and 1921, when the average fell to $627. In the same period, the actual real earnings slipped twice, once between 1909 and 1914, from $390 to $344, and between 1919 and 1921, from $406 to $356. In addition to this fact of halting advance, attention should be likewise directed to the difference between the earnings of men and women. Similar failures to advance are noted, but always, as the Census puts it, there is a "wide margin" by which the earnings of women (and children) fall short of the earnings

---

[1] *Report of the U. S. Industrial Commission*, 1899, VII, 55–68.
[2] Brissenden, *op. cit.*, p. 85.

of men."[1] The extent of this disparity varies greatly in the
different industries. The Census points out,[2] for example, that
in 1919 the per capita earnings of men in the glass industry were
three times the per capita earnings of women in that industry,
i.e., $1,420 as compared with $464, whereas in the electrical
machinery, apparatus and supplies, the earnings of men, per

TABLE 38.—ESTIMATED AMOUNTS OF NOMINAL HOURLY EARNINGS, BY SELECTED
INDUSTRIES, FOR WOMEN WAGE EARNERS ONLY, CENSUS YEARS:
1899–1921[a]

	Cents per hour					
	1899	1904	1909	1914	1919	1921
All industries..........................	10.3	12.0	13.3	15.3	33.1	34.1
Bread and other bakery products...........	8.33	10.02	11.74	12.85	25.69	30.46
Confectionery............................	9.17	10.19	11.20	13.12	25.04	28.61
Mineral and soda water...................	8.04	9.05	9.56	12.17	18.32	22.36
Tobacco, cigars and cigaretts.............	10.17	11.06	11.70	13.55	23.92	24.35
Carpets and rugs, other than rag...........	11.49	12.63	14.39	15.27	37.13	46.87
Shirts...................................	10.62	11.45	12.92	14.38	28.26	31.90
Clothing, men's..........................	11.35	12.50	14.24	15.18	39.59	47.80
Clothing, women's........................	12.21	14.31	16.74	18.64	46.58	50.59
Dyeing, finishing textiles..................	10.88	11.47	12.81	14.20	31.85	35.11
Knit goods...............................	10.38	11.10	12.69	15.35	30.37	34.13
Silk goods...............................	11.81	12.72	14.60	15.03	37.68	40.99
Boots and shoes, not including rubber boots and shoes.............................	13.81	15.90	17.44	19.80	40.04	45.05
Printing and publishing, book and job.......	11.88	14.05	16.49	18.85	31.34	42.47
Printing and publishing, newspapers and periodicals............................	11.17	13.30	14.84	16.96	26.45	36.31
Glass....................................	7.93	9.41	9.29	11.05	20.72	23.03
Electrical machinery, apparatus and supplies	11.16	12.55	13.66	15.40	30.28	33.15

[a] Brissenden, *op. cit.*, p. 125.

capita, were not quite twice those of women, $1,007 as compared
with $545; and in cotton the women earned $816 to the men's
$1,043. Evidently there are questions of relative degrees of skill,
as well as differences of sex; but lack of opportunity to acquire
skill is a "function of difference of sex," as the mathematicians
might say.

It is not possible here to state all the reservations and cautions
with which the Census presents the figures; what the author is
willing to have the reader understand is that there was a pre-war

[1] *Ibid.*, p. 83.
[2] *Ibid.*, p. 111.

[217]

period of low earnings when, as he puts it, the "style for averages for men's earnings was between $500 and $600, and of women's earnings from 60 to 75 per cent of that amount; and a later period of higher earnings, when there could hardly be said to have been a style, because of the great variation among industries; but if there was any, it would have been between about $1,000 and $1,300. And always, however the estimates were made, or whatever the unit, the women's wages or earnings are lower than those of men.[1]

TABLE 39.—SUMMARY OF ESTIMATED AMOUNTS OF EARNINGS, PER CAPITA, IN THE UNITED STATES, ALL INDUSTRIES COMBINED, BY SEX AND AGE GROUPS, CENSUS YEARS; 1899–1923[a]

Sex, age group, and type of per capita earnings	1899	1904	1909	1914	1919	1921	1923
All groups:							
Full-time earnings:							
Nominal....................	$525	$590	$643	$719	$1,433	$1,462	$1,548
Real.......................	710	711	739	719	801	831	927
Actual earnings:							
Nominal....................	446	483	557	576	1,212	1,047	1,401
Real.......................	603	582	640	576	677	595	839
Women:							
Full time earnings:							
Nominal....................	314	353	391	430	858	875	925
Real.......................	424	425	449	430	479	497	547
Actual earnings:							
Nominal....................	267	289	339	344	726	627	837
Real.......................	361	348	390	344	406	356	495

[a] Brissenden, op. cit., p. 85.

The differences between the earlier and the later period are much more marked in the hourly rates, as shown in Table 38, in which there were increases, than in annual earnings, on which seasonal employment or unemployment laid its devastating hands. For the normal hourly earnings in selected industries, the increases ran from 10.3 cents for all industries in 1899 to 34.1 in 1921. The highest rate in 1899 was the rate 13.81 cents for boots and shoes. The lowest, for 1921, was 22.36 in minerals and soda waters, while the highest was 50.59 in women's clothing.

When the question of purchasing capacity is asked, the progress is not quite so smooth. This can be seen in Tables 39 and 40.

[1] Ibid., pp. 117, 123.

That is, there are increases in 1919 and 1921 and 1923 as compared with 1899, but there remain great differences between the real earnings of men and of women, and wide divergences in these differences; so that the influence of other factors must be kept in mind if the shifting occupational position of women is to be eventually understood. Factors of sex operate in an atmosphere likewise affected by activities of racial loyalty and prejudice[1] and of competition among and between national groups.

TABLE 40.—PURCHASING POWER (AT 1914 PRICES) OF ACTUAL AND FULL-TIME EARNINGS, PER CAPITA, IN THE UNITED STATES, ALL INDUSTRIES COMBINED, BY SEX AND AGE GROUPS, CENSUS YEARS: 1899–1923[a]

Year and type of annual earnings	All wage earners	Men	Women	Children
1899—full-time earnings	$710	$ 793	$429	$242
Actual earnings	603	673	361	205
1904—full-time earnings	711	794	425	241
Actual earnings	582	651	348	198
1909—full-time earnings	739	838	449	255
Actual earnings	640	725	390	221
1914—full-time earnings	719	804	430	244
Actual earnings	576	644	344	195
1919—full-time earnings	801	894	479	272
Actual earnings	677	756	406	195
1921—full-time earnings	831	928	497	282
Actual earnings	595	665	356	230
1923—full-time earnings	927	1,021	547	311
Actual earnings	839	924	495	281

[a] Brissenden, op. cit., p. 156.

What can be said is that, while during the period from 1899 to 1914 there was no appreciable gain in purchasing power, between 1914 and 1927 there was a gain corresponding to 131 as compared with 99, and the rates of pay, if not the real wages and earnings, increased by something like threefold.[2]

To come nearer the present (1932), it is possible to refer to the reports[3] of the National Industrial Conference Board which publishes figures for average hourly earnings for (1) male common

[1] See Herbst, op. cit., p. 97 ff.
[2] Brissenden, op. cit., p. 156.
[3] Wages in the United States, 1914–1927; Wages in the United States, 1931.

and unskilled, (2) male skilled workers, and (3) women, in twenty-four manufacturing industries, the data being obtained from 1,440 plants employing an average of 634,000 workers[1] and covering the period 1914–1930, compared with 1923 as a base. That authority estimates that the average weekly earnings of female wage earners increased by 1.9 per cent between 1927 and 1929.[2] According to these estimates, hourly earnings for all wage earners combined averaged the same in 1930 as in 1929 and were higher than at any time since 1920. There was, however, a decline during the last quarter of 1930 as compared with the first three-quarters of that year. Hourly earnings of the individual labor group showed a slight reduction in 1930 as compared with 1929, this decline being less for the female labor (.4 cents) than for either the unskilled (.8 cents) or for the semi-skilled and skilled male workers (0.6 cents). In 1930, the hourly earnings for female labor were near the 1923 level, being only 0.8 per cent above, when the two male groups were 5.8 per cent and 6.3 per cent higher than in 1923.

If a comparison be made by industries of the earnings of all wage earners in separate industries in the fourth quarter of 1930, five industries—silk, wool, northern cotton, and boots and shoes—show declines from 2.4 per cent to 9.9 per cent. In the other nineteen industries, the average hourly earnings in the last quarter of 1930 were higher than in 1923. For women, the minimum average hourly earnings were in leather tanning and finishing (32.7 cents), while the highest were in news and magazine printing (44.3 cents). The weekly earnings, however, of course went down. The decline in 1930 over 1929, which manifested itself every quarter, amounted to 9.4 per cent. In the fourth quarter of 1930, average weekly earnings were still higher than the level during the depression of 1921. This relative reduction in 1930 as compared with 1929 was slightly less characteristic of the women's weekly earnings than of either group of men workers; and while the earnings of the other two declined steadily, women's earnings rose slightly during the last quarter of the year. There were seven industries in which weekly earnings were higher than in 1923. In all others they were markedly lower. They ranged

---

[1] It is not necessary to describe all the methods used in dealing with the figures. The Board's publications are not difficult to obtain.

[2] National Industrial Conference Board, *Wages in the United States, 1914–1930; ibid., 1931.*

from $13.37 in leather tanning to $19.44 in meat packing.[1] As to average hourly real earnings, these were higher for all groups in 1930 as compared with 1929.[2] They were at this time, however, 3.7 per cent lower than in 1923.

As to working hours, the women's working time showed a decline of 2.2 hours between the first and the fourth quarter of 1930. In the last quarter of that year, too (1930), the employment index approached that of 1921 and was 22.1 per cent below that of 1923. As for 1928, it may be noted that average annual hourly earnings increased in all industries except northern cotton, foundries, wool, silk, rubber, paper products, panel and varnish, meat packing, and paint and varnish.[3]

In 1931, hourly earnings averaged 4.1 per cent less than in 1929 and 1930. In the last quarter of 1931, average hourly earnings were still 12.1 per cent higher than after the 1920–1921 depression had run its course. During the two years, 1930–1931, the relative reductions in the average hourly earnings of women were larger than in those of male labor. The decline between the last quarters of 1930 and of 1931 amounted to 7.3 per cent for female labor, as compared with 6.3 per cent for skilled and 6.1 per cent for unskilled male labor. The declines between 1929 and 1931 were for female labor, 10.1 per cent; for skilled male labor, 8.4 per cent; for unskilled male labor, 9.2 per cent; while the percentage decline was greater for women, the actual money reduction was less for them, being 4.0 cents for women between 1929 and 1931, 4.5 cents for unskilled and 5.6 cents for skilled labor.

In the same way, average weekly earnings declined, the decline being greater than in 1920–1921, and actual average weekly earnings fell to lower levels than 1921. The decline in earnings, too, has been greater than the decline in the cost of living, though not to the lowest point of the 1920–1921 depression. In the matter of hours of work, the women had less reduction than either group of men.[4]

What can be said as to the outlook? That possibly growing out of wider discussion of the cost of living, out of the rationalization of men's claims, out of the lip-service paid the principle of the equal wage, the influence of the community attitude on both

[1] *Ibid.*, p. 32.
[2] 3.1 per cent for women, *ibid.*, p. 33.
[3] *Ibid.*, p. 24.
[4] These data apply, as has been said, only to occupations in the manufacturing group of industries.

employer and employee looks toward both a closer approxima-
tion of earnings to needs, and wider application of the principle
of the wage for the job.

Yet the author of the Census study thought in 1927 that it
was[1]

probably true, unfortunately, that in manufacturing industry generally
there is not evident any consistent long-time trend toward the closing
up of the gap between actual and full-time earnings by elimination of the
causes for the existence of that gap, namely, unemployment and irregular
employment. It is evident . . . however, that in some of the industries
represented, there has been appreciable improvement in this respect.
Such improvement appears to have taken place in the printing and
publishing industry (book and job), and in the paper and wood pulp
industry. Unhappily, however, other industries such as chemicals,
cotton manufactures, and woolen goods, show a tendency toward a
greater loss in purchasing power attributable to lost time.

What these figures mean is revealed to a certain extent in
studies of industrial and other occupations in a number of selected areas. The conditions prevailing during the first half of
the decade are described, for example, in a study covering groups
of workers in the women-employing industries in thirteen states.
Data were assembled in regard to 100,967 white and 3,141
Negro women in 1,472 plants.[2] Of these, 79,162 white women and
3,141 Negro women were in manufacturing industries, the others
in stores and laundries. Although this inquiry was made two
decades after the Woman and Child Wage Earners investigation
referred to above, the figures are not strikingly different. As
before, there were differences in different sections of the country.
In Alabama, Mississippi, and South Carolina, half the women
earned less than $8.35. In New Jersey, Ohio and Rhode Island
the median was $19.13. The earnings were still universally low
in the cotton industry and, with one exception,[3] in the hosiery
and knit goods·industries, while, if the earnings were higher, it
was in manufacture of electrical appliances or rubber, or, less
so, in metals, shoes, or tobacco.

Attention has been called to the shifting of the age groups
between 1900 and 1930, and to the fact that it is among the
older workers that increases in number are taking place. In this

---

[1] Brissenden, *op. cit.*, p. 162.
[2] U. S. Women's Bureau Publication No. 85 (1930), *Wages of Women in Thirteen States*, p. 3.
[3] *Ibid.*, p. 34.

study, earnings and age were reported for 39,141 women in manufacturing in eleven states. In each of these, the group of younger women was relatively numerous, from one half to almost two-thirds being in the group under twenty-five. The highest earnings were, however, in six states, found in the group between thirty and forty years of age; in four states in the group between twenty-five and thirty.[1]

As among the occupations, the earnings (median) were highest in general mercantile establishments, at least this is true in nine of the thirteen states, and the earnings in laundries were between those in manufacturing and those in five-and-ten cent stores, which were the lowest, at least in eleven states.

As to national and racial affiliations, the median earnings of native born workers were above those of foreign born in general mercantile establishments and laundries, while below in manufacturing establishments or in five-and-ten cent stores. The earnings of the Negro workers were lowest of all. In nine states the median earnings of Negro women workers were from $4.89 to $8.92. As far as yearly earnings were concerned, the median earnings of the Negro women ranged from $263 to $563 in manufacturing, and from $306 to $550 in laundries. Earnings for a year were obtained for a considerable number of those who had been employed for the preceding year and had had forty-four weeks of work in that year. In all but two of the states the highest median earnings were in the general mercantile establishments, the lowest in the five-and-ten cent stores.[2]

If the earnings are compared with the estimated cost of living it is found that large numbers of women earned less than the amounts designated as necessary for health and decency. The Women's Bureau estimated a general level of $18.38 weekly as necessary for 1920, $15.98 for 1921; $15.54 for 1922; $15.88 for 1923; $15.82 for 1924; $16.31 for 1925; $15.71 for 1928; and concluded that more than half the women in manufacturing in six states earned less than such a minimum and that in 1928, the minimum would be above the median for full time workers in manufacturing in all but four of the states surveyed.

A study of women's wages from a wider range in 1919 reviewed the development up to that time, pointed out the reasons for the segregation of women from men's jobs, calling attention to

[1] *Ibid.*, pp. 74–79.
[2] *Ibid.*, p. 90.

the changes apparently brought about by the war, and empha-
sizing the dangers inherent in the cheapness of women's work.[1]
At that time the minimum wage laws that had been enacted in
seventeen jurisdictions were generally in force, and the effects
of that legislation were being studied both by those who had
advocated the enactment of the laws and by the United States
Bureau of Labor. The war had seemed to give a new impetus to
women's organization into unions, and the movement for vocational guidance and vocational education had gained some
momentum. The writer looked to these three lines of effort as
offering hope of improvement, although she was inclined to limit
the application of the minimum wage legislation to minors, trust-
ing to the development of the trade union or to industry through
better selection, for the improvement in the situation of adult
women. This was probably because the constitutional limitations
on the regulation of men's wages were foreseen as perils to the
regulation of women's wages, although an extension of the argument based on a relation between low income and health had
already been suggested by the data concerning infant mortality
and low income; and the acceptance of that view could and was
expected by distinguished students of the police power to find
acceptance on the part of the United States Supreme Court.
It was four years later that the United States Supreme Court
held the District of Columbia Minimum Wage Act unconstitutional,[2] so that that method of dealing with the subject has been
generally thought of as for the time inapplicable.[3]

[1] Emilie J. Hutchinson, Ph.D., *Women's Wages, A Study of the Wages of Industrial Women and Measures Suggested to Increase Them*, Columbia University
Studies, Whole No. 202, pp. 66–67.

[2] *Children's Hospital* v. *Atkins*, 261 U.S. 526 (1923).

[3] This is not entirely accurate, since the advisory character of the Massachusetts Act and the acquiescence of California employers leave the acts operative in those two commonwealths. There is, in fact, not infrequent legislation
on the subject in a number of states. See, for example, *Sixth Report of Industrial
Commission of California*, 1926–1928, pp. 12, 21, 134–36; *Tenth Report of Industrial Commission of Colorado*, 1926–1928, p. 67; *Eleventh Report*, 1928–1930, pp.
28, 33; *Fifth Biennial Report Minimum Wage Department*, North Dakota, Workmen's Compensation Bureau, 1926–1928, pp. 3, 7–8; *Eighth Report of Industrial
Welfare Commission, State of Oregon*, 1927–28, pp. 3, 4; *Ninth Report*, 1929–1930,
p. 5. *Oregon Laws*, 1931, Ch. 394, Sec. 3, p. 843; *Session Laws of South Dakota*,
1931, Ch. 74, Sec. 1, pp. 218–19; *Fourteenth Annual Report of the South Dakota
Industrial Commissioner*, 1931, p. 9. "No woman or girl over the age of fourteen
years shall be employed or permitted to work in any factory, work shop, mechanical or mercantile establishment, laundry, hotel, restaurant or packing house, at
less than a living wage of Twelve Dollars per week, or a proportionate amount for

The war had exercised a catastrophic influence on the occupational situation. Men were drained off to the service, immigration stopped, the Negro became available for industrial employment in northern communities and women took men's places in innumerable establishments, and when this substitution of women for men took place, there was a tendency to fix the wage scale at points more nearly approaching the rates at which men had been paid, which were of course higher than women's rates had ever been. In April and May, 1918, for example, an inquiry was made on the employment of women in metal-working establishments,[1] by which it was learned that out of 127 establishments from which information was sought, 53 paid wages equal to men's wages, 29 paid piece rates equal to men's time rates, 24 paid less, and from 21 no information was obtained. The figures seem to indicate that the principle of an equal wage for equal work was more extensively adopted among employers in industries where the use of women was a comparatively new thing than where their employment was of long standing.

Through the decisions and awards of the War Labor Policies Board[2] and the Railroad Administration,[3] the principle that pay should be based on the nature and complexity of the work and

---

periods of employment of less than a week, the same to be paid in cash or by check." *Session Laws of South Dakota*, 1931, Chap. 173, sec. 1, p. 218. And a recent report of the Ontario Board calling attention to the relative stability of wages in that Province during the years 1929–31 (*United States Daily*, July 14, 1932) and the *Report of the Department of Labor and Industry of Pennsylvania* (*Labor and Industry*, XIX, No. 5, p. 24) seem to bring the question again into the area of practical politics. For extended discussion of the subject, see Barbara Nachtreeb Armstrong, *Insuring the Essentials* (New York: The MacMillan Company, 1932), Part II, *Minimum Wage*. See also, U. S. Women's Bureau, *News Letter*, No. 92, November 1, 1932, p. 2, for communications about wages from the Massachusetts Minimum Wage Commission and from the Wisconsin Industrial Commission on the subject of their respective activities.

[1] *I.e.*, automobile necessaries, typewriters, electrical machinery apparatus and supplies, foundries, machine shop products, munitions, railway equipment, tools, cutlery, hardware. United States Bureau of Labor Statistics, *Monthly Labor Review*, IX (1919), 192.

[2] Established April 8, 1918.

[3] General Order No. 27 issued by the office of the Director General, U. S. Railroad Administration, Mr. McAdoo, on May 25, 1918, provided for equal pay for equal work. The article providing this reads as follows: "When women are employed, their working conditions must be healthful and fitted to their needs. The laws enacted for the government of their employment must be observed and their pay, when they do the same class of work as men, shall be the same as that of men." *Official Bulletin*, May 29, 1918, p. 15.

not on sex[1] and the phrase "equal pay for equal work" gained wide publicity, received general verbal acquiescence and, under the pressure of immediate demand, affected the rates of pay of many women workers.

When the war was ended, however, and account was taken of its general results, they were found to be on the whole meager from the point of view either of widened occupational opportunity for women or of increased rates of pay.[2] Women were often either still excluded or still paid at inadequate rates.

For wages and earnings in the fields of clerical and business employment, attention may again be directed to the researches of the National Federation of Business and Professional Women's Clubs[3] which are interesting. The median earnings of a group of 14,073 women engaged in the occupations classed as Clerical, Trade, Transportation, Communication, Professional, Public not elsewhere classified, and Executives in Manufacturing, were $1,548, while the average was higher by $114, or $1,668. The lower quartile was at $1,213, the upper quartile at $2,004. In other words, one in four earned less than $1,213, and one in four more than $2,004; while one earned between $1,213 and $1,548, and one between $1,548 and $2,004.

It is also true that the urban centers offer a wider range of opportunity for women, especially in the field of finance, sales, and publicity. In this group, the findings with reference to the relative earnings of single and of married workers are interesting. Among these groups, the earnings of single women tend to exceed those of married women of the same age and experience. In fact, single women earn consistently not only more than married women but more than widows and women divorced or separated from their husbands.[4]

---

[1] For example, in the case of the Corn Products Refining Co., the Board took this position. It studied the factory and graded the positions in four classes on a functional basis. The minimum wage in grade one was set at 35 cents an hour, for grade 4, at 70 cents an hour (*Monthly Labor Review*, VIII, 31–32). For a number of positive statements and determinations to this effect see *ibid.*, VIII, 203, 205–208, "Laundry Workers, Little Rock, Arkansas"; 262–63, "The Worthington Pump and Machinery Co. on May 25, 1918."

[2] New York State Department of Labor, 1919, pp. 22, 23. Quoted, Wolfe and Olsen, *Journal of Political Economy*, XXVII (1919), 639, 658. For other studies, see U. S. Bureau of Labor, *Monthly Labor Review*, VIII (March, 1919), 212. See also the *Fourth Report of the New York State Factory Investigating Commission*, 1915.

[3] Quoted in *Recent Social Trends in the United States*, Chap. XIV. Elliott and Manson, *op. cit.* As this is readily available, only the results will be noted.

[4] Elliott and Manson, *op. cit.*, p. 47.

The important point is that the difference between low and high, while of very great significance to the worker, is a slender difference, and the earnings of the higher paid group are still very modest. It is true, however, that those women who are independently engaged earn considerably more than those employed on a salary basis. Their earnings were $503 above those of salaried workers and one in three of them earns $3,000 a year or more, while among the salaried workers only one in twenty earns that amount.[1] A few spectacular exceptions are 174 who earn $5,000 or more. Of these, 83 earn between $5,000 and $6,000, 32 earn between $6,000 and $7,000; 16 between $7,000 and $8,000; 18 between $8,000 and $9,000 thousand; and 25 over $9,000.

There are wide differences in the range of earnings in these different groups. Median earnings vary from $68.2 for 23 telephone operators to $3,088 for 55 physicians in private practice. Of course, too, there are great differences in the proportions of workers in the different groups who earn $5,000 or more. Only 2.6 per cent of the clerical workers, 4 per cent of the teachers and 7 per cent of the whole group earn that much; while 13.7 per cent of the welfare group, 14 per cent of the health group, 18 per cent in the legal and protective group and 21.6 per cent of the personnel group earn $3,000 or more. The two points to be kept in mind are that some are earning in the higher levels, but that on the whole the rewards are low and where the content of the pay envelope or the amount of the salary check constitutes most of the reward, if not all the return for the labor expended, the picture is not a very cheerful one. This is, of course, not true of those occupations like teaching, welfare work, librarianship or other occupations giving opportunity for the use of one's intelligence and opening up constantly more interesting fields of endeavor.

A few of the conclusions drawn by the investigators are of such special interest in this connection as to justify quotation at length. (1) The earnings increase with experience for about the first twenty years of work, remain fairly constant for the next ten years and then decline; (2) they increase with age up to fifty, vary but little between fifty and sixty, and then decline; (3) they tend to increase with the years of general education, so that women with a college degree earn more than those without; (4) earnings, living expenses and savings increase with the size of the com-

[1] *Ibid.*, p. 13.

munity in which the women are working, the proportion of earnings which goes with living expenses and savings remaining about the same, regardless of the size of the community; (5) the charge of occupational instability often brought against women is thought untenable; and (6) for most women, earnings in their chief occupation are the only source of income.[1]

The facts with reference to 1,025 women holding the degree of Doctor of Philosophy,[2] for a group of 844 university or college women,[3] have been discussed elsewhere. The figures with reference to the earnings of 3,521 women who had been land-grant college students have recently been made available.[4] The median for all is $1,655; for those teaching, $1,640; for those in other positions, $1,677. The lower quartile, the figure below which the earnings of one-fourth of those reporting were found, showed earnings were $1,280; the upper quartile, $2,089. Of the 3,521 women, 5.1 per cent received $3,000 or over. These figures are slightly higher than those of the business and professional women, whose lower quartile was $1,213 instead of $1,280; whose median was $1,548 instead of $1,655, and whose upper quartile was $2,007. Among that group, however, 6.7 per cent instead of 5.1 per cent earned $3,000 or more. The figures differ slightly if they are separated into occupational groups. The teachers, for example, earned a median of $1,640, or $15.00 less than the group median; their lower quartile was $1,291, the upper $1,985. There were only 3.6 per cent earning $3,000 or more. Those women who earned $5,000 or more were from the older group. They had matriculated between 1889 and 1902, and had held administrative as well as teaching positions. The salaries in this group were, in fact, somewhat higher than those of the teachers in the business and professional women's group, whose median salary was $1,557, with the lower quartile at $1,253, and the upper quartile at $1,965.

---

[1] Women in the federal civil service are discussed elsewhere; there are available, however, two competent studies of women in municipal civil service to which reference may again be made: *Recent Social Trends in the United States*, Chap. XIV. "Women in Public Service, Berkeley," *Public Personnel Studies*, VIII, No. 7, p. 105; "Oakland," *ibid.*, No. 8, p. 117.

[2] Emilie J. Hutchinson, *Women and the Ph.D.*, Bulletin No. 2 of the Institute of Women's Professional Relations (Published by the North Carolina College for Women).

[3] Marion O. Hawthorn, "Women as College Teachers," *Annals of the American Academy of Political and Social Science*, CXLIII No. 232, May, 1929, p. 146.

[4] *After College What?*, Bulletin No. 4, Institute of Women's Professional Relations (1932), p. 29. Published by the North Carolina Women's College.

In all these groups, length of experience told in the salary, and both in the business and professional and in the land-grant college groups, those who earned larger sums had changed their positions more frequently than those who earned the smaller sums. The capacity that registers in higher earnings seems to obtain those higher earnings rather by finding opportunities in connection with different institutions than through promotion in the same institution.

THE EQUAL WAGE

It has proved impossible to separate the two questions of the low rate of women's pay and the relationship between women's remuneration and men's earnings. And it has seemed inevitable that reference be made to this problem, which, as has been pointed out, is often referred to as the "problem of the unequal wage" giving rise to the slogan, "Equal pay for equal work." It has long been clear that there are two problems rather than one.[1] In manual work it is difficult to discover more than a very few instances in which men and women do the same work, in the same place, at the same time, so that the question is rather that of segregation of jobs than of equal pay.

It is true that women often do the work requiring little training, what has been called the "unskilled work"; that is, however, by no means all the story; there has been the limitation of opportunity to which attention has been called, and the influence of custom and tradition to which women themselves adhere. "It's not bad for a woman" may be the statement of a woman about a woman as well as the statement of a man about a woman. There is the lack of organization; the working conditions of all women have been affected by the youthfulness of large numbers of them, and the prospect of marriage has had perhaps as disastrous an effect as marriage itself.

The equal wage is, of course, a protection of the man against underbidding on the part of women. It is the only safeguard for the man's scale in time of real pressure. The application of the principle is, however, possible substantially only when there are

[1] Emilie J. Hutchinson, *Women in the Modern World* (*Annals of the American Academy of Political and Social Science* Vol. CXLIII, No. 232, May, 1929), p. 132.
  These subjects were discussed at great length by certain British official bodies during and after the war. Reference may be made to the War Cabinet Committee, and the Successive Royal Commissions on the British Civil Service. For a very interesting statement see Silvia Anthony, *Women's Place in Industry and Home* (London: George Routledge and Sons, Ltd., 1932), Chaps. VII, VIII, XII.

objective tests for the jobs and those tests are open to both men and women, that is chiefly in the school system or under the civil service system.

In connection with the relative scales of women in the civil service and in academic institutions, it should be pointed out that the question is not only one of getting the same pay if one has the same job, but of getting the opportunity to do the interesting and important work at any scale of pay. The figures given in connection with women in the land-grant colleges and with women in the federal service illustrate this difficulty. Those figures show a very slow advance in the direction of occupational opportunity but through women's admission on some of the lower levels a considerable increase in the numbers of positions affected by the equal pay principle.

The proposal for the equal wage should perhaps not be discussed without reference to the factors determining wage scales. That subject in general does not belong in this monograph, but attention must be again called to the interest of gainfully occupied women in the question. It cannot be claimed that anywhere in the United States the remuneration of men is fixed with reference to their responsibility for dependents. It should therefore be entirely possible to discuss the subject of women's wages without raising the question of responsibility for dependents. On that subject, therefore, no special study has been made for this report. Reference has been made to the effect of the study of Woman and Child Wage Earners upon the "pin-money" myth. Fifteen years later, the United States Woman's Bureau, supplemented those inquiries by an investigation, concluding with reference to the contributions of the mother and of sons and daughters to the family budget, that the exclusion of the earnings of the wife or the mother would lower considerably the standard "of economic well-being" in the families concerned, although her earnings seldom equaled in importance those of other members of the families, and that, although sons earned more than daughters, the daughters contributed a far larger proportion to the total family income than did the sons.[1]

The subject has likewise been the object of scholarly analyses and three interesting views formulated in the years since the close of the war may be cited.

[1] *The Share of Wage Earning Women in Family Support*, U. S. Department of Labor, Women's Bureau, Bulletin No. 30 (1923), p. 60.

One view enunciated in 1919 was to the effect that since scientifically accurate studies of the relative output of men and women were not available, it would be easy for unscrupulous employers to misrepresent women's efficiency and delay equal standards of pay, that equal pay was more likely with union organization of women, that to have a higher industrial status women must be as valuable to the employers as the men, and that the restriction of immigration would aid in the accomplishment of equal pay for equal work.[1]

In a study of the cost of living for working women, another student, in 1920, discussed four theories: the joint-cost theory which emphasizes the norm of family life and family economy; the temporary independence theory, the needs of the girl adrift; the theory of permanent independence, the value of provision for old age and unemployment; and the family support theory, "the prevalence of need in the families of women workers." Her conclusion was that, realizing its revisability, the working woman's standard should be the cost of independent living and that a full temporary independence minimum should be allowed for items other than board as they are practically identical whether the woman lives at home or not.[2]

A third distinguished scholar in 1925 said that "The provision of an equal minimum wage for both sexes based on the cost of living for a single person and with allowances made for dependents would prevent the undercutting of the men's rate by women and would protect them from the competition of cheap labor." The wage for men is higher for women even when they perform practically the same work because of the present assumption that men have dependents and women do not. Consequently the employer has an inducement either to substitute women for men or to cut the wages of men to an equality with those of women. The range and the intensity of competition between the sexes increases as the increasing automatization of industry widens the area of work which both men and women can perform. Men will try to keep women out from these positions as long as this condition continues.[3]

[1] Wolfe and Olson, *op. cit.*

[2] Dorothy W. Douglas, "The Cost of Living for Working Women: A Criticism of Current Theories," *Quarterly Journal of Economics*, XXXIV (1920), 225–59.

[3] Paul H. Douglas, *Wages and the Family* (University of Chicago Press, 1925), p. 273.

The question is, of course, one that presents itself wherever professional women are entering the labor market, so that literature and proposals for community action have been developed in jurisdictions as remote as New South Wales, where the family allowance plan was first elaborated, and Belgium where that plan is put into effect in a considerable number of occupations. As has been pointed out, the United States Government and the Boards of Education in a number of cities have embodied the principle of equal pay in their legislation. Whether with equal pay goes equal opportunity for appointment and promotion, it is probably not possible to say. Certainly the economic basis of wider occupational opportunity is a sounder ground for satisfaction than statutory requirement.[1] Nor can the fact be ignored that a basis for hope for some may be a cause for despair for others. For to the extent to which women abandon the advantage of cheapness will they be dependent upon objective views and purposes on the part of employers.[2]

[1] The following discussions of the subject are of interest. *Report of Royal Commission on the Civil Service*, 1929–1931. In this report the discussion of an earlier Royal Commission, *The MacDonnell Report*, is summarized and the views of the women in the civil service and the commission are given. *The Report of the War Cabinet Committee on Women in Industry, Minority Report, The Home Office Report on the Substitution of Men by Women in Non-munition Factories During the War;* Eleanor F. Rathbone, *The Disinherited Family* (London: Edward Arnold and Co., 1924).

For figures with reference to the opportunities of university faculty members, see *Recent Social Trends in the United States*, Chap. XIV.

[2] For example, in the report of the War Cabinet Committee only Mrs. Sidney Webb stood strongly for the principle and as recently as 1930, a Royal Commission on the Civil Service found irreconcilable differences of opinion in the staff of the service (Cd. 3909). It is difficult to leave the subject without calling attention to the difference in the position of women in the United States and in Great Britain. In the United States, as has been pointed out, the authorities proclaimed the principle of equal pay. Congressional legislation has always rested on that basis. The Administration of the United States Civil Service Act and of the Reclassification Act have departed at times from the principle, but the women have the letter of the statute as a basis for their claim. In Great Britain, on the other hand, during the war, agreement to the principle could not be obtained and a very recent statement by an important public authority rejects the principle for the women in the Civil Service of Great Britain.

CHAPTER XIV

WOMEN AND UNEMPLOYMENT

THERE are several features that distinguish the problem of unemployment of women from that of men. First, the different wage scale is always tempting the employer in time of pressure to substitute cheaper women for dearer men workers. This may account in part for the fact that, in the reports of various earlier official commissions[1] on unemployment, the subject of women was given relatively little consideration.

Often the line between gainful employment and domestic duty is not very clear to the girl or woman; or she hopes to obscure it to the outside world and, when at home, she is just a woman and neither employed nor unemployed. There is sometimes a way out, that is, rather into matrimony, and she takes up marital, when before she performed filial, obligations. And, there is always the street![2] At any rate the "homeless woman" has not in the United States presented a problem comparable with that of the "homeless man." In older countries, the lodging house for vagrant homeless women has been found necessary; in the United States, it has rather been the boarding home for the girl who worked for wages too low to meet the costs of life of a "woman adrift."

The figures presented by the Census for earnings[3] showed, in fact, a slight advantage for women and children in respect to purchasing power lost because of failure to work full time. The discrepancy between full time and actual employment is greater with men than with women or children. These differences vary

---

[1] This was true of the two Commissions that sat in Chicago in 1914, namely, the Mayor's Commission on Unemployment of which the distinguished Dr. Charles Richmond Henderson was Secretary, and the City Council Committee on Markets Commission on A Practical Plan for Relieving Destitution and Unemployment of which Professor Charles E. Merriam was a member. It was also true of the President's Conference on Unemployment (1921) of which President Hoover, then Secretary of Commerce, was Chairman. Mayor Mitchell's Committee on Unemployment (New York, 1917) of which Mr. J. R. Shillady was Secretary, was concerned for the young girl out of work. See pp. 39, 42, 79.

[2] What Dr. Charles G. Hyde calls "Spilling over into Prostitution," *Journal of Social Hygiene*, XVIII, p. 321.

[3] Brissenden, *op. cit.*, pp. 7, 15.

with the industry and the location. Periods of lost time or interruptions in work are of course very different in different industries, and very different possibly in the same industry in different localities. And, with the exception of a few industries, such as printing and publishing, and the paper and wood pulp industries, there was, as has been pointed out above, no sign of any consistent long time trend toward reducing the difference between possible full time earnings and actual earnings by stabilizing the industry and doing away with the causes of interruption and underemployment.[1]

Of course, there are many facts which suggest that women workers have suffered. In 1921, for example, many women-employing industries, such as the textile industries, clothing, hosiery, underwear, and boots and shoes,[2] were hard hit, and reduced their working staffs. The industries that employ large numbers of women, like clothing and the canning industry, are highly seasonal. The actual effect of unemployment, however, on women is still to be understood. Nor can such effects as are generally recognized be set out here when the purpose is to try to discover whether occupational life is offering relatively greater or less security than at earlier times. It is perhaps safe to say that it is offering a degree of security slightly nearer than before to that offered the man, because of the larger number of older, of native born, and of married women who are found to be gainfully occupied.

To return to the Census, it may be noted that the fact that the census data now supply information on unemployed women as constituting a problem, is itself perhaps likewise evidence of their belonging in the occupational world, consciously sharing its vicissitudes as workers.

It should be kept in mind that when the unemployment Census was taken there were two groups of persons about whom information was sought: those in Class A, who were persons out of work, able to work, and looking for work; and those in Class B, who, having a job, were laid off without pay, excluding of course the sick and the voluntarily idle.

Of the 10,788,794 women and girls over ten years of age reporting a gainful occupation, 370,000, or 3.4 of one per cent, were, on the day of the enumeration, out of a job, looking for work and

---

[1] *Ibid.*, p. 162.
[2] Theresa Wolfson, *The Woman Worker and the Trade Union*, p. 50.

able to work, while 131,178, or 1.2 per cent, were laid off without pay.[1] From the Census figures the duration of the unemployment can be learned by age groups, and it can also be seen how, except for the younger persons, the percentage remains about the same for the different groups, while the amount of employment remains surprisingly constant. Again the Census fails to indicate special disabilities for the older women.

It is interesting to note the occupations in which the proportions run high and also the areas in which the percentages are large.[2] As to occupations, the large numbers of women out of work are in manufacturing and mechanical occupations where 9.7 per cent were out of work, of which number the Textile industry provides 23,355. In Trade, 55,712, or 3.2 per cent, were out of work; in the professional group, 33,043; among the Domestic and Personal Service, 122,178, or 3.9 per cent.

As to the states in which the percentage rose above the percentage for the whole country, 3.4 per cent, in California it was 4.6; in Colorado, 3.8; in Connecticut, 3.3; in Delaware, of the night workers, 6.2; in Florida, 5.6; Idaho, 3.5; Illinois, 4.4; Maryland, 4.0; Massachusetts, 4.3; Missouri, 3.4; New Jersey, 4.3; New York, 3.9 Ohio, 3.6; Oregon, 5.1; Pennsylvania, 3.4; Rhode Island, 5.6; Washington, 4.4 per cent.

As to the occupations in which the percentages were high, there were 17,727, or 4.3 per cent, of Class A, and 13,686, or 3.3 per cent, of Class B in clothing; in cotton mills, 7,386, or 4.6 per cent of Class A, and 10,069, or 6.3 per cent, of Class B; 1,133, or 3.1 per cent, in paper and allied industries; 2,436, or 5.6 per cent in silk and 3,457, or 4.0 per cent, in woolen and worsted mills; 1,951, telegraph or telephone operatives, or 1.4 per cent of the total employed group. In Trade there were 44,363, or 3.6 per cent of Class A in wholesale or retail trade, and 9,576, or 0.8 per cent, of Class B. In Public Service there were 1,458, or 1.2 per cent of Class A, and 414, or 0.3 per cent, of Class B. In the Professional group, there were 33,043, or 1.9 per cent of Class A, and 9,867 or 0.6 per cent, of Class B. Of the women in Domestic and Personal Service the numbers were 26,324, or 4 per cent, of Class A, and 4,458, or 0.7 per cent, of Class B, in hotels, restaurants, and boarding houses; while 6,993, or 3.4 per cent of

---

[1] *U. S. Summary of Unemployment, Fifteenth Census,* 1930, Table 1, p. 6.

[2] These figures taken from the Summary include the ten to seventy-five year old group.

Class A, and 1,698, or 0.8 per cent of Class B were from laundries.[1] As to family relationship, the Census shows, of the entire group of unemployed women, that is Class A, 9.8 per cent were heads of families, 69.6 per cent were related to a member of the family, 20.6 per cent were lodgers. Of those laid off, 9.4 per cent were heads of families, 77.9 per cent related to a member of the family, 12.7 per cent lodgers.[2] These are very different figures from those for men where 47.7 per cent or almost half of the unemployed were heads of families, 34.2 per cent were related, and 18.2 were lodgers, or in the case of those laid off, 59.1 per cent, 28.4 per cent, and 12.5 per cent. However, if the number of heads of families and of those related are added, the numbers of persons usually contributing to the family income are not so different in the case of women as compared with men.

It was pointed out above that the percentage of professional women was small; however, the number that might be classified as business women was considerable.

The limited character of the Census data gives significance to special studies of gainfully occupied women and there is available an extremely interesting study of the effect of the depression on the members of the American Woman's Association in cooperation with the President's Organization for Unemployment Relief. This Association is composed of professional and business women living, almost all of them, in New York City, or within a fifty-mile radius of the city, and employed there. Questionnaires were sent to 4,800 members between April 1, 1929, and February 1, 1930, with reference to their being laid off, having their earnings reduced by cuts in salary, or reduced bonus, or loss of patronage if they were independent workers.[3] The women from whom data were obtained were persons employed in one of the business or professional groups, or holding administrative positions in connection with an occupation classified as "domestic or personal" or "manufacturing and mechanical." In Table 41 are found the percentage distribution of members of these organizations and of the business and professional women to whom refer-

[1] *Ibid.*, Table 21, p. 49.
[2] *Ibid.*, Table 7, p. 10.
[3] *The Trained Woman and the Economic Crisis.* A study made by the American Woman's Association in cooperation with the President's Emergency Committee for Employment (1931).

ence was made above. The largest number represents the clerical workers; and, secondly, the teachers. In these groups the nurses are a smaller contingent than those connected with selling activities, and librarians in the one case and influential executives in the other.

TABLE 41.—SHOWING VOCATIONS OF MEMBERS OF THE REPORTING GROUP AND OF MEMBERS OF THE NATIONAL FEDERATION OF BUSINESS AND PROFESSIONAL WOMEN[a]

Vocation	Reporting group, per cent	N. F. of B. P. W. clubs,[b] per cent
All vocations...	100.0	100.0
Clerical executives..	5.4	6.6
Clerical, other than executives............................	25.6	35.7
Dentists, chiropractors, health specialists....................	0.7	1.5
Doctors, surgeons, osteopaths............................	1.0	1.6
Editors and editorial workers.............................	2.5	1.2
Financial executives and experts..........................	2.7	4.3
Food and housing executives.............................	1.8	0.9
Home economics experts.................................	0.6	0.3
Lawyers and judges.....................................	0.6	0.6
Librarians...	4.0	1.5
Nurses, executives......................................	1.0	0.4
Nurses, other than executives............................	2.8	2.4
Personnel workers......................................	1.5	0.5
Production and planning executives........................	0.9	1.8
Production and planning operators and technicians...........	1.2	1.4
Professions n.e.c.......................................	4.6	0.8
Public health workers...................................	0.6	0.5
Purchasing..	0.6	1.0
Sales, advtg., publicity and misc. exec's...................	6.3	5.1
Sales, advtg. and publicity, other than exec's...............	3.3	6.0
Social workers...	2.3	2.4
Teachers, executives....................................	4.9	4.7
Teachers, other than executives..........................	22.3	14.4
Miscellaneous and n.s...................................	2.6	4.4

[a] *The Trained Woman and the Economic Crisis.* A study made by the American Woman's Association in Cooperation with the President's Emergency Committee for Employment (1931), p. 73.
[b] Margaret Elliott and Grace E. Manson, *op. cit.* Based on Table 1, Appendix II.

The first point of interest is the number of "independent" workers. It is not possible, by examining the Census category, to separate all the independent workers. Attention has been called to the increase in the group known as managers and officials in connection with manufacturing and mechanical occupations, but they may or may not be managing their own business.

Of the two groups about whom special information is available among the Business and Professional Women, to whom extended

[237]

reference was made above, 6.9 per cent were "on their own," while of the members of the American Woman's Association, 11.6 per cent were managing their own business or carrying on their own professional practice. For the members of the American Woman's Association the earnings are on a higher level than those of the Business and Professional Women. The median earning rate for the American Woman's Association was $3,030, while that for the Business and Professional Women was $1,675. The lower quartile of the American Woman's Association was $2,195, while for the Business and Professional Women it was only $1,315; the upper quartile in the one case, $3,890, and in the other, $2,170. The largest group in one case, the modal group, earned between $2,000 and $2,500, while in the other case, the largest single class earned between $1,085 and $1,625.[1] The American Woman's Association were a more select group, even more mature and with better educational equipment than the Business and Professional Women. The statement of their findings is of such significance and is so ably formulated, that it might well be quoted at length. It is to be hoped that similar bodies of fact may in the coming decade make clearer the significance to women of the loss or reduction in employment and earnings. The most important findings may be summarized as follows:

Extent of Unemployment: The proportion of unemployed in the total salaried group is only 6.5 per cent (as of February 1, 1931).

Earnings Reduction versus Unemployment: More than a quarter of the total group had their earnings fall between November, 1929, and February, 1931. Of the independent workers, with their own business or professional practice, more than half reported a loss in earnings through loss of patronage. Salary cuts were slightly more widespread than unemployment and bore most heavily upon the same workers as suffered from unemployment—those at the bottom of the earnings scale (making less than $3,000) and those at the top (making more than $7,000).

Duration of Unemployment: The typical (median) length of unemployment was eight months. Of every ten unemployed women, four were unable to find a tide-over job, three found employment lasting three months or less, and three secured longer employment. Ninety-six per cent of the unemployed group found the irregular earnings from such jobs insufficient to maintain the customary standard of living. Sixty-five per cent were not able to earn sufficient for necessities. Prac-

[1] American Woman's Association, *The Trained Woman and the Economic Crisis*, p. 74. These are figures obtained by questionnaires made comparable by correcting in accordance with *National Conference Board Estimates and U. S. Bureau of Labor Statistics Estimates*, Vol. 32, p. 487.

tically the entire group found it necessary to draw on savings or other resources.

Resources of the Unemployed: In tiding over the unemployment period the majority of women were forced to draw on savings (67.8 per cent). Others sold securities, borrowed against insurance policies or, in 30.0 per cent of the cases, from friends or relatives. Only 1.1 per cent were protected by any form of social unemployment insurance.

Age of the Unemployed: There was relatively more unemployment among women under 35 than among the more mature workers. In fact, the proportion of unemployed decreased in each successive age group up to 45 years after which it showed an increase.[1]

There are also available[2] the results of an inquiry made by the Industrial Assembly of the Y. W. C. A. in the first half of 1932 at the request of a number of the wage-earning members of the Association. A questionnaire sent out brought in 603 replies from many types of industry and from varied parts of the state. All who sent in schedules were asked to tell the amount of their last pay.

The 603 who sent in the histories of their pay envelopes for the last year are a fairly representative sample of the industrial membership. Of the 603, the largest single group (177) were household employees; 80 were textile workers, 71 were garment workers, 36 in the electrical industry, 32 in stores, 28 in the food industries, 23 in shoe factories, and smaller numbers in the metal trades, in rubber factories, in hotels and restaurants, laundries, printing establishments and many miscellaneous trades. . . .

The median rate for all included is $11.13 (half earning less and half earning more), and that for the largest single occupation group, the household employees, is $10.54. The latter amount does not include room and board so that it shows a rate actually somewhat higher than for the total group. The following table gives the wages paid to these 603 women during the early months of 1932:

Up to $5	8%	$15–$19.99	18%
$5–$9.99	32%	$20–$24.99	5%
$10–$14.99	36%	$25–$29.99	1%

Half of these women are getting less than $11.13 (the median) and 74 per cent are getting under $15 which shows that wages are dropping down below anything current in recent years. Information also was secured as to wages received a year ago.

. . . There has been a drop in the cost of living since the depression began, and between December, 1931, and December, 1930, a decline of

[1] *The Trained Woman and the Economic Crisis,* Study of the American Woman's Association, New York, 1931, p. iii.

[2] *U. S. Women's Bureau, News Letter,* November 1, 1932. Grace L. Coyle, in *The Women's Press,* October, 1932.

about 9.2 per cent. At the same time the wage of this group had declined from a median of $14.83 for that received a year back to a median of $11.13, a drop of 24.9 per cent. This means, of course, that there was a real drop in the standard of living during the last year.

Of 584 women reporting wages for both 1930 and 1931, 35 had an increase in earnings and 107 were earning the same. The remaining 442, almost three-fourths, reported reductions ranging from $1 to $15 or more, the median being just under $5. The lowering of earnings by 10 per cent—for this group an average of about $1.50—would have more than equalled the reduction during the year in cost of living, yet the median loss in earnings, instead of $1.50 was $4.93.

The catastrophe, when it came, had not been wholly unforeseen, for as has been pointed out, no nation lives unto itself alone. And with the situation so unhappy in other countries, the International Labour Office at Geneva had undertaken to assemble facts with reference to the situation among intellectual workers. In the United States, therefore, the Institute of Women's Professional Relations cooperated with the International Labour Office in such a study of unemployment among intellectual workers with special reference to the situation in the United States.[1] The results of this study dealt largely with teachers, but contained information with reference to women in other professions as well. This showed an over-supply of teachers, meaning more teachers than could be placed under the prevailing conditions of pay and rank; not more than would be needed if the purpose of the educational organization were to enlighten all young persons needing or seeking an education. For it must be recalled that the total demand is not one comprehensive demand, but the sum of a multiplicity of local demands varying greatly in resources and in understanding of the problem. For example, one excess was found in the unplaced college graduates in California who wanted to teach academic subjects, especially English and History, in high schools. It was pointed out that while those teachers could not find positions, the need of teachers with experience in the elementary schools who could serve on faculties in the normal or teacher training schools was far from met. Lack of experience is in many cases a factor in over-supply, but that merely means that the supply is not composed of adequately equipped candidates: in physical education the supply

[1] Chase Going Woodhouse, "The Demand for College Trained Women in the United States, A Study of the Employment Situation," *Journal of the American Association of University Women*, XXIV, 61.

was inadequate, in the scientific and mathematical lines in which men still enjoy special prestige, the demand for women was low.

Among the graduates of the other professional schools, the experience was varied. Of 76 professional schools and independent agencies, 9 reported a surplus, 19 a light surplus, 41 said that they had met no difficulty; 5 said they had found a shortage rather than a surplus, and 2 had no data to give. Nine out of 14 library schools reported no difficulty in placing their graduates. Teachers of public school music and art teachers seemed to be finding employment; and secretarial jobs seemed available, though public accounting was found to be closed to women, and salaries as high as $45.00 a week in the secretarial field seemed available only as the result of promotion, never as a beginning salary. Women were not desired in statistical divisions of financial organizations, though jobs in department stores for women willing to begin at the bottom in the hope of promotion were not difficult to find. In advertising there were opportunities for the ostensibly journalistic aspirant rather than for the person concerned for the more strictly selling organization.

The situation has, of course, changed greatly for the worse since that study was made. The Schools are almost universally facing a crisis justifying a special White House Conference, and persons equipped to teach are unable to find employment; the American Library Association, in January of 1932, called attention to the serious amount of unemployment among experienced librarians and the number of new graduates of Library schools who were not finding employment. It was later recommended that in the library schools the size of classes be reduced by more rigid scrutiny of applicants, both as to scholarship and personality.[1]

Reference has been made to the fact that at earlier times of depression, the question of women has been relatively ignored. It is not meant that there were not innumerable women needing aid but there was at no earlier time so widespread a program of relief. It is, therefore, interesting to note in a community in which the relief program has been put on a sound basis of service the way in which what might be called work relief has been given unemployed women. In New York State, more than 3,000 women were given employment between November, 1931, and

[1] American Library Association *Bulletin*, 1932. 26: 337. See the *Library Journal* 57: 774, 968, 1000.

August, 1932.[1] The types of work included clerical and professional positions, such as stenographic, typing, bookkeeping, nursing, teaching. They were also employed in manufacturing, cleaning, altering and repairing clothing; they used their specialized knowledge to study food prices, catalogued in public libraries, made surveys, gave instruction to bedridden children. They were in many parts of the state: 500 in New York City, 700 in Binghampton, 278 in Troy, 216 in Buffalo, 114 in Utica, 100 in Schenectady, 100 in Nassau County, and 100 in Westchester County. Later reports may show similar work being done in other jurisdictions.

The question may be raised as to whether or not there could have been discovered trends toward unemployment. What may be noted is the degree to which the planlessness of productive activity renders the choice and tenure of employment accidental and precarious. The factors are, however, evidently such that if women become gainfully occupied persons, their employment, once obtained, is possibly less insecure than that of men.

[1] Release New York State Temporary Emergency Relief Administration, August 29, 1932.

PART III
WOMEN AND GOVERNMENT

Chapter XV

WOMEN AS VOTERS[1]

IN THE preceding pages, attention has been directed to two great general aspects of women's life and of their activities in other than family relationships.

In the following pages, an attempt is made to examine and set out the general course of development, especially since 1920, taken by women's activities in relation to the single problem of government.

In 1920, women were granted the right to vote throughout the United States and one era in the movement toward equality between the sexes was closed. Women have now, 1932, voted in their fourth presidential election. They have already participated in local, state and national campaigns, been candidates for office and assumed responsibility in high official positions. Can the direction in which they are going be ascertained and pointed out?

First in interest, if not in order of performance, is the question of voting. Having secured the right, do they exercise that right? If not universally, do they exercise it with increasing or decreasing interest? With increasing or declining effectiveness?

It must be recalled that since the ratification of the Nineteenth Amendment, men and women use the same ballots and that it is therefore a matter of practice in the various states, if records are kept in such a way as to distinguish the women from the men. It should also be recalled that the problem of the non-voters, whether men or women, has been one cause of grave concern to students of our political development.[2]

The admission of women to the electorate is not the only change in the suffrage during the period under consideration. Between 1900 and 1930, changes were made in four states in the property qualifications of voters and in nine states in the matter of ability to read and write. In spite, then, of the addition of women, the percentage of the electorate participating is estimated

[1] Again special obligation to Miss Marguerite Owen is gratefully acknowledged.
[2] *Recent Social Trends in the United States*, Chap. XXIX, p. 1489.

as having dropped from 79 per cent in 1900 to 53 per cent in 1920. This is in general explained by the southern one-party system, to general indifference, and in part to the newness of the women's ballot.[1]

Although the autumn elections of 1920 were the first in which women all over the country joined, it should not be forgotten that some form of suffrage for women existed in twenty-nine states before the federal constitution was amended.

The situation in 1920 has been summarized by historians who were party to the movement as follows:

> The total number of fully enfranchised women was now over seven and a quarter million in fifteen states. And so successful had been the work for presidential suffrage that these seven and a quarter million fully fledged voting women were flanked by eight million more who could vote for President in twelve other states—thirteen, if Vermont, where the legislative grant of Presidential suffrage was in question, be included. Moreover, Texas, another one party state, had followed the lead of Arkansas and granted primary suffrage to women.[2]

The women of Wyoming had voted since 1869, and in dealing justly with the record of the past it should be said that Wyoming was not the ultimate pioneer in granting suffrage to women. Two days before the independence of the colonies was declared the tax-paying women of New Jersey were given the vote by the Constitution of July, 2, 1776. In 1790 and 1797 legislative enactments confirmed them in the right.[3]

A century was nearly over before women voted again in the United States, and a second century was almost at its halfway mark before the women of the whole country voted.

The vanishing voter then, who was revealed in 1920, caused widespread concern. The National League of Women Voters, the lineal descendant of the National American Woman's Suffrage Association, was the first of a number of organizations to enlist jointly or independently in a pursuit. A crusade was inaugurated to "get out the vote" before the next quadrennial election. The League's special concern was the woman voter, and effort was

---

[1] *Ibid.* It may be noted that the percentage rose in 1928 to 61.

[2] Carrie Chapman Catt and Nettie Rogers Shuler, *Woman Suffrage and Politics; the Inner Story of the Suffrage Movement* (New York: Charles Scribner's Sons, 1926), p. 305.

[3] *Ibid.*, p. 9. It was a distinction briefly held however, for in 1807 a chastened legislature terminated their enjoyment of the franchise. The candid explanation was that although women had used the ballot quite generally, they had failed to support the proper candidates in the election!

particularly directed to the problem of arousing her interest and stimulating her participation before the habit of indifference should be deeply graven on her political character. A variety of devices were used, and immense energy was expended. But when the polls were closed after the national election of 1924, the preference of just a little more than half the eligible voters had been recorded. The estimated percentage for that year was a little more than 51 per cent.

In New Hampshire, for example, the proportion voting of those on the so-called "check lists" were estimated by the Secretary of State as declining from 68.9 per cent in 1921, to

TABLE 42.—GIVING PROPORTION OF REGISTERED PERSONS IN NEW HAMPSHIRE WHO VOTED BY BIENNIUMS*

Year	Population	Names on checklists	Ballots cast	Percentage voting
1920[1].....................	442,440	191,561	161,626	84.4
1922[2].....................	....	196,921	135,692	68.9
1924[3].....................	....	209,554	171,031	81.6
1926[4].....................	....	207,055	132,520	64.0
1928[5].....................	....	234,522	200,143	85.3
1930[6].....................	465,293	224,876	134,198	55.2

* Letter from Secretary of State, July 19, 1932.
[1] *Manual for General Court*, 1921, p. 140.
[2] *Ibid.*, 1923, p. 288.
[3] *Ibid.*, 1925, p. 364.
[4] *Ibid.*, 1927, p. 440.
[5] *Ibid.*, 1929, p. 442.
[6] *Ibid.*, 1931, p. 389.

55.2 per cent in 1931. These were, however, the figures for the non-presidential years. In those years the proportion remained as high as in 1920. The figures in Table 42 were supplied by the Secretary.

These figures are obviously not classified by sex, since the sex of voters is not indicated on the ballot.

There is no way by which an accurate share of the credit or blame for voting or non-voting can be given to women as against men. The responsibility for government by a minority cannot be fixed. It remains a question. No one knows exactly how many of the voters at any general election are women. Only a few studies have been made. Of as great interest perhaps as any attempt to set out the subject are those which were stimulated by the National League of Women Voters, and conducted by state and local leagues in the period from 1926 to 1929. Although those inquiries were conducted by amateurs, they were under skilled direction. In the limited areas surveyed the information was assembled by an examination of the official poll lists and by house-to-house canvassing. The reports from one state where the work appears to have been admirably conducted may be quoted.[1]

In Minnesota the voting record of twelve districts was traced back through a four-year period with as many as eight elections. Seven districts were in first class cities, two were in a city of about 4,000 people, and three were in villages of about 1,000 population. A total population of more than 13,000, of whom 56 per cent were of voting age, was covered.

The surveys showed that the voting records of men in the selected districts were better than those of women. So far as occupational groups were studied the poorest voting record was held by women in domestic service. Of both sexes it appeared to be true that married people had a better voting record than the unmarried and that permanence of residence and property ownership coincided with regular voting habits. It is of general interest to note that the range of percentage was all the way from 30 per cent in a transient city rooming house district to 94 per cent in one of the villages.

The rise in 1928, when 61.04 per cent of the eligible voters cast their ballots, might seem to indicate that the initiation of women had taken place. Only time and the percentages of the future can tell whether the explanation is adequate. The estimated percentage for 1928 still falls short of any low mark before the spiritless sag of 1920 was reached. Certainly in 1928, as in 1916, there were special reasons why interest in the contest was acute. In contrast with 70.5 per cent in 1916, the 61.04 per cent in 1928 seems low.

The question is not only do women vote less universally than men, but as the years pass, are they voting in larger or in smaller proportions than they have voted before or than the men vote? Voting is, of course, the ultimate expression of interest, of responsibility, and of choice. Registration is one step, an essential step, in the direction of that exercise, and figures with reference to

[1] Made to the Conference on Voting and Non-Voting—a feature of the meeting of the General Council of the National League of Women Voters in Washington, April 23, 1929.

registration therefore are not irrelevant, and the figures with reference to the registration of men and women are available for several jurisdictions. In Chicago, as shown in Table 43, it appears that, between 1914 and 1932, there has been a fairly steady increase in the proportion which women have made of the registered group.[1] Whereas, in 1914, out of 100 registered persons, 68 were men, in 1931, only 58 were men. What the number was of either sex eligible to register, cannot be told.

TABLE 43.—MEN AND WOMEN REGISTERED TO VOTE IN CHICAGO, 1914–1932[a]

Year	Number		Per cent	
	Men	Women	Men	Women
1914	455,283	217,614	67.7	32.3
1915	486,815	282,291	63.3	36.7
1916	470,029	261,172	64.3	35.7
1917	490,604	297,931	62.2	37.8
1918	493,578	286,634	63.3	36.7
1919	473,124	266,904	63.9	36.1
1920	550,060	334,060	62.2	37.8
1921	552,101	334,834	62.2	37.8
1922	511,284	293,364	63.5	36.5
1923	539,063	313,381	63.2	36.8
1924	654,640	410,255	61.5	38.5
1925	666,674	420,495	61.3	38.7
1926	556,735	318,546	63.6	36.4
1927	705,489	440,919	61.5	38.5
1928	787,498	599,133	56.8	43.2
1929	766,994	583,735	56.8	43.2
1930	736,343	527,891	58.2	41.7
1931	817,703	594,432	57.9	42.1

[a] Figures obtained from *Chicago Daily News Almanacs*, 1915–1932.

In Louisiana, in the same way, as can be seen from Table 44, between 1920 and 1930, registered women rose from 18 to 30 per cent of the registered voters, while among white voters the increase was from 14 to 34 per cent of the registered citizens.

The figures for a more recent period have been graciously supplied from some jurisdictions. In Arizona, for example, the figures indicate a higher percentage increase among the women voters than among the men.

A study of voting in the November election of 1930 was made by the Registrar of Los Angeles, California. It appears that 853,676 citizens registered and were eligible to vote. Of these,

[1] *Recent Social Trends in the United States*, Chap. XIV.

439,062, or a few more than half, were men, and 414,614, or a few less than half, were women. On election day, only 500,801 of those registered presented themselves to vote. Of these, 227,744 were women. They were 45.5 per cent of those who voted; and the women who voted were 55 per cent of those women who registered. The men who voted were 54.5 per cent of the voters and 66 per cent of those who had registered. In twenty-three of the incorporated cities in the county outside of Los Angeles City more women than men registered, but in only six of those did a larger number of women actually vote.

TABLE 44.—NUMBER MEN AND WOMEN REGISTERED TO VOTE IN LOUISIANA, BY RACE, 1920–1928

Year	White men	White women	Colored men	Colored women	Total women	Per cent women of total registered voters
October 2, 1920ᵃ	211,831	45,451	1,632ᶠ	1,901ᵍ	47,352	18.15
October 7, 1922ᵇ	153,159	38,032	508	90	38,122	19.87
March 22, 1924ᶜ	220,691	87,929	599	99	88,028	28.45
October 4, 1924ᶜ	227,035	90,101	791	164	90,265	28.37
October 2, 1926ᵈ	194,596	79,936	828	160	80,096	29.07
March 17, 1928ᵉ	254,575	108,482	1,653	307	108,769	29.79
October 6, 1928ᶜ	261,827	115,136	1,734	320	115,456	30.46

ᵃ Report of the Secretary of State to His Excellency the Governor of Louisiana, January 1, 1921, pp. 336–37.

ᵇ Ibid., January 1, 1923, pp. 306–307.

ᶜ Ibid., January 1, 1925, pp. 340 and 342.

ᵈ Ibid., January 1, 1927, p. 368.

ᵉ Ibid., January 1, 1929, pp. 328 and 330.

ᶠ 802 of these were registered in the Parish of Orleans.

ᵍ 1,797 of these were registered in the Parish of Orleans.

So far as registration is concerned, the records of men and women in the county outside Los Angeles City were almost alike. The number of men who registered was 188,475, and of women, 188,466. On election day, however, 177,672, or 94 per cent of the registered men, voted and only 103,329, or 54.8 per cent of the registered women, voted. In Los Angeles City, 250,587 men registered, and only 155,385, or 62 per cent of those registered, voted. The number of women registered was 226,148, of whom only 55 per cent came to the polls on election day. Women were 47 per cent of those registering and only 44 per cent of those voting.

On the other hand, on May 2, 1932, in St. Paul, at the city election, of 106,283 registered voters, of whom 61,898 were men and 44,385 were women, 75 per cent of the men and 79.57 per cent of the women voted; at the Presidential election in 1928, 71 per cent of the registered men voted, and 75 per cent of the registered women.[1]

TABLE 45.—NUMBER OF MEN AND WOMEN REGISTERED TO VOTE IN THE STATE OF PENNSYLVANIA, 1925 AND 1931[a]

Year	Number registered			Per cent registered		Per cent of increase	
	Men	Women	Total	Men	Women	Men	Women
1925	1,886,820	1,358,145	3,244,965	58.15	41.85		
1931	2,144,713	1,715,272	3,859,985	55.56	44.44	0.137	0.263
Total	4,031,533	3,073,417	7,104,950	56.74	43.26		

[a] Courteously supplied by the Secretary of State, to whom appreciative acknowledgments are made.

TABLE 46.—NUMBER OF MEN AND WOMEN REGISTERED TO VOTE IN THE STATE OF RHODE ISLAND, 1920–1930[a]

Year	Number registered			Per cent registered		Percentage of increase	
	Men	Women	Total	Men	Women	Men	Women
1920	122,120	77,836	199,956	61.07	38.93		
1922	121,019	81,245	202,264	59.83	40.17	−0.009	0.057
1924	137,493	108,586	246,079	55.87	44.13	0.119	0.336
1926	120,685	90,290	210,975	57.20	42.80	−0.122	−0.168
1928	147,986	121,874	269,860	54.84	45.16	0.226	0.350
1930	146,281	121,516	267,797	54.62	45.38	−0.012	−0.003
Total	795,584	601,347	1,396,931	56.95	43.05		

[a] Courteously supplied by the Secretary of State, to whom appreciative acknowledgments are made.

In Pennsylvania, too, the figures are available by sex for a few years, and are shown in Table 45. In 1925, for example, 41.8 per cent of the registrants were women, 1,368,395 women out of a total of 3,244,965, while in 1931, they were 44 per cent, or 1,715,-292 out of a total of 3,859,985. That is, the percentage increase of women registering was 21, of men 13 per cent. In Rhode

[1] Letter from the City Clerk and Commissioner of Education.

WOMEN IN THE TWENTIETH CENTURY

Island, as shown in Table 46, of the 199,956 registrants in 1920, 38.93 per cent were women. In 1922, the percentage was 40.16; in 1924, 44.12; in 1926, women were only 42.79 per cent of those voting; in 1928 they were 45.16 per cent; in 1930, 45.37 per cent. That is, at no time have they been half of those who registered, but there has been an increase in the number of women during the decade of 43,680, or a percentage increase of 56, while the increase in the number of men voting has been 24,161 or less than 20 per cent. The numbers are smaller in the years that are not presidential for both men and women.

TABLE 47.—NUMBER OF MEN AND WOMEN REGISTERED TO VOTE IN THE STATE OF VERMONT, 1924-1930[a]

Year	Number registered			Per cent registered		Percentage of increase	
	Men	Women	Total	Men	Women	Men	Women
1924	90,012	71,271	161,283	55.81	44.19		
1926	87,768	71,119	158,887	55.24	44.76	−0.025	−0.0007
1928	92,503	82,845	175,348	52.75	47.25	0.053	0.165
1930	89,490	79,029	168,519	53.10	46.90	−0.032	−0.046
Total	359,773	304,264	664,037	54.18	45.82		

[a] Courteously supplied by the Secretary of State, to whom appreciative acknowledgments are made.

In Vermont, as shown in Table 47, women registrants increased from 44 to 47 per cent of those registering. Again 1928 was the high water level, both in the total and in the percentage women make of the total.

Besides figures of this kind, it is possible to obtain opinions on the subject, and in asking for such statistics as are available the secretary of state was asked, as was the National Committee woman of each major party in each state, to give an opinion as to whether or not women's interest in government and politics was increasing.

Of the secretaries of state, 39 replied. Of these, 30 reported that no figures were available. Some, however, express quite definite views which may be quoted, and nine gave some figures or referred to sources from which figures might be obtained. The Secretary of State for Arizona, for example, writes, "From what we hear around the State, there will be a larger number of women

candidates for the legislature and for state and county officers
than ever before."[1] From Florida, the Secretary writes, "My
opinion is that there is a slightly increasing interest of the women
in voting and government affairs."[1]

From Indiana, the Secretary writes, "It is the opinion of the
writer that the men and women are equally divided."[2] In Iowa,
on the basis of a questionnaire sent out in 1929 to the Committee
women, the vice-chairman of the Republican State Committee
thought that women were very nearly half the voters.

From Minnesota, the Secretary[2] writes that he thinks the
economic situation has stimulated an increasing interest on the
part of both men and women. Similar opinions testifying to a
general increase in interest is expressed in letters from Utah,[1]
Washington,[1] and Wisconsin.[1] There are several women holding
the office of Secretary of State.[3] One of them writes:

We do not have any compiled figures judging the relative interest of
men and women in governmental affairs in this State.
However, from personal observation, I can state that the growing
interest of women in politics throughout the State is very noticeable.
More women run for public office every year, and more are receiving
appointments to public and semi-public office. I am sorry that there are
no figures published to substantiate such statements.

An interesting statement comes from Hawaii showing that in
1920, 65.4 per cent of the registered men voted and 43.8 per cent
of the women, while in 1930, 63.4 per cent of the registered men
and 57.8 per cent of the registered women voted. The increases
of the different population elements are interestingly varied, as
can be seen from the following tables:

The percentage of male registered voters is consistently larger
than the percentage of female registered voters except for the
American, British, Germans and others in 1930. There is a small
decrease in the percentage of the male registered voters in 1930
but a fairly large increase in the female registered voters in
the same year.

For the most part there has been an increase in the percentages
for each race every two years and there has been a varying
increase in the totals without exception.

[1] Letter dated July 18, 1932.
[2] Letter dated July 16, 1932.
[3] *e.g.*, Kentucky, New Mexico and South Dakota.

TABLE 48.—THE PERCENTAGE OF REGISTERED VOTERS OF THE CITIZENS OF
VOTING AGE IN THE TERRITORY OF HAWAII IN 1920 AND 1930,
ACCORDING TO RACE AND SEX

Race	Percentage of registered voters			
	1920		1930	
	Male	Female	Male	Female
Hawaiian.............................	(ᵃ)	90.7	(ᵃ)	(ᵃ)
Part Hawaiian........................	(ᵇ)	(ᵇ)	54.9	42.6
Portuguese...........................	73.7	15.4	98.3	57.0
Chinese..............................	57.1	9.3	76.6	43.0
Japanese.............................	43.4	4.6	77.3	27.2
Americans, British, Germans and others........	45.9	45.7	32.2	51.4
Total.............................	65.4	43.8	63.4	57.8
Grand total.........................	53.6		61.1	

ᵃ Number of registered voters exceeds number of citizens of voting age.
ᵇ Number of registered voters omitted.

TABLE 49.—PERCENTAGE OF INCREASE IN THE NUMBER OF FEMALE REGISTERED
VOTERS IN THE TERRITORY OF HAWAII IN BIENNIAL PERIODS FROM
1920 TO 1930, ACCORDING TO RACE

Race	Percentage of increase				
	1922	1924	1926	1928	1930
Hawaiian........................	23.6	−22.7	5.5	21.0	0.1
Part Hawaiian...................	(ᵃ)	(ᵃ)	18.1	−30.6	37.5
Portuguese......................	96.9	53.2	23.8	25.0	17.0
Chinese.........................	65.9	55.1	77.4	73.2	20.4
Japanese........................	112.3	69.4	67.3	108.7	64.9
American........................	36.0	3.0	19.5	5.0	16.0
British..........................	83.5	−28.5	10.5	23.4	19.0
German.........................	(ᵃ)	(ᵃ)	−4.3	50.0	14.3
Others..........................	66.3	13.5	22.5	38.5	11.1
Total..........................	33.1	10.6	11.8	17.0	13.9

ᵃ Figures omitted.

In Porto Rico, women have for the first time gained the right
to vote, and 120,000 women have registered, together with
108,000 new men registrants. However, there were already
266,000 men on the lists. The superintendent of elections com-

ments, "It will be several years before we can judge of the women's interest."

The question is not merely how many women vote, but how they vote. There, however, the reply must be less definite than the question of numbers. Before 1920, questions like this could be answered in such jurisdictions as Illinois where different voting capacity led to the use of different ballots for men and women.

The effect of the ratification of the Nineteenth Amendment has been likened not inaptly to the demobilization of the defense forces after a war. Such demobilization is followed, naturally, first by a great letting-down of moral energy and force, and second by the development of a diversification of aims and interests among and between those who have been united in the attack upon a common enemy. It is unnecessary to point out into what a confused and difficult situation the women were thrown by the ratification of the Amendment. How they had voted was a question which had already aroused interest, and in 1914 and 1915, data were supplied by the *National Municipal Review* with reference to the effects of women's votes in the Chicago elections of those years.[1] In 1919, a study was made of an election in Portland, Oregon, and on the basis of certain assumptions and of certain statistical calculations, it was concluded that, on the whole, women were conservative voters.[2]

In 1924, again, the statistician attacked the question, and although it was clear that since women's ballots were not separated from men's ballots definite conclusions could not be drawn, the impression was definitely made that women's use of the vote had been "ineffective," while it was admitted that with time and practice, they might overcome this ineffectiveness.[3]

In 1928, it seemed to be accepted that, whereas before 1920 they may not have "known what they wanted,"[4] they had "arrived in politics."[5] One student estimated that 18,000,000

[1] *National Municipal Review* (Published by the National Municipal League, 261 Broadway, New York, N. Y.), IV: 437; V: 460.

[2] William F. Ogburn and Inez Goltra, "How Women Vote: A Study of an Election in Portland, Oregon," *Political Science Quarterly*, XXIV (1919), 413–33.

[3] S. A. Rice and M. M. Willey, "American Women's Ineffective Use of the Vote," *Cur. Hist. M., N. Y. Times*, XX (1924), 641–47.

[4] M. Adams, "Did They Know What They Wanted?" *Outlook*, XLVII, 528–30.

[5] E. F. Barnard, "Madame Arrives in Politics." *North American*, 226 (1928), 551–56.

women may have voted in 1928 and commented that, "Having at length developed effective organizations and having got their names at last on the poll books, the women of America may reasonably be depended upon in future presidential campaigns to do their part in elections."[1]

There will undoubtedly be many interpretations of the part played by women in the campaign of 1932, but the results of that campaign will, of course, be fully known only after a considerable period of time. In the meantime, by reference to the registration figures in a number of states, and by consultation with public officials, men and women alike in many jurisdictions, some impressions may be gained of the course of women's experience and participation as voters during the years since the ratification of the amendment.

An interesting editorial comment to that effect concludes with the words:

No one will ever know exactly what part the women played in the final result, since voting machines tell no tales on them. But it is fairly certain that they are playing an increasingly important rôle in national elections. The rise in the popular vote from 29,000,000 in 1924 to 37,000,000 in 1928 undoubtedly reflected their increasing participation. One expert, Simon Michelet, estimates that women cast 30 per cent of the total vote in 1920, 35 per cent in 1924 and 45 per cent in 1928.[2]

[1] Simon Michelet (Chairman of the Get Out the Votes Committee, Washington, D. C.), *The Election of 1928*, p. 13.
[2] New York *Times*, October 25, 1932.

CHAPTER XVI

THE WOMEN'S BLOC

OTHER aspects of women's participation in political activity
offer perhaps more rewarding data than those testifying
to their use of the ballot. There is lobbying. For to women,
long denied the right to express their political convictions directly
through their ballots, lobbying seemed to become a natural
channel for exercising influence.

It began with anti-slavery. To the National Anti-Slavery
Society, formed in 1833, is given the honor of being not only the
first organized woman's society, but also "the first effort of
women to affect a political question."[1] Women held meetings,
they addressed petitions to Congress. In 1837, John Quincy
Adams introduced their anti-slavery petition in the House of
Representatives as a part of his campaign to establish the right
of petition for all, a right which had been hitherto believed to
belong only to electors.

The cause of temperance followed. After 1865, the fight for
equal suffrage with men was continuously advanced. In the
nineties the reports of women's meetings show that a variety of
social welfare measures were being advocated at state capitols
and in council chambers. Ever since, and in increasing numbers,
women have lobbied for causes they thought good.

As a matter of history, the first woman lobbyist to enjoy more
than local influence advocated a particular reform not related to
those other three causes which women so early espoused. She was
Dorothea Lynde Dix and it was the care of the indigent insane
which in the forties and fifties excited her continuous solicitude
and drove her in her devoted championship from state to state
and finally to the Congress in Washington.[2]

Clara Barton was another pioneer lobbyist. The adherence
of the United States to the treaty of 1864 by which the Red
Cross was recognized as an international agency of mercy was

[1] Catt and Shuler, *op. cit.*, p. 14.
[2] Tiffany, *op. cit.*, 1890, pp. 77–82, 90.

[257]

the objective sought by Clara Barton during seven long years.[1]

In the meantime the suffrage lobby grew and the records of suffrage associations show how faithfully the women struggled with state legislatures, with constitutional conventions, attended and organized political meetings, and in Washington year after year tried to secure congressional action. The reports of less agitating groups of other women reveal that they, perhaps too fearful to ask for the vote as yet, were willing to lobby for the welfare measures which are still thought of as their special concern.

In 1900, the General Federation of Women's Clubs resolved at its Biennial meeting to work for legislation for women and children so that "every state will equal the best already enacted," and a paragraph in the Proceedings of the 1904 Biennial reads, "The Legislative Committee of the General Federation recommends the formation of legislative committees in every department club, the duty of which shall be to keep the clubs informed as to bills pending in municipal, state, and national legislatures. There are many questions, which for special reasons, are of paramount interest to women. Marriage and divorce, child protection, child labor, pure food, forestry and libraries, are subjects which the clubs are asked to follow." Lobbying at Washington was reported too. In 1905, the Industrial Committee worked "to secure the passage of a bill through Congress for an appropriation to enable a bureau of experts to investigate industrial conditions of American working women."

Lobbying was thus a well recognized form of activity for public spirited women long before the franchise was granted. As early as 1906 the reports of women's organizations contain reference to Legislative Councils in which the constantly increasing number of women's organized groups united to advocate their common interests. An admirable speech on lobbying appears in the record of the 1904 Biennial of the General Federation. And ten years later, in 1914, and again in 1916, there were conferences at which the technique of lobbying was discussed apart from the subject matter of the measures to be advanced. In 1914, the Minnesota Federation testified to its intention to have in the future a paid legislative worker at the Capitol.

[1] William Barton, *Life of Clara Barton, Founder of the American Red Cross* (Boston: Houghton Mifflin Co., 1922), II, Chaps. I, II, VIII, IX, X.

In 1920 then, when they finally achieved the ballot, women had lobbied for over fifty years and in growing numbers. Child labor laws had been passed, educational facilities had been improved, and women had been liberated from outworn laws governing family relationships and protected against newly recognized industrial hazards—all due in considerable measure to the efforts of women lobbying in state capitols from coast to coast and in Washington.

After 1920, the right to vote stimulated the activities of women as lobbyists. They remembered, perhaps, the testimony of Idaho women[1] after state suffrage was won by constitutional amendment, " . . . The innovation has brought in its train a disposition to give greater consideration to women's clubs and the work they undertake," and of California, whose delegates to the 1914 Biennial stated that they had perceived a more sympathetic and favorable attitude toward their interests after they became voters. The women of Oregon had written in a similar vein. It was to be expected then that with women voting all over the country the measure of their influence at the national Capitol and the record of their accomplishments would be sharply increased.

A Woman's Joint Congressional Committee was organized in Washington; its purpose was to serve as a clearing house for the federal legislative activities of member organizations, and its plan of organization was similar to the Legislative Councils which had flourished in the states for over a decade. Ten national organizations[2] were charter members. They were: The American Association of University Women, The American Home Economics Association, The General Federation of Women's Clubs, The National Congress of Mothers and Parent-Teachers Associations, The National Consumers' League, The National Council of Jewish Women, The National Federation of Business and Professional Women's Clubs, The National League of Women Voters, National Women's Christian Temperance Union, and National Women's Trade Union League.

Two more organizations joined in the second year of its existence, namely, The Girls' Friendly Society of America and the

---

[1] At the Biennial Convention of the General Federation of Women's Clubs in 1898.

[2] Something of the history and purpose of these organizations is given in the chapter on Women's Organizations.

National Board of Young Women's Christian Association. In 1922 The National Council of Women and The Service Star Legion came in.

In 1923, the membership had increased to seventeen.[1] The Woman's Joint Congressional Committee has functioned without interruption. Although the Committee itself has neither supported nor opposed any legislation, its member organizations working together on common measures have come to be recognized as the "Women's Lobby on Capitol Hill," which was in hostile irony, perhaps, described as the "most highly organized and powerful lobby ever seen in Washington."[2] Not every national organization of women belongs, of course, but an examination of its membership and its progress since 1920 gives perhaps as good an indication as any of the trend of women's interests in lobbying. In 1923 the American Federation of Teachers, the National Education Association and the National Committee for a Department of Education joined. In 1924 the American Nurses Association, the Council of Women for Home Missions, the Medical Women's National Association and the National Association of Colored Women joined. In 1925 the Medical Women of the Institute of Homeopathy, the Women's Homeopathic Medical Fraternity, and in 1931, the American Dietetic Association joined. In 1927 the National Women's Christian Temperance Union withdrew, as did the General Federation, the National Association of Colored Women and the National Council of Women in 1928.

Two federal legislative victories rewarded women's efforts during their first two years of lobbying as voters. The *Maternity and Infancy* Law,[3] which enabled the federal government and the states to cooperate in the preservation of the lives of mothers and babies, was enacted in 1921, and the *Nationality of Women* Act, which granted married women a citizenship status independent of their husbands, became a law September 22, 1922.[4]

[1] In 1925, there were 21 organizations who were members, in 1927 there were 21, in 1929 there were 18, and 19 in 1931 and 1932. (From letter from Secretary, June 4, 1931, also on November 9, 1932.)

[2] *Journal of the American Medical Association*, 1922, p. 1542.

[3] 42 *U. S. Statutes at Large*, p. 224, Sixty-seventh Congress, First Session, Ch. 135. U. S. Children's Bureau Publication No. 203, reviews the history of that Act. See also White House Conference Publications. See also, *Modern Social Trends*, Frank, Chapter on Childhood and Youth.

[4] 42 *U. S. Statutes at Large*, p. 1021, Sixty-seventh Congress, Second Session, Ch. 411; 46 *U. S. Statutes at Large*, p. 854, Seventy-first Congress, Second Session,

These were women's measures, proposed and advanced through their initiative and energy and designed to affect their lives directly. They were major achievements and seemed to assume the more generous consideration for women's interests in government which was to be expected in the future.

The prevention of child labor, as has been pointed out, had been one of the first causes which women embraced to advance through legislation. State laws were unequal and two federal laws designed to correct the evil had been declared unconstitutional.[1] In 1924, therefore, every organization in the Woman's Joint Congressional Committee united with groups outside and, with the approval of the President and of influential leaders of both Houses, advocated an amendment to the Federal Constitution which would enable the Congress to legislate on the subject of child labor.

In April of 1924, the legislative achievements of women since 1920 were summarized as including in addition to the Maternity and Infancy Act and the Nationality of Women Act:

Appropriations for the U. S. Children's Bureau carried in the Appropriation Acts for the years 1922, 1923, and 1924.

An Act to extend the Federal aid provisions of the Sheppard-Towner Maternity and Infancy Act to Hawaii. (March 10, 1924.)[2]

An Act to provide for the classification of civilian positions within the District of Columbia and in the field services, carrying the proviso that in determining the rate of compensation for equal work irrespective of sex shall be followed. (March 4, 1923.)[3]

An Act to regulate interstate and foreign commerce in livestock, livestock products, dairy products, poultry products and eggs and for other purposes. (August 15, 1921.)[4]

An Act to prohibit the shipment of filled milk in interstate and foreign commerce. (March 4, 1923.)[5]

An Act to establish a commission to be known as the United States Coal Commission for the purpose of securing information in connection

---

Ch. 835; *ibid.*, p. 1511, Seventy-first Congress, Third Session, Ch. 442. See *The American Journal of International Law* 36: 700, Ernest J. Hover, "Citizenship of Women in the United States." See *Equal Rights*, XVIII, 315, "Nationality of Women."

[1] 39 *U. S. Statutes at Large*, p. 677, Sixty-fourth Congress, First Session, Ch. 432; *Hammer* v. *Dagenhart*, 247 U. S. 251 (1917); *Bailey* v. *Drexel Furniture Co.*, 259 U. S. 20 (1918).

[2] 43 *U. S. Statutes at Large*, p. 17, 68th Congress, First Session, Ch. 46.

[3] *U. S. Statutes at Large* 42: 1488; 67th Congress, Fourth Session, Ch. 265.

[4] *Ibid.*, 42: 181; 67th Congress, First Session, Ch. 80.

[5] A part of the Pure Food Control Movement. *Ibid.*, 42: 1486; *ibid.*, Fourth Session, Ch. 262.

with questions relative to interstate commerce in coal. (September 22, 1922.)[1].

An Act to amend the Coal Commission Act (September 2?, 1922)[2] for the purpose of strengthening the original act. (March 4, 1? ?3.)[3]

The proposed Child Labor Amendment[4] and the bill to provide an institution for federal women prisoners[5] were both passed by the Congress shortly after this summary had been made.

The adoption of the child labor amendment by the necessary two-thirds majority of both Houses and its submission to the states for ratification was heralded as the third major legislative victory for enfranchised women, and there was much rejoicing. Women seemed to be marching steadily toward the realization of a more influential participation in the law making process.

In June of 1924 the National Party Conventions met. The plank on Child Labor which the Republican convention adopted, read:

We commend congress for having recognized this possibility in its prompt adoption of the recommendation of President Coolidge for a constitutional amendment authorizing congress to legislate on the subject of child labor, and we urge the prompt consideration of that amendment by the legislatures of the various states.

It commended the Congress for the adoption of the proposed amendment and urged its prompt consideration by the states. The Democratic platform recited boastful history:

Without the votes of Democratic members of the Congress the proposed Child Labor amendment would not have been submitted for ratification.

In spite, however, of the ardent solicitation of women who appeared before the Resolutions Committee of both major parties, and the earnest persuasion of women supposed to have influence in party councils, neither platform contained a positive statement in favor of the new amendment. Only the Progressive Conference, meeting after the two parties had acted, adopted a candid plank urging ratification of the women's major measure.

In January, 1925, forty-two state legislatures were in session. Arkansas[6] had ratified at a special session in 1924, and only

[1] *Ibid.*, 42: 1023; 67th Congress, Second Session, Ch. 412.
[2] *Ibid.*, 42: 1464; 67th Congress, Fourth Session, Ch. 248.
[3] *Ibid.*, 68th Congress, First Session 6/4/24.
[4] *Ibid.*, 43: 670.
[5] *Ibid.*, 43: 473, 68th Congress, First Session, Ch. 287.
[6] *Annual Report of the Chief of the Children's Bureau*, 1924, p. 8.

three, those of Arizona, California, and Wisconsin, took similar action in 1925.[1] When the sessions had all adjourned, overwhelming defeat had overtaken this most cherished and most conspicuous of women's measures. While Montana[2] ratified in 1927, it was clear that the winter of discontent in politics had come for women, and when the year 1932 came to an end only Colorado[3] had acted.

For the purposes of this study it is unnecessary to analyze or even outline the bewildering campaign by which an immensely popular measure became the most despised. Unquestionably neither the women's organizations nor the representatives of organized labor upon whose efforts the campaigns for ratification usually rested were adequately prepared for its defense. Women particularly, and there were women champions in states where labor's force was small, had depended upon the general public approval of their cause and were innocent with the false sense of security which their earlier triumphs had fostered. To recite and interpret statistics, to explain administrative practices, to expound constitutional law, above all to meet misleading, deliberately fabricated, insinuations as to the domestic consequences of the amendment, those were tasks essential for the amendment's advocates to master. If they were too difficult who could quite wonder?

The records of meetings of women's organizations in 1925 and afterward reveal lively debate on the subject, ending in most cases with a reaffirmation of their support. Their steady faithfulness to this cause has not yet been rewarded by favorable legislative action. Since 1925, four state legislatures, as has been pointed out, have reconsidered their first rejection. In the meantime, although there has been some improvement in state standards, there is still the inequality that had called for action on a national scale. The modest standards of the first federal child labor law which was enacted in 1916[4] are not yet realized by state action, and thirty years after the adoption of the resolution of the General Federation that club women should work so

[1] *Ibid.*, 1925, p. 7.
[2] *Ibid.*, 1927, p. 27.
[3] *Ibid.*, 1931, p. 42.
[4] The law was in effect for nine months—from September 1, 1917 to June, 1918. See United States Children's Bureau Publication No. 79. *The Administration of the First Federal Child Labor Law.* See also White House Conference Publications on *Child Labor* and on *Vocational Guidance.*

that every state should "Equal the best" is still a goal toward which it is necessary to strive.

The fate of the child labor amendment was disheartening to women, and equally encouraging to those who distrusted an increase in the influence of women as voters. Today, as women's organizations survey the past twelve years, they must reflect that so far as federal legislation is concerned the cause of Child Welfare, which they had so long ago espoused, has advanced little, if any, since 1921.

In that year the Maternity and Infancy Act was passed, with a five-year limit on the appropriation which it authorized to match the funds which states accepting the benefits of the Act would make available. On January 22, 1927, the termination date of the federal appropriation was advanced two years. But in spite of the devoted and persistent efforts of every large national organization of women, the federal program for Maternity and Infancy Hygiene was allowed to lapse seven years after it was inaugurated.

The character of the measures which seemed the women's undoing should be briefly explained. Apparently, they were not radical measures; they set out no dream of a Utopian commonwealth. They seemed harmless. And they were, in fact, highly conservative, if one thinks of the values on which the enduring life of the community must draw. The lives of mothers and infants is the life of the nation, and the protection of the childhood against early exhaustion is likewise essential to a vigorous and competent citizenship. It seemed as though the women were just doing on a larger platform what women had been always supposed to do—care for women in childbirth, welcome the newborn and nurture the children. But there is an essential conflict between the purpose of making the United States everywhere a fit and safe place in which mothers may confidently anticipate the coming of their children, in which infants can safely enter on life, in which children can pass into adolescence, and that of securing marketable products whose sale will bring a profit to the producer. It is in a future not yet attained in which Scripture will be fulfilled and the guiding hand of the child's leadership brings the community to the place where the lamb of general welfare and the lion of competitive gain find their interests reconciled and "lie down together."

This does not mean that there have been no successes to reward the efforts of women lobbying in Washington these past ten years. They have been less conspicuous than the failures, but it is fair to record that sub-committees of the Woman's Joint Congressional Committee have supported and secured amendments to the Cable Act removing almost all of the disabilities of married women which remained in respect to their citizenship after the original act was secured. They have championed adequate appropriations for the work of bureaus of special interest to women, they have been interested in child welfare measures passed for the District of Columbia. Two measures in the field of international relations—one the proposal that the United States should adhere to the Permanent Court of International Justice, and the other the Kellogg Multilateral Treaty—were supported by active sub-committees and received favorable Senate action. Neither of these, however, could be said to be women's measures.

It should be explained that the measures whose advocacy prompts the organization of a sub-committee is only a partial list of the legislative activity of those same organizations. A sub-committee of the Woman's Joint Congressional Committee is formed whenever a certain number of member organizations unite to support or oppose a given measure. In the beginning only three interested organizations were required. At one time the number was raised to seven. For several years now it has remained stationary at five. Obviously, therefore, there are measures supported by member groups in respect to which there are not a sufficient number of other organizations interested to make possible the organization of a sub-committee. Some of these should be mentioned. The National Council of Jewish Women, for example, has opposed any plan of calendar simplification which would change the Sabbath Day; and, like the National Board of the Y. W. C. A., has concerned itself with various legislative proposals affecting the welfare of immigrants and immigration problems. The General Federation of Women's Clubs has been concerned with legislation affecting the care of American Indians and supported a prison labor bill, which was adopted. The League of Women Voters supported the Norris plan for government operation of Muscle Shoals, and the so-called "Lame Duck" amendment to the Constitution which was finally submitted in 1931–1932 and was ratified within a record breaking period. The National Association of Business and Professional Women's Clubs recently favored an increase in the income tax exemption allowed for single persons. And no summary can omit the constant vigilance of the National Women's Christian Temperance Union in behalf of the legislation falling in its special field. Nor can the success of the women's organizations for so-called prohibition reform be ignored. The recent swift change of public opinion, as at least registered in the 1932 platforms of the two parties, owes much of its momentum to the effective organization of the women to secure the repeal of the Eighteenth Amendment.

Unquestionably, the sphere of women's interest in government has widened. That the list of their accomplishments has not been lengthened correspondingly is likewise evident. What is true of federal legislation is also true of the states.

It was to the 1904 Biennial of the General Federation of Women's Clubs that Idaho reported, "Candidates for the legislature will be asked for their position on these bills in advance of election, and if they take adverse stands they will never pass the stage of being candidates if women's votes are numerous enough."

In 1924, the reports of state legislation enacted with the support of the League and other women's organization enacted with the adoption of the suffrage amendment were summarized. The record was complete for only three years as the legislative sessions of 1924, less than twelve in number, were at the time not yet adjourned. The years included two sessions in thirty-six states, three sessions in six states and one session in six states. The summary follows:

TABLE 50

Subject	No. of states	Bills supported by state Leagues passed	Bills opposed by state Leagues defeated
Child welfare.................................	45	130	3
Uniform laws concerning women (i.e., removal of legal discriminations against women)......................	30	86	19
Social hygiene..	19	45	3
Education...	22	43	5
Efficiency in government.............................	31	27	27
Women in industry....................................	14	18	5
Living costs..	6	7	1
Miscellaneous..	23	64	1

Four hundred and twenty bills approved by the League had become laws since 1920, and, in the states, as in the national Congress, child welfare held first place, with the removal of the legal discrimination against women second.

In 1930, at the ten-year anniversary convention of the League of Women Voters, the president of the League recapitulated the state legislative achievements which the League claimed alone or shared with other organizations. In 1930, the sum of state laws concerning the legal status of women included 130 enactments in 32 states, the District of Columbia and Hawaii during the ten-year period. Of the total, it is of interest to note that the largest number—24 measures in 12 states—related to property rights of married women. Equal guardianship measures had totaled 21 enactments in 17 states, and office-holding and voting rights came next with 20 enactments in 13 states.

In the effort toward Efficiency in Government, 76 state legislative victories had been won, and 60 measures which had been opposed had been defeated. The enactments included election law reforms in 16 states, with Permanent Registration a feature in 4 states, and measures for improved state administration in 11.

Sixty-one child welfare measures had been enacted with League support; 22 of them in 16 states were laws to limit working hours, and 39 measures in 23 states were enacted for the protection of dependent, delinquent, neglected and handicapped children. The Education Committee boasted compulsory education laws in 9 states and 60 additional laws for the improvement of school administration and finance in 27 states. Seventy-five measures are credited to the Social Hygiene Committees in the various states, and 25 victories are classified as relating to the work of the Committee on Women in Industry. The legislative achievements of the Committee on Living Costs in the States are not listed.

In 1930, then, looking backward a decade, the League of Women Voters pointed to a total of 436 laws enacted with its support. Presented as the record of 1924 was shown, the ten-year summary is as shown in Table 51.

It is true that in 1924 already 420 laws had been claimed as victories, and in 1930 only 436 were counted as in that category; it would, however, be misleading to contend by the obvious subtraction that only 16 victorious measures had been supported by state Leagues of Women Voters since 1923, and that the enactment of over 400 had been secured in the three years before that date.

The leaders of the state Leagues of Women Voters have had almost ten years' training in collecting and classifying reports. The figures of 1930 are more accurately reported and analyzed than those of 1923. Unquestionably the first census was swollen with enthusiasm. Probably slight amendments to existing laws were listed as separate bills. Perhaps administrative rulings and routine appropriations were included. The contrast in numbers must not be taken too somberly.

TABLE 51

Subject	Bills supported by state Leagues passed	Bills opposed by state Leagues defeated[a]
Child welfare...	61	
Uniform laws concerning women (*i.e.*, removal of legal discriminations against women).................................	130	
Social hygiene...	75	
Education...	69	
Efficiency in government....................................	76	60
Women in industry...	25	
Living costs (not reported).................................		

[a] The number of states reporting and the record of bills opposed is incomplete and therefore not included.

Nevertheless, although allowance is made for better reporting and more precise classification, there is still a startling drop. And women leaders in almost every state admit it. The demands of women voters were not receiving great consideration at the hands of legislators in the various states.

The reasons generally advanced are varied. One is entirely political. It is said that the woman vote was dreaded by the politicians who had delayed its coming as long as they were able. So for a brief time they were willing to make concessions, to tease with promises, to placate with welfare legislation. The sorry sequel to this theory is that with acquaintance, the threat of the woman vote diminished. The party bosses found that things were much the same after all. They grew thrifty with their gifts, took courage to deny, and about 1925 the down-hill road for women's bills began, in Washington and in the states.

The minds and habits of those who control political machinery are not open for objective inspection. The theory can be accepted or rejected. There seems a certain quality of simple truth about it.

Social advances by legislation have been few these past years. The women's measures were the first to suffer. Not because their advocates are women but because measures designed to protect the underprivileged, to remedy inequalities, to prevent distress are among the first to be sacrificed when economy programs are inaugurated. Those measures suffer in days of spiritual depression and economic misery. The failure of such legislation is, however, accepted by women as their failure, its continued advocacy as their responsibility. Even the most cursory examination of the standards adopted by women's organizations demonstrates that year after year they endorse better education laws, improved child labor standards, a shorter work week for women, adequate institutional care for delinquents. Their programs are monotonous with the weight of unfinished business. Who can say what would happen if large groups of men demanded consideration of the same measures? That is another question. But perhaps until there is some such group to act as a control, and men in great numbers unite to support measures of social welfare, and without money, and with complete integrity fail or succeed, it is too soon to say that women have failed in this aspect of their political life.

A very real question is whether great numbers of women can survive in political activity the period of discouragement into which they have been plunged. For there is some evidence that genuine and widespread interest has slackened.

Although the General Federation of Women's Clubs, and the Women's Christian Temperance Union withdrew from the Women's Joint Congressional Committee, both of them continue to advocate programs of legislation, so that their absence from the Joint Committee need not be taken to mean a lessened interest in legislative work.

The National League of Women Voters still belongs and the American Association of University Women. The American Home Economics Association is a member, and the full list includes the American Federation of Teachers; the American Nurses Association; the Council of Women for Home Missions; the Girls Friendly Society of the U.S.A.; the Medical National Association; the National Association of Business and Professional Women; the National Board of the Y.W.C.A.; the National Committee for a Department of Education; the National Congress of Parents and Teachers; the National Consumers' League; the National Council of Jewish Women; the National Education Association; the National Woman's Trade Union League; the Service Star Legion, Inc., and the Women's Homeopathic Medical Fraternity.

Nine legislative subcommittees functioned in 1931 to support legislation related to: The World Court, maternity and infancy hygiene, a department of education, independent citizenship, adequate appropriation for the Children's Bureau, adequate appropriation for the Woman's Bureau, reclassification in the Civil Service, unemployment legislation, opposition to the so-called Equal Rights Amendment.

Legislative councils in the states continue. There were in 1931 at least eighteen states where women's organizations cooperated in support of desired legislation.[1]

In general the methods of women lobbyists have been above reproach. They have performed a genuine service in informing legislators and constituents alike. A few of them at Washington and in the states are celebrated for the skill with which they pilot legislation. They are expert in the subjects they advocate, and familiar with legislative procedure, they know the human beings whose votes control their measures' destinies. To these leaders in women's organizations lobbying has brought some influence and rich rewards in the sense of achievement. For the majority of women who have participated it has provided an unrivaled school of political education. Its graduates are in elective and appointive office. They sit in party committees. It is safe to guess that they vote more regularly than their non-lobbying sisters. They care immensely about the election. To them it means the roll call later on.

For lobbying has changed somewhat since the days of Dorothea Dix. She inevitably succeeded in arousing public opinion by direct appeals to the press. But when the legislatures were in

---

[1] The comment that Legislative Councils have been abandoned has been heard. An attempt was made to secure a record of the dates of organization, fluctuations in membership, and length of life of the various groups. It proved to be impossible to secure as the Committees are informal, have no permanent offices and generally no useful records. An inquiry was generously made by the League of Women Voters of its State Leagues. The statement given above is based on League sources.

session she concentrated her effort on the task of "leading the leaders." "Personally she never cared to appear in public. It was thoroughly distasteful to her to do so. She made no addresses, she gathered no meetings. To come to close quarters of eye, conscience, and heart with impressionable and influential minds, to deliver her burden as from the Lord to them, and let it work on their sensibility and reason—this was her invariable method."[1] Lobbying today does not stop with that. It goes back and is inextricably mingled with the whole election process.

The organizations advocate programs of legislation, address questionnaires to candidates before the primary as well as before the general election; and publish records. Lobbying includes interviews with candidates and their managers individually and in deputations. It flowers in such unexpected beauties as luncheons for departing legislators.

At state capitols and in Washington it involves interviews with senators and representatives. Lobbying today means preparing printed material, informing constituents, soliciting letters and telegrams from constituents back home, arranging hearings, releasing supporting publicity. Remember that back in 1896 the club women of the District of Columbia were lobbying, "and every Senator will know before the measure comes up who wants it passed, and why."

Lobbying means appearing before political party conventions, writing letters and interviewing the delegates beforehand. With painful regularity the suffragists sought a woman suffrage plank. In 1920, with the suffrage amendment pending for ratification as the conventions met, women widened their demands. In 1924, 1928, and 1932, and at state conventions, women have appeared to urge their parties to assume responsibility for the interests they represent. They have not found exceeding hospitality for their claims, although the noble ambiguity of party platforms prevents any useful comparison and makes a critic seem too churlish.

And in 1927, when the Pan-American Conference met in Havana, delegates of the National Woman's Party were there to advocate the adoption of an Equal Rights Treaty. When the Conference for the Codification of International Law met at the Hague in 1930 representatives of the National League of Women Voters attended as well as spokesmen of the National Woman's

[1] Tiffany, *op. cit.*, p. 92.

Party. The interest of both groups was focused on the question of the nationality of married women, a problem affected by the passage of the Cable Act in the United States.

In outline then, this is the story of women as lobbyists. Since the days of anti-slavery agitation women leaders with energy, devotion and intelligence have accepted lobbying as an inevitable responsibility in their zeal for the advancement of causes. In general social welfare legislation has been their field and throughout the country mothers' pension laws exist, child labor standards have been improved, educational opportunities have been advanced because of the activities of the Woman's Lobby.

Since suffrage their interests have widened. But after the first few years of victory their achievements have diminished. To what extent with that diminishing there has come a slackening of interest is impossible to measure. It is true that fewer organizations are members of the Woman's Joint Congressional Committee in Washington than there were in 1925; it is reported that Legislative Councils have been abandoned in a few states, and competent observors report some lessening of active interest in the work; whether it means lessened interest or a pause during which new methods may perhaps be developed, no one can say at the moment. The outward appearances are ambiguous to say the least.

Outside the Joint Congressional Committee, but always active, the Woman's Party has urged the Equal Rights Amendment to the United States Constitution, has secured the enactment of their blanket statute in several states,[1] and has opposed before numerous state legislative committees the enactment of protective legislation for women that does not apply to men.[2]

[1] Louisiana, for example, and Wisconsin. The Wisconsin act reads:
"Sec. 1. A new section is added to the statute to read as follows: *6.015*: Women shall have the same rights and privileges under the law as men in the exercise and suffrage, freedom of contract, choice of residence for voting purposes, jury service, holding office, holding and conveying property, care and custody of children, and in all other respects. The various courts, executive and administrative officers shall construe the statutes where the masculine gender is used to include the feminine gender unless such construction will deny to females the special protection and privileges which they now enjoy for the general welfare. The courts, executive and administrative officers shall make all necessary rules and provisions to carry out the intent and purposes of this statute.
"Sec. 2. Any woman drawn to serve as a juror upon her request to the presiding judge or magistrate before the commencement of the trial, or hearing, shall be excused from the panel or venire.
"Sec. 3. This act shall take effect upon passage and publication." (*Session Laws, Wisconsin*, 1921, Ch. 529, p. 869.)
[2] Such as minimum wage legislation for women.

[272]

So far no investigation of lobbying has disclosed the representatives of women's organizations failing in integrity, or seeking selfish ends. Almost without exception legislators accord them credit for honor and sincerity. A few have been distinguished leaders. Almost every state holds some woman lobbyists in reverence. For example, the story of Miss Dix and her devotion to the indigent insane is unmatched, and Clara Barton is a name to honor. But one need not go so far back. For years Mrs. Andreas Ueland of Minneapolis lobbied in the Minnesota capitol for woman suffrage. When that was won she continued to advance the varied program of public welfare measures which the League of Women Voters advocated. When she was tragically killed by an automobile in the winter of 1927 on her way home from the capitol after a discouraging day of work, the whole state mourned. Formal resolutions were passed by both houses of the legislature. An official delegation attended her funeral. Later the House Chamber was the scene of a public memorial service which was infinitely moving. The Governor was there, the presiding officers of House and Senate. Men with whom she had pleaded the cause of the child laborer, the working woman, the dependent and infirm, came to do her honor. A year afterward, in 1928, a tablet was unveiled in the rotunda of the State Capitol of Minnesota to which it had been admitted by special legislative act in memory of Mrs. Andreas Ueland inscribed with the words:

May her memory save us from all pettiness, all unworthy ambitions, all narrowness of vision, all mean and sordid aims.

Her claim to honor was the influence she had exerted in behalf of woman's suffrage and social welfare measures.

The legacy to government of woman lobbyists like these is not a substance to be measured.[1]

[1] The following is a story of a person who might be thought of as a sister of the Unknown Soldier:

A Light under a Bushel

Her name may not be immediately recalled, for there was little that was exciting in the life of Mary Elizabeth Wood. And when she died there was no long obituary notice to blaze her story.

Yet she must always be remembered in connection with one outstanding event in the recent history of China.

A teacher in the Central China University, she laid the foundation of modern library science in the scene of her missionary endeavor, and her work was so successful, we read, that her students are found serving as librarians wherever modern libraries exist in China.

She was the recognized leader of the so-called library movement. But money was always lacking, of course.

Opportunity for the purse came suddenly. When it began to be rumored that the United States Government intended to return to China the balance of the American portion of the Boxer indemnity, amount to approximately $12,000,000, The China Weekly Review (Shanghai) tells us, Miss Wood conceived the idea of inducing the United States Government to earmark a portion of the money for the construction of modern libraries in China.

Her secluded life as a missionary did not fit her for the rôle of lobbyist, but she went to Washington, anyway, to see what could be done. She didn't receive much encouragement from the State Department, we read; so she consulted a newspaper correspondent, who "knew the ropes." She got from him a copy of the Congressional Directory and the advice that she see all the members of Congress. She did just that, for we read:

"Taking them alphabetically, she actually called on ninety-two Senators and 435 members of the House of Representatives and pledged them to support her scheme. More, she got them to sign a petition.

"Later, when President Harding (then Senator) introduced a resolution in Congress providing for the return of the indemnity, the committees having charge of the bill specified that a portion of the money should be devoted to the construction of modern libraries in China. The remainder of the fund went for the purposes of higher education.

"Miss Wood's propaganda was not only successful in connection with her library scheme, but also had much to do in causing Congress to pass the Indemnity Return bill.

"Since few persons who use modern libraries in China are familiar with the great service of Mary Elizabeth Wood, we take pleasure in printing this testimonial to her work. She died in Wuchang, on May 1, at the age of seventy years." (*Literary Digest*, June, 1931, p. 22.)

CHAPTER XVII

WOMEN AND PARTY ORGANIZATION
ACTIVITIES

IT IS difficult to discover and hazardous to estimate the extent
to which women have been influential in partisan politics.
They have official titles now and they sit on party committees.
Their names are listed in party records.

Certain land marks on the road of women's progress in the major
political parties[1] can be noted. Their participation in national
party conventions and their relation to the organization of
national party committees are matters of record.[2]

Women and National Republican Conventions.—In accordance
with the Washington custom the history of women in the majority
party will be presented first.

So far as party records disclose, women made their first official
appearance at a National Republican Convention in 1892.

[1] There is no disposition to ignore the existence of minority parties. They are
always more generous to women. The Prohibition party in 1924 advanced a
woman nominee for Vice-President. A letter of inquiry to the National Socialist
party brought the following courteous reply, June 22, 1921. "Women have
always been well represented in activities of the Socialist Party. Out of the eight
members of the National Executive Committee at this time, two, Meta L. Berger
of Milwaukee, Wisconsin, and Lilith Wilson of Reading, Pennsylvania, are
women. The National Secretary of the Party for many years was Bertha H.
White, a woman. Women are almost regularly named by the Party as candidates
for public office. Lilith Wilson above referred to was nominated and elected on the
Socialist ticket as a member of the Pennsylvania assembly. In all nation, state and
local conventions of the Party, women as a rule represent a substantial proportion
of the delegates."

[2] There is, however, one impediment to accuracy in the persistent sense of
insecurity with which one must depend upon the recognition of essentially
feminine names. Some allowance for error must be made. As the following tabula-
tion was prepared there were times when the prevalence of "Allies" and "Ollies,"
"Marions," "Shirleys," and "Merles" caused apprehension. Discretion had to
be used. When "Ruby" appeared as a member of the Resolutions Committee
of the Republican Convention some years ago, the name was judged to be that
of a man. A gallant "May" of an early day was reluctantly surrendered when the
delegate proved to be "Max." "Louise" was moved into the longer column of
alternates when more careful searching removed the printer's "e." The record
therefore is subject to correction, although every effort has been made to present
the truth.

[275]

Then three women were seated as alternates, and one of them addressed the convention as chairman of the Women's Republican Association of the United States. Four years later there were no women members of the convention although the adopted platform piously declared:

> The Republican Party is mindful of the rights and interests of women. Protection of American industries includes equal opportunity, equal pay for equal work, and protection to the home. We favor the admission of women to wider spheres of usefulness, and welcome their cooperation. . . .

In 1900, one lonely woman was seated as a delegate. Four women were alternates in 1904. Two women were full-fledged delegates in 1908 and 1912 and in 1916, when the platform included the first woman suffrage plank, 5 delegates and 9 alternates represented Republican women.

When the 1920 Republican Convention was held two months prior to the ratification of the suffrage amendment, 27 women delegates[1] were seated and 129 alternates, and for the first time women were appointed to official positions in the convention.

One woman was appointed to the Committee on Permanent Organization[2] and chosen as its secretary. Four were members of the Committee on Rules and Order of Business. Seven women spoke to second the nominations of various candidates, one woman made a brief address celebrating the significance of the year to women, and one formal resolution relating to committee organization was offered by a woman. A woman was one of the committee of three appointed to escort the Permanent Chairman of the Convention to the platform. Three women were members of the Committee to notify the candidate for President of his selection, although the Vice-Presidential nominee was acquainted with the news by a committee composed entirely of men.

The platform spoke out boldly:

> We welcome women into full participation in the affairs of government and the activities of the Republican Party. We earnestly hope that Republican legislatures in states which have not yet acted on the Suffrage Amendment will ratify the Amendment, to the end that all of

[1] There was 984 delegates seated at the convention.

[2] This committee and the other regular committees of the National Party Conventions are made up of one member selected by the delegation from each state and territory. Unless otherwise stated this committee composition can be assumed in the following pages.

the women of the nation of voting age may participate in the election of 1920, which is so important to the welfare of the country.

So much for the convention background which Republican women recalled when the suffrage amendment was proclaimed in August of 1920. From 1892 to 1920 inclusive 37 Republican women had been seated in the National Conventions as delegates. One hundred and forty-five had been alternates. And in 1920 they had a modest representation among the officers and committee members of the convention.

Women and the National Democratic Conventions.—The record of the Democratic party prior to the enfranchisement of women is not dissimilar, although 109 Democratic women had been delegates and 220 alternates up to and including the 1920 convention.

In 1900, the name of a delegate from Utah is starred in the convention lists and a footnote gives a woman's name as its representative. In the course of the convention she was escorted to the platform, and there she was gallantly introduced to the assembly as "the lady delegate." From the platform she seconded the nomination of William Jennings Bryan, who was chosen as the Democratic standard bearer that year.

There were no women in the next convention, but in 1908 the suffrage states of Colorado, Utah and Wyoming sent 2 delegates and 3 alternates. In 1912, there were 2 women delegates and one alternate representing Colorado and Washington. Four years later, 1916, the representation jumped to 22, equally divided between delegates and alternates, and for the first time women appeared as members of a convention committee. California's member on the Credentials Committee was a woman and Illinois and Utah appointed women to represent them on the Committee to notify the nominee for President. The nominee for Vice-President was notified by a committee on which California, Idaho and Utah were represented by women.

At the convention of 1916, a suffrage plank was adopted for the first time by the Democratic party, declaring, "We recommend the extension of the franchise to the women of the country by the states upon the same terms as men." There was vigorous debate and the political possibilities of the woman vote in the western suffrage states was stressed by suffrage advocates.

In 1920, there were 93 women present at the Democratic Convention as delegates and 206 wore alternates' badges. They were more generously represented on the convention committees. Two women were on the Credentials Committee this time and 5 were appointed to the Committee on Rules and Order of Business. There were 4 women members and one alternate appointed to the Committee on Permanent Organization. Seven, and one alternate, were selected to notify the candidate for President. Ten members and one alternate on the Committee appointed to notify the Vice-President were women. Fifteen women were assistant secretaries, sharing the honor with an equal number of men. Of 6 tally clerks, one was a woman. Another woman was on the Committee of Three to escort the chairman to the platform.

One woman addressed the Convention in a congratulatory speech on the party's record in relation to women's interests. Fourteen women made seconding speeches, and in the debate on prohibition one woman defended a minority report which was presented from the Resolutions Committee by William Jennings Bryan.

A plank advocating ratification of the pending suffrage amendment was adopted and the imminent enfranchisement of women probably encouraged the inclusion of a plank favoring the maternity and infancy legislation which was urged by women and which was enacted by the Congress the following year in response to the demand of women of all parties.

One other party convention should be mentioned in the pre-franchise period.

Women and the Progressive Conventions.—In August of 1912, a Progressive Convention met in Chicago. There are no printed proceedings available to examine but a contemporary newspaper account[1] relates that Colonel Roosevelt's nomination was seconded by Miss Jane Addams and comments that, "It was the first time a woman ever has seconded the nomination of a candidate of a great party for president of the United States," a statement that was not strictly accurate.[2]

A dozen women were delegates in contrast with the two who had been seated in the Republican and Democratic Conventions

---

[1] The Chicago *Daily Tribune*, August 8, 1912.

[2] It was the first nominating speech to be made by a woman, but in 1900, as was noted above, the woman delegate from Utah had seconded the nomination of Mr. Bryan at the Democratic Convention.

alike just a few weeks earlier. A woman sat on the Resolutions Committee[1] and the platform declared:

> The progressive Party, believing that no people can justly claim to be a true democracy which denies political rights on account of sex, pledges itself to the task of securing equal suffrage to men and women alike.

It was four years later when woman suffrage was mentioned in the platforms of both of the older parties.

Women and the Party Committees.—When women became voters all over the country the question arose of their participation in the National Committees of the parties. A careful summary of the situation has been made by the National League of Women Voters.

Immediately after the federal suffrage amendment was ratified, an effort was begun to secure the representation of women on governing committees of the political parties in equal numbers and in positions of equal responsibility with men. Attempts to make such equal (or as it is commonly called, "50-50") representation compulsory resulted in the passage of legislation in several states, although the laws passed do not in every case include all party committees within the state.

The Democratic Party in 1920 recognized the claims of women to a voice in its counsels by providing that men and women should be equally represented on the Democratic National Committee which should thereafter consist of two members from each state. In 1923 the Republican National Committee directed its members in each state to appoint immediately women associate members, and in 1924 by action of the Republican Convention officially provided that women should be equally represented on the National Committee from every state.[2]

As a matter of fact, such efforts appear to have preceded enfranchisement and somewhat informal organizations of women had been fostered by both parties before official action was taken.

In 1918, the chairman of the Republican National Committee appointed a woman to take charge of women's activities in connection with the work of the National Committee, and in 1919 there was created a "Women's Division" and a "Republican Women's National Executive Committee." In the same year a

---

[1] Representing Massachusetts (The Chicago *Tribune*, August 6, 1921). No woman was appointed to membership on that important committee by either of the major parties until 1932 when one woman appeared as a member in both the Republican and Democratic Conventions.

[2] *The Legal and Political Status of Women in the United States*, a statement issued by the National League of Women Voters, November, 1927; Headquarters, 532 Seventeenth Street, N.W., Washington, D. C.

"Committee of One Hundred" women was selected from the country at large and headquarters for Republican women were opened in Washington.

In the presidential campaign of 1920 Republican women maintained an organization with a woman director in connection with the headquarters of the National Committee in New York, in Chicago, and in Marion, Ohio.

In 1921, the Woman's Executive Committee was discontinued, and a Women's Division was made a permanent part of the organization of the National Republican headquarters. A prominent suffrage leader was appointed vice-chairman of the National Republican Executive Committee and placed in charge. Seven other women were appointed[1] to serve with her on the Executive Committee which had more than twenty members in all.

The question of the propriety of permitting women to be members of the National Committee until the National Convention had acted on the subject, was referred to a sub-committee of the Committee on Rules, and was unfavorably reported on. As a substitute, associate members[2] were appointed. Forty-five states had such associate members in 1923 when the following rule was proposed by the Committee on Rules to the National Committee:

> The Republican National Committee having appointed a woman from each state as associate member; Be it Therefore Resolved by the Republican National Committee that they instruct the Rules Committee of the National Convention of 1924 that they report a rule that in future the National Committee be composed of one man and one woman from each State.

And in 1924, the Convention adopted such a rule. In the meantime, a year earlier, two additional women, one called assistant vice-chairman and one assistant secretary, had been appointed to be officers of the National Committee.

Democratic women had enjoyed a similar pre-ratification relationship with the national organization and had been more promptly admitted to actual representation. It was some time after the 1916 Convention that the acting chairman of the Demo-

---

[1] *The Woman Citizen* on June 28, 1924, in an article reporting the 1924 Convention, states that a group of Republican women headed by Miss Hay asked for full equality of representation between men and women on the National Committee. The plea was denied and the seven members were appointed to the Executive Committee instead.

[2] Without a vote.

cratic National Committee appointed a woman "to consider an organization among the women." In February, 1919, she attended a meeting of the National Committee as a proxy for the committee member from Illinois. The minutes disclose that she was referred to once as the "female member of the Committee" and in the chairman's report the following paragraph occurs:[1]

> The work of the Women's Bureau under the direction of Mrs. Bass was all that could be desired within the limits of the means afforded. It would not be fair to conclude a report of the campaign of 1918 without paying tribute to the loyalty and efficiency of Mrs. Bass and those associated with her in the work.

At this meeting the chairman presented a report including a plan for the organization of an Associate National Committee of Women which, after some discussion, was adopted. The first recommendation of this report and an excerpt from the second paragraph outline its purpose:

> First: We recommend the selection of a woman in each state as an associate member of the National Committee to be appointed by the Chairman of the Democratic National Committee, upon the nomination of the member of the committee in each state and territory respectively. The associate member so chosen shall exercise in large measure, among the women of the respective states, the functions of members of the National Committee, and she shall also act as State Chairman for Women in her state until such office is otherwise provided for by party custom or state law.
>
> Second: We recommend that the National Committee propose to the various state committees that representation in their respective bodies should be provided for the women of their states. This representation shall include both officers and members, so far as practicable. . . .

Nine months later[2] a call was issued to the members of the "Democratic National Committee and the Women's Associate National Committee" to attend a meeting to be held January 8, 1920. The records disclose that 22 states were represented by women members of the Associate Committee. Some question about the length of term of the Associate members had arisen. A sub-committee was appointed to settle the question and make a report, one paragraph of which is of interest:

[1] Minutes of the meeting of the Democratic National Committee, February 26, 1919. During the 1916 campaign Mrs. Bass had been in charge of women's activities in the Chicago headquarters. The organization of the Women's Bureau, which she headed, was an outgrowth of that work.

[2] On November 24, 1919.

We recommend that the term of office of the Women's Associate members of the National Committee shall terminate upon the expiration or termination of the term of office of the member of this Committee recommending said appointment, that upon the resignation, death or removal of the member of this committee who recommends said appointment, the office of the Associate member recommended by him shall ipso facto become vacant.

At the Convention of 1920, a Resolution was adopted, to the effect that from that time the National Committee should consist of one man and one woman from each state and territory, the women for the next four years to be selected by the delegations to the convention and after that in the same manner as the men were selected.[1]

In 1924, then, with their rights as voters and party workers recognized by official standing, the attendance of women as delegates and alternates was increased at both conventions. At the Republican Convention in Cleveland 120 women were delegates[2] and 277 of their sisters were present as alternates.

Two women were tally clerks at this convention. One was an assistant secretary. One of the formal resolutions authorizing the organization of the convention committees was presented by a woman. Fourteen women were members of the Committee on Permanent Organization—one of them was its chairman. Two women delegates were appointed to membership on the Credentials Committee and 9 were named to the Committee on Rules and Order of Business—one of them acting as secretary. Three seconding speeches were made by women and nine were appointed to notify the nominee for President of his selection by the Convention. An equal number were named to notify the Vice-President. One of the courtesy resolutions was offered by a woman at the Convention's adjournment.

The platform declared:

We extend our greeting to the women delegates who, for the first time under Federal authorization sit with us in full equality. The Republican Party from the beginning has espoused the cause of woman suffrage, and the presence of these women delegates signifies to many here the completion of a task undertaken years ago. We welcome them not as assistants or as auxiliary representatives but as co-partners in the great political work in which we are engaged, and we believe that the actual partnership in party councils should be made more complete.

[1] Mrs. Emily Newell Blair was in 1922 named vice-chairman of the National Committee and placed in charge of the Woman's Division.

[2] There was a total of 1,109 delegates seated.

It is interesting to note that when the vice-chairman of the National Executive Committee at the convention, who had been identified with the suffrage cause, retired from her position in 1924, she was succeeded by a woman who had not been associated with the woman suffrage movement nor with those aspects of government usually identified as women's interests, but was the widow of a prominent Republican politician.

Democratic Women in 1924.—There were 199 delegates and 310 alternates at the Democratic Convention in 1924. A woman was vice-chairman of the Convention. Twelve women were on the Credentials Committee. One was its chairman, another acted as secretary. Seven women were members of the Committee on Permanent Organization. One was appointed to the Committee on Rules and Order of Business and chosen as its secretary. Ten women were members and one was an alternate on the Committee to notify the nominee for President, and 21 were selected by their states to notify the nominee for Vice-President with 4 expectant alternates likewise chosen. Twenty-three women and 9 men made up the list of assistant secretaries. Twelve seconding speeches were made by women. One woman debated a contested plank. Two women offered resolutions and the name of one woman was placed in nomination for the vice-presidency by the delegation of her state.

Women and the Progressives.—The Republican Convention was followed shortly by another meeting in Cleveland in 1924. Progressives, discontented with the policies of the major parties, met to nominate the late Senator LaFollette of Wisconsin for the Presidency. The Convention was distinguished by two keynote speeches. One was by a woman, and her selection was heralded as evidence of a new recognition of woman's place in politics.

One woman was on the Rules Committee. The Committee on Organization and Campaign had 3 women members and 4 women served on the Resolutions Committee.[1]

In the campaign which followed 9 women made up the Executive Committee of the National Woman's Division which established its headquarters in Washington, with one member in charge

[1] Unlike the other National Conventions referred to, the Progressive Assembly was not made up of regularly elected state delegations. Labor, social and political groups composed it. Outstanding members of the conference were appointed to the Committees.

of a Western Divisional Office located in Chicago. In August a woman member[1] of the Conference rejoiced that not a single committee or sub-committee had failed to include at least one woman member, and that on the Joint Executive Committee of eleven, which determined campaign strategy, there were 2 women. During the campaign 35 state committees of women were reported to be active, and even in the unorganized states many women were reported to be participating actively in behalf of the LaFollette-Wheeler ticket.

As the Progressive campaign was carried on without permanent organization it is difficult to measure and impossible to compare the opportunity which it presented for the active work of Progressive women. "Several thousand" is the summarizing total of the women who were actively concerned in the national work or the Women's Divisions in the various states.

Some of the women were protesting members whose previous political activity had been in the existing political parties. Others without previous campaign experience were attracted to the program and loyal to the leadership of the group which in 1924 promised generous consideration for social welfare legislation. They were social workers, feminists, crusaders. LaFollette's candidacy and the Progressive platform seemed a cause.

The Republican Convention of 1928.—Four years later the number of Republican women delegates diminished. There were 70 seated in Kansas City to be compared with the 120 who had qualified four years earlier. Only 264 women alternates were in reserve in 1928.[2] Four nominations were seconded by women, but there were only 8 women delegates appointed to membership on the Standing Committees.[3] One was a member of the Committee on Permanent Organization. Two were on the Credentials Committee and 5 were selected to represent their states on the Committee on Rules and Order of Business. There were 6 women chosen as convention vice-presidents.[4] There was one woman tally clerk, one assistant secretary and one assistant reporter.

Eleven women were appointed on the notification committees. So far as the recognition or the achievements of women are concerned the Convention of 1928 is undistinguished. In feminist

---

[1] Miss Ethel M. Smith, writing in *The Woman Citizen*, August 9, 1924.
[2] At Cleveland in 1924 there had been 277 alternates.
[3] There were 43 in 1924.
[4] This seems to be a new and apparently entirely honorary position.

annals this convention will be remembered for a single triumph—
the selection of a woman,[1] an assistant attorney general of the
United States, to act as chairman of the Committee on Credentials, for the judgment of the Credentials Committee was crucial
at this Convention.

The platform, drafted by a Committee of which no woman was
a member, read:

Four years ago at the Republican National Convention in Cleveland,
women members of the National Committee were welcomed into full
association and responsibility in party management. During the four
years which have passed they have carried with their men associates an
equal share of all responsibilities, and their contribution to the success
of the 1924 campaign is well recognized.

The Republican party, which from the first has sought to bring this
development about, accepts whole-heartedly equality on the part of
women, and in the public service it can present a record of appointments
of women in the legal, diplomatic, judicial, treasury and other governmental departments. We earnestly urge on the women that they participate even more generally than now in party management and activity.

In 1930, Mrs. Lenna Lowe Yost was appointed director of the
Woman's Division and Mrs. Hert, relieved of the executive
responsibility, retained her position as the vice-chairman of the
Executive Committee.

Democratic Women—1928.—In 1928, there were 151 women
delegates at Houston with 263 women present as alternates.
The roll of assistant secretaries includes the names of 11 women
and 3 men. There were 3[2] women on the Credentials Committee
and 6 were appointed to the Committee on Permanent Organization. One of the 6 was chosen to be the Committee's Secretary.
The Committee on Rules and Order of Business had 3 women
members. Three women (and 4 alternates) were named to notify
the nominee for President and 14 women (with 4 alternates) to
notify the Vice-Presidential nominee. There were 10 women
honorary vice-presidents of the Convention and thirteen honorary
vice-secretaries, and an alternate.[3] Four seconding speeches were
made by women; a routine resolution was offered by a woman,
and the name of Mrs. Nellie Tayloe Ross was placed in nomination for the vice-presidency. The official reporter of the Conven-

[1] Mrs. Mabel Walker Willebrandt.
[2] One dubious "Jean" included.
[3] One vice-president and a vice-secretary were appointed from each state and
territory. It seems to have been an innovation.

tion was a woman whose name had appeared as an assistant secretary at the two preceding conventions.

At its meeting held July 11, 1928, the Democratic National Committee passed the following resolutions:

BE IT RESOLVED, That the chairman of the National Committee be and is hereby authorized to appoint five vice-chairmen of said committee, two of whom shall be women, all of whom shall be members of the Democratic National Committee, and to assign to such vice-chairmen such powers and duties as he may designate.

Subsequently, the chairman announced the appointment of the following vice-chairmen under the resolution just adopted: Nellie Tayloe Ross,[1] Wyoming; Frank Hague, New Jersey; Florence Farley, Kansas; Harry F. Byrd, Virginia; Scott Ferris, Oklahoma.

An Innovation in 1928.—Women were more active in the presidential campaign of 1928 than ever before. One vice-chairman of the Republican Committee was in charge of the activities of Republican women at the headquarters in Washington with another member representing her in the Chicago headquarters. There was a Bureau of Women Speakers in New York and one in Chicago and an effort was made to attract every group and all kinds of women by the organization of special bureaus or divisions. The chairmen of most of these groups were women whose names would be known throughout the country.

The Democratic headquarters were not dissimilarly organized. The first vice-chairman of the National Committee went about the country speaking. A College Woman's Bureau was organized. A woman, the daughter of a former Secretary of Labor, and herself a candidate for the House of Representatives, headed the Division of Women in Industry. A distinguished social worker was in charge of the Women in Social Service Group. There was a Speaker's Bureau and a Woman's Publicity Bureau. Most important to remember perhaps is the fact that a woman, often referred to in the press as the candidate's confidential adviser, was a member of the National Executive Committee which directed the entire campaign policy. The Democratic headquarters were similarly organized with distinguished women in strategic

---

[1] Since that time, Mrs. Ross, who has the distinction of having served one term as governor of her state, has been in charge of the women's activities in the National Democratic Committee as the successor of Mrs. Blair who retired as first vice-chairman in 1928.

positions. In addition to these regular partisan organizations, each candidate was supported by a National Committee of women working somewhat independently although in cooperation with the National Committees.

There was great publicity value to both candidates in these imposing lists of eminent women, and members of the Committees did valiant work as speakers in the campaign. Their existence may be said to suggest the thought that the regular party machinery has found inadequate place to enlist the loyalty and energy of women of talent and independence, and may indicate that women's interest is in candidates and not in parties, and that the position of women in the parties is less gratifying than that of women outside who supplement party programs and aid, on occasions, party candidates.[1]

Women and the Conventions of 1932.—In both Conventions in 1932, the number of women increased over 1928, although not quite equal to those of 1924.

There was a total number of 395 women on the permanent roll of delegates and alternate delegates to the Republican National Convention in Chicago on June 14, 1932. Of this number, 50 were delegates-at-large, 108 were alternates-at-large, 37 were district delegates, and 198 were district alternates from the states.[2] There also was a woman delegate from Porto Rico and a woman alternate from the Philippine Islands. There were three states, in whose delegation there was no woman, but New York had 34 women of whom, to be sure, 25 were district alternates, in its delegation. There was one woman on the Resolutions Committee; there were 2 on the Committee on Rules and Order of Business, 5 on the Credentials, and 9 on the Committee on Permanent Organization, or 17 in all. This was 9 more than in 1928 but 8 fewer than 1924.

In the Democratic Convention, too, the number rose as compared with 1928, but not quite to the level of 1924. There were 478 women delegates and alternates in the Democratic National Convention. Of these, 127 women were delegates-at-large, 99 were alternates-at-large, 76 were district delegates, and 165 were district delegates from the states. The Canal Zone had one woman delegate and 2 women alternates, the District of Columbia had

---

[1] It is significant that both the Republican and the Democratic chairman had been officers of the State and National League of Women Voters.

[2] Alabama, Georgia, and New Mexico.

one woman delegate and one woman alternate, and Porto Rico had 3 women delegates and 3 women alternates. There were 2 states[1] from which no women came, while California had 13 delegates and Texas had 38 women in its delegation of whom 10 were district delegates and 26 district alternates.

All of the major committees of the Convention had at least one woman member. There was a woman on the Resolutions Committee; there were 2 on the Credentials Committee; 2 on the Rules Committee; and 3 on the Permanent Organization Committee.[2]

Women in the Socialist Convention.—Only 2 women were mentioned in connection with the Socialist National Convention which opened in Milwaukee on May 21, 1932. Mrs. Meta Berger, widow of Representative Victor L. Berger, was placed in nomination for Vice-President but declined in favor of James H. Maurer.[3]

Mrs. Rachel Panken was one of the principal speakers at the dinner in New York on June 12th at which Norman Thomas and James H. Maurer were formally notified of their nominations for President and Vice-President.[4]

Women are in the parties today. Since 1924 they have represented their states on the National Committees equally with men, That equal representation does not extend to local committees is freely admitted by both parties, although the pattern is recommended and a genuine effort is made to advance its acceptance. Even if the plan were completely carried out down to the last precinct, it would not necessarily forecast any change in party policies or any special acceptance of the women voters' point of view. The Committee woman is often the shadow of the Committee man; but she is a woman. The door has opened a little.

It is likewise difficult to judge how much weight to place on women's participation in party conventions. It counts somewhat. In 1924, the vice-chairman of the Democratic National Committee said:[5]

[1] Alabama and New Mexico.
[2] The "Women of the Press" were well represented at the Democratic Convention.
[3] *New York Times*, May 23, 1932, p. 1.
[4] *Ibid.*, June 13, 1932, p. 2.
[5] *Woman Citizen*, April 19, 1924.

The number, great or small, of women delegates and alternates in the forthcoming national party conventions will be an authoritative test of women's interest in politics and of the recognition given them by the major parties.

If this is so, to compare the conventions of 1924, 1928, and 1932, is the sad duty of an observer of the trend in that interest and recognition. It will be observed from Table 52 in which are given the figures for the conventions since 1916, the first year when there was a substantial attendance of women, that in

TABLE 52.—THE ATTENDANCE OF WOMEN AND DELEGATES AND ALTERNATES TO NATIONAL PARTY CONVENTIONS

Republican		Democratic	
1916			
Delegates.....................	6	Delegates.....................	11
Alternates....................	9	Alternates....................	11
Total......................	14	Total......................	22
1920			
Delegates.....................	27	Delegates.....................	93
Alternates....................	129	Alternates....................	206
Total......................	156	Total......................	299
1924			
Delegates.....................	120	Delegates.....................	199
Alternates....................	277	Alternates....................	310
Total......................	397	Total......................	509
1928			
Delegates.....................	70	Delegates.....................	152
Alternates....................	264	Alternates....................	263
Total......................	334	Total......................	415
1932			
Delegates.....................	88	Delegates.....................	208
Alternates....................	307	Alternates....................	270
Total......................	395	Total......................	478

both party conventions, the number of women delegates and alternates was reduced in 1928 as compared with 1924, and did not recover full equality in 1932. But the question may well be raised as to whether the test was really a final one. That there was some recovery is to be kept in mind.

If the responsibilities to which they were assigned are examined, omitting the complimentary offices, counting the representation of women as *members* of the Committees on Credentials, on Permanent Organization, on Rules and Order of Business, the figures are like these:

TABLE 53.—REPUBLICAN

Committee	1924	1928	1932
Permanent organization................................	14*	1	9
Credentials..	2	2*	5
Rules and order of business........................	9†	5	2
Platform and resolution...............................	0	0	1
	25	8	17

   * A woman chairman.
   † A woman secretary.

TABLE 54.—DEMOCRATIC

Committee	1924	1928	1932
Permanent organization................................	7*	6*	3
Credentials..	12*	3	2
Rules and order of business........................	1†	3	2
Platform and resolution...............................	0	0	1
	20	12	8

   * Woman chairman and secretary.
   † Woman secretary.

Both parties show a curve first downward, and then one shows an upward, the other a continued downward, curve. Honorary title and complimentary offices are not included in these lists. There is no protest from the men when the women softly or vehemently offer resolutions, and second nominations with deferential grace. The decorative aspects of women delegates are appreciated. If, however, the appointment of women to positions of potential responsibility is a guide they have not gained in influence in the brief time during which it is possible to compare their opportunities.

If, however, the voice of women in the parties is still perhaps faint, it should never be forgotten that many, if not most, men voters dwell likewise in dim remoteness from the center of party control. The women of the parties are not solitary in their isolation.

The personnel of each National Committee now includes 53 women, just half of the total membership of the National Committee of 106. In the case of the Republican Committee there are 11 women members on the Executive Committee of 26, and of 9 officers 2 are women.

Each state has a director of Women's Activities, and the conventional pattern for all committees appears to include an equal number of men and women, although it is an ideal far from realization.[1]

To describe at length the part played by women, to count them, name their offices or describe their activities, is still to reveal inadequately the volume or force of their influence. That they find or use slighter opportunity so far as numbers or as official recognition goes is, however, part of the story. Whether or not it is misleading cannot now be said. Attention[2] was called in another connection to the demand that they should have told when they were seeking political emancipation, what they would do with their new freedom and why they desired a new and outward evidence of equality. A few points about their experiences with and in the conventions were significant.

The first perhaps was that the only amendment to the platform as it came from the Committee on Platform to the Democratic

---

[1] Like the first chairman of the National Republican Committee, Woman's Division, the present chairman was identified with the woman suffrage movement, and in common with most men of influence in national party councils, she began her political career in her own state. She was the first chairman of the West Virginia Republican Women's State Executive Committee (1920–1922). In 1920, she was the first woman teller in a Republican National Convention. In that same year she was the first woman to preside over a state Republican convention. In the year 1921 and since, she has served by appointment as a member of the West Virginia State Board of Education and since 1924 she has been the woman member from West Virginia of the Republican National Committee. Hers is a background of genuine political experience in state and local committees. It should be added that for years she was the legislative representative in Washington of the National Woman's Christian Temperance Union, one of the most experienced band of women lobbyists whose activities have been mentioned.

[2] See *Women in the Modern World* (*Annals*, CXLIII, No. 232, May, 1929), p. 14.

Convention was one proposed by a delegate long active in the State and National League of Women Voters[1] which read:

We favor continued responsibility of government for human welfare, especially for the protection of children.

A second was that while the representatives of organized groups appeared as usual before the Resolutions Committees urging the recognition of their interests, they showed in general little hope of success. The Committee listened courteously to Jane Addams while she presented the program of the League for Peace and Freedom, and to the representatives of the League of Women Voters who argued for sound economy which is wise use rather than reduced spending, but there was little sense of reality.[2]

There was, in fact, little reality; and while delegates to the conventions were absorbed in problems of candidates versus candidates and wet versus dry, as human beings all were aware of the proximity of Madison Street, the great thoroughfare of the Hobo and the present abiding place of unnumbered unemployed men. For women and men alike in their consciousness of the realities of life, it was all like a child's game. But, it is an important point that in that game, in one capacity or another, women are accepted as participants. How eventually that participation will develop is as yet impossible to say.

However, because they have a definite experience and are conscious of the problem, the women members of the National Committees of the two major parties have been asked to say something of their view on the subject (1) of the parties and women, and (2) of women and the parties.

Twelve Republican National Committee-Women replied. Three of these have held public office, one in a Rocky Mountain state has been a precinct committee-woman for the last ten years; one from a southern state was clerk to the Insular Affairs Committee, 1922–1924; and one from the Northwest was a member of the 1931 State Legislature. Four had been definitely interested in securing the ballot for women, 3 were not interested, although only one was really opposed, while 2 were too young,

[1] Mrs. Caroline O'Day of Westchester County, New York, vice-chairman of the New York State Convention.
[2] The Platform of the League was a statesmanlike document and is given in the Appendix. (See below, p. 351.)

and 2 lived in states that had suffrage prior to 1920. These 12
women expressed their interest in such subjects as child welfare,
prohibition, public health, registration of women voters, and
legislation pertaining to co-guardianship of children, property
rights of women, education of children, and women in industry.
Six were satisfied with the record of women in their states while
the other 5 suggested that it was difficult to get the "right type"
of women into official positions and that women have not taken
the interest in politics that they should. One thought that women
still had much to learn. Just one committee-woman was dis-
satisfied with the treatment of women by the party, as she said
that they were not allowed to sit in on the inside business. The
suggestions with reference to the future of women in government
were that women prove their ability in the small places first,
that they unite their political efforts and work with men not
against them, and that they take a more active part in the
mechanics of the government.

Replies were received from 11 Democratic National Committee-women, 4 of whom have held public office. One has been
governor, one was appointed as state tuberculosis commissioner,
the third a member of a commission to investigate conditions
regarding the Minimum Wage or Industrial Welfare Commission
in her state, a fourth on the Board of Trustees of the State School
for the Deaf and Blind. Only 2 of the 11 had not been interested
or active in the suffrage movement and 2 lived in states that had
suffrage before 1920. Their present interests include the League
of Women Voters, property rights of married women,
prohibition reform, welfare legislation, child welfare (including
infancy and maternity measures), peace movements, international relations, education, and labor problems, those particularly
affecting women workers. Only 2 women expressed their
dissatisfaction with the record of women in their states. The
other 7 said that the women had been efficient, satisfactory,
more faithful, and less self-seeking than men were. All except
2 have been satisfied and proud of the recognition which the
Democratic Party has accorded women although one woman
says,

Yet we do not find women on a parity with men in party councils nor do
we find women getting party support, that is, if a woman seeks office
the fact she is a woman handicaps her regardless of qualifications.

Another adds,

This generous national policy is not carried out by the lesser men leaders. In my state, many of these are of the older generation who feel that politics is not a woman's business and they are far from cooperative. Women are encouraged to run for office only when defeat is certain. If victory seems possible, the nomination is always claimed by men.

The fact was generally conceded that the position of women in government will advance but slowly until women study and learn about the affairs of the government and develop their own political leadership. "Study, study, study, especially within the parties" is the admonition of one.

CHAPTER XVIII

WOMEN OFFICE HOLDERS

I F VOTING, lobbying, taking part in party conventions fail adequately to reveal the trends of women's political activity, something may possibly be learned from a study of the extent to which women have been admitted to public office.

Among the arguments advanced by women in the days of the suffrage struggle, in support of their claim, were three with reference to women and public employment. One was that there were positions for which the experience of women especially qualified them. Such would be inspectorships in establishments employing girls and women, judgeships in juvenile courts, directorships of institutions in which women and girls or young children of either sex, or possibly the aged and infirm, were cared for. The idea was to transfer to the larger platform the services rendered by women in the home; that women should be able to follow their job even when that job took on aspects of public authority. A second argument supported the admission of women to legislative bodies for the same reason, that many laws embodied principles truly domestic in character, though now affecting all families in their corporate capacity. A third and very important plea was that to open for women the door of public employment was to widen that occupational opportunity of which the limitations were made so clear during the decade 1900 to 1910. From a study of women in public office, therefore, light should be thrown on the question whether or not in increasing numbers they are obtaining the opportunities (1) to do on a wider platform what women have done in earlier times in the home, (2) to embody their experience and judgment in legislation, (3) through holding positions hitherto not open to women to widen women's general opportunity for employment.

With the ratification of the Nineteenth Amendment women became eligible for elective offices hitherto closed to them. Since 1920, then, they have been elected to the United States Congress, to governorships, to state legislatures, to the offices of judge, sheriff, mayor. By appointment, they have become collectors of internal revenue, heads of state departments, and superintendents of institutions.[1]

It is not the task of this inquiry to compile a complete account of the public offices which women have held in the last decade, and that would be too formidable a task to undertake. There are more than 3,000 counties in the United States, there are over 15,000 cities of the first, second, and third class, and the hamlets and villages are uncounted. With the never-ceasing changes in public employment, of which, because of the unequal standards of recording and reporting it is impossible to learn, it is probable that thousands of women citizens have held office of whom no report can be given here. Hence, no attempt will be made in the following pages to set out the development in the local jurisdictions. An effort will be put forth, however, to include a record of the women who have been elected to serve in the Congress, and so far as possible, those who have been candidates but who have been defeated. The statement includes, too, the names of the women appointed to important federal office. The women who have served in state legislatures are counted and some indication is given of the extent to which they have been elected or appointed to other important state offices. An idea can certainly be obtained as to the opportunity opening before women and as to the extent to which they are grasping that opportunity. Since these are matters of public record, names will be more freely used than has been appropriate in the earlier discussion.

Women in the Congress.—One woman had been elected to the House of Representatives before the adoption of the Nineteenth Amendment. She was Miss Jeanette Rankin of Montana, elected in 1916 to represent her state at large. At the conclusion of her term she did not seek renomination, engaging instead in the first of two unsuccessful campaigns for the Senate. There was no woman member of the House of Representatives to succeed her in the next Congress, which convened in December, 1919.

A melancholy fate decreed that the first woman to sit in the House of Representatives after women all over the country were enfranchised should be an anti-suffragist, Miss Alice Robertson of Oklahoma, who served only one term, received the nomina-

---

[1] The subject of women in federal and municipal civil service has been studied in a competent manner by Miss Croice Marion Saint. See *Public Personnel Studies*, VIII, No. 4, p. 46, No. 7, p. 104, No. 8, p. 119; IX, No. 1, p. 14.

tion of the Republican party a second time but failed of election in 1922.

Miss Robertson was the only woman in the Congress during her first session. In the second, or short session, Mrs. Winifred Mason Huck, a Republican of Illinois, who had been elected in November, 1922, to fill the unexpired term left vacant by her father's death, was the first of a series of women to whom membership in the Congress came, as it were, through descent. Later, Mrs. Huck failed to secure the nomination for a full term which she subsequently sought in the primaries.

In January of 1923, Mrs. Mae Nolan of California joined Miss Robertson and Mrs. Huck, having been elected to fill the vacancy which her husband's death created. Mrs. Nolan was elected for the unexpired portion of her husband's term in the sixty-seventh Congress, and also to the sixty-eighth Congress to which Mr. Nolan had been elected in November of 1922. When, therefore, the sixty-eighth Congress convened in December of 1923 she was the only woman member. Mrs. Nolan was not a candidate for renomination in 1924 and retired when her term expired on March 4, 1925.

Three women were among the new Representatives sworn in when the sixty-ninth Congress met in December, 1925. Two of these, Mrs. Florence Prag Kahn of California and Mrs. Edith N. Rogers of Massachusetts, had been widowed by the deaths of members and elected to fill the resulting vacancies. The new third-comer, Mrs. Mary T. Norton, a Democrat, of New Jersey, was the first woman to represent her party in the House. These three have been in continuous service since their first elections.

Mrs. Katherine Langley of Kentucky was the next woman to be elected.[1] She came to the seventieth Congress to fill the vacancy created when her husband was convicted and sentenced to the federal prison for violation of the prohibition law, and was reelected to the seventy-first Congress, but was defeated in November, 1930.

In the seventy-first Congress the peak of woman membership was reached. Mrs. Kahn, Mrs. Norton, and Mrs. Rogers were veterans. Mrs. Langley was returned and three new women members were elected in November, 1928. Another was chosen at a special election in January, 1929, so that there were eight women

[1] She was elected on December 5, 1927.

[297]

members at the beginning of the Congress[1] and the ninth was soon added.[2] The newcomers were Mrs. Ruth Hanna McCormick of Illinois, Mrs. Ruth Bryan Owen, and Mrs. Ruth Pratt of New York. Mrs. Pratt was the widow of a prominent Republican, but her political experience had been won in her own right, for she had twice been elected to membership on the Board of Aldermen of New York City. On January 9, 1929, following the death of her husband, Mrs. Pearl Peden Oldfield of Arkansas was elected to his unexpired term in the seventieth Congress and to his full term of the seventy-first. Mrs. Oldfield was not a candidate in 1930.

The death of Representative Wingo of Arkansas brought a second widow to represent that state.[3] Mrs. Effie Gene Wingo was elected to fill her husband's unexpired term in the seventy-first Congress to replace him, and held his seat in the seventy-second Congress, but did not offer herself for reelection in the seventy-third.

This completes the roll of women who had served in the House of Representatives prior to March 4, 1893. They were 13 in all, of whom 7 illustrated the interesting attitudes toward the effect of marriage on a woman's qualifications for office,[4] to which reference was made in the introductory chapter. But 2 of the 7, Mrs. Kahn and Mrs. Rogers, who, with Mrs. Norton, have been returned to the seventy-third Congress, have held their seats in their own rights for so long that the sympathetic compliment of their first election has been forgotten.

Two of the 13, Miss Rankin and Mrs. McCormick, retired from the House to fail in the stiffer competition for the Senate. Three—Miss Robertson, Mrs. Huck, and Mrs. Langley—have been defeated in primary or general elections. Mrs. Nolan and Mrs. Oldfield did "not choose to run" when their terms of condolence were ended. Of the 6 women members of the seventy-second Congress when it convened in December, 1931 Mrs. Kahn, Mrs. Norton, Mrs. Owen, Mrs. Pratt, Mrs. Rogers, and Mrs. Wingo—only one, Mrs. Wingo, owed her election to any influence other than her individual capacity and service. Five of the 13

---

[1] Which convened in December, 1928.
[2] During the entire period under discussion the membership of the House of Representatives has been 435.
[3] Mrs. Wingo was elected December 1, 1930.
[4] Eight, if Mrs. McCormick's indirect inheritance may be added.

were Representatives for whom their constituents had cast one or more votes of confidence.

Mrs. Kahn and Mrs. Rogers were both considered to have been closely associated with the work of their husbands. Indeed Mrs. Kahn was appointed to membership on the Committee on Military Affairs, of which Mr. Kahn had long been chairman. Earlier Mrs. Nolan had been assigned to the Labor Committee of which her husband was a member. The late Mr. Rogers had been distinguished for his work in advancing the legislation which bears his name and under which the Foreign Service of the United States was reorganized. Mrs. Rogers came to Congress with a special personal interest—the care of World War Veterans. President Harding had appointed her his representative to inspect veterans' hospitals throughout the country, and she had been reappointed in 1923 by President Coolidge. Her service in the House, therefore, has been characterized by special concern for veterans' legislation. Her three committee assignments in the seventy-first Congress were Civil Service, Indian Affairs, and World War Veterans' Legislation.

Mrs. Norton came to Washington with a conventional party organization background. With the exception of Mrs. Langley, whose history reveals that she was the first chairman of the Kentucky Woman's Republican State Organization and delegate at large to the Republican National Convention in 1924, and with only slight rivalry from Mrs. Pratt, Mrs. Norton appears to be the most "regular" in her partisan progress to Congress. In 1920, she was appointed to represent her county on the New Jersey State Democratic Committee. She was elected a member of that committee in 1921, and later served as its vice-chairman. She, too, was a delegate-at-large to her party convention in 1924. In the Congress she has been a member of the Committees on Labor, World War Veterans' Legislation, and the District of Columbia.

Mrs. Pratt, whose biography recites the fact that she has been associate leader of her party's organization in the fifteenth assembly district of New York, and twice an alderman, sits on the Committee on Banking and Currency and the Library. Mrs. Owen, the only Congresswoman who made one unsuccessful campaign before she was finally elected to the Congress in 1928, and has been defeated on renomination for the seventy-third

Congress, sat on the Committee on Foreign Affairs, the committee of her selection.

There is no standard by which the achievements of the women in the House can be measured. Their committee assignments appear to be no better nor worse than many men receive. The women who have survived have satisfied the majority of their own constituents. That is the only test of fitness yet devised. They are regular party followers. Mrs. Owen was the only one who appears to make an effort to advance what is generally considered to be the women's point of view. She proposed, for example, the creation of a Department of Home and Child in the federal government. She often spoke in behalf of Mothers' Pensions, and advocated similar accepted forms of social legislation. The necessity to defend her own right to her seat when her election was contested identified her with those feminists who had had the principle of independent citizenship for married women written into federal law.[1] With the election for the seventy-third Congress, other changes must be noted. Mrs. Owen failed of renomination; Mrs. Pratt went down in the Democratic landslide, so that Mrs. Norton and Mrs. Rogers will be alone when they welcome the new members of the group, Mrs. Virginia Jenckes of Indiana, who was elected largely on a wet platform to secure a market for the grain of her constituents, and Miss Katherine O'Loughlin, of Kansas, who was victorious in a campaign in which general capacity to represent the interests of her district was recognized rather than any special claim as a woman.

While these women were pioneering in the House there was, until 1931, no woman in the Senate—although to see the pattern of the last decade wholly the woman "senator for-a-day" should not be forgotten. Mrs. Rebecca Latimer Felton was appointed senator by the Governor of Georgia when Senator Thomas E. Watson's death during the recess left the seat vacant. His elected successor, Senator George, courteously withheld the presentation of his credentials one day in order that Mrs. Felton might be sworn in. Accordingly for one day in 1922 Georgia had a woman senator. Then in the summer of 1931, Arkansas again recognized the principle of entrusting to a widow her deceased husband's unfinished task. Mrs. Hattie Caraway was elected senator in the

[1] Mrs. Owen had married a British subject, and the challenge of her regained citizenship was raised by contest, which was decided in her favor. See p. 260, reference to the "Cable Act."

autumn of 1931 under the Arkansas statute to serve out her husband's unfinished term. Since then, the Senate, too, has become accustomed to the presence of a woman; she has been called to preside in the absence of the Vice-President and has been elected to succeed herself. She is a member of the Committees on Agriculture and Forestry, Enrolled Bills, and the Library.

It is easy to recount with barren accuracy the names of the women who have been elected to the Congress. Their elections testify to the success of a few women in one political relationship. The interest of women is really better shown by the number of candidates who have presented themselves; for, although many are called, exceedingly few are chosen.

A Few Candidates Are Mentioned.—In 1920, 7[1] women were reported to have received the nomination of the two major parties to represent their districts in the Congress. Six of them were nominated by the party which was habitually in a minority in their districts, and it will be remembered that Miss Robertson was the only woman to be elected that year.

Two years later 8 women candidates were reported[2] of whom only one was elected—Mrs. Huck. Six of the aspirants were candidates of the minority party for the Senate. Mrs. Anna Dickie Oleson had been nominated by the Democrats in Minnesota, Mrs. Jessie Jack Hooper was the Democratic candidate in Wisconsin. Both of these women were well known suffrage leaders. In Ohio, Mrs. Virginia Darling Green ran as an Independent. Mrs. Maud C. Mandell was an Independent candidate in New Mexico. In Pennsylvania, Rachel C. Robinson was the candidate on the Prohibition ticket. Esther Lefkowitz ran as a Socialist and Farmer Labor candidate in New York. They were minority candidates.

Three other women with senatorial aspirations had failed in the primaries. Mrs. Frances C. Axtell of Bellingham, who was in 1912 the first woman in the Washington legislature, had been defeated in the Republican primaries. Miss Belle Kearney lost in the Democratic primaries in Mississippi, as did Mrs. Izetta Jewell Brown in West Virginia.

[1] *The Woman Citizen*, November 13, 1920. Eight were first reported but a later correction reduced the number to seven. In addition, it is of interest that Mrs. Ella Boole, later President of the National W.C.T.U., was a candidate for the Senate in the Republican Primaries in New York. She was defeated, but later ran in the general election as the nominee of the Prohibition Party.

[2] *Ibid.*, November 18, 1922.

The record of 21 disappointed candidates for the House of Representatives contains the names of 5 Republican candidates,[1] all but one striving against unequal odds in Democratic districts, 10 Democratic candidates[2] nominated in districts almost all of which were indisputably Republican. The Prohibition party named 2,[3] the Socialist party 1,[4] and 3[5] had the combined endorsement of the Socialist and Farmer Labor parties.[6]

Women's organizations and women leaders were greatly disappointed at the meager showing. A comment in the *Woman Citizen*[7] voiced the disillusionment:

First of all it is clear (the editorial runs) that the barriers in the way of women being elected to any political office are almost insurmountable. The dominant political parties do not nominate women for political office if there is a real chance for winning. Political offices are the assets of the political machine. In general, they are too valuable to be given to women. They are used to pay political debts or to strengthen the party, and so far the parties are not greatly in debt to women, and it has not been shown that it strengthens a party to nominate them.

The list of all the women who had failed to be nominated is not obtainable. The conspicuous Senate aspirants have been noted. In both Alabama and Mississippi where a primary victory is equivalent to election a woman had announced her candidacy for the House. Undoubtedly there were many others whose ambitions and names are lost.

In 1924,[8] Mrs. Izetta Jewell Brown of West Virginia again made an early announcement of her candidacy for the Senate, and shortly afterward Mrs. Menley Fosseen, a prominent Re-

---

[1] Mrs. H. Guild in Arizona; Mrs. Winnifred Mason Huck (elected) from Illinois-at-large; Mrs. Lindsay Patterson, North Carolina; Miss Alice Robertson, Oklahoma; and Adeline Otero, New Mexico.

[2] Mrs. Ellen Duane Davis, Pennsylvania; Mrs. Jett Wickersham Douglas of Iowa; Mrs. Lillien Cox Gault of Minnesota; Mrs. Luella St. Claire Moss, Missouri; Mrs. Esther K. O'Keefe of Indiana; Martha Riley, Wisconsin; Miss Jane E. Leonard of Pennsylvania, who was eighty-one years old; Miss Seneca Cleveland of Kansas; Mrs. Irene C. Buell of Nebraska; Mrs. Maggie Smith Hathaway of Montana.

[3] Julia R. Hazard, Pennsylvania; and Mamie Colvin, New York.

[4] Mrs. Elvia S. Beals, California.

[5] Jessie Wallace Hughan, New York; Mina Eskenazi, New York; Helen Murphy, Pennsylvania.

[6] The names and addresses of the twenty-one of the twenty-two candidates who were defeated in the election are given in the *Woman Citizen*, August 26 and October 1, 1922.

[7] November 18, 1922.

[8] *Ibid.*, March 8, 1924.

publican of Minnesota, was in the race. Mrs. Benjamin F. Perry of Kentucky announced her candidacy and, undaunted by the failure of women candidates in 1922, Mrs. Huck announced her candidacy for the House again. Four Democratic women, Miss Nellie Cline, a Kansas legislator; Mrs. Helen F. Greenfield of Colorado; Miss Julia Landers of Indianapolis; and Mrs. Genevieve Clark Thompson of Louisiana, sought their party's favor. A little later, Mrs. A. H. Hoffman of Iowa, formerly a county superintendent of schools, announced her candidacy.[1] There was much interest when, at the conclusion of the Republican Convention, Mrs. Harriet Taylor Upton filed as a candidate for Congress.

In 1924, only one[2] of those early entrants survived the primary test, but as election day approached the names of 19 women candidates for Congress were announced, one Republican, 5 Democrats, 4 on the Prohibition ticket, 7 Socialists, and 2 Progressives,[3] but no woman was nominated for the Senate in 1924, although 6 had been listed in 1922.

In 1926, the story was much the same,[4] although there was some comfort to be taken in the fact that three women members of Congress, Mrs. Kahn, Mrs. Norton and Mrs. Rogers, were reelected. It was the first regular election in which Mrs. Kahn and Mrs. Rogers competed, as their first victories had been won in special elections; but no woman was nominated for the Senate by a major party, although the attention of women all over the country had been focused on a distinguished aspirant, Judge Florence Allen of Ohio, who sought to be the candidate of the Democratic party in Ohio. Judge Allen's defeat was more than

---

[1] *Ibid.*, April 19, 1924.

[2] Miss Nellie Cline, D., Kansas.

[3] The Republican was Mrs. Mary Giles Howard of Tennessee.

The Democrats were: Mrs. Mary Ward Hurt of Benton, Illinois; Miss Nellie Cline, Larned, Kansas; Mrs. Mary T. Norton, Jersey City, New Jersey; Miss Phebe T. Sutliff, Warren, Ohio; and Mrs. Jessie L. Collett, Philadelphia, Pennsylvania.

The Prohibitionists were: Luella Barton, Nebraska; Mrs. L. Blankenburg, Anna Van Skite, and Mrs. Elizabeth R. Culbertson, from Pennsylvania.

The Socialists were: Miss Isabelle King, San Francisco; Mrs. Junia Sisaman, Evanston, Illinois; Amy R. Juengling, Eden, New York; Jessie Wallace Hughan, and Lucille E. Randolph, New York City; Mrs. Minnie McFarland, Umatilla, Oregon; Mrs. Ruby Herman, Seattle, Washington.

The Progressives were: Miss Jennie Dornblum and Miss Daisy Detterline of Pennsylvania.

[4] With this election the *Woman Citizen* ceased publication of names of women candidates.

the failure of an individual candidate. It was a reverse in a cause which, to many women, they embodied.

Mrs. Lillian Ford Feickert sought, but did not gain, the Republican senatorial nomination in New Jersey in 1928, and Mrs. Virginia Peters Parkhurst of Maryland was similarly disappointed in her aspiration to the Senate through the Democratic primaries. In April, Mrs. Gifford Pinchot was a candidate in the Pennsylvania primaries to represent her district in the Congress. She failed to receive the nomination. Mrs. Minnie Fisher Cunningham was a candidate for the Senate in the Democratic primaries of Texas.[1] Like Mrs. Pinchot, she was well known to women's organizations all over the country and her defeat, although not unexpected, was a sharp disappointment. But the much publicized "three Ruths" came into Congress, so that women's hurt was somewhat soothed.

Two years later, in 1930, there were 19 women competing for congressional seats in the general election.[2] Six members[3] of Congress were campaigning for reelection. One of their colleagues, Mrs. Ruth Hanna McCormick had won the Republican nomination for the Senate in Illinois, and was engaged in a hot three-cornered fight in which another woman, Mrs. Lottie Holman O'Neill, the first woman member of the Illinois legislature, was one of her opponents. In New Jersey 2 women had been nominated[1] for the Senate, and in 5 other states women[2] were campaigning for election to the House.

Only 5 of the 19 candidates were elected, and all of these were incumbent members of Congress campaigning to hold their seats. It should be added that 17 victories was the possible total as in the 2 senatorial contests women were pitted against each other.

The name of Mrs. Effie Wingo was omitted in the preceding paragraph. It would have raised the total to 6 victories out of

[1] These are the only names which appear in the pages of the *Woman Citizen* or in the bulletins of organizations interested in the woman movement.

[2] *The Woman Citizen* issues of November-December, 1930.

[3] Mrs. Owen, Mrs. Pratt, Mrs. Kahn, Mrs. Rogers, Mrs. Norton, and Mrs. Langley. All but the last named were victorious.

[4] Miss Thelma Parkinson, Democrat, and Esther H. Elfreth, Prohibitionist.

[5] Mrs. J. N. Fickel (D), Iowa; Mae Clausen (D) and Stella B. Haines (R), Kansas; Mrs. P. Gehrig (R), Missouri; Izetta Jewell Miller (formerly Izetta Jewell Brown), twice defeated as a senatorial candidate in the primaries of West Virginia; and Hattie de Lone (D), Laura Treadwell (R), and Hilda Claesseus (R) all from New York; Ann W. Dillad (R), Oklahoma.

20 contestants. But both parties endorsed her candidacy which carried out her husband's dying wish that she should succeed him, so that her election was unopposed.

Somehow, then, from 1922 to 1930 the number of women nominated to the Congress has sagged from 28 to 20.[1] There were 6 women in the House of Representatives of the seventy-second Congress, none of them newcomers.[2] Once there were 9.

Women in Federal Office.—Although until 1931 there was no woman in the Senate, a few women have taken their places in the governmental scheme by Executive appointment "with the advice and consent" of that body. The list is not imposing in length, for it is still true that the majority of women in government service find their way into the classified service through competitive examination.[3]

It should be remembered that it was only in November, 1919, that all competitive examinations were thrown open to women, and not even after the enactment of the Reclassification Act of March 4, 1923, when the principle of equal pay for equal work without regard to sex was expressly written into the law regulating government employment,[4] was the principle generally applied. Evidence is given in another place that relatively few women reach the higher grades of service, and that to women advancement comes slowly. It is evident that women workers in government have not been freed from the occupational disability of sex. Their progress and their difficulties are, however, different from those of women in politics, who are affected by considerations which the merit system is designed to remove from the classified service.

There are positions in the government service outside the classified service—those where the incumbents are appointed by bureau chiefs or department heads or where the power of selection is vested in the President. In some cases the Civil Service Commission gives examinations to test the qualifications of the

---

[1] Including Mrs. Wingo.

[2] For Mrs. Wingo served in the short session of the seventy-first Congress (December, 1930–March, 1931).

[3] On December 31, 1930, there were 595,456 government employees in the executive civil service. Of these, 94,163 were women. See *Recent Social Trends in the United States*, Chap. XIV.

[4] Reference should be made to the General Order No. 27, issued during the war by Mr. McAdoo in the Railroad Administration in which equal pay for women doing the same work as men was ordered.

candidates appointed by the President or some other administrative officer even though the positions are not under its jurisdiction. This is true of the trade commissioners in the Department of Commerce, and of postmasters.

The Foreign Service appointees in the State Department are selected by examination, although, like postmasters, they are nominated by the President and their nominations are confirmed by the Senate.

Political influence is reflected most clearly in Executive appointments. Therefore it is of importance to trace the place which women take in the lists; and to add the measure to the record of women's influence in politics in this decade of their enfranchisement. It has already been pointed out that the appointment of women did not have to wait upon the suffrage. The selection of a few for positions of responsibility came more swiftly than the right of all to vote.

In the years just prior to the ratification of the amendment a number of substantial appointments were made. Probably the first major appointment in the federal government was welcomed when the Children's Bureau was created in 1912 and Julia C. Lathrop of Illinois was selected by President Taft to be its head. In 1916, Mrs. J. Borden Harriman was appointed to the United States Industrial Commission. When the Tariff Commission was organized in 1916, Miss Ida Tarbell was offered a position as a member, which she declined. In January of 1917, Mrs. Frances Axtell was appointed for a four-year term as a member of the United States Employees' Compensation Commission, and in June, 1920, Mrs. Annette Abbot Adams of California was appointed to the office of assistant attorney general. Previously, in August, 1919, Mrs. Adams had been appointed United States attorney for the Northern California District and confirmed by the Senate, although she had held the position since 1914 "under appointment by the court." Her salary was $1,800, when, it might be added, male assistants were receiving $2,150. She retired from that office a fortnight before her new appointment as attorney general was confirmed.

The Women's Bureau in the Department of Labor was established in 1918 as a war service to Women in Industry with Mary Van Kleek of New York in charge. In August, 1919, Mary Anderson was appointed as its chief and in June, 1920, the Bureau was given a permanent statutory status in the Department of Labor.

Kathryn Sellers was named judge of the juvenile court in the District in 1918 and in December, 1920, Mabel Boardman was appointed to be one of the three commissioners of the District of Columbia. She served until March of 1921, when, under the new administration, her place was given to a man. Mrs. Virginia Cross was appointed to the Board of Charities in the District in the same year.

In March, 1920, Mrs. Helen H. Gardner was appointed to the United States Civil Service Commission, and it is interesting that in that same year a woman, Miss Viola Smith, was for the first time given office in the foreign field of the Department of Commerce. She was named clerk to the American Commercial Attaché in Peking.[1] Mrs. Clara Sears Taylor was appointed to the Rent Commission in the District of Columbia,[2] and Mrs. Anna C. Tillinghast was appointed commissioner of immigration for District 3, with headquarters at Boston. When, therefore, the Federal Suffrage Amendment was ratified, the pioneering was over. Women were chiefs of bureaus, a woman was assistant attorney general, another was on the District Bench. A woman was a commissioner of the District and women served on the staff of other District governmental agencies. Mrs. Axtell and Mrs. Gardener sat on Federal Commissions, all by Presidential appointment. And a beginning had been made in the field of foreign commerce.

Voting women looked forward to a wider recognition of their talents and influences. In July of 1921, a woman, Mary Rutter Towle, was appointed assistant United States attorney for the Southern District of New York; one month later, another (Miss Mary O'Toole) was appointed municipal judge for the District of Columbia. In November the Senate confirmed the appointment of Mrs. Mabel Pound LeRoy of Michigan as recorder of the General Land Office.[3]

These new offices were filled by women in the first year of their enfranchisement, and before the year had ended women were appointed to succeed the first encumbents in the offices of chief

[1] This is not a Presidential appointment but illustrates an entrance into a new field outside the classified service. Miss Smith was promoted first to the position of assistant trade commissioner. Later she was made trade commissioner. Now she is registrar.

[2] She served until the Rent Commission was terminated.

[3] On December 16, 1930, Mrs. Emma L. Warren was appointed to succeed Mrs. LeRoy who resigned.

of the Children's Bureau, the U. S. Compensation Commission, and assistant attorney general.

In that year, too, 1922, the first woman was appointed to the diplomatic service of the United States. The name of Lucille Atcherson of Ohio was sent to the Senate for confirmation in September. Mrs. Jennie P. Musser had been appointed collector of customs in the district having Salt Lake City as its head-quarters, and in September Miss Sophie McCord was made appraiser of merchandise at St. Louis, so that two outposts in the Treasury Department were thus claimed as within the field of women's employment.

In 1923, Mrs. Mabel Reinecke was appointed collector of internal revenue in Chicago, after five months' experience as acting collector. She was the first woman to hold the position, and two years later Mrs. Jennette A. Hyde was appointed collector of customs in Hawaii. Since that time, three other women have received similar appointments. Mrs. Eddie McColl Priest was appointed collector for the Tennessee district in January, 1926, and in March of that year Mrs. Nellie Gregg Tomlinson was placed in charge of the Iowa district. In 1930, Mrs. Fannie Sutton Faison was made collector at Wilmington, N. C., and Miss Margaret Ellis was appointed an examiner in the United States Appraiser's Office in Baltimore.

Three years earlier, Mrs. Anna C. Tillinghast had been appointed to succeed herself as a member of the Civil Service Commission. In 1925, Dr. Helen Strong, a highly qualified woman, was appointed by President Coolidge to serve as a member of the United States Geographic Board, and progress in the diplomatic service could be noted, for one woman received her first foreign assignment and another was appointed and assigned. Judge Kathryn Sellers was reappointed in 1925.

In 1926, two women, Miss Julia Jaffray and Mrs. Alvin Dodd,[1] were appointed by the President to be members of the Advisory Board of the new Federal Women's Prison, of which Dr. Mary B. Harris had been selected as superintendent by the attorney general.[2] It is of interest to recall in this connection that

[1] Mrs. Dodd resigned in 1928. Miss Jaffray is still a member, and Mrs Frederick Upham of Chicago and Mrs. Frederick Mann of West Virginia have been added.

[2] Dr. Amy N. Stannard of the staff of St. Elizabeth's Hospital was appointed to the Federal Parole Board by the attorney general in 1930.

Mrs. J. Ellen Foster, in 1908, had been made inspector of women prisoners for the Department of Justice.

A third woman diplomat appeared in 1927, and Miss Florence Willis of California, who was later transferred to the vice-consulship at Valpariso, Chile, and two more were appointed in 1929, Miss Nelle Stogsdall of Indiana, later vice-consul at Beiruit, Syria, and Miss Margaret Warner of Massachusetts, vice-consul at Geneva. Miss Constance Harvey of New York was appointed in 1930 vice-consul in Ottawa, and on June, 1931, she was transferred to Milan. In the meantime the number of women in foreign service under the Department of Commerce increased. In 1931, three women were serving as trade commissioners and five women were serving as assistant trade commissioners. Unlike the State Department representatives, none of these is a Presidential appointment. One of them is a registrar at Shanghai, China. Her first appointment as clerk to the American Commercial Attaché[1] in Peking was in 1920. There is a woman trade commissioner at Oslo, Norway, appointed January 1, 1929; one at Rome, Italy, appointed January 1, 1929; one at Bogota, Colombia, appointed July 1, 1930; one at Barcelona, Spain, appointed July 1, 1930; one at Madrid, Spain, appointed July 1, 1930; one at Santiago, Chile, appointed July 1, 1930; and one at Havana, Cuba, appointed July 1, 1930. One trade commissioner, Miss Margaret Goldsmith who was appointed in 1923, and assigned to Berlin, Germany, resigned in 1925.

In 1928, a woman became for the first time head of a division in the State Department; Mrs. Ruth B. Shipley, chief of the passport division, is the pioneer. Another, who had been appointed a custom's appraiser at Cleveland by President Harding, was named a judge of the Customs Court in New York by President Coolidge in 1928 and in the same year Miss Amy Wren was appointed to serve the Eastern District of New York as a United States Commissioner. The President's selection of Dr. Bess Goodykoontz to be assistant commissioner of the Office of Education on October 1, 1929, was confirmed by the Senate on June 16, 1930.

In 1929, Mrs. Myrtle Tanner Blacklidge was appointed to succeed Mrs. Reinecke as collector of internal revenue in Chicago,

---

[1] This is not a Presidential appointment. It is mentioned because it appeared to be of widespread interest.

WOMEN IN THE TWENTIETH CENTURY

only to resign in January, 1931. Her successor is a man.[1] When Mrs. Willebrandt resigned in 1929 as assistant attorney general her place was likewise given to a man.

One new position of importance was opened to women in 1930 when Miss Annabel Matthews, an attorney since 1925 in the office of the solicitor of internal revenue, was appointed to the Board of Tax Appeals. With Judge Cline of the Customs Court, Miss Matthews shares the honor of being the highest salaried woman employed in the government. Both receive $10,000 a year. Judge Cline's appointment is for life. Miss Matthews was appointed to fill the unexpired portion of a term of ten years which ends June 1, 1936.

After a decade, then, it appears that in addition to the 4 women in the diplomatic service[2] and not including post office appointments, 15 women hold significant federal office[3] by appointment of the President, 5 of which were held by women in 1920.[4] Six of them are in the Customs Service, one is a commissioner of immigration. Three are bureau chiefs. There is a woman civil service commissioner, a woman is chairman of the United States Employees Compensation Commission, a woman sits on the Board of Tax Appeals, three are assistant chiefs in the Children's Bureau, the Woman's Bureau, and the office of Education. Three women judges, one of the Customs Court in New York, one presiding over the Juvenile Court, and one assigned to the Municipal Court in the District of Columbia, have been selected by the President. With these the list is finished. There has been no woman appointed to succeed Miss Boardman as commissioner of the District of Columbia. No woman is assistant attorney general now, nor is there a woman collector of internal revenue.[5] There have obviously been losses as well as gains.

[1] Gregory T. Van Meter.

[2] In 1927, Miss Atcherson resigned to be married. Miss Field resigned in 1929 to enter private employment.

[3] Receivers of public moneys are omitted from this list. At least four have been appointed since 1920. Also a register of the Land Office, Mrs. Minnie L. Bray, was appointed at Carson City, Nevada, July, 1919. In 1930, Miss Clara Crisler was appointed to the same position.

[4] The chief of the Children's Bureau, the chief of the Woman's Bureau, the Civil Service Commission, the member of the United States Employees' Compensation Commission, the judge of the Juvenile Court of the District of Columbia.

[5] The Presidential appointments mentioned in the preceding pages include all those in the list furnished by the Civil Service Commission entitled, "Women in

So large a number of the Executive appointments relate to the Postal Service that some mention of women postmasters should be made. Candidates for appointments as postmaster are examined by the Civil Service Commission. The three highest are certified to the Department—any one of the three may be chosen.

In 1919, there were 255 women postmasters appointed out of a total of 2,487, or 10.26 per cent. Of 2,855 appointed in 1921, 321, or 11.24 per cent, were women. A year later 629 women were appointed when there were 3,402 in all, or 18.48 per cent. Of 2,019 postmasters appointed in 1925, 397 were women, or 19.66 per cent. Four hundred and seventy-four women were appointed in 1927 when the total was 3,890, or 12.18 per cent. In 1930, there were 940 women appointed, or 17.60 per cent. The total number appointed was 5,338.[1] The proportion has increased from a little more than one-tenth in 1920 to nearly a fifth in 1930. In all that time, however, no one of the large city postmasterships has gone to a woman. In 1923, when Miss Elizabeth Barnard was made postmaster of Tampa, Florida, she was reported[2] to be "the first woman in that office to receive a salary of $6,000 a year. The highest salary previously given to a woman had been $2,500."

In addition to the regular administrative responsibilities to which women are eligible in the federal government[3] the past ten years have seen special opportunities.

---

the Federal Government." Reports of the civil appointments sent to the Senate for confirmation have been examined. Lists from the League of Women Voters, and the *Woman Citizen* have also been consulted.

[1] Some years are omitted because the lists rely so much upon initials that comparisons are impossible. It is hoped that the years selected are adequate illustrations.

[2] *Woman Citizen*, March 24, 1923. Miss Barnard is still (January, 1933) in office. Tampa is a post office of the first class.

[3] The following responsible positions, not Presidential appointments, are among those now held by women:

Miss Adelaide S. Baylor	Chief, Home Economics Service, Federal Board for Vocational Education
Dr. Louise Stanley	Chief, Bureau of Home Economics, United States Department of Agriculture
Mrs. Lulah T. Andrews	Director, Bureau of Industrial Housing and Transportation, United States Department of Labor
Miss Mary Stewart	Assistant Director of Education, Indian Service
Miss Margaret M. Hanna	Chief of the Office of Coordination and Review in State Department
Miss Ethel L. Lawrence	Assistant Solicitor of the State Department

[311]

When the Disarmament Conference met in Washington from November, 1921, to February, 1922, four women were on the American Advisory Committee. In 1922, the chief of the Children's Bureau was appointed to the League of Nations Advisory Commission for the Protection and Welfare of Children and Young Persons as the representative of the United States in an "unofficial and consultative capacity," and in 1926 the former chief of the Bureau, Miss Julia C. Lathrop, was appointed as "assessor" to that Commission, representing the National Conference of Social Work. In 1923, Mrs. Hamilton Wright was appointed "assessor" for the United States on the League of Nations Commission on Traffic in Opium, and in 1929, President Hoover appointed a distinguished citizen of New Jersey, Mrs. C. B. Wittpen, as American Commissioner of the International Penitentiary Association.

During the past three decades it has been the practice to set up commissions or committees or to organize conferences. These have been of three kinds: (1) Temporary bodies created by the President's order for the determination of policy or for giving advice as to policies on special subjects; these are usually privately financed: (2) Commissions or committees created by Congress on recommendation of the President; for these it is common to appropriate: (3) Commissions created by Congress on its own initiative; for these it is common that an appropriation be made. President Roosevelt set up 107, President Taft 63, President Wilson 150, President Harding 44, President Coolidge 118, President Hoover, prior to February 19, 1932, had appointed 44, of which he had either set up or recommended 29, while 15 had been authorized by Congress on his suggestion and financed by public appropriations. A list of these with a statement of the purpose of each is available in a speech by Representative Will R

Miss Marjorie M. Whiteman	Assistant Solicitor of the State Department
Miss Mary M. O'Reilly	Assistant Director of the Bureau of the Mint
Major Julia Stimson	Head of the Army Nurses Corps, U.S. Department of War (Only woman with rank, insignia and rights of major in the U.S. Army)
Miss Beatrice Bowman	Head of Navy Nurses' Corps, U.S. Department of the Navy
Miss Lucy Minnigerode	Superintendent of Nurses, U.S. Public Health Service, Department of the Treasury
Mrs. Mary A. Hickey	Superintendent of Nurses, Medical Section, U.S. Veterans' Bureau

Many in the U.S. Children's Bureau and the U.S. Woman's Bureau are not listed.

Wood of Indiana.[1] The list includes, however, such varying groups as the Federal Power Commission, the United States Tariff Commission, the London Naval Conference, and the Geneva Arms Limitation Conference. Twenty-one names of women appear among the total of 230 appointed on these commissions. The appointment of a woman, President Mary E. Woolley of Mt. Holyoke College, as a member of the Arms Limitation Conference, was one of the important evidences of interest in women's advancement to which President Hoover called special attention during the campaign.

Then there is the decennial Census to consider. Its field appointees are outside the classified service. In 1920, there were 5 women out of 372 supervisors, or between 1 and 2 per cent. Thirty were appointed in 1930 out of a total of over 575 selected, or something over 5 per cent.[2]

Such is the record of what might be called the voluntary recognition of women in the federal government. Their opportunities under the Civil Service have been described somewhat in another place.[3]

Women in State Governments.[4]—Long before women had served the federal government in public office they were repre-

---

[1] *Congressional Record*, Vol. 75, Part IV, p. 4355.

[2] *Annual Reports of Director of the Census*, 1920, p. 8; 1930, p. 5.

[3] See *Recent Social Trends in the United States*, Chap. XIV.

[4] In an effort to compile a complete record of women office holders in state governments during the past ten years an inquiry was addressed to the Secretary of State of every commonwealth. All but two replied but the replies are exceedingly unequal in scope and precision. From some states an elaborate report of membership on all boards and commissions, and elective and appointive offices was submitted. A complete set of abstracts of votes cast was sent in some cases. Other replies omitted all reference to anything other than the membership of women in state legislatures. In many of the replies submitted as complete, essential data such as the length of term or the date of appointment failed to be included. For example, the Legislative Bureau of Indiana in a memorandum accompanying a letter dated March 6, 1931, listed 18 women who have held state office with the dates of their terms, and 88 women members of various permanent boards and commissions. The Secretary of State of South Carolina replied March 2, 1931, "There is no publication which would show what other state appointive or elective offices have been held by women during the last ten year period." The Division of Records in the Department of State of Wisconsin sent an admirable list of 72 women who had served on the various boards and commissions of the state. A similar report was received from the State Library of Connecticut.

Which does not always mean that women in those states of scant reports have been less recognized than in the others. Indeed one letter from the Secretary of State in New Jersey, March 13, 1931, said of women holding other than

sented in the governments of the respective states. In the nineties and early in the present century, the proceedings of the General Federation of Women's Clubs and the pages of women's magazines reported the widening scope of the activities of women in relation to state government. It would appear that administrative positions on the boards of state institutions engaged their first attention.

As early as 1875 the legislature of Wisconsin is reported[1] to have "appropriated $1,000 to secure a record of 'women's labor of life.'" It was discovered that Wisconsin women "had been most active and influential in founding orphanages, hospitals, industrial homes for delinquent girls, colleges for the education of young men and women, besides holding many positions of trust and responsibility in state institutions."

In 1893, the governor of Illinois appointed Mrs. Florence Kelley state factory inspector, and for four years she served in that capacity, directing a staff composed of one assistant and ten deputies. The club women of Michigan reported to the Biennial Convention in 1896 that "Women's clubs were also a potent factor in securing the appointment of a woman professor in our University, upon the same terms and with the same salary as is given the other professors." In 1899, Mrs. Elizabeth C. Earl was made a member of the Public Library Commission in Indiana. In 1906, a woman, Kate Barnard, was influential in the Constitutional Convention in Oklahoma, supported a program which included in the proposed state government an elective office of commissioner of charities,[2] and was elected to that office which she held until 1915. Each time, the appointment or election of women to public office was hailed as an advance for the woman's cause. In 1910, Illinois and Kentucky delegates rejoiced that women, and "club women," had been appointed to the State Library Commissions.

---

legislative jobs, "There have been many instances when they have done so, such as on boards pertaining to education, libraries, reformatories, the blind, deaf, epileptics, tubercular, health, various prisons, insane, etc."

The files of the *Woman Citizen* have been carefully searched, the records of the League of Women Voters, and the proceedings of various women's organizations were examined. From these sources as well as the direct inquiry, news about women in state government has been assembled and is presented. But hope of reporting the complete roster cannot be cherished.

[1] This was in preparation for the Wisconsin Exhibit at the Philadelphia Centennial Exhibition, 1876. *Wisconsin Laws*, 1875, p. 391.

[2] *Constitution of the State of Oklahoma*, Art. VI, Secs. 27–30.

It is impossible to mention each new responsibility assumed. In 1912, Washington women gloried in a woman deputy labor commissioner, a woman member of the State Board of Health and a feminine superintendent of public instruction.[1] Kentucky reported a woman on the Forestry Commission, two women on the Tuberculosis Commission and a state bacteriologist. Minnesota boasted a woman at the head of the State Library Commission, a woman in charge of a Department for Women and Children in the State Labor Bureau and "several club women" on the Board of the State Art Commission.[2]

Three years later, Governor Capper appointed a woman to the State Board of Control in Kansas. In 1916, the club women of Arkansas reported that the Governor, "at the request of the Federation," had appointed a woman to be a member of the Minimum Wage Commission. In Georgia the Governor had appointed a woman as member of the board of five to manage the Training School for Wayward Girls, and in Nevada in 1917 a woman was appointed to the governing board of the Industrial School at Elkao.

So, in 1920, when the suffrage amendment was ratified there was a history of women in state government. Women were factory inspectors, members of state boards of education, charities and health. Appointment to responsible positions was no longer a glamorous novelty. Reports of progress still are noted and self-conscious in their suffrage and their records, women of all states have checked the advances of the past ten years with more reserved enthusiasm. In some states special legislation was required after the federal amendment was ratified in order that women should be eligible to hold some state offices. Indeed it was only in 1926 that the word "male" was stricken from the qualification of legislators in Iowa. Variation in titles and ambiguity in duties prevent analysis or classification. Comparison between states and between years is therefore unfair.

First, women governors. Only two women have been elected to gubernatorial office, Mrs. Nellie Tayloe Ross of Wyoming and

[1] Mrs. Evelyn Chantler, Mrs. R. C. McCredie, and Mrs. Josephine Corliss Preston. Mrs. Preston served four terms of four years each as state superintendent of public instruction. The reports were made to the Biennial of that year. The names have been checked.

[2] Oklahoma, Minnesota, and Washington were reported as having women assistant commissioners of labor and New York "has one for all practical purposes, although not called by that name."

Mrs. Miriam Ferguson of Texas. Both inherited their places. Mrs. Ross was nominated by a Democratic Convention held in October and elected in November, 1924, to fill out the unexpired term of her husband who had died in office. Mrs. Ferguson was nominated in the Democratic primaries and elected that same November in lieu of her husband who was physically alive but civilly dead. Mr. Ferguson was a former governor who was ineligible to be a candidate himself because impeachment proceedings, which had been brought against him for misappropriation of state funds during his previous administration, disqualified him.[1] It was generally understood that a vote for her was vote for him. Mrs. Ferguson's election was not applauded by feminists. There is something piquant in the recollection that it was the then Governor Ferguson who led the fight against the adoption of the suffrage plank in the Democratic platform at the Convention of 1916. Then his impeccable objective was "to keep women free from the entanglements and the degrading influence of politics and politicians," a depth to which his loyal pioneering wife descended in his behalf less than ten years later.

Governor Ross was the first woman elected governor to be sworn in. On January 5, 1925, she took the oath of office, for her first term which ended two years later. Although her party renominated her she was not reelected in 1926. Mrs. Ferguson was sworn in on January 20. A single term was the length of her first service. In the Democratic primaries of 1925 she was not renominated,[2] but in those of 1932 she was one of the two highest, and was successful and elected again on November 8, 1932.

While Mrs. Ross enjoys the distinction of being the first elected woman governor to take the oath of office, it is to Mrs. Soledad C. Chacon of New Mexico that the honor of acting first as governor of a state is due. Mrs. Chacon was elected secretary of state for New Mexico in 1922. The lieutenant governor died during her term, so that when the governor left the state to

[1] Early in her term Mrs. Ferguson had the satisfaction of signing the amnesty bill which restored the rights of citizenship to her husband. She has now entered upon her second term.

[2] Few women have been candidates for the office of governor. Mrs. Alice Lorraine Daly was nominated for the governorship by the Non-Partisan League of South Dakota but was defeated in the election of 1922. Mrs. Lilith Martin Wilson was the Socialist nominee in Pennsylvania in 1922. Miss Gladys Pyle was a candidate but failed to receive the Republican nomination in South Dakota in 1930, and the same year Mrs. Clara Shortridge Foltz was rejected in the Republican primaries in California.

attend the Democratic National Convention in 1924, Mrs. Chacon was "acting governor" in his absence.

This second-in-line-of-descent in state government is a position which has been given to women a considerable number of times. Mrs. Chacon was elected in 1922. She was reelected in 1924 and New Mexico has had a woman secretary of state ever since Miss Jennie Fortune was elected in 1926. She was followed by Mrs. Edward Perrealut in 1928 and Mrs. Marguerite P. Baca, the present incumbent, who was elected in 1930.

In 1924, Mrs. Florence M. S. Knapp was elected secretary of state in New York and Mrs. Emma Guy Cromwell was elected in Kentucky. She was succeeded by Miss Ella Lewis in 1928, who was again succeeded by Miss Sarah M. Mahan in 1930. In 1925, Mrs. Emma Grigsby Meharg was appointed secretary of state of Texas. June Y. McCallum succeeded her in 1927 and is now serving her third term.

South Dakota twice elected Miss Gladys Pyle, formerly a member of the legislature for two terms, to the office of secretary of state. She was elected first in November, 1926, and retired in 1930 when she became a candidate for governor.[1] Mrs. Elizabeth Coyne was then elected to succeed her as secretary of state. On November 4, 1925, Miss Fannie Herrington, appointed to be secretary of state for Delaware, was sworn in by Governor Robinson. A man, elected to the position, had been missing since October 24th. Miss Herrington was appointed to his place but after three months' service resigned. In 1927, Helen E. Burbank was made deputy secretary of state of Vermont, a position she still holds. Miss Alice Lee Crosjean was appointed secretary of state in Louisiana in the autumn of 1930.

In all, 13 women held the position of secretary of state during the decade 1920–1930. There were 5[2] secretaries and one deputy[3] in office in 1931. There has never been a woman state

---

[1] In her gubernatorial campaign Miss Pyle received the plurality vote against four men—her adversaries in the Republican primaries. She did not however receive the required 35 per cent of the vote which is necessary for selection under South Dakota law. In the convention which followed she was defeated on the twelfth ballot by a combination of the strength of the two remaining men candidates (from a letter from Miss Pyle, March 31, 1931).

[2] In Kentucky, South Dakota, Texas, New Mexico, and Louisiana, two serving by appointment, in Texas and Louisiana. The rest are elected.

[3] There have been a number of assistant secretaries, but no effort has been made to check and compile the list.

attorney general, although women have served as deputies or assistants.[1]

Four[2] women have been chosen clerks of their State Supreme Court. In October, 1921, Miss Eugenia Davis was appointed clerk of the Supreme Court of Arizona. She has served continuously ever since. Mrs. Grace Kaercher Davis, still clerk in Minnesota, was elected in 1922.[3] Mrs. Eva Hatton is now holding the position in Nevada.[4] Miss Jessie Elizabeth Moore was elected in 1926 to a four-year term as clerk of the Supreme Court of Oklahoma. In Georgia Mrs. K. C. Beckley is now serving as deputy clerk.

Mrs. Edward F. White was elected to be reporter of the Supreme Court in Indiana in 1925. In 1929, she was succeeded by Miss Genevieve Brown whose term will expire in 1933.

A unique position in state government is that of Mrs. Esther Andrews of Massachusetts. She is now (1933) serving her fifth term as one of the governor's councillors, a position to which she was elected first in 1928. The Governor's Council of eight members has considerable power over appointments, clemency, expenditures, and other aspects of the state administration.

Three states have had women treasurers since 1920. In Indiana[5] Mrs. Grace B. Urbahns was appointed in January, 1926, to fill the unexpired term of her husband. In February, 1927, she was elected to a term which expired in February, 1931. In 1928, Mrs. Emma Guy Cromwell of Kentucky advanced from secretary of state to state treasurer, a position she now holds. Mrs. Bertha E. Baker is now serving her second term as state treasurer of North Dakota.[6] The fiscal departments of two state governments

---

[1] Mrs. Edward Franklin White was deputy in Indiana in 1920. Miss S. M. R. O'Hara and Miss M. Vashti Burr have been deputies in Pennsylvania. Miss Burr resigned, but Miss O'Hara, appointed in 1927, is still in office. Women have also served as assistants in Texas and Massachusetts, according to authoritative replies to this inquiry. The 1931 report of the National League of Women Voters adds New York and Arkansas too.

[2] A fifth, Miss Anne Foley of South Dakota, has been mentioned in some reports as serving in 1929. Several inquiries failed to substantiate her selection. Through the courtesy of the office of Senator, formerly Governor Bulow of South Dakota, a thorough search revealed a Miss Anna Foley as clerk of the county court in Beadle County in that year. It is believed that that is her correct title and that she was never clerk of the supreme court.

[3] The term in Minnesota is four years. Mrs. Davis was reelected in 1926 and again in 1930 for a term expiring in 1935.

[4] Mrs. Hatton was first elected in 1926. She was reelected in 1930.

[5] Letter from librarian of Indiana Legislative Bureau, March 6, 1931.

[6] She was elected for the first time in 1926.

have had the additional representation of women in the capacity of assistant treasurer and as auditors.[1] In 1931, the appointment of Mrs. F. W. Wittick[2] as budget director of the new Farmer-Labor administration in Minnesota was a substantial innovation.

The total number of women who have been governors, secretaries of states, and treasurers is small. Enfranchisement has not changed the most familiar state governmental activity for women. Since 1920, as before, they are most frequently listed as members of boards of commissions. A few are of special significance.

Miss Frances Perkins was appointed to the State Industrial Board of New York in 1919. With the exception of a two-year interval in 1921–1923, when a Republican administration was inaugurated, Miss Perkins served continuously until she was made head of the State Labor Department in 1929. From 1926 to her promotion she was chairman of the State Industrial Board.[3] Mrs. Alice Curtis Moyer Wing was appointed industrial commissioner of Missouri in 1921.[4] In that same year Mrs. Kate Burr Johnson was appointed commissioner of public welfare in North Carolina, after two years service as director of child welfare.[5] She was succeeded by a woman, Mrs. W. Thomas Bost. In 1922,[6] Mrs. Mabel Bassett reclaimed for women the office of state commissioner of charities and corrections of Oklahoma. Mrs. Alice Warren began in 1921 her six years of service on the State Board of Regents.

By 1923, the number of comparable appointments had been increased. Mrs. Charles Bennett Smith was president of the New York Civil Service Commission. Dr. Ellen Potter was appointed commissioner of public welfare in Pennsylvania, January, 1923.

[1] Wisconsin and Texas.

[2] Mrs. Wittick, a prominent member of the Minnesota League of Women Voters, who had been active in Governor Olson's campaign, had made a special study of tax matters.

[3] Miss Nelle Swartz succeeded Miss Perkins on the State Industrial Board in 1929. Miss Swartz had been head of the Women's Bureau of the New York State Labor Department. Miss Frieda S. Miller is now director of the Division of Women in Industry of the State Labor Department.

[4] Mrs. Armanda D. Hargis of Springfield is the present commissioner of labor and industrial inspection in Missouri, appointed by Governor Caulfield.

[5] She served until 1930 when she was succeeded by Mrs. W. T. Bost who is now in office.

[6] She is now serving her third term.

The title of her position was changed in June to secretary of welfare.[1] Mrs. Katherine Phillips Edson was executive commissioner of the Industrial Welfare Commission in California,[2] having been a member of the Commission since 1913.

Miss Caroline Crosby and Mrs. Blanche La Du had been appointed in 1922 to the State Board of Control in Minnesota.[3] Miss Maud Neprud had been similarly honored in Wisconsin in 1919.[4] In Virginia Mrs. Emma Speed Sampson was appointed to the State Board of Censors that same year and has served continuously ever since. In Michigan Mrs. Dora Stockman was elected to the State Board of Agriculture. In 1925 she was selected for a second term.

The census of women participating in state government in some capacity might be prolonged. As it cannot be completed no attempt at copious illustration will be made. A few unexpected assignments stand out. In 1928, Miss Caryll Hoffman was deputy state game warden in South Dakota. In 1929, Mrs. Belva Martin was appointed commissioner of state lands in Arkansas. In 1930 she was elected to the position for a second term. At her husband's death, Mrs. Mamie G. Eaton was appointed in March of 1927 to succeed him as railroad commissioner of Florida. Her appointment ran until the election in November, 1928. At that time she was elected for his unexpired term. In 1930, she was reelected and began in January of 1931 the four-year term she is now serving.

In Oregon Mrs. Ella S. Wilson, as secretary of the Board of State Fair Directors, has direct charge of the annual state fair.

Interesting as these responsibilities are, it is still in the fields long accepted as engaging women's special interests that women have most persistently appeared. There were in 1930 13 women who were state librarians.

---

[1] Dr. Potter retired in January, 1927. Mrs. E. S. McCauley, who was appointed to succeed her, served until January, 1931. She was succeeded by Hon. John L. Hanna, who served for a brief period and was succeeded by Mrs. Alice F. Liveright, the present director of the Department.

[2] Mrs. Edson has served continuously since her appointment. In 1930, Governor Young of California appointed a second woman to the Commission, Mrs. Parker Maddeux of San Francisco.

[3] Miss Crosby resigned in 1923. Mrs. La Du is still a member.

[4] Mrs. Elizabeth Kading was also appointed to the Wisconsin Board of Control in 1923. Prior to that she had been a member of the Civil Service Commission, having been appointed in 1921.

Ten states have had state superintendents of public instruction since 1920. Several of them have given the office to women repeatedly.[1]

In twenty-six states women head Divisions of Child Welfare or Hygiene organized in State Boards of Health, largely as a result of the same interest which resulted in the enactment of the Maternity and Infancy Law in response to the demand of women.[2]

Women as Judges.—As reporters or clerks to the supreme courts of their states, as assistants to attorneys general, women have been associated with the judicial branch of state governments. Women as judges present a special classification, for although judges achieve their places by political processes, professional equipment is generally a prerequisite.[3] Only a comparatively small number of women are available.

Judge Florence Allen is the one whose record stands out as especially distinguished. In 1920 she was elected as Common Pleas Judge in Cuyahoga County, Ohio. In 1922, and again in 1928, she was elected to sit as Justice on the Supreme Court of

[1] Colorado—Mary C. C. Bradford was elected in 1922 and 1924. Katherine L. Craig in *1926 and 1927.* Inez Johnson Lewis is the present incumbent, having been reelected and having received "the largest vote of any candidate on any ticket."—Letter from chief clerk, W. E. Alexander, November 14, 1932.

Idaho—Since 1921 the office has been continuously held by women. There have been four different incumbents. This position is not, however, in Idaho the chief educational position. Miss M. R. Davis is superintendent of public instruction, but a man is commissioner of education.

Iowa—Miss Mae Francis was elected for four-year term in 1922. Miss Agnes Samuelson succeeded her in 1926. She is now serving her second term.

Kansas—Corraine Elizabeth Wooster, elected in November, 1918. She served two terms.

Montana—May Trumper 1921–1928. Elizabeth Ireland is the present incumbent (1932).

New Mexico—Miss Isabel Eckles was elected 1922 and 1924. Mrs. Georgia Lusk is the present incumbent.

North Dakota—Miss Minnie J. Neilson. She was succeeded by Mrs. Bertha P. Palmer who is now in office.

Texas—Miss Annie Webb Blanton was elected in 1918 and reelected in 1920.

Washington—Joseph Corliss Preston was elected in 1912 and served four terms of four years each.

Wyoming—Mrs. Katherine Norton, now in office.

[2] Before the enactment of the Maternity and Infancy Act there were Child Hygiene Divisions in thirty-six states. Many of these were organized in anticipation of the federal law and twelve more were added later making a total of forty-eight now.

[3] Exceptions to the rule may be found in the case of juvenile court judges in New York. It is no longer essential for them to be members of the Bar.

Ohio, the only woman in this country so honored. A partial list of judgeships which have been held by women during the ten years 1920–1930 includes the following: Judge Mary M. Bartelme, first associated Judge of Chicago Juvenile Court, in 1923 elected Judge of the Circuit Court and since then continuously Judge of the Cook County Juvenile Court; Catharine Waugh McCulloch, Justice of the Peace; Kathryn Sellers, Judge of the Juvenile Court of the District of Columbia; a City Magistrate, New York City; a Judge of the Juvenile Court of Seattle; of the Los Angeles Juvenile Court; the Municipal Court in the District of Columbia; the Municipal Court in Los Angeles; the Municipal Court, Plymouth, Michigan; the Children's Court of Christian County, New York; the Morals Court in Cleveland; the City Magistrate's Court in Brooklyn; the Juvenile Court in Miami, Florida; the Children's Court in Memphis; the City Magistrate's Court of Philadelphia; the County Court of Allegheny County. Two women were appointed in Massachusetts in January, 1931. One of them had been the first woman assistant attorney general serving from 1927, and was reappointed in 1931. She was succeeded in that position by another woman.

In connection with the administration of justice, it should be noted that there are 27[1] states in which women are not yet eligible for jury service. It might also be noted that an important State Commission on Criminal Justice recently remarked cautiously that women would "probably *be found as well qualified for jury service as men.*"[2]

Women in State Legislatures.—There were women in state legislatures before the Federal Suffrage Amendment was ratified.[3] Indeed in several states the ratification resolution was presented to the legislature by a woman member.[4] But since 1920, the number of women in legislative bodies has notably increased. In presenting the following figures it must be admitted that they do not agree with the totals offered in other compilations. In some statements the number of women elected seems to be treated as synonomous with the women who sit when the legis-

---

[1] *Equal Rights* XVIII, 395.

[2] The Illinois Association for Criminal Justice, *Illinois Crime Survey* (1929), 240.

[3] According to an estimate made by the National League of Women Voters about sixty women had served prior to 1920.

[4] Women members had some part in the ratification proceedings in New York, Nevada, Oregon, Montana, Kansas, Utah, Colorado, and probably others.

latures meet. They seem to disregard the holdover women who have been elected as senators or representatives in states where the term is four years.[1] The following list has been checked with other sources, ambiguous letters from secretaries of state have been clarified by second inquiries, and by correspondence with responsible persons in the state. It is believed to be accurate. The membership of the legislatures in the odd years is given as the majority of states are then in session. Women elected in the states which meet biennially in the even years[2] have been included in the odd year which these two-year terms encompassed. Technically they were members of the legislature then, although the body was not in session.[3]

When the legislatures of 1921 assembled there were 37 women members,[4] 34 members of the House and 3 in the Senate.[5] In 1923, the number jumped to 98.[6] Seven of these sat in the Senate, 6 newly elected[7] and one holding over from the previous session.[8] Of the newly elected senators 2 had been members of the House in the preceding session.[9] Ten members of the Houses had been reelected. More women came to join them in 1925. Then, 141 women were making laws in 38 states.[10] Forty of these had been reelected. One former member returned to her seat in the House after an absence of one session. There were 9 women senators in 1925.

In 1927, the number dropped. One hundred and twenty-seven women were members in 36 states.[11] Thirteen were in the Senate, 3

[1] The legislative tenures in the various states have been conveniently summarized by the American Legislators Association. The senatorial term is 4 years in 26 states, 2 years in 21 states, and 3 years in one state. Members of the House are elected for one year in 2 states, 2 years in 42 states, and 4 years in 4 states.

[2] Kentucky, Virginia, Mississippi, Louisiana. In the first two sessions reported Maryland was also an even year state. It has now changed to the odd year biennial session.

[3] New York and New Jersey elect their House members for one year and have annual sessions. Therefore, the women serving in the even years in those states are not included in the totals presented.

[4] In 26 states, including Kentucky, where the session is in the even year.

[5] Michigan, Oklahoma, and Utah.

[6] Elected in 35 states.

[7] Mississippi, 2 in Ohio, Oregon, Vermont, Washington.

[8] In Oklahoma.

[9] In Oregon and Vermont.

[10] Including Virginia where 2 women had been members in 1924. This total does not include one woman in New Mexico who was elected but whose election was contested and she was unseated.

[11] And Kentucky whose single member is included in the total although it was not a legislative year.

newcomers there being former members of the lower House.[1] Forty-nine of the women members had been reelected and 3 former members were returned after an interruption in their service. Two years later the largest number of women yet recorded was reached. One hundred and forty-nine are reported for 1929 in 38 states.[2] Fifteen were senators, 4 reelected and 4 holdovers. Of the 7 novices in the upper chamber, 3 came up from their respective Houses. In all, 54 of the 149 were reelected, and one was a former member with interrupted service.

In 1931, the number dropped a little. Thirty-nine states[3] had a woman membership of 146. Twelve were senators. Fifty-two had been reelected, 3 to the Senate and the rest to the House. Ten were former members and one newcomer to the Senate had been a member of the House, so that there were 65 to whom the legislative business was not new. One new member had been appointed at her husband's death to fill out his term.[4]

Louisiana is the only state which has never elected a woman to its legislature. Alabama, Florida, and Iowa have each had one, although Florida has made some slight reparation by electing that woman twice. Kentucky, Delaware, and Michigan each have elected 2 since 1920. Wyoming and Georgia have chosen 3 although one of Georgia's 3 has been three times a member of the House.

Connecticut with its total of 82 has elected the largest number of women legislators.[5] New Hampshire is next with 64 and Vermont third with 50. The peak of women members in any legis-

[1] In Maine 2 senators were former House members, and one was promoted in Ohio.

[2] And Virginia (with 4 women 2 of whom had been reelected).

[3] With Virginia the number would be 36.

[4] Mrs. W. Carlton Smith of Oregon. Mrs. Laura Naplin of the Minnesota Senate was elected to fill her husband's unexpired term at his death in 1927. She has been reelected. In 1928, Mrs. Howard Harper of West Virginia was appointed to the seat her husband's death left vacant. She is the first Negro woman to be a member of a state legislature, Mrs. Charles E. Cannon sat in the State Senate of Georgia at its extraordinary session in 1931. She was elected to fill her late husband's unexpired term. The total number of women in the legislatures in 1933 of 33 states is 131, which is 15 fewer than the number serving in 39 states in 1931, and 18 below the total of 149 in 38 states in 1929. These 131 are 65 Democrats, 58 Republicans, one Socialist, three Non-Partisans, and four elected by both Democrats and Republicans. Twelve are in the Senate, and 56 have served before. (National League of Women Voters, *New York Times*, January 1, 1933.)

[5] This means 82 terms in which women have been elected—not 82 individual women.

lature in one session was reached in 1929 when Connecticut had 20.

Only 19 of Connecticut's 82 have served more than one term. Of those, 8 were twice elected, and one, after two terms in the House was elected to the Senate. Only 2 of Connecticut's women legislators have served continuously since 1923.[1]

And gratifying as is the number of women who have served in these three New England states, it must be pointed out that in relation to the size of the legislature Connecticut's 20 in 1929 does not bulk so large. There are 262 members in the Connecticut House and 35 in the Senate. And New Hampshire's 17 women members of the House in 1931 would scarcely be noted in its total membership of 424. In Vermont there were 16 women members in 1931, 15 in the House and one in the Senate—not a substantial proportion of its membership of 247 in the House and a Senate of 30. The great majority of the women have been one termers. Only a half dozen in all the country have served five terms. No one has seen continuous service since 1921.

It is, of course, impossible to measure the contribution women legislators have made to state government. Two of them[2] achieved the minority leadership. But their way is not easy. In August, 1923, Mrs. Ira Couch Wood of Chicago commented in the *Woman Citizen* on the discouraging fact that Mrs. Lottie Holman O'Neill, in spite of much ability, had lost ten out of the thirteen measures she sponsored:

Perhaps never before (she wrote) have the women's organizations of the state considered legislation so carefully, discussed it so fully and agreed so heartily in their endorsement of several measures introduced, so that their failure to achieve success is all the more conspicuous. The three measures which were passed in response to the women's urging were "to save the wild flowers, to help the crippled children, and to assure some added rights of inheritance to wives."

In the hope of adding some fresh material to this study, and discovering more about the qualifications and successes of women legislators a letter was directed to every one whose address could be secured. Letters were sent to 320 women. Replies were received from 124.

[1] Mrs. Clarissa Nevius and Mrs. Helen E. Lewis.
[2] Mrs. Maggie Smith Hathaway, a Democrat, was chosen by her party caucus in Montana in 1921 and Miss May Carty, a Democrat in New Jersey in 1930, came into leadership through seniority.

The 124 correspondents were divided by states as follows: Alabama 0, Arizona 3, Arkansas 3, California 1, Colorado 4, Connecticut 6, Delaware 1, Florida 1, Georgia 0, Idaho 0, Illinois 0, Indiana 6, Iowa 1, Kansas 4, Kentucky 1, Louisiana 0, Maine 6, Maryland 1, Massachusetts 6, Michigan 0, Minnesota 3, Mississippi 0, Missouri 0, Montana 4, Nebraska 0, Nevada 0, New Hampshire 17, New Jersey 4, New Mexico 0, New York 0, North Carolina 1, North Dakota 0, Ohio 5, Oklahoma 4, Oregon 2, Pennsylvania 4, Rhode Island 2, South Carolina 0, South Dakota 2, Tennessee 1, Texas 0, Utah 6, Vermont 14, Virginia 0, Washington 4, West Virginia 2, Wisconsin 2, Wyoming 3.

The Women Legislators Themselves.—No special type predominates among them, no common qualifying experience can be found. Pioneering women in the West have turned legislators when their other work was done. College graduates have gone swiftly from the campus to legislative halls. Old women and young women have made up the band of women legislators in this decade. Some were suffragists, some were antis. Others took no part in the struggle. A few had previous political experience. To some their legislative service was a surprising innovation. Others entered the competition with a definite intention to accomplish some objective. Many of them championed measures of special interest to women. Others made a conscious effort to avoid adherence to the feminist tradition. A few were disillusioned when their terms were over. Some were happy with the compliments and honor. The letters from over a hundred women legislators tell a varying story.

Only 48 women mentioned any occupational training as a qualifying experience. The largest number of these—26—were school teachers. And 6 of the teachers had added some other occupation to pedagogy—one was a lawyer too, another had been an editor, one was a lecturer, two were also nurses, and one had been in government service. The lawyers came next to the teachers. There were 9 Portias, 2 doctors, 3 social workers, one of these also a nurse, 6 business women, one newspaper woman and one lecturer.

Sixty, almost one half of the writers, had advocated woman suffrage. From one who wrote, "In the early eighties I joined Susan B. Anthony's Suffrage Society in Washington, D. C.," to another who confessed, "I marched in two parades." Thirteen more professed sympathy with the cause, but for various reasons had never been identified with the movement. Of these, 3 were too young for participation. Nineteen were either entirely indifferent or hostile to the step. Seventy-two of the women elected had been identified with women's organizations in their communities, the interest of 2 of these being confined to activity in a fraternal order, The Eastern Star.

Only 26 of the women reported that they had held political office prior to their legislative service, although in addition to those another group of 35 women had been active in party work, as organizers of partisan clubs, as precinct and county or state committeewomen, as workers at the polls, on campaign committees, as ballot clerks.

The women who had previously enjoyed political office had been members of boards of education or school committees, members of city councils, county superintendents of schools, members of library boards, justices of the peace, town clerks, treasurers, city prosecutors, state's attorneys, city or county treasurers, state librarians, chief examiners of city civil service commissions, members of boards of control of state institutions, postmasters.

For almost 60[1] women their legislative service was the first political office, and whatever party experience they may have had was not sufficiently substantial to merit mention.

A few legislators described the way in which their candidacy began. One woman wrote:

> . . . The county chairman appointed a committee of, I believe, 16 men and 3 women to meet on a certain day and name a ticket to make the race for county offices and representative in the Legislature and I was one of the three women. After the naming of all the ticket but representative I was asked to name someone for representative and I put in nomination an attorney of_____, when someone remarked, "Why not nominate Mrs._____?", and then they yelled, "You are nominated."
> I got the floor and told them I would not accept as it would practically be impossible to elect a Democrat, much less a woman. This did not still the clamor. . . . The Chairman exclaimed, "You are nominated—the Convention's adjourned," and they scattered in every direction.

Match that happy informality of the South with this decision in the Rockies:

> My entry into politics was not very regular. I had never been associated with any organizations, or had any experience other than a keen

---

[1] One or two letters were without information on most points.

interest since childhood in elections. I happened to read Roosevelt's
"The Strenuous Life" just as the caucus was called before last election,
and decided to go to the caucus. As the Republican party in————
is very weak, and no one likes to have much to do with it, the leaders
seized upon me as a newcomer, made me delegate to the local convention
and then made me vice-chairman of the county central committee, and
candidate for the general assembly.

I ran without much thought of being elected. . . .

A scattering few report that party leaders asked to put their
names on the ticket. "I attracted the attention of the political
minded men," one wrote. But the majority ambiguously refer
to the "group," or "delegation" or "the friends" who suggested
their candidacy.

Although women who were identified with suffrage work,
and with the activities of other women's organizations may be
assumed to be sympathetic and somewhat representative of
women's interest, only 3 mentioned that they ran at the solicitation of women's organizations. One of these campaigned "at the
insistence of the W. C. T. U.," 2 others reported that they were
drafted "by the League of Women Voters."[1]

A few women identified in their letters the impulse which made
them enter the legislative race.

During the World War I had charge of a Venereal Clinic for women.
I examined at the city jail all the women arrested. I came to realize the
need for a Detention Hospital for their cure and rehabilitation. The
legislature was the obvious place to get action. A bill had been passed
creating a State Detention Home, but with a wholly inadequate appropriation. The next session I ran for the legislature and was elected.

Another spoke of devastating forest fires against the recur-
rence of which existing law did not give adequate protection.
"I resolved that day to run for the office and get that law changed
—which I did."

Another wrote from New England:

Through my work as chairman of the Civics Committee of the
Federation of Women's Clubs I became interested in state problems
involving the welfare of children. Because of my interest in obtaining the
Sheppard-Towner appropriation for maternity and infancy work I
consented when asked to run for the State Legislature. I was elected
and served two years.

[1] A branch not affiliated with the National League which discourages the
policy of endorsing candidates.

[328]

And very similar is this paragraph from Florida,

I had for years been identified with Woman's Club work and I had been intensely interested in Public Welfare work thereby coming in contact with so much of human need that I began to think of the legislation which hedged about all our activities as citizens.

From the West Coast comes this:

My first personal contact with politics was when as a high school teacher in Portland, Oregon, I went with a group of instructors to the state capitol to lobby for the Teacher's Tenure Act. . . .

During their legislative service the majority of the women writers—all but 26 in fact—displayed by their membership on appropriate committees or through their authorship of certain bills a genuine concern for questions affecting child welfare, education, state institutions, public health, in general, social legislation and problems affecting the legal and political status of women.

Sixty-five of the writers, more than half, are not now serving in their legislatures. Three New England women legislators retired involuntarily when their term was ended because the inconstant representation of their towns temporarily removed the opportunity. "Our town only has a representative once in ten years," one wrote in explanation. Four others cited the precedent of one or two terms only, a precedent one of them had vainly tried to shatter. Two women moved, one to another state, the second to a new district.

This is why the rest retired.

Twelve aspired to some other elective or appointive office. Two ran for secretary of state, one to victory, and one to defeat. Another was defeated in a campaign for state auditor. One retired to run for county commissioner but lost the race. Two women retired from the House in order to run for the State Senate, and lost membership in the legislature when they failed to be elected to the upper body. One ran for the office of county treasurer, but was defeated. Three retired to run for Congress,[1] 2 to take state appointive positions—one in the New Jersey Department of Labor, the other field inspector of the Board of Cosmetic Therapy in Arkansas.

[1] They were unsuccessful. No woman had, until 1932, when Miss O'Loughlin was elected in Kansas, been elected to Congress with a state legislative experience as a background.

Nineteen were rejected by the voters. Of these, 11 were renominated by their parties but failed of election, "in the Republican landslide of 1928," "in the Democratic landslide of 1930," as the case may be. Only 6 who wanted to be nominated clearly failed to be selected by their parties for continued service, although in 2 additional cases the wording is ambiguous.

Twenty-three women voluntarily retired for a variety of reasons. Home duties had prior claim on 4. One served in the legislature when her children were babies, now they need her personal care. When they are grown she hopes to serve again. One of the 4 added her age of seventy-two as a contributing factor. Two others of over seventy surrendered the work to younger hands. Ill health removed 2 others from the active political field. One good "organization representative" loyally withdrew because her party thought a man would be more effective in an approaching legislative battle over good roads. Another yielded to a "gentleman's agreement" that another town should have its turn for the district. Subsequently she ran for the Congress but was defeated in the primaries.

Another wrote that she retired when success in larger political fields seemed probable, "becoming an addict to individualism in place of political socialism—and feeling I had a right to life, liberty and happiness apart from constituents' views of it."

For the rest of these 23 voluntary retirements—12 in number— no reason is given. Nine reported that they simply did not choose to run again; 3 made no comment on the question.

So if this small group of legislators representing states may be considered typical of all, these appear to be the facts. More than half were in sympathy with or participated in the woman suffrage movement. Nearly two-thirds of the women elected since 1920 have been identified with women's organizations in their communities and states. Over three-fourths of them showed a special interest in that which is generally called women's legislation. To satisfy this interest was the motive which prompted many of them to seek legislative service.

For 65 of the women their legislative service was their first experience in political office, and they had had no outstanding record of party allegiance prior to their election.

Only a few women were prevented from continuing their legislative duties because of home responsibilities; a negligible number failed to be nominated. Most of them retired for unknown reasons. The smallest number of all found it a stepping stone to other political office.

Most of the writers indicated that their legislative experience was an interesting and happy one. Many of them speak of the courtesies of the men. A few acknowledge that the courtesy does not imply admission to full equality. A few general observations in the letters will be quoted.

I am still interested in Politics but can see no future for women . . . Women must not be content to do things in a man's way. The obligation rests upon them to think and to act together as women if they wish advantages to women as a group. Women do not frame the policies, build the platforms, or shape the political ideas. When they organize as women and support women in politics—then and not 'till then will they be a real force.

Another, equally somber:

In my opinion it will take years of experience before women play any considerable part in law making bodies. For one reason, because men do not as a rule want them there, and another, the unfitness of a great many because of an inferior complex concerning such matters. As a matter of fact they are just as able as men. . . .

This, happily, is not disillusion:

I did not advocate woman suffrage and feel now that woman has done little or nothing in politics. She has allowed man to shift much of the hard work in party organization to her for which she gets small pay and small places of influence.

Although this one may be:

It is my opinion that men do not want women in office, they only put them in for expediency:—to keep the women voting and working for them politically. Usually they do not give them offices of leadership but chiefly honorary positions.

That accusation finds an echo:

I feel that the men do not support the women candidates of their own party to the same extent that they support their men candidates. . . .

And is re-echoed many times:

The men do not want the women to come in, only to help on election day. . . .

A thoughtful veteran wrote:

Many of our women feel that the women of_____have not received as much consideration politically the last three or four years, as was given to them when the franchise was first granted. They have been regular and stood by their parties, both the Republican and Democratic women. They know that they have done 50 per cent of the work and the voting too. We hear this question often, "How many women are permitted to be nominated?" And they are getting a little bit weary of political speakers coming before them and telling them that all the women have to do is put their shoulder to the wheel and they can put the ticket over.

A question in this comment is unanswered:

When we think of the power of an unseen force, that of the women's vote, it is hard to understand why more women are not elected to office.

Women in County and Local Government.—It is in county and local government that women have participated most largely in the United States. Competition for power is not so great in that dark continent of American politics. And while modest progress in conspicuous federal or state offices has been hailed with joy and desired with fervor, the substantial advance in local office holding has been almost entirely ignored.[1]

True, the women's press has been reporting with increasing frequency appealing items for feminist appreciation: that a complete woman slate was elected in Yoncalla, Oregon, a town of 700 inhabitants, in preference to a ticket of men, for example,[2] or that in 1922 Des Lacs, North Dakota, and Randalia, Iowa, elected administrations completely feminine too. Women mayors are a novelty no longer, although the frequency of their selection diminishes as the size of the towns and cities rises. In spite of the substantial list[1] it is still true that only one woman had been elected to be mayor of a large city. That is Mrs. Bertha

[1] I mean ignored by the general public. It has been noted by political scientists, for example, see Charles Edward Merriam, *Chicago: A More Intimate View of Urban Politics* (New York: Macmillan Co., 1929), p. 155, and William Anderson, *American City Government* (New York: H. Holt and Co., 1925), pp. 141–42.

[2] In June, 1922, less than two years after the ratification of the federal suffrage amendment an article by Mildred Adams entitled, "What Are Women Mayors Doing?" appeared in *The American City*. It reported the activities of women mayors in 16 communities: Rochester, Ohio; St. Peter, Minnesota; Thayer, Kansas; Jackson, Wyoming; Fairport, Ohio; Magnetic Springs, Ohio; Salina, Utah; Cohato, Minnesota; St. James, Missouri; Red Cloud, Nebraska; Waterloo, Nebraska; Langley, Washington; Brewton, Georgia; Cokesville, Wyoming; Rendalia and Lehigh, Iowa.

The comment of one of the mayors reported in Miss Adams' article is of interest. She said, "I might say here that our election was due to the fact that in small towns men best fitted for public office often refuse to serve on the plea that they would 'hurt their business.' We had no business to hurt."

Landes who was elected in 1926 to one term as mayor of Seattle and who had first served as a member of the City Council.

The election of women to Councils or Boards of Aldermen is frequently reported: in Macon, Georgia; Gloucester, Massachusetts; Des Moines, Iowa; Cambridge, Massachusetts; Cleveland, Ohio; and New York. Those are only a few and indicate the variation of the cities in size and in geography. The list might be extended immeasurably, and their tenure in other jobs recited.

In 1922 a woman was comptroller of Nashville, Tennessee, and another woman was city clerk in Tacoma, Washington; and Miss Frieda Mueller was appointed a member of the Public Debt Commission by the mayor of Milwaukee in 1924. In Albany, New York, the first woman to head a municipal department was Mrs. Elizabeth V. Colbert who in 1923 was appointed registrar of vital statistics. To be sure, Katharine Bement Davis had been commissioner of corrections in New York City under Mayor Mitchell's administration in 1914–1915. In 1925, when Mrs. Ruth Pratt was elected to the Board of Aldermen of New York City, Miss Annie Mathews was a second time elected registrar of New York County, the $12,000 salary marking it as the highest paid public office which a woman has ever held in this country.

In 1923, a woman was elected to be commissioner of Cook County and one was made a commissioner of public welfare in Chicago and sat in the mayor's cabinet. Another woman was appointed to the same position in 1928. At the last election four women commissioners of Cook County were successful.

The two women who were elected to the Cleveland City Council in 1930 were not pioneers, although one of them, Miss Susan Bebhan, had formerly served as the first woman deputy of insurance in Ohio. Honors for being a "first" went to Mrs. Mary Brown Martin who was elected to the Board of Education in Cleveland in 1930. She is only one of three women members, and a newcomer, yet she is a pioneer because she is a Negro, and the first woman of her race to be so honored.

In 1930, a woman was appointed by the mayor to a regular term on the New York Municipal Parole Commission after filling out an unexpired term, and a highly qualified woman was appointed director of the Crime Prevention Bureau of New York City. She is now a deputy police commissioner.

[333]

These are examples of achievement in city government which have been noted. The records of women in county offices, like those in towns and villages, become too numerous to mention. It is likely that the number is increasing for women in local offices are no longer novices.[1] As far back as 1920 every one of the twenty-one counties in Wyoming elected a woman superintendent of education. In 1922, Connecticut reported[2] that 138 women had been elected to minor offices, and were serving throughout the state as selectmen, members of school committees, and in a variety of local offices. In 1920, there were 81 women serving on school boards in Pennsylvania. In 1922, there were more than 600. In 1925, there were almost 2,100.[3] The election returns in Nebraska that year brought in the names of 97 victorious women, and in Cuyahoga County, Ohio, 41 women had been chosen for various county jobs.[4]

As it is obviously impossible to submit a complete list of positions held by women in local government, and the few examples given illustrate either the common experience or the exceptional recognition, no attempt to prolong the report will be made. Instead a summary of the history in four states will be quoted. Although no general review of women's office holding in local jurisdictions is undertaken, the following figures are of too great interest to omit.

The Leagues of Women Voters in Minnesota, Wisconsin, Connecticut, and Michigan made detailed surveys of the offices in local government which had been filled by women, comparing the results of their inquiries for the years 1925,[5] 1927, 1929, or 1930.

A summary of those returns are shown on p. 335.

This summarizes[6] what appears to be the only available study of comparable offices over a period of years. It indicates that the woman in politics goes ahead more rapidly at home than in the larger political units. It is of interest that women superintendents

---

[1] *The Biennial Report of the Secretary of State of Texas for the Years 1929–1930* contained the following record of women office holders for the two-year period:

County Treasurers 109, County School Superintendents 47, County Clerks 39, District Clerks 33, County Tax Collectors 13, County Tax Assessors 7, Constables 5, Justices of the Peace 3, Public Weighers 2, County Commissioners 1.

[2] *Woman Citizen*, January 28, 1922, Vol. X.

[3] Data supplied by National League of Women Voters from memorandum, 1925.

[4] *Woman Citizen*, February 25, 1922.

[5] The Michigan report omits 1925.

[6] The state reports are complete with names, dates, and places carefully shown.

of schools, and women city, town, and county treasurers appear most frequently. The schools have long been considered the special responsibility of women. Their concern with fiscal responsibilities is more surprising.

So in the field in which women have figured most conspicuously, this survey will be most brief. The multiplicity of data is too great to tabulate. The surveys quoted are submitted in the belief that the increase they illustrate is widely characteristic of the participation of women in local government in the United States today.

TABLE 55.—NUMBER OF WOMEN IN OFFICE IN FOUR SELECTED STATES[a]

State	Date	Elected	Appointed	Total
Connecticut...........................	1925	29	105	134
	1927	67	349	416
	1929	178	474	652
Michigan............................	1927	277	90	367
	1929	590	203	793
Minnesota...........................	1926	127	100	227
	1927	209		
	1930	245	103	348
Wisconsin...........................	1926	58	4	62
	1927	64	9	73
	1929	158	13	171

[a] City, village and township offices are not covered in Wisconsin in 1926 and 1927 reports. Of the 171 women officials reported in 1929, 80 were in county and state offices.

It may be noted that the several aspects of the question of women in politics are generally confused when the problem is explored. There is comment on their interest and their influence as if the two were inseparably related. The extent of their participation presents still a different question.

Apparently in the twelve years of their enfranchisement the number of women holding office in local and county government has steadily increased. The only available studies would indicate that to be true, and scattered items from all over the country support the assertion. As sheriffs, city clerks, treasurers, and comptrollers as well as members of school and library boards, women have taken their places in local government and have invaded fields which men have hitherto regarded as their own.

Some substantial interest in politics and government must be demonstrated by their persistent advance.

Yet, according to the opinion of the editors of certain women's magazines, the interest of women has diminished.[1] They testify that the peak of their subscribers' concern with politics was reached about 1925. After that there was slighter response to articles of a political nature. The editor's mail box reflected little preoccupation with public affairs. Sad to relate, additional evidence is found in the fact that with the issue of June, 1931, the one magazine[2] which chose women in relation to public affairs as its special field, gave up the long unequal struggle and suspended publication.

It must be noted, too, that the increase in office holding is not sustained when more coveted positions are surveyed. In conspicuous federal offices there is scarcely any net gain to show in 1931–1932 as compared with 1921–1922, for there have been losses for women in the decade, too, as well as advances. The failure to search for qualified women for important offices indicates the limitations of the political influence of women. The ill fortune which has attended the legislation sought by women's groups gives further evidence to which there is no answer.

And yet women have been more active in campaigns than ever before. Party leaders say so. The general comment agrees. Women are welcomed by party leaders in times of campaigning, after policies have been laid down, when candidates have been selected and platforms adopted—when there is work to be done. After 1928, for example, the new administration certainly had political debts to pay. That women could be safely ignored argues that the women who have the confidence of the men in power are themselves unconvinced of the capacity of the woman vote to reward or punish.

Two of those who have had conspicuous positions in the party organizations comment on the subject. One[3] writes:

When it appeared that women might be given the right to vote before the next national election, politicians of both parties rushed to place women on their party committees. In their choice, the men paid women a high compliment. They believed, it was evident, that women would

[1] Editors or editorial writers and staff members of *Good Housekeeping, The Woman's Home Companion, Pictorial Review,* and *The Farmer's Wife* were interviewed.

[2] The *Woman's Journal.*

[3] Emily Newell Blair, *ibid.*, January, 1931.

want the highest type of women to represent them. And in their eagerness to capture the women's votes for their party they put this type on
their committees. They also believed that women would want women on
these committees who could lead women. They therefore named women
whose leadership had been tried and tested. And then these men listened
to these women whom they had chosen; even when they did not have a
vote on the committees, their opinions had weight. And why? Because
the men saw them as powerful leaders of women.

Since then, women have come officially to have a place on party
committees. They are elected to them as are the men. But in too many
cases these first women have been succeeded by a different type, who
give their proxies at committee meetings to the men by whose influence
they have been elected, who do what they are told by these men to do,
and who are without achievement or previous leadership of women.

The same thing is true of the women delegates to conventions. There
has been a steadily decreasing number of independently-minded women,
of eminent women among them. The kind of woman who could or would
urge her state's member on a Resolutions Committee to vote for a
measure which she thought was based on women's values, who could
sway delegates at a convention, has all too often been succeeded by the
wife of some office-holder whose aim in politics is to help him to success,
or a woman who follows instructions from some men in order to advance
herself to office.

Naturally the same kind of women are elected to the party offices.
They become the women vice-chairmen of state and county committees. I make no attack on the ability or integrity of these women.
Some of them are very fine. Many of them have real political gifts. I
have known one or more of them who ran the men on their state committees. For this reason they have sometimes been cited as proof of
women's participation in politics. On the contrary, such women are
evidence that women do not participate. For they participate in politics
by ignoring other women. They have few women followers. For their
power and success they depend upon men.

Such women never bother with so-called women's measures or movements. They have no use for feminism. The League of Women Voters,
for instance, is anathema to them. And so they do nothing to forward
the participation of women in politics. Small wonder that politicians
think woman suffrage a success. The bogie of the feminine influence, of
the woman-vote has been laid.

Another[1] equally conspicuous in the party activity is likewise
candid in admitting the imperfections of the woman representation within the parties:

The truth is, [Mrs. Ross wrote in the July, 1931 number of The
Democratic Bulletin] women have been floundering ever since they got
the ballot and they will continue to flounder until they find adequate
representation in the councils of the party from the precinct committees

[1] Nellie Tayloe Ross.

up, and stand side by side with their husbands and brothers, pursuing with them an intelligently conceived co-ordinated plan. It is time for us, men and women, to drop the word "auxiliary" from our vocabulary. There is no more justification for our thinking of women as auxiliary to men in the political world than there would be for thinking of a girl in a family as auxiliary to her brother.

Mrs. Ross quoted a recent statement of James A. Farley, chairman of the New York State Democratic Committee, in which he "pledged himself to strive for the equal representation of women with men in county committees throughout his state." "In one county," said Mr. Farley, "there were 32 election districts and only one woman co-leader because the men leaders will not allow the women to participate in the work."

More optimistic opinions can, however, be quoted.

In April, 1931, *The Woman's Journal* carried a reply to Mrs. Blair by Sarah Schuyler Butler, vice-chairman of the New York State Republican Committee.

For example,[1]

The first forward step was taken when women in the political parties managed to write into the election laws of the various states the provision that they, like men, should be elected and not appointed to the regular party committees. So long as they remained appointees they were not only under obligation to the man who named them, but they had no constituency to appeal in case of necessity. They were dependents rather than equals. In some states the necessary changes in the election laws have not yet been made, but every year a few more states are added to the list of those that have given this just recognition to their women.

Or, again,[2]

Ten years in national politics have given women a practical experience which they needed, and by which they have profited; have given them, too, as much official recognition as they might reasonably have expected. Countless women throughout the Nation are taking an active part in regular elections, municipal, state and national, and their influence in choosing and electing candidates and shaping civic and social policies has increased immeasurably since the passage of the Nineteenth Amendment. In point of fact women's interest and influence in politics is probably proportionately greater than men's. It is well to remember that we sought the franchise primarily as a human, not a divine right. Our claim was that we were people, not paragons. We wanted to share the duties and privileges of citizenship in proportion to our abilities, interests, and opportunities.

[1] Sarah Schuyler Butler, *Woman's Journal*, April, 1931.
[2] Mrs. Ellis Yost, director of the Women's Division of the Republican National Committee, has contributed a more hopeful expression for this study.

One does not learn to be an effective citizen in a day. Millions of men have not yet learned it; millions more are, apparently, indifferent to their responsibilities as citizens. Why exact super-citizenship of women?

The success of women as citizens cannot be measured by the number of political offices to which they are elected or appointed. However, political preferment is the yardstick by which many measure the progress of women in the task of sharing in governmental responsibilities, so that record merits consideration.

Ten years ago there was not a woman in the diplomatic service; hardly a handful were holding important Federal government positions; only one woman in Congress; no women on Presidential Commissions; no woman had been elected governor of a state; and no woman held high judicial positions. Women now occupy important positions of high honor and great responsibility in all of these fields in the national government service; while the list of women in state offices is long and imposing. One hundred and forty-three women were elected last year to the legislatures of thirty-eight states. Women of outstanding ability now speak with authority from official positions in both state and nation that, ten years ago, seemed at least a score of years beyond our grasp. A goodly number of women have been both elected and appointed to high office for sheer ability and recognized worth.

It will thus be seen that women are playing an important part in governmental affairs; and they are bringing to their work an enthusiasm and efficiency that is noteworthy and altogether creditable.

The problem, unquestionably, is one of relationship to the parties. If the independent woman voter shows no disposition to reward or punish at the polls, and the women in the party organization are complacent, the road ahead will be a difficult road for feminists in politics to face. Two schools of thought emerge. Those who believe that wider participation in government will come when women who are organized to support measures and advocate policies outside the parties are sufficiently numerous to tempt party organizations to woo them. The other theory is that every effort must be made within the party.

It should be remembered that there were a few campaigns in the decade where enfranchised women did rebuke or reward. There are a few issues which the activities of women voters vitalized.

In its issue of June 3, 1922, the *Woman Citizen* carried an article signed by Mary B. Warburton, vice-chairman of the Republican State Committee. She wrote:

There never was a greater opportunity nor a more clearly cut moral issue presented than the recent primary election in Pennsylvania. Ninety per cent of the women voters of the state took occasion to raise their voices against hand picked candidates, secret political combinations and the vilest type of personal vilification. The result is the dawn of a new political day for the Republican party not only of Pennsylvania, but throughout the country. The decent element of the Republican party was shown the way by the women, and I am proud to have been one of them. . . .

Reciting the history which made this primary election of such particular importance, Mrs. Warburton quoted the statement she had issued to the women voters in her party:

In view of the announcement that a compromise candidate for Governor has been agreed upon, it is only fair to inform the women of Pennsylvania that I as their representative was not included in the negotiations conducted by the state leaders. The women of Pennsylvania will not be deceived into thinking that a so-called compromise candidate will be free to act for the best interest of the state, and the women recognize in this action an attempt to break down the direct primary in the interests of a small group.

In the campaign which followed Republican women deserted the candidate chosen by their party leaders and worked for his opponent. "All over the state a house-to-house campaign of the voters was made, often followed by telephone calls, the women dividing up the telephone book and canvassing every name in it—many of them two or three times."

After his election Governor Pinchot publicly gave the women credit for a large share in his victory.

Mrs. Warburton's story is not cited because of the belief that its enthusiastic prophecy has been realized. It simply illustrates *one* occasion in the decade when women voters and women leaders were not amenable to dictatorship within the party. It tells of a time when rebellion was effective but it challenges the theory that independence leads to permanent influence in party councils.

In Cleveland it was a woman's organization which twice within the decade led the fight to defend a city charter from attack. In Cincinnati and in Rochester women played a large share in the work of securing a change in the form of city government. Although a campaign for a new city charter in Minneapolis ended in defeat for the project, a proposal for the reorganization of the state government originating with a women's group was effectually carried out in the state. In none of these campaigns did women play an exclusive part. But in all of them women were active leaders, and in some of them the initiative came from women. The ten years' total reckoning should give great credit to them.

Before the summary is complete it should be noted that three women officials have been found unworthy of public trust. The first was a secretary of state for New York in 1924. Before the enfranchisement of women in New York, she had held the only political office open to them—that of district superintendent of schools. After her election as secretary of state, the efficiency with which she organized the census was praised and her foresightedness in beginning to instal voting machines was noted. But in 1927 it appeared that her efficient organization of the census had involved the misappropriation of funds. In 1928, she was convicted and sentenced to serve a thirty-day term of imprisonment.

The next conspicuous offender was one who in 1931 resigned as collector of internal revenue for Illinois following the discovery of her participation in a faro game patronized by politicians. Apparently there was no dishonor attached to the conduct of her office.

The last was a magistrate in Manhattan who in June of 1931 was convicted of unfitness and removed from office. All of the charges against her were sufficiently grave—her financial interest in the bonding company active in relation to the business of her court, and the alteration of court records. But to women the most disturbing count was the allegation of her unjudicial attitude toward women offenders. Apparently so-called vice cases were allocated to her on the easy theory that any woman could deal with women. Her conduct, when it was exposed, caused her dismissal from the Bench where, as the first woman magistrate of New York, she had served for more than a decade.

One unsuccessful candidate for office might also be mentioned in the roll of women of prominence who have brought disservice to the women's cause. She spent more than $300,000 to secure the nomination in the Republican primaries in Illinois. To be exact. the sum was $319,786.40.

These records are disappointing, but of the majority of women office holders no great incompetence is known, no suggestion of dishonor is recorded. Those women who have taken public office as a dower right in their husband's estates have had unblemished records for integrity and generally have maintained an equal standard of capacity. It is perhaps disappointing to some that more women have failed to be elected or appointed, that the women chosen have not more widely shared the feminist tradition, and that the women's point of view has seemed to be progressively neglected by the men.

If suffrage had come earlier, the story might have been different. In 1900, for example, even in 1910, there were fewer women in professions. It was not unnatural then for a college-trained woman to remain economically dependent upon the men of her household. The problems of government might perchance have engaged the attention of the younger woman as the fight for suffrage did her mother. But economic independence came first. Young women of training now accept earning a living as a first responsibility. Married women increasingly have jobs. Leisure for politics is lacking and recognition in other fields is perhaps easier for women to secure, at any rate, and other interests compete with the political interest.

Chapter XIX

CONCLUSION

IN THE preceding pages an attempt has been made to set out the developments that have taken place during these three decades of the twentieth century in the relation of women under three sets of conditions: (1) those characteristic of their incalculably varied organization on a voluntary basis for the accomplishment of innumerable purposes; (2) those characteristic of their relationship as employed or employer; and (3) those determining their success or failure in their relation to government. The three phases of their activity have seemed to call for different methods of treatment and discussion.

In the case of the clubs or organizations, an attempt was made by a chronological account to suggest the response of women in their leisure time to the great numbers of stimuli to which they were subjected. By 1900, the separate clubs had federated, national affiliations were being developed, women associated themselves with other women for the accomplishment of innumerable common purposes. It is hoped that something of the variety has been suggested, and that with the increasing freedom from occupational, pecuniary, political and domestic restraints, the possibly increasing emphasis on individual satisfactions may have emerged.

It likewise seems clear that as the home offers less opportunity for girls both to be educated for adult life and to contribute by services to the well-being of the family life and as the standard of educational requirements are raised, young persons between ten and twenty are going in larger numbers to school and into the labor market.

It also appears that as the home offers fewer opportunities for the wife and mother to render services that make a definite contribution to the family income, more adult women, and among them more married women, are entering the labor market. This subject needs, however, more complete information, since the mothers' pension movement should remove from the market those whose presence there is due largely to the inadequate income of the husband and father or to the lack, through his incapacity, of any income from that source. There should also be further analysis to determine the counter-balancing influence of the professional woman's demand for opportunity to continue in the wage-earning group and the influence of migration or of changed economic status on the attitude of men who under the earlier situation felt compelled to acquiesce in their wives' remaining wage earners and who now find their own prestige affected by so doing.

With reference to the choice of employment, the range is still restricted although it is not possible at the moment to say whether or not it is more or less so than at the beginning of the century. The demand for women's labor, as for men's, has been so affected by the reorganizations that have taken place, that for the time the old avenues of employment in manufacturing and in certain forms of domestic or personal service and agriculture are less wide. What the implications of these changes are can only be definitely stated when certain terms such as "operatives" and "laborers" have been more fully discussed and expounded by the census; on the other hand, new chances are found in the distributive services and in the adjustments among and between administrative divisions of activity. A great variety of situations and relationships and activities are concealed under the term "clerical." In the levels of employment calling for more extended training or for professional education, there are still natural resistances on the part of men, who see not only the readjustment necessary if the marginal level is raised but the threat of cheapness which has been the weapon of all groups handicapped by non-occupational prejudices, the Negro, the alien, as well as the woman.

In the strata of higher business, of the professions, and of the academic world, there are evidences of the same resistances, but likewise of a steady wearing away of the oppositions. In university faculties a few more women are admitted to higher rank and pay; in the world of research, of athletics and sport, they likewise widen the sphere and make possible an objective testing of achievement.

As to unemployment, the relative cheapness of women may keep them in where it has got them in, and may get them in where they have not been before. On the other hand, many of the newer occupations in which they have found opportunity are greatly affected, and the evidence as to their occupational opportunity shows how accidental and precarious all employment is—being determined as between men and women or between older and younger or between more skilled and less skilled by the profitable use of the invention. That subject, too, is discussed elsewhere.

With reference to their public activity, the moment seems an unhappy one at which to attempt to take account of stock. Great effort had been necessary to secure the ballot, and much was expected from its possession. Women thought that they could by the ballot more easily rectify the mistakes that had been made in the governmental field, and men expected that within a brief period evil or anti-social situations would be constructively dealt with. Disappointment and disillusionment are therefore expressed by both men and women. Yet it seems clear that women are increasingly learning to use the governmental agencies that had been developed and they will be increasingly clear as to whether the older forms of organization should or should not be discarded. In the meantime, in the organization of clubs and the provision of club houses, through the demand to be allowed to continue in gainful employment after marriage, in discarding the older social restraints, they are widening the spiritual bounds within which both men and women must find their fullest satisfaction. It is in the college and university gymnasiums that preparation is being made for full participation by women in the activities requiring continuity and stability. It is in the laboratories and libraries of colleges and universities that scientific bases for emancipation are being assembled. In building upon those bases, women are experimenting in the adjustment of their needs as individuals to their requirements as members of families, whether as wife, mother, daughter or sister, and as members of the larger group. It is of interest that of the amendments to the proposed platforms suggested by various delegates to the Democratic convention the only one accepted by the convention was one pledging protection to childhood, offered by a woman who had been for years active in the so-called woman's movement.

It seems incomplete and fragmentary to close any discussion of women's place in the community organization without renewed reference to their earlier responsibility for the distribution of goods, and without discussion of their important services in the protection of the adolescent and the safe conduct of young persons from the simpler conditions of childhood through the confusions of the years between childhood and adult life. Those topics belong to other sections of the inquiry, however, and here reference to them is made only that frank acknowledgment may again be expressed of the fragmentary character of this presentation. In that connection the reader may be reminded of the development, meager but observable, in the use of women as juvenile court judges, as policewomen, as probation officers and as members of staffs of correctional institutions where girls and women are under custody. The presence of an able woman as head of the Labor Department[1] of the most populous and industrialized state, of a woman[2] in the cabinet of the commissioner of police in the greatest city,[3] of a woman at the head of the department of public welfare in each of three great states, and of a woman chief of the Federal Bureau[4] steadfastly demanding that the needs of the children and young persons of the whole country be recognized and dealt with after the principle of adequate care, suggests a recognition on the wider platform of national development of those same services as essential to the community well-being.

[1] Hon. Frances Perkins.
[2] Hon. Henrietta Additon.
[3] California, North Carolina and Pennsylvania.
[4] Hon. Grace Abbott.

DECLARATION OF SENTIMENTS—1848

DECLARATION OF SENTIMENTS[1]

When, in the course of human events, it becomes necessary for one portion of the family of man to assume among the people of the earth a position different from that which they have hitherto occupied, but one to which the laws of nature and of nature's God entitle them, a decent respect to the opinions of mankind requires that they should declare the causes that impel them to such a course.

We hold these truths to be self-evident: that all men and women are created equal; that they are endowed by their Creator with certain inalienable rights; that among these are life, liberty, and the pursuit of happiness; that to secure these rights governments are instituted, deriving their just powers from the consent of the governed. Whenever any form of government becomes destructive of these ends, it is the right of those who suffer from it to refuse allegiance to it, and to insist upon the institution of a new government, laying its foundation on such principles, and organizing its powers in such form, as to them shall seem most likely to effect their safety and happiness. Prudence, indeed, will dictate that governments long established should not be changed for light and transient causes; and accordingly all experience has shown that mankind are more disposed to suffer, while evils are sufferable, than to right themselves by abolishing the forms to which they were accustomed. But when a long train of abuses and usurpations, pursuing invariably the same object evinces a design to reduce them under absolute despotism, it is their duty to throw off such government, and to provide new guards for their future security. Such has been the patient sufferance of the women under this government, and such is now the necessity which constrains them to demand the equal station to which they are entitled.

The history of mankind is a history of repeated injuries and usurpations on the part of man toward woman, having in direct object the establishment of an absolute tyranny over her. To prove this, let facts be submitted to a candid world.

He has never permitted her to exercise her inalienable right to the elective franchise.

He has compelled her to submit to laws, in the formation of which she had no voice.

He has withheld from her rights which are given to the most ignorant and degraded men—both natives and foreigners.

Having deprived her of this first right of a citizen, the elective franchise, thereby leaving her without representation in the halls of legislation, he has oppressed her on all sides.

He has made her, if married, in the eye of the law, civilly dead.

[1] Stanton, Anthony, and Gage, I, pp. 70–73. Woody, *op. cit.*, II, 416.

He has taken from her all right in property, even to the wages she earns.

He has made her, morally, an irresponsible being, as she can commit many crimes with impunity, provided they be done in the presence of her husband. In the covenant of marriage, she is compelled to promise obedience to her husband, he becoming, to all intents and purposes, her master—the law giving him power to deprive her of her liberty, and to administer chastisement.

He has so framed the laws of divorce, as to what shall be the proper causes, and in case of separation, to whom the guardianship of the children shall be given, as to be wholly regardless of the happiness of women—the law, in all cases, going upon a false supposition of the supremacy of man, and giving all power into his hands.

After depriving her of all rights as a married woman, if single, and the owner of property, he has taxed her to support a government which recognizes her only when her property can be made profitable to it.

He has monopolized nearly all the profitable employments, and from those she is permitted to follow, she receives but a scanty remuneration. He closes against her all the avenues to wealth and distinction which he considers most honorable to himself. As a teacher of theology, medicine, or law, she is not known.

He has denied her the facilities for obtaining a thorough education, all colleges being closed against her.

He allows her in Church, as well as State, but a subordinate position, claiming Apostolic authority for her exclusion from the ministry, and, with some exceptions, from any public participation in the affairs of the Church.

He has created a false public sentiment by giving to the world a different code of morals for men and women, by which moral delinquencies which exclude women from society, are not only tolerated, but deemed of little account in man.

He has usurped the prorogative of Jehovah himself, claiming it as his right to assign for her a sphere of action, when that belongs to her conscience and to her God.

He has endeavored, in every way that he could, to destroy her confidence in her own powers, to lessen her self-respect, and to make her willing to lead a dependent and abject life.

Now, in view of this entire disfranchisement of one-half the people of this country, their social and religious degradation—in view of the unjust laws above mentioned, and because women do feel themselves aggrieved, oppressed, and fraudulently deprived of their most sacred rights, we insist that they have immediate admission to all the rights and privileges which belong to them as citizens of the United States.

In entering upon the great work before us, we anticipate no small amount of misconception, misrepresentation, and ridicule; but we shall use every instrumentality within our power to effect our object. We shall employ agents, circulate tracts, petition the State and National legislatures, and endeavor to enlist the pulpit and the press in our behalf. We hope this Convention will be followed by a series of Conventions embracing every part of the country.

RESOLUTIONS

WHEREAS, The great precept of nature is conceded to be, that "man shall pursue his own true and substantial happiness." Blackstone in his Commentaries remarks, that this law of Nature being coeval with mankind, and dictated by

God himself, is of course superior in obligation to any other. It is binding over all the globe, in all countries and at all times; no human laws are of any validity if contrary to this, and such of them as are valid, derive all their force, and all their validity, and all their authority, mediately and immediately, from this original; therefore,

Resolved, That such laws as conflict, in any way, with the true and substantial happiness of woman, are contrary to the great precept of nature and of no validity, for this is "superior in obligation to any other."

Resolved, That all laws which prevent woman from occupying such a station in society as her conscience shall dictate, or which place her in a position inferior to that of man, are contrary to the great precept of nature, and therefore of no force or authority.

Resolved, That woman is man's equal—was intended to be so by the Creator, and the highest good of the race demands that she should be recognized as such.

Resolved, That the women of this country ought to be enlightened in regard to the laws under which they live, that they may no longer publish their degradation by declaring themselves satisfied with their present position, nor their ignorance, by asserting that they have all the rights they want.

Resolved, That inasmuch as man, while claiming for himself intellectual superiority, does accord to woman moral superiority, it is pre-eminently his duty to encourage her to speak and teach, as she has an opportunity, in all religious assemblies.

Resolved, That the same amount of virtue, delicacy, and refinement of behavior that is required of woman in the social state, should also be required of man, and the same transgressions should be visited with equal severity on both man and woman.

Resolved, That the objection of indelicacy and impropriety, which is so often brought against woman when she addresses a public audience, comes with a very ill-grace from those who encourage, by their attendance, her appearance on the stage, in the concert, or in feats of the circus.

Resolved, That woman has too long rested satisfied in the circumscribed limits which corrupt customs and a perverted application of the Scriptures have marked out for her, and that it is time she should move in the enlarged sphere which her great Creator has assigned her.

Resolved, That it is the duty of the women of this country to secure to themselves their sacred right to the elective franchise.

Resolved, That the equality of human rights results necessarily from the fact of the identity of the race in capabilities and responsibilities.

Resolved, therefore, That, being invested by the Creator with the same capabilities, and the same consciousness of responsibility for their exercise, it is demonstrably the right and duty of woman, equally with man, to promote every righteous cause by every righteous means; and especially in regard to the great subjects of morals and religion, it is self-evidently her right to participate with her brother in teaching them, both in private and in public, by writing and by speaking, by any instrumentalities proper to be used, and in any assemblies proper to be held; and this being a self-evident truth growing out of the divinely implanted principles of human nature, any custom or authority adverse to it, whether modern or wearing the hoary sanction of antiquity, is to be regarded as a self-evident falsehood, and at war with mankind.

At the last session Lucretia Mott offered and spoke to the following resolution:

Resolved, That the speedy success of our cause depends upon the zealous and untiring efforts of both men and women, for the overthrow of the monopoly of the pulpit, and for the securing to woman an equal participation with men in the various trades, professions, and commerce.

The only resolution that was not unanimously adopted was the ninth, urging the women of the country to secure to themselves the elective franchise. Those who took part in the debate feared a demand for the right to vote would defeat others they deemed more rational, and make the whole movement ridiculous.

NATIONAL LEAGUE OF WOMEN VOTERS, PLATFORM—1932

A PLATFORM FOR THE LEAGUE OF WOMEN VOTERS
1932–1934[1]

The platform here presented is of immediate and pressing importance. It is selected from the program of work for study and support of the National League of Women Voters. Leagues that are not yet prepared by study and planning should prepare themselves as speedily as possible for effective action.

The need is urgent

The country faces an emergency

The League of Women Voters faces an opportunity

CONSTRUCTIVE ECONOMY IN GOVERNMENT

Reorganization of governmental units, especially local units, to prevent waste.

Establishment of budget systems to promote efficiency.

Reduction of expenditures for war to release funds for other governmental services which now receive only 31% of the federal budget.

Maintenance of standards and opposition to destructive "economy" which threatens essential services such as public schools, public health nursing, child welfare, labor inspection and agricultural extension services; which threatens commissions and agencies designed to lower living costs and prevent unfair trade practices; and which threatens the status of women in governmental employ.

Readjustment of tax burdens.

PREVENTION AND RELIEF OF UNEMPLOYMENT

Provision for public relief funds to be administered by trained personnel.

Establishment of a co-ordinated system of federal and state employment exchanges as one factor in the prevention as well as the relief of unemployment; and regulation of private employment agencies.

State legislation for unemployment insurance.

INTERNATIONAL CO-OPERATION

Economic international conferences on war debts and tariffs to remove causes of war and maintain standards of living.

Adherence of the United States to the World Court.

Devices to make effective the Pact of Paris.

International reduction of armaments.

[1] This Platform was accompanied by a List of Publications of the League in support of each of the three Planks.

INDEX

A

Abdominal breathing theory, 2, 104
Absenteeism, 162–163
Accountants, 176–178
Actors, 188, 189, 190
Adams, Mrs. Annette Abbot, 306
Addams, Jane, 21, 29, 292
Adult education, 66
　rural women, 43, 72
Age, of child workers, 113
　of women workers, 111 *ff*., 222
　　and earnings, 227
　　unemployed, 239
Agriculture, women in, 72, 126–128
Air transportation, women in, 169, 195
Aircraft manufacture, 155
Alabama, earnings of women, 222
　women legislators, 326
Alcoholic beverages, 196, 208
Allen, Judge Florence, 303, 305 *n*., 321
Alpha Kappa Alpha, 80
Altrusa Clubs, 37, 179
　activities, 37
　membership, 37
　organization of, 37
Alumnae education, 55
Alumnae organizations, 16, 54
　of colored women, 79
American Association of University
　Women, 16, 54–55, 85, 88, 121,
　198, 259, 269
　activities, 55
　budgets and support, 90
　headquarters, Washington, D. C., 83
　Journal, 55
　membership, 55
　organization of, 54
　scholarships, 55
American Federation of Labor, 27, 33,
　35, 166

American Federation of Teachers, 260,
　269
　membership, 62
American Home' Economics Associa-
　tion, 27, 59, 259, 269
American Institute of Accountants,
　180
American Institute of Homeopathy, 27
American Legion Auxiliary, 43, 44, 86,
　88
　budgets and support, 90
　membership, 44
American Library Association, 93
　and unemployment, 241
American Medical Association, 34, 88
American Nurses Association, 24, 60,
　88, 260, 269
　activities, 60
　membership, 60
　organization of, 24
American Osteopathic Association, 63
American Red Cross, 54, 76, 257
American Woman's Association, 236–
　238
　Club House, New York, 83
　earnings of members, 238
　effect of depression, 236
Americanization, and the D. A. R., 47
Anti-slavery, 257, 272
　societies, 1, 257
Architects, 188–190
Arizona, child labor law, 263
　Secretary of State, 252
　women legislators, 326
　women office holders, 318
　women voters in, 249
Arkansas, child labor law, 262
　Edelweiss Circle, 20
　State Farm for Women, 212
　women legislators, 326
　women office holders, 320

INDEX

INDEX

INDEX

Transportation, women in, 126, 167, 226

Truant officers, 203–209

Turnover, women workers, 162

Typing, 175–177

U

Ueland, Mrs. Andreas, 273

Unemployment, 154, 233–242, 344–345

U. S. Civil Service Commission, 3, 70, 305, 307

U. S. Woman's Bureau, 3, 106, 156, 157, 159, 160, 230

Universities, women in, 196–201
organizations, 16, 54
(*See also* Colleges.)

Utah, women legislators, 326

V

Vermont, voters in, 252
women legislators, 326

Veterans organizations, 48

Vice commissions, 210

Virginia, women legislators, 326

Vocational education, 31, 224

Vocational guidance, 100, 124, 178, 182, 185, 224, 263*n.*

Voters, women, 66–70, 245–256

W

Wages, 100–101, 147–148, 199, 215–232
and cost of living, 216, 219
effect of World War on, 224
equal, 225, 229–232
factory workers, 182, 215
in industries, 216–223
men workers, 217–221
office work, 180–182
(*See also* Earnings.)

Waiters, 130–132, 136

Waitresses, 129–132, 136

Warburton, Mary B., 339, 340

Washington, unemployment in, 235
women legislators, 326

West Virginia, women legislators, 326

Willard, Frances E., 87

Window dressers, women, 168, 174

Wingo, Mrs. Effie Gene, 298, 304

Wisconsin, women legislators, 326
women office holders, 314, 320, 334–335

Wolman, Dr. Leo, 166

Woman suffrage, 1, 3, 40, 66, 101, 245 *ff.*
effect of, 255
in England, 36
lobby, 258
organizations, 14, 36, 66, 246

Woman Suffrage Association (*see* National American Woman Suffrage Association).

Woman's Bureau (*see* U. S. Woman's Bureau).

Woman's Christian Temperance Union, 14, 34, 76, 269
membership, 92*n.*

Woman's Joint Congressional Committee, 85, 259–261, 265, 269, 272

Woman's Party, 272

Women's bloc, 257–274

Women's courts, 210

Women's Patriotic Conference on National Defense, 47, 86–87

Wood, Mrs. Ira Couch, 325

Woolf, Virginia, 84

Woolley, Mary E., 313

Working hours, 147–148

World War, 207–208
effect on wages, 224
women veterans, 48
and women workers, 152
women's organizations, 43

Wyoming, women legislators, 326

Y

Young Women's Christian Association, 15–16, 28, 35, 56–67
activities, 56
budgets and support, 89
City Association, 57
colored branches, 57
development, 56
educational work, 56

American Women: Images and Realities
An Arno Press Collection

[Adams, Charles F., editor]. **Correspondence between John Adams and Mercy Warren Relating to Her "History of the American Revolution," July-August, 1807.** With a new appendix of specimen pages from the **"History."** 1878.

[Arling], Emanie Sachs. **"The Terrible Siren": Victoria Woodhull, (1838-1927).** 1928.

Beard, Mary Ritter. **Woman's Work in Municipalities.** 1915.

Blanc, Madame [Marie Therese de Solms]. **The Condition of Woman in the United States.** 1895.

Bradford, Gamaliel. **Wives.** 1925.

Branagan, Thomas. **The Excellency of the Female Character Vindicated.** 1808.

Breckinridge, Sophonisba P. **Women in the Twentieth Century.** 1933.

Campbell, Helen. **Women Wage-Earners.** 1893.

Coolidge, Mary Roberts. **Why Women Are So.** 1912.

Dall, Caroline H. **The College, the Market, and the Court.** 1867.

[D'Arusmont], Frances Wright. **Life, Letters and Lectures: 1834, 1844.** 1972.

Davis, Almond H. **The Female Preacher, or Memoir of Salome Lincoln.** 1843.

Ellington, George. **The Women of New York.** 1869.

Farnham, Eliza W[oodson]. **Life in Prairie Land.** 1846.

Gage, Matilda Joslyn. **Woman, Church and State.** [1900].

Gilman, Charlotte Perkins. **The Living of Charlotte Perkins Gilman.** 1935.

Groves, Ernest R. **The American Woman.** 1944.

Hale, [Sarah J.] **Manners; or, Happy Homes and Good Society All the Year Round.** 1868.

Higginson, Thomas Wentworth. **Women and the Alphabet.** 1900.

Howe, Julia Ward, editor. **Sex and Education.** 1874.

La Follette, Suzanne. **Concerning Women.** 1926.

Leslie, Eliza . **Miss Leslie's Behaviour Book: A Guide and Manual for Ladies.** 1859.

Livermore, Mary A. **My Story of the War.** 1889.

Logan, Mrs. John A. (Mary S.) **The Part Taken By Women in American History.** 1912.

McGuire, Judith W. (A Lady of Virginia). **Diary of a Southern Refugee, During the War.** 1867.

Mann, Herman . **The Female Review: Life of Deborah Sampson.** 1866.

Meyer, Annie Nathan, editor.**Woman's Work in America.** 1891.

Myerson, Abraham. **The Nervous Housewife.** 1927.

Parsons, Elsie Clews. **The Old-Fashioned Woman.** 1913.

Porter, Sarah Harvey. **The Life and Times of Anne Royall.** 1909.

Pruette, Lorine. **Women and Leisure: A Study of Social Waste.** 1924.

Salmon, Lucy Maynard. **Domestic Service.** 1897.

Sanger, William W. **The History of Prostitution.** 1859.

Smith, Julia E. **Abby Smith and Her Cows.** 1877.

Spencer, Anna Garlin. **Woman's Share in Social Culture.** 1913.

Sprague, William Forrest. **Women and the West.** 1940.

Stanton, Elizabeth Cady. **The Woman's Bible** Parts I and II. 1895/1898.

Stewart, Mrs. Eliza Daniel . **Memories of the Crusade.** 1889.

Todd, John. **Woman's Rights.** 1867. [Dodge, Mary A .] (Gail Hamilton, pseud.) **Woman's Wrongs.** 1868.

Van Rensselaer, Mrs. John King. **The Goede Vrouw of Mana-ha-ta.** 1898.

Velazquez, Loreta Janeta. **The Woman in Battle.** 1876.

Vietor, Agnes C., editor. **A Woman's Quest: The Life of Marie E. Zakrzewska, M.D.** 1924.

Woodbury , Helen L. Sum n er. **Equal Suffrage.** 1909.

Young, Ann Eliza. **Wife No. 19.** 1875.